SPANISH
FOR HEALTH CARE
PROFESSIONALS

Second Edition

William C. Harvey

BARRON'S

The author wishes to thank Anaheim Memorial Medical Center in Southern California, and Mr. Dimitry Popow for their help during the creation of this book.

© Copyright 2000 by William C. Harvey.

All rights reserved. No part of this book may be reproduced in any form, by photostat, microfilm, xerography, or any other means, or incorporated into any information retrieval system, electronic or mechanical, without the written permission of the copyright owner.

All inquiries should be addressed to:
Barron's Educational Series, Inc.
250 Wireless Boulevard
Hauppauge, NY 11788
http:www.barronseduc.com

International Standard Book No. 0-7641-1138-8

Library of Congress Catalog Card No. 99-76147

PRINTED IN UNITED STATES OF AMERICA

9 8 7 6 5 4 3 2

Table of Contents

Introduction for the *gringo*

The first thing you should know about me is that I'm a *gringo*. I was born in Michigan and raised in California where everyone I knew at that time spoke only English. I didn't hear someone speak Spanish until I was 12 years old, but my life changed dramatically in 1967 when I landed a job as a busboy at a local Mexican restaurant.

The Hispanic employees took me under their wings and introduced me to a whole new world of language and culture. Although I was studying Spanish in school like other American teenagers, nothing compared to those real-life experiences at the restaurant. I remember writing down key expressions and phrases on the back of napkins, and then sharing them with my friends at school. It was an effective way to learn the language because I wasn't intimidated. I used only everyday conversations instead of the formal dialogues my teacher forced me to memorize.

Years later, my life took another turn. I was teaching English to immigrant children during the day and Spanish to grown-ups in the evening. One night after class, my supervisor asked me if I would like to teach Spanish to the doctors and nurses at a local hospital. I jumped at the opportunity. But in place of textbooks I pulled out the old napkins. My goal was to reduce the language to its simplest form. I spent countless hours interviewing health care professionals to pinpoint key terms and expressions. Within weeks, staff members were jabbering away in *español*. The non-threatening "gringo" approach had worked.

The key to learning Spanish is self-confidence. To build self-confidence you must first realize that the entire learning experience is painless and fun. What they told you in the traditional foreign language classroom was wrong. In fact, research has revealed some startling information. Consider these tenets to acquiring basic Spanish skills:

• Thousands of words are similar in both Spanish and English, which makes it easier for you to remember vocabulary.

• Grammar and pronunciation don't have to be "perfect" in order to be understood.

- Messages in Spanish can be communicated with a few simple expressions.
- As the number of Hispanics in the United States increases, so do the opportunities to practice new Spanish skills.
- Motivation shouldn't be a problem. Businesses across the country are making efforts to recruit employees who speak two or more languages.
- People who relax and enjoy their learning experiences seem to acquire Spanish at a much faster pace than everyone else.
- Even a little Spanish allows doctors, nurses, technicians, and support staff to help people in need of medical assistance.

Feel better? Trust me. When it comes to learning a new language, believing in yourself can make all the difference.

Before you begin

This book provides all the practical vocabulary and phrases you need to communicate with non-English speaking patients and their families. Each chapter introduces several new language skills, along with suggestions on how to use these skills in everyday situations. Read along at your own pace. If you get frustrated, review the material from previous chapters.

Most of the material is presented in a user-friendly format. Chapters One and Two, for examples, teach you how to speak and understand Spanish almost immediately. Chapters Three through Eleven follow members of a non-English speaking Hispanic family as they receive medical treatment from various hospital departments. At the end of the book is a section on cognate words along with an index that lists, in alphabetical order, words and expressions for the health care professional. Use this list as a quick reference point for immediate conversation.

Throughout each chapter are signposts to help you find your way around the language. The ¡**No Se Olvide!** *('noh seh ohl-'bee-deh)* (Don't Forget!) sections give you tips on how to learn Spanish more effectively. The ¿**Cuánto Aprendió?** *('kwahn-toh ah-prehn-dee-'oh)* (How Much Did You

Learn?) sections are for easy review and practice. You will often find these sections preceded by a number within a circle, indicating that the answers are located on pages 213–220. The **Dos Culturas** *(dohs kool-'too-rahs)* (Two Cultures) segments provide you with valuable information on Hispanic customs. You will also find sections titled **Más Acción** *(mahs ahk-see-'ohn)* (More Action). Use these signposts as tools to improve your skills and to better understand your patient's needs and desires.

So, let's get started … and have fun. ¡**Diviértase!** *(dee-bee-'ehr-tah-seh)*.

Chapter One

Basic Information
Información Básica
(een-fohr-mah-see·'ohn 'bah-see-kah)

This first section is an easy-to-follow introduction to survival Spanish. Before you learn all the job-related words and expressions, take time to review how the Spanish language is put together. Focus on the inside tips and practice the suggestions for successful communication. You soon will discover that learning Spanish is really **no problema** *(noh proh-'bleh-mah)*.

The sound system

One of the biggest concerns people have about acquiring a second language is speaking with improper pronunciation. Fortunately, Spanish is close enough to English that minor mistakes won't hurt communication. In fact, you need to remember only five sounds in order to speak well enough to be understood. Here are the vowels—each one is pronounced the way it is written:

a *(ah)* as in yacht
e *(eh)* as in met
i *(ee)* as in keep
o *(oh)* as in open
u *(oo)* as in spoon

Now, using your new sound system, try pronouncing these words:

a: **banana** *(bah-'nah-nah)*, **gas** *(gahs)*, **plasma** *('plahs-mah)*
e: **Pepe** *('peh-peh)*, **bebé** *(beh-'beh)*, **excelente** *(ehk-seh-'lehn-teh)*
i: **sí** *(see)*, **Trini** *('tree-nee)*, **sífilis** *('see-fee-lees)*
o: **loco** *('loh-koh)*, **no** *(noh)*, **doctor** *(dohk-'tohr)*
u: **mucho** *('moo-choh)*, **pus** *(poos)*, **Lulú** *(loo-'loo)*

¡ N O   S E   O L V I D E ! *(noh seh ohl-'bee-deh)*
D O N ' T   F O R G E T !

• Did you notice the accent (´) mark on some words? That part of the word with the accent mark should always be pronounced LOUDER and with more emphasis (i.e., **Lulú** *[loo-'loo]*). If there's no accent mark, say the last part of the word LOUDER and with more emphasis (i.e., **doctor** *[dohk-'tohr]*). For words ending in a vowel, or in **n** or **s**, the next to the last part of the word is stressed **excelente** *(ehk-seh-'lehn-teh)*. You'll get the hang of this once you begin to practice.

• In some cases, the letter **u** doesn't make the "oo" sound as with **guitarra** *(gee-'tah-rrah)* or **guerra** *('geh-rrah)*. Don't worry about these words right now. They're few and far between.

• **Note:** The word **si** *(see)* without an accent mark means "if."

Now let's take a look at the other sounds you'll need to remember. And don't forget—these sounds are always the same:

Spanish Letter	English Sound
c (after an e or i)	s as in Sam (**cerebral**, *seh-reh-'brahl*)
g (after an e or i)	h as in Harry (**general**, *heh-neh-'rahl*)
h	silent, like the k in knife (**hombre**, *'ohm-breh*)
j	h as in hot (**Julio**, *'hoo-lee-oh*)
ll	y as in yellow (**tortilla**, *tohr-'tee-yah*)
ñ	ny as in canyon (**español**, *ehs-pah-'nyohl*)
qu	k as in kit (**tequila**, *teh-'kee-lah*)

rr	The "rolled" r sound (**burro,** *'boo-rroh*)
v	b as in blood (**viva,** *'bee-bah*)
z	s as in son (**Gonzales,** *gohn-'sah-lehs*)

The rest of the letters in Spanish are very similar to their equivalents in English. Although some dialects may vary, these will work fine:

b	**bueno** (*'bweh-noh*)	**p**	**papá** (*pah-'pah*)
d	**disco** (*'dees-koh*)	**r**	**tres** (*trehs*)
f	**flan** (*flahn*)	**s**	**salsa** (*'sahl-sah*)
l	**Lupe** (*'loo-peh*)	**t**	**taco** (*'tah-koh*)
m	**más** (*mahs*)	**x**	**México** (*'meh-hee-koh*)
n	**nada** (*'nah-dah*)		

Take a few minutes to practice your new sounds in Spanish. Read the following words aloud. You should have no trouble figuring out what they mean.

accidente (*ahk-see-'dehn-teh*)	**medicina** (*meh-dee-'see-nah*)
anestesista (*ah-nchs-teh-'sees-tah*)	**menopausia** (*meh-noh-'pow-see-ah*)
colesterol (*koh-leh-steh-'rohl*)	**sexo** (*'sehk-soh*)
intestinos (*een-tehs-'tee-nohs*)	**tableta** (*tah-'bleh-tah*)

Some words are spelled the same in both languages, but are pronounced differently. (Don't forget the rules about accent marks.) Most medical terms in Spanish are easy to remember because they share common roots.

abdomen (*ahb-'doh-mehn*)	**hospital** (*hos-pee-'tahl*)
dental (*dehn-'tahl*)	**saliva** (*sah-'lee-bah*)
doctor (*dohk-'tohr*)	**tendón** (*tehn-'dohn*)
epidermis (*eh-pee-'dehr-mees*)	**vertebral** (*behr-teh-'brahl*)

Here are some more words in Spanish you may already know. People who speak English use them all the time!

adiós *(ah-dee-'ohs)*
amigo *(ah-'mee-goh)*
amor *(ah-'mohr)*
bueno *('bweh-noh)*
casa *('kah-sah)*
dinero *(dee-'neh-roh)*
español *(ehs-pah-'nyohl)*
Feliz Navidad *(feh-'lees nah-bee-'dahd)*
fiesta *(fee-'ehs-tah)*
gracias *('grah-see-ahs)*
grande *('grahn-deh)*
hombre *('ohm-breh)*

macho *('mah-choh)*
más *(mahs)*
muchacho *(moo-'chah-choh)*
mucho *('moo-choh)*
patio *('pah-tee-oh)*
plaza *('plah-sah)*
problema *(proh-'bleh-mah)*
pronto *('prohn-toh)*
rancho *('rahn-choh)*
señorita *(seh-nyoh-'ree-tah)*
sí *(see)*
uno *('oo-noh)*

¡NO SE OLVIDE!

Here's another hot tip for learners: The trend to mix Spanish and English has created a new language called *"Spanglish."* Millions of immigrants use it so don't be afraid to stick in an English word whenever you forget a Spanish word. Here are a few examples:

La "nurse"   El "hospital"
La "maternity"   El "bill"

The Spanish alphabet

At some point during the early stages of learning the language you may be forced to spell out a word in Spanish. In case of an emergency, you should know the letters of the alphabet in Spanish:

a	*(ah)*	g	*(heh)*
b	*(beh-'grahn-deh)*	h	*('ah-cheh)*
c	*(seh)*	i	*(ee)*
ch*	*(cheh)*	j	*('ho-tah)*
d	*(deh)*	k	*(kah)*
e	*(eh)*	l	*('eh-leh)*
f	*('eh-feh)*	ll*	*('eh-yeh)*

m	*('eh-meh)*	**s**	*('eh-seh)*
n	*('eh-neh)*	**t**	*(teh)*
ñ	*('eh-nyeh)*	**u**	*(oo)*
o	*(oh)*	**v**	*(beh-'chee-kah)*
p	*(peh)*	**w**	*(beh-'doh-bleh)*
q	*(coo)*	**x**	*('eh-kees)*
r	*('eh-reh)*	**y**	*(ee-gree-'eh-gah)*
rr	*('eh-rreh)*	**z**	*('seh-tah)*

* Recently, these letters were cut from the official Spanish alphabet. However, people do refer to them when spelling out a word.

With each bit of new information, you should be growing in self-confidence. However, if you're still having problems with the sounds of Spanish, try listening to the language for a few minutes each day. Radio, audiocassettes, television, plays, and musical performances provide fun and effective ways to help you become familiar with the pronunciation patterns.

Beginner's babble

On page 3 we mentioned a few Spanish words you may already know: now read these popular expressions and practice them aloud.

Excuse me!	**¡Con permiso!** *(kohn pehr 'mee-soh)*
Go ahead!	**¡Pase!** *('pah-seh)*
Good afternoon.	**Buenas tardes.** *('bweh-nahs 'tahr-dehs)*
Good-bye.	**Adiós.** *(ah-dee-'ohs)*
Good evening or Good night.	**Buenas noches.** *('bweh-nahs 'noh-chehs)*
Good morning.	**Buenos días.** *('bweh-nohs 'dee-ahs)*
Hi.	**Hola.** *('oh-lah)*
How are you?	**¿Cómo está?** *('koh-moh eh-'stah)*
How's it going!	**¡Qué tal!** *(keh tahl)*
I'm sorry!	**¡Lo siento!** *(loh see-'ehn-toh)*
May I come in?	**¿Se puede?** *(seh 'pweh-deh)*
Nice to meet you!	**¡Mucho gusto!** *('moo-choh 'goos-toh)*
Please!	**¡Por favor!** *(pohr fah-'bohr)*
Thank you!	**¡Gracias!** *('grah-see-ahs)*
Very well.	**Muy bien.** *('moo-ee 'bee-ehn)*

What's happening?	**¿Qué pasa?** *(keh 'pah-sah)*
What's wrong?	**¿Qué pasó?** *(keh pah-'soh)*
You're welcome!	**¡De nada!** *(deh 'nah-dah)*

1* ¿CUÁNTO APRENDIÓ? *('kwahn-toh ah-prehn-dee-'oh)*
HOW MUCH DID YOU LEARN?

Can you fill in the blanks with the appropriate response?

¿Cómo está? *('koh-moh eh-'stah)* ¡ _____ !

¡Gracias! *('grah-see-ahs)* ¡ _____ !

¿Se puede? *(seh 'pweh-deh)* ¡ _____ !

* To check your answers to these practice questions, see the ANSWERS section at the back of the book.

It is important to learn as many friendly exchanges as possible:

I appreciate it!	**¡Muy amable!** *('moo-ee ah-'mah-bleh)*
See you tomorrow!	**¡Hasta mañana!** *('ah-stah mah-'nyah-nah)*
We'll see you!	**¡Nos vemos!** *(nohs 'beh-mohs)*

Check out these "Excuse me" phrases:

Excuse me, if you cough or sneeze.	**¡Perdón!** *(pehr-'dohn)*
Excuse me, if you need someone's attention.	**¡Disculpe!** *(dees-'kool-peh)*

Note: The upside-down exclamation point (¡) and question mark (¿) must be used when you write in Spanish.

DOS CULTURAS *(dohs cool-'too-rahs)*
TWO CULTURES

Friendly greetings in Spanish are used all day long. Being courteous is the key to establishing trust with your patient. Throughout the Spanish-speaking world, a smile and kind word can lead to respect and complete cooperation.

Do you understand?

¿Entiende? *(ehn-tee-'ehn-deh)*

Let's be honest. One of the reasons you may be hesitant to speak Spanish is that you're afraid people might try to answer back and you won't understand them. You fear that all sorts of information will be given in return and you'll be totally confused.

Instead of running for help, search for clues as to what the person in front of you might be saying. If necessary, use your hands and facial expressions to help convey meanings. Then ask them to speak more slowly. Here are some phrases that will help you:

Again.	**Otra vez.** *('oh-trah behs)*
Another word, please.	**Otra palabra, por favor.**
	('oh-trah pah-'lah-brah, pohr fah-'bohr)
Do you speak English?	**¿Habla inglés?** *(ah-blah een-'glehs)*
How do you say it?	**¿Cómo se dice?** *('koh-moh seh 'dee-seh)*
How do you write it?	**¿Cómo se escribe?**
	('koh-moh seh ehs-'kree-beh)
I don't understand!	**¡No entiendo!** *(noh ehn-tee-'ehn-doh)*
I speak little Spanish.	**Hablo poquito español.**
	('ah-bloh poh-'kee-toh ehs-pah-'nyohl)
More slowly!	**¡Más despacio!** *(mahs dehs-'pah-see-oh)*
Thanks for your patience.	**Gracias por su paciencia.**
	('grah-see-ahs pohr soo pah-see-'ehn-see-uh)
What does it mean?	**¿Qué significa?** *(keh seeg-nee-'fee-kah)*
Word by word!	**¡Palabra por palabra!**
	(pah-'lah-brah pohr pah-'lah-brah)

The key here is not to panic. No doubt, they're having as much trouble understanding you, as you are understanding them. Make an attempt, and between the two of you, some kind of communication will take place.

Simple expressions
Expresiones simples
(ehks-preh-see-'oh-nehs 'seem-plehs)

Beginning conversations usually consist of nothing more than a brief exchange of words. To sound more natural when you speak, try running your words together. Go ahead—express yourself.

Bless you!	¡Salud! *(sah-'lood)*
Congratulations!	¡Felicitaciones! *(feh-lee-see-tah-see-'oh-nehs)*
Don't worry!	¡No se preocupe! *(noh seh preh-oh-'koo-peh)*
Good luck!	¡Buena suerte! *('bweh-nah 'swehr-teh)*
Go with God!	¡Vaya con Dios! *('bah-yah kohn 'dee-ohs)*
Happy Birthday!	¡Feliz cumpleaños! *(feh-'lees koom-pleh-'ah-nyohs)*
Have a nice day!	¡Que le vaya bien! *(keh leh 'bah-yah 'bee-ehn)*
Sure!	¡Claro! *('klah-roh)*
Take it easy!	¡Cúidese bien! *('kwee-deh-seh 'bee-ehn)*
That's great!	¡Qué bueno! *(keh 'bweh-noh)*
Very good!	¡Muy bien! *('moo-ee 'bee-ehn)*
Welcome!	¡Bienvenidos! *(bee-ehn-beh-'nee-dohs)*
Wow!	¡Caramba! *(kah-'rahm-bah)*

¡ N o   S e   O l v i d e !

- To improve your vocabulary, try writing the name of an object on removable stickers and placing them on objects you're trying to learn.

- Notice that the names for people, places, and things have either **el** *(ehl)* or **la** *(lah)* in front. Generally, if the word ends in the letter **o** there's an **el** in front (i.e., **el cuarto** *[ehl 'kwahr-toh]*, **el niño** *[ehl 'nee-nyoh]*). Conversely, if the word ends in an **a** there's a **la** in front (i.e., **la mesa** *[lah 'meh-sah]*, **la persona** *[lah pehr-'soh-nah]*). Some Spanish words are exceptions: **el agua** *(ehl 'ah gwah)*, **la mano** *(lah 'mah-noh)*, **el sofá** *(ehl soh-'fah)*. But relax. There aren't that many.

- Words not ending in either an **o** or **a** need to be memorized (i.e., **el hospital** *[ehl ohs-pee-'tahl]*, **la mujer** *[lah moo-'hehr]*). In the case of single objects, use **el** and **la** much like the word **"the"** in English: The hospital is big (**El hospital es grande** *[ehl ohs-pee-'tahl ehs 'grahn-deh]*).

- Remember too, that **el** and **la** are used in Spanish to indicate a person's sex. **El doctor** *(ehl dohk-'tohr)* is a male doctor, while **La doctora** *(lah dohk-'toh-rah)* is a female doctor. Here's how we change words to refer to the female gender: **la muchacha** *(lah moo-'chah-chah)*, **la niña** *(lah 'nee-nyah)*, **la enfermera** *(lah ehn-fehr-'meh-rah)*, **la paciente** *(lah pah-see-'ehn-teh)*, **la visitante** *(lah bee-see-'tahn-teh)*.

- Learn how to say "this" and "that" in Spanish.

that	**ese** *('eh-seh)* or **esa** *('eh-sah)*
these	**estos** *('eh-stohs)* or **estas** *('eh-stahs)*
this	**este** *('eh-steh)* or **esta** *('eh-stah)*
those	**esos** *('eh-sohs)* or **esas** *('eh-sahs)*

Vocabulary

El vocabulario *(ehl boh-kah-boo-'lah-ree·oh)*

Now that you're using hand signals, greeting people with simple expressions, and getting a general idea of what people are telling you, it's time to take on the next series of survival words and expressions. These are divided into separate lists for easy practice and review. No doubt you'll hear other words in Spanish that mean the same as the words being introduced here. Vocabulary often differs from one region to the next, but don't worry—these are general enough to be understood by most Hispanics.

Everyday things

Las cosas diarias *(lahs 'koh-sahs dee-'ah-ree·ahs)*

bathroom	**el baño** *(ehl 'bah-nyoh)*
bed	**la cama** *(lah 'kah-mah)*
book	**el libro** *(ehl 'lee-broh)*
chair	**la silla** *(lah 'see-yah)*
desk	**el escritorio** *(ehl ehs-kree-'toh-ree·oh)*
door	**la puerta** *(lah 'pwehr-tah)*
floor	**el piso** *(ehl 'pee-soh)*
food	**la comida** *(lah koh-'mee-dah)*
light	**la luz** *(lah loos)*
office	**la oficina** *(lah oh-fee-'see-nah)*
paper	**el papel** *(ehl pah-'pehl)*
pen	**el lapicero** *(ehl lah-pee-'seh-roh)*
pencil	**el lápiz** *(ehl 'lah-pees)*
room	**el cuarto** *(ehl 'kwahr-toh)*
table	**la mesa** *(lah 'meh-sah)*
trash	**la basura** *(lah bah-'soo-rah)*
water	**el agua** *(ehl 'ah-gwah)*
window	**la ventana** *(lah behn-'tah-nah)*

People
La gente *(lah 'hehn-teh)*

baby	**el bebé** *(ehl beh-'beh)*
boy, child	**el niño** *(ehl 'nee-nyoh)*
doctor	**el doctor** or **el médico**
	(ehl dohk-'tohr, ehl 'meh-dee-koh)
girl	**la niña** *(lah 'nee-nyah)*
in-patient	**el paciente interno**
	(ehl pah-see-'ehn-teh een-'tehr-noh)
man	**el hombre** *(ehl 'ohm-breh)*
nurse	**el enfermero** *(ehl ehn-fehr-'meh-roh)*
outpatient	**el paciente externo**
	(ehl pah-see-'ehn-teh ehks-'lehr-noh)
patient	**el paciente** *(ehl pah-see-'ehn-teh)*
person	**la persona** *(lah pehr-'soh-nah)*
teenager (male)	**el muchacho** *(ehl moo-'chah-choh)*
teenager (female)	**la muchacha** *(lah moo-'chah-chah)*
visitor	**el visitante** *(ehl bee-see-'tahn-teh)*
woman	**la mujer** *(lah moo-'hehr)*

The colors
Los colores *(lohs koh-'loh-rehs)*

black	**negro** *('neh-groh)*
blue	**azul** *(ah-'sool)*
brown	**café** *(kah-'feh)*
gray	**gris** *(grees)*
green	**verde** *('behr-deh)*
orange	**anaranjado** *(ah-nah-rahn-'hah-doh)*
pink	**rosado** *(roh-'sah-doh)*
purple	**morado** *(moh-'rah-doh)*
red	**rojo** *('roh-hoh)*
white	**blanco** *('blahn-koh)*
yellow	**amarillo** *(ah-mah-'ree-yoh)*

¿CUÁNTO APRENDIÓ?

• **Los colores** *(lohs koh-'loh-rehs)* play an important role in conversations. Find creative ways to practice. For example, form your own sentence using colors from the above list.

El papel es *(ehl pah-'pehl ehs)* _____ .

El libro es *(ehl 'lee-broh ehs)* _____ .

La silla es *(lah 'see-yah ehs)* _____ .

El cuarto es *(ehl 'kwahr-toh ehs)* _____ .

The numbers

Los números *(lohs 'noo-meh-rohs)*

0	**cero** *('seh-roh)*	14	**catorce** *(kah-'tohr-seh)*
1	**uno** *('oo-noh)*	15	**quince** *('keen-seh)*
2	**dos** *(dohs)*	16	**dieciseis** *(dee-ehs-ee-'seh·ees)*
3	**tres** *(trehs)*	17	**diecisiete** *(dee-ehs-ee-see-'eh-teh)*
4	**cuatro** *('kwah-troh)*	18	**dieciocho** *(dee-ehs-ee-'oh-choh)*
5	**cinco** *('seehn-koh)*	19	**diecinueve** *(dee-ehs-ee-noo-'eh-beh)*
6	**seis** *('seh·ees)*	20	**veinte** *('beh·een-teh)*
7	**siete** *(see-'eh-teh)*	30	**treinta** *('treh·een-tah)*
8	**ocho** *('oh-choh)*	40	**cuarenta** *(kwah-'rehn-tah)*
9	**nueve** *(noo-'eh-beh)*	50	**cincuenta** *(seen-'kwehn-tah)*
10	**diez** *(dee-'ehs)*	60	**sesenta** *(seh-'sehn-tah)*
11	**once** *('ohn-seh)*	70	**setenta** *(seh-'tehn-tah)*
12	**doce** *('doh-seh)*	80	**ochenta** *(oh-'chehn-tah)*
13	**trece** *('treh-seh)*	90	**noventa** *(noh-'behn-tah)*

For all the numbers in-between just add **"y"** *(ee)*:

21 **veinte y uno** *('beh·een-teh ee 'oo-noh)*,

22 **veinte y dos** *('beh·een-teh ee dohs)*

23 **veinte y tres** *('beh·een-teh ee trehs)* . . .

Practice your numbers in Spanish every day. Reciting addresses, phone numbers, and license plate numbers are just a few ways to learn them quickly.

Sooner or later, you'll also need to know how to say the larger numbers in Spanish. They aren't that difficult, so practice aloud:

100	**cien** *(see-'ehn)*
200	**doscientos** *(dohs-see-'ehn-tohs)*
300	**trescientos** *(trehs-see-'ehn-tohs)*
400	**cuatrocientos** *('kwah-troh-see-'ehn-tohs)*
500	**quinientos** *(keen-ee-'ehn-tohs)*
600	**seiscientos** *(seh-ees-see-'ehn-tohs)*
700	**setecientos** *(oh-choh-see-'ehn-tohs)*
800	**ochocientos** *(oh-choh-see-'ehn-tohs)*
900	**novecientos** *(noh-beh-see-'ehn-tohs)*
1000	**mil** *(meel)*
million	**millón** *(mee-'yohn)*
billion	**billón** *(bee-'yohn)*

② ¿CUÁNTO APRENDIÓ?

- Translate the following:

200 rooms	_____
80 tables	_____
3 nurses	_____
75 books	_____
10 floors	_____
361 babies	_____

A beginner's list

appointment	**la cita** *(lah 'see-tah)*
care	**el cuidado** *(ehl kwee-'dah-doh)*
emergency	**la emergencia** *(lah eh-mehr-'hehn-see-ah)*
form	**el formulario** *(ehl fohr-moo-'lah-ree-oh)*
health	**la salud** *(lah sah-'lood)*

help	**la ayuda** *(lah ah-'yoo-dah)*
injury	**la herida** *(lah eh-'ree-dah)*
medicine	**la medicina** *(lah meh-dee-'see-nah)*
pain	**el dolor** *(ehl doh-'lohr)*
sickness	**la enfermedad** *(lah ehn-fehr-meh-'dahd)*

③ ¿CUÁNTO APRENDIÓ?

If you've been following closely, the following expressions should be easy for you to translate into English:

Mucho dolor *('moo-choh doh-'lohr)*

Tres formularios *(trehs fohr-moo-'lah-ree·ohs)*

Herida y enfermedad *(eh-'ree-dah ee ehn-fehr-meh-'dad)*

Dos citas *(dohs 'see-tahs)*

Más ayuda *(mahs ah-'yoo-dah)*

Commands
Las órdenes *(lahs 'ohr-deh-nehs)*

You could not survive in a medical situation without a set of command words that can quickly get the job done. Instead of trying to always speak perfect Spanish, you'll sometimes need to take control of a situation. Try using these phrases, and don't forget to emphasize the letter with the accent mark.

Calm down!	**¡Cálmese!** *('kahl-meh-seh)*
Get undressed.	**¡Desvístase!** *(dehs-'bees-tah-seh)*
Hurry up!	**¡Apúrese!** *(ah-'poo-reh-seh)*
Lie down!	**¡Acuéstese!** *(ah-'kwehs-teh-seh)*

Open your mouth.	**¡Abra la boca!** *('ah-brah lah -boh-kah)*
Sit down!	**¡Siéntese!** *(see-'ehn-teh-seh)*
Stand up!	**¡Levántese!** *(leh-'bahn-teh-seh)*
Take a deep breath.	**¡Aspire profundo!** *(ahs-'pee-reh proh-'foon-doh)*
Turn around!	**¡Voltéese!** *(bohl-'teh-eh-seh)*
Wait!	**¡Espérese!** *(ehs-'peh-reh-seh)*
Wake up!	**¡Despiértese!** *(dehs-pee-'ehr-teh-seh)*

¡ N O   S E   O L V I D E !

These two words can be used by themselves:

¡Venga! *('behn-gah)*	Come!
¡Vaya! *('bah-yah)*	Go!

The rules
Las reglas *(lahs 'reh-glahs)*

As you begin to describe things in Spanish, you will notice that the words are positioned in reverse order: The descriptive word goes <u>after</u> the word being described. Try to keep this general rule in mind, even though you'll still be understood if you should forget!

The big hospital	**El hospital grande** *(ehl ohs-pee-'tahl 'grahn-deh)*
The blue medicine	**La medicina azul** *(lah meh-dee-'see-nah ah-'sool)*

You'll need to make a few other changes when referring to more than one item. The words **el** and **la,** for example, as discussed on page 9, become **los** and **las,** respectively.

el cuarto *(ehl 'kwahr-toh)*	**los cuartos** *(lohs 'kwahr-tohs)*
la mesa *(lah 'meh-sah)*	**las mesas** *(lahs 'meh-sahs)*
el doctor *(ehl dohk-'tohr)*	**los doctores** *(lohs dohk-'toh-rehs)*
la mujer *(lah moo-'hehr)*	**las mujeres** *(lahs moo-'heh-rehs)*

In addition, not only do all the nouns and adjectives need **s** or **es** to make the sentence plural, but when they are used together, the **o**'s and **a**'s (masculine and feminine) must match as well. This may seem foreign at first, but you'll get the hang of it the more you listen and speak in Spanish.

Many good doctors   **Muchos doctores buenos**
       (*'moo-chohs dohk-'toh-rehs 'bweh-nohs*)

Three white tables   **Tres mesas blancas** (*trehs 'meh-sahs 'blahn-kahs*)

Two yellow rooms   **Dos cuartos amarillos**
       (*dohs 'kwahr-tohs ah-mah-'ree-yohs*)

¡ N o   S e   O l v i d e !

- To say "a" in Spanish, use **un** or **una**:

  A hospital   **un hospital** *(oon ohs-pee-'tahl)*
  A nurse   **una enfermera** *('oo-nah ehn-fehr-'meh-rah)*

- To say some, use **unos** or **unas**:

  Some hospitals   **unos hospitales** *('oo-nohs ohs-pee-'tah-lehs)*
  Some nurses   **unas enfermeras**
             ('oo-nahs ehn-fehr-'meh-rahs)

- Use these words to link everything together:

  y *(ee)*= and   **o** *(oh)* = or   **pero** *('peh-roh)* = but
  Thank you and goodbye!
  ¡Gracias y adiós! *('grah-see-ahs ee ah-dee-'ohs)*
  Juan and María   **Juan y María** *(wahn ee mah-'ree-ah)*
  money or love   **dinero o amor** *(dee-'neh-roh oh ah-'mohr)*
  Many patients, but few doctors.
  Muchos pacientes, pero pocos doctores.
      ('moo-chohs pah-see-'ehn-tehs, 'peh-roh 'poh-kohs dohk-'toh-rehs)

- Are you ready to form a few phrases? You'll need the following:

  for   **para** *('pah-rah)*   **para el paciente**
                           ('pah-rah ehl pah-see-'ehn-teh)
  in, on, at   **en** *(ehn)*   **en el hospital**
                           (ehn ehl ohs-pee-'tahl)
  of, from   **de** *(deh)*   **de la doctora**
                           (deh lah dohk-'toh-rah)
  to   **a** *(ah)*   **a la oficina**
                           (ah lah oh-fee-'see-nah)
  with   **con** *(kohn)*   **con cuidado**
                           (kohn kwee-'dah-doh)
  without   **sin** *(seen)*   **sin la comida**
                           (seen lah koh-'mee-dah)

- There are only two contractions in Spanish:

  to the   **al** *(ahl)*   **al baño** *(ahl 'bh-nyoh)*
  of the, from the   **del** *(dehl)*   **del paciente**
                           (dehl pah-see-'ehn-teh)

Do you have a question?
¿Tiene una pregunta?
(tee-'eh-neh 'oo-nah preh-'goon-tah)

Understanding and using question words in Spanish is crucial in gathering information. The best way to learn how to use question words in a foreign language is to focus on the first word of each sentence, and then try to get a general feel for what the person might be asking. Attempting to translate every word will only lead to frustration.

In a medical situation, it is essential that staff members memorize as many of the following "question words" as they can:

How?	**¿Cómo?** *('koh-moh)*
How many?	**¿Cuántos?** *('kwahn-tohs)*
How much?	**¿Cuánto?** *('kwahn-toh)*
What?	**¿Qué?** *(keh)*
When?	**¿Cuándo?** *('kwahn-doh)*
Where?	**¿Dónde?** *('dohn-deh)*
Which?	**¿Cuál?** *(kwahl)*
Who?	**¿Quién?** *(kee-'ehn)*
Whose?	**¿De quién?** *(deh kee-'ehn)*

¡No Se Olvide!

- "There is" and "there are" are very simple: in both cases you use **hay** *('ah-ee)*.

| There is one boy | **Hay un niño** *('ah-ee oon 'nee-nyoh)* |
| There are two girls | **Hay dos niñas** *('ah-ee dohs 'nee-nyahs)* |

- **¿Por qué?** *(pohr keh)* means "why?" in English. To respond, simply repeat the word **porque** because it means "Because."

You soon will discover that daily conversations are filled with common question phrases. Take a look at these examples:

How are you?	**¿Cómo está?** *('koh-moh eh-'stah)*
How much does it cost?	**¿Cuánto cuesta?** *('kwahn-toh 'kwehs-tah)*
How old are you?	**¿Cuántos años tiene?**
	('kwahn-tohs 'ah-nyohs tee-'eh-neh)
What's happening?	**¿Qué pasa?** *(keh 'pah-sah)*
Where are you from?	**¿De dónde es?** *(deh 'dohn-deh ehs)*

(4) **¿C U Á N T O   A P R E N D I Ó ?**

Match the following question with the appropriate response.

¿Qué pasa? *(keh 'pah-sah)*	**Verde.** *('behr-deh)*
¿Cómo está? *('koh-moh eh-'stah)*	**Kathy.**
¿Quién es la enfermera?	**Mucha.** *('moo-chah)*
(kee-'ehn ehs lah ehn-fehr-'meh-rah)	
¿Cuál color? *(kwahl koh 'lohr)*	**Muy bien.** *('moo-ee bee-'ehn)*
¿Cuántos visitantes?	**Nada.** *('nah-duh)*
('kwahn-tohs bee-see-'tahn-tehs)	
¿Cuánta medicina?	**Seis.** *('seh-ees)*
('kwahn-tah meh-dee-'see-nah)	

What's your name?
¿Cómo se llama? *('koh-moh seh 'yah-mah)*

The popular phrase "**¿Cómo se llama?**" *('koh-moh seh 'yah-mah)* is usually translated to mean "What's your name?" However, you may also hear "**¿Cual es su nombre?**" *(kwahl ehs soo 'nohm-breh)*, which means "Which is your name?" You should also know these:

first name	**primer nombre** *(pree-'mehr 'nohm-breh)*
last name	**apellido** *(ah-peh-'yee-doh)*

It really helps if you are able to pronounce people's names correctly, as it makes patients feel much more at ease. Always remember that

Spanish is pronounced the way it is written. Also, it is not uncommon for someone in Spain or Latin America to have two last names. Don't get confused. Here's the order:

First name	Father's last name	Mother's last name
primer nombre	apellido paterno	apellido materno
(pree-'mehr	*(ah-peh-'yee-doh*	*(ah-peh-'yee-doh*
'nohm-breh)	*pah-'tehr-noh)*	*mah-'tehr-noh)*
JUAN CARLOS	**ESPINOZA**	**GARCÍA**
(wahn 'kahr-lohs)	*(ehs-pee-'noh-sah)*	*(gahr-'see-ah)*

¡Dos Culturas!

• Not all Hispanic people have two first names, and there is no "middle name" as we know it.

• When a woman marries, she keeps her father's last name, followed by her husband's.

• Learn these abbreviations:

Mr.	**Sr.** *(seh-'nyohr)*
Mrs.	**Sra.** *(seh-'nyoh-rah)*
Miss	**Srta.** *(seh-nyoh-'ree-tah)*

The missing link

Now that you're beginning to form simple questions and answers, it's time to link everything together. To accomplish this, you'll need to understand the difference between **está** and **es.** Both words mean "is," but they're used differently.

The word **está** *(eh-'stah)* expresses a temporary state, condition, or location.

The patient is fine.	**El paciente está bien.**
	(ehl pah-see-'ehn-teh eh-'stah 'bee-ehn)
The patient is in bed.	**El paciente está en la cama.**
	(ehl pah-see-'ehn-teh eh-'stah ehn lah 'kah-mah)

The word **es** expresses an inherent quality or characteristic, including origin and ownership.

The patient is big.	**El paciente es grande.**
	(ehl pah-see-'ehn-teh ehs 'grahn-deh)
The patient is Carlos.	**El paciente es Carlos.**
	(ehl pah-see-'ehn-teh ehs 'kahr-lohs)
The patient is Cuban.	**El paciente es cubano.**
	(ehl pah-see-'ehn-teh ehs koo-'bah-noh)
The patient is my friend.	**El paciente es mi amigo.**
	(ehl pah-see'ehn-teh ehs mee ah-'mee-goh)

Although this might seem confusing, these two wonderful words can really help put your Spanish together. You'll also need to talk about more than one person, place, or thing. To do so, replace **está** with **están**, and **es** with **son**. Don't forget that everything changes when you shift to plurals.

The patient is in the office.	**El paciente está en la oficina.**
	(ehl pah-see-'ehn-teh eh-'stah ehn lah oh-fee-'see-nah)
The patients are in the office.	**Los pacientes están en la oficina.**
	(lohs pah-see-'ehn-tehs eh-'stahn ehn lah oh-fee-'see-nah)
It's a child.	**Es un niño.** *(ehs oon 'nee-nyoh)*
They are children.	**Son niños.** *(sohn 'nee-nyohs)*

The best way to remember how to use these four words correctly is to follow them closely in sentences from real-life situations. Concentrate as you read aloud the following examples:

Dr. Ramírez is a big man.	**El Dr. Ramírez es un hombre grande.** *(ehl dohk-'tohr rah-'mee-rehs ehs oon 'ohm-breh 'grahn-deh)*
Hospitals are very important.	**Los hospitales son muy importantes.** *(lohs ohs-pee-'tah-lehs sohn 'moo·ee eem-pohr-'tahn-tehs)*
How are the patients?	**¿Cómo están los pacientes?** *('koh-moh ehs-'tahn lohs pah-see-'ehn-tehs)*

The medicines are in Chicago.	**Las medicinas están en Chicago.** *(lahs meh-dee-'see-nahs eh-'stahn ehn Chee-'cah-goh)*
The office is in the hospital.	**La oficina está en el hospital.** *(lah oh-fee-'see-nah eh-'stah ehn ehl ohs-pee-'tahl)*
When is the appointment?	**¿Cuándo es la cita?** *('kwahn-doh ehs lah 'see-tah)*
Where is the nurse?	**¿Dónde está la enfermera?** *('dohn-deh eh-'stah lah ehn-fehr-'meh-rah)*
Who are the doctors?	**¿Quiénes son los doctores?** *(kee-'eh-nehs sohn lohs dohk-'toh-rehs)*

To say "I am" and "We are" in Spanish, you must also learn the two different forms. **Estoy** *(eh-'stoh·ee)* and **Estamos** *(eh-'stah-mohs)* refer to the location or condition of a single person, place, or thing. **Soy** and **Somos** *('soh-mohs)* are used with everything else.

I am in the house.	**Estoy en la casa.** *(eh-'stoh·ee ehn lah 'kah-sah)*
I am well.	**Estoy bien.** *(eh-'stoh·ee 'bee·ehn)*
We are in the hospital.	**Estamos en el hospital.** *(eh-'stah-mohs ehn ehl ohs-pee-'tahl)*
We are sick.	**Estamos enfermos.** *(eh-'stah-mohs ehn-'fehr-mohs)*
I am Juan.	**Soy Juan.** *('soh·ee)*
I am a visitor.	**Soy un visitante.** *('soh·ee oon bee-see-'tahn-teh)*
We are Cuban.	**Somos cubanos.** *('soh-mohs koo-'bah-nohs)*
We are tall.	**Somos altos.** *('soh-mohs 'ahl-tohs)*

You also may hear people use the words **estás** or **eres**, which are the informal ways of saying "you" **tú.** The "you" **(usted)** we are using in this book has a polite and respectful connotation, and is appropriate for communication between the health-care provider and the patient. The informal "you" is **tú,** it is used among friends and acquaintances, and requires additional verbal conjugation. For these reasons, **tú** has been left out. Let us see now the complete present tense of **estar** and **ser.**

TO BE	ESTAR *(eh-'stahr)*	SER *(sehr)*
I'm	estoy *(eh-'stoh-ee)*	soy *('soh-ee)*
you're, he's, she's, it's	está *(eh-'stah)*	es *(ehs)*
they're, you (plural) are	están *(eh-'stahn)*	son *(sohn)*
we're	estamos *(eh-'stah-mohs)*	somos *('soh-mohs)*

⑤ ¿CUÁNTO APRENDIÓ?

Match the question with the appropriate answer.

¿Quiénes son? *(kee-'eh-nehs sohn)*

¿Dónde está? *('dohn-deh eh-'stah)*

¿Qué medicinas son blancas?
(keh meh-dee-'see-nahs sohn 'blahn-kahs)

¿Cuánta agua hay en el baño?
('kwahn-tah 'ah-gwah ah-ee ehn ehl 'bah-nyoh)

¿Qué comida es buena?
(keh koh-mee-dah ehs 'bweh-nah)

¿Cuántas camas hay en el hospital?
('kwahn-tahs 'kah-mahs ah-ee ehn ehl ohs-pee-'tahl)

Mucha. *('moo-chah)*

250. *(dohs-see-'ehn-tahs seen-'kwehn-tah)*

Estoy en el cuarto.
(eh-'stoh-ee ehn ehl 'kwahr-toh)

Pizza.

Somos enfermeros.
('soh-mohs ehn-fehr-'meh-rohs)

Las aspirinas.
(lahs ahs-pee-'ree-nahs)

Do you have problems?

¿Tiene problemas? *(tee-'eh-neh proh-'bleh-mahs)*

Another common linking verb is **tener**, which means "to have." You will need to use this word a lot as a health care professional. Although we'll be discussing **tener** in more detail later, here are the basic forms to get you started:

I have	tengo *('tehn-goh)*
you have, she has, he has, it has	tiene *(tee-'eh-neh)*

| they have, you (plural) have | **tienen** *(tee-'eh-nehn)* |
| we have | **tenemos** *(teh-'neh-mohs)* |

To practice, read these simple sentences aloud:

I have a lot of pain.
Tengo mucho dolor. *('tehn-goh 'moo-choh doh-'lohr)*
The doctor has the medicine.
El doctor tiene la medicina.
  (ehl dohk-'tohr tee-'eh-neh lah meh-dee-'see-nah)
The hospitals have many beds.
Los hospitales tienen muchas camas.
  (lohs ohs-pee-'tah-lehs tee-'eh-nehn 'moo-chahs 'kah-mahs)
We have an office.
Tenemos una oficina. *(teh-'neh-mohs 'oo-nah oh-fee-'see-nah)*

As you can see, the word **tener** (to have) is extremely practical. Also keep in mind that **tener** sometimes is used instead of the verb **estar** to express a temporary condition.

(I am) afraid	**(tengo) miedo** *(mee-'eh-doh)*
(we are) at fault	**(tenemos) la culpa** *(lah 'kool-pah)*
(they are) cold	**(tienen) frío** *('free-oh)*
(she is) 15 years old	**(tiene) quince años** *('keen-seh 'ah-nyohs)*
(I am) hot	**(tengo) calor** *(kah-'lohr)*
(they are) hungry	**(tienen) hambre** *('ahm-breh)*
(he is) sleepy	**(tiene) sueño** *('sweh-nyoh)*
(we are) thirsty	**(tenemos) sed** *(sehd)*

To say "not" in Spanish, interject the word **no** in front of the verb:

Kathy is a nurse.	**Kathy es una enfermera.**
	(K. ehs 'oo-nah ehn-fehr-'meh-rah)
Kathy is not a nurse.	**Kathy no es una enfermera.**
	(K. noh ehs oo-nah ehn-fehr-'meh-rah)
I have the paper.	**Tengo el papel.** *('tehn-goh ehl pah-'pehl)*
I don't have the paper.	**No tengo el papel** *(noh 'tehn-goh ehl pah-'pehl)*

6 ¿CUÁNTO APRENDIÓ?

Read the following story. How much of it can you understand?

Yo soy Roberto. (yoh 'soh-ee roh-'behr-toh) *Estoy en el hospital.* ('eh-stoh-ee ehn ehl ohs-pee-'tahl) *Tengo un dolor en el estómogo.* ('tehn-goh oon doh-'lohr ehn ehl eh-'stoh-mah-goh) *Hay una enfermera en el cuarto.* ('ah-ee 'oo-nah ehn-fehr-'meh-rah ehn ehl 'kwahr-toh) *Ella tiene la medicina blanca.* ('eh-yah tee-'eh-neh lah meh-dee-'see-nah 'blahn-kah)

Action!
¡Acción! *(ahk-see·'ohn)*

As we begin to express ourselves in Spanish, it becomes obvious that we're limited without verbs or "action words." Although **estar, ser,** and **tener** are extremely useful, they do not express action. Learning Spanish verbs will allow us to talk about what's going on in the hospital.

Fortunately, action words are easy to use. The best method is to first learn the basic forms, then practice them as parts of common expressions and commands. We'll acquire our action words through short practical phrases, and then use them in various forms as parts of our work-related comments and questions.

Let's open with a brief list of helpful beginning verbs. Please notice that Spanish action words end in the letters **ar, er,** or **ir.**

to drive	**manejar** *(mah-neh-'hahr)*
to eat	**comer** *(koh-'mehr)*
to go	**ir** *(eer)*
to read	**leer** *(lee-'ehr)*
to run	**correr** *(koh-'rrehr)*
to sleep	**dormir** *(dohr-'meer)*
to speak	**hablar** *(ah-'blahr)*
to write	**escribir** *(ehs-kree-'beer)*
to work	**trabajar** *(trah-bah-'hahr)*

Notice what happens when you place a verb after the following pattern: **tiene que** *(tee-'eh-neh keh)* (you have to, she/he has to):

You have to read the book.	**Tiene que leer el libro.**
	(tee-'eh-neh keh leh-'ehr ehl 'lee-broh)
You have to speak Spanish.	**Tiene que hablar español.**
	(tee-'eh-neh keh ah-'blahr ehs-pah-'nyohl)

Since we already have worked with the verb **tener** *(teh-'nehr)* (to have), you should have no trouble with **tener que** *(teh-'nehr keh)* (to have to). Here are the forms:

I have to	**tengo que** *('tehn-goh keh)*
you have to, she/he has to	**tiene que** *(tee-'eh-neh keh)*
you (plural)/they have to	**tienen que** *(tee-'eh-nehn keh)*
we have to	**tenemos que** *(teh-'neh-mohs keh)*

This is only one of the many patterns you'll encounter in this book. Soon you'll be introduced to a variety of verb phrases that target specific areas of medical care. Each new phrase will show how action words can be altered to communicate different messages.

In Spanish, one of the easiest verb forms to use is the Present Progressive. It refers to actions that are taking place at this moment. Simply combine the four forms of **estar** with any verb. Notice how the ending of the verb changes slightly.

eat	**comer** *(koh-'mehr)*
He is eating well.	**Está comiendo bien.**
	(eh-'stah koh-mee-'ehn-doh 'bee-'ehn)
gain	**ganar** *(gah-'nahr)*
They are gaining weight.	**Están ganando peso.**
	(eh-'stahn gah-'nahn-doh 'peh-soh)
leave	**salir** *(sah-'leer)*
We are leaving now.	**Estamos saliendo ahora.**
	(eh-'stah-mohs sah-lee-'ehn-doh ah-'oh-rah)

The **ndo** is similar to our "ing" ending. The **ar** verbs become **ando** while the **er** and **ir** verbs become **iendo**. Look at the first example and create "ing" phrases with the verbs that follow.

to cook	**cocinar** *(koh-see-'nahr)*
cooking	**cocinando** *(koh-see-'nahn-do)*
They are cooking without salt.	**Están cocinando sin sal.** *(eh-'stahn koh-see-'nahn-doh seen sahl)*

to cure	**curar** *(koo-'rahr)*
curing	**curando** *(koo-'rahn-doh)*
_____.	_____.

to find	**encontrar** *(ehn-kohn-'trahr)*
finding	**encontrando** *(ehn-kohn-'trahn-doh)*
_____.	_____.

to function	**funcionar** *(foon-see-oh-'nahr)*
functioning	**funcionando** *(foon-see-oh-'nahn-doh)*
_____.	_____.

to gain	**ganar** *(gah-'nahr)*
gaining	**ganando** *(guh-'nahn-doh)*
_____.	_____.

to lose	**perder** *(pehr-'dehr)*
losing	**perdiendo** *(pehr-dee-'ehn-doh)*
_____.	_____.

to measure	**medir** *(meh-'deer)*
measuring	**midiendo** *(me-dee-'ehn-doh)*
_____.	_____.

to follow	**seguir** *(seh-'geer)*
following	**siguiendo** *(see-ghee-'ehn-doh)*
_____.	_____.

to observe	**observar** *(ohb-sehr-'bahr)*
observing	**observando** *(ohb-sehr-'bahn-doh)*
_____.	_____.

to recuperate	**recuperar** *(reh-koo-peh-'rahr)*
recuperating	**recuperando** *(reh-koo-peh-'rahn-doh)*

_____ . _____ .

¡ N o S e O l v i d e !

A couple of verbs change in spelling when you add the **ndo** ending. Study this example:

to follow **seguir** *(seh-'geer)* Are you following the instructions?
¿Está siguiendo las instrucciones?
(eh-'stah see-gee-'ehn-doh lahs een-strook-see-'oh-nehs)

The majority of verbs used in medicine are similar to English. Look at these examples:

consult	**consultar** *(kohn-sool-'tahr)*
control	**controlar** *(kohn-troh-'lahr)*
disinfect	**desinfectar** *(dehs-een-fehk-'tahr)*
evaluate	**evaluar** *(eh-bah-loo-'ahr)*
recommend	**recomendar** *(reh-koh-mehn-'dahr)*

By now you may have noticed that some action words include the word **se,** which has many meanings. Here are some important action words in which **se** indicates that the action is self-directed (e.g., **lavar** means "to wash" but **lavarse** means "to get washed").

to bathe oneself	**bañarse** *(bah-'nyahr-seh)*
to brush oneself	**cepillarse** *(seh-pee-'yahr-seh)*
to faint oneself	**desmayarse** *(dehs-mah-'yahr-seh)*
to fall down	**caerse** *(kah-'ehr-seh)*
to get better	**mejorarse** *(meh-hoh-'rahr-seh)*
to get dressed	**vestirse** *(behs-'teer-seh)*
to get drowned	**ahogarse** *(ah-oh-'gahr-seh)*
to get sick	**enfermarse** *(ehn-fehr-'mahr-seh)*

to get washed   **lavarse** *(lah-'bahr-seh)*

to remember   **acordarse** *(ah-kohr-'dahr-seh)*

¿ C U Á N T O   A P R E N D I Ó ?

- Practice the following dialogue with a friend.

  "Hola, Doctora Smith. ¿Cómo está?"

  ('oh-lah, dohk-'toh-rah S. 'koh-moh eh-'stah)

  "Buenos días, Francisco. Estoy bien. ¿Qué pasa?" *('bweh-nohs 'dee-ahs, frahn-'sees-koh. eh-'stoh-ee 'bee-ehn. 'keh 'pah-sah)*

  "Mi amigo está en el hospital. Tiene muchos problemas."

  (mee ah-'mee-goh eh-'stah ehn ehl ohs-pee-'tahl. tee-'eh-neh 'moo-chohs proh-'bleh-mahs)

- If you were asked the following questions, what would you say?

  ¿Cómo se llama? *('koh-moh seh 'yah-mah)*

  ¿Cuántos años tiene? *('kwahn-tohs 'an-nyohs tee-'eh-neh)*

  ¿Quién es su amigo? *(kee-'ehn ehs soo ah-'mee-goh)*

  ¿Cómo está? *('koh-moh eh-'stah)*

  ¿De qué color es el hospital?

  (deh keh koh-'lohr ehs ehl ohs-pee-'tahl)

  ¿Tiene mucho dolor? *(tee-'eh-neh 'moo-choh doh-'lohr)*

  ¿Tiene que trabajar? *(tee-'eh-neh keh trah-bah-'hahr)*

Chapter Two

The Patient
El Paciente
(ehl pah-see-'ehn-teh)

In Chapter One you learned survival skills, basic vocabulary, and a few rules related to the Spanish language. Here you will learn all there is to know about the patient. In Chapters Three through Eleven, you'll be following various members of a Latino family, the Espinozas, as they receive specialized medical attention.

The body
El cuerpo *(ehl 'kwehr-poh)*

In order to discuss in Spanish any form of medical treatment, you must first learn the words for parts of the body. These are only the basic body parts. We will discuss more of them in the following chapters. The best practice technique is to touch, point to, or move these body parts as you say them aloud:

Move the	**Mueva** *(moo-'eh-bah)* . . .
Touch the	**Toque** *('toh-keh)* . . .
Point to the	**Señale** *(seh-'nyah-leh)* . . .
arm	**el brazo** *(ehl 'brah-soh)*
back	**la espalda** *(lah ehs-'pahl-dah)*
blood	**la sangre** *(lah 'sahn-greh)*
bone	**el hueso** *(ehl 'weh-soh)*
chest	**el pecho** *(ehl 'peh-choh)*
ear	**la oreja** *(lah oh-'reh-hah)*

eye	**el ojo** *(ehl 'oh-hoh)*
elbow	**el codo** *(ehl 'koh-doh)*
face	**la cara** *(lah 'kah-rah)*
finger	**el dedo** *(ehl 'deh-doh)*
foot	**el pie** *(ehl pee-'eh)*
hair	**el cabello** *(ehl kah-'beh-yoh)*
hand	**la mano** *(lah 'mah-noh)*
head	**la cabeza** *(lah kah-'beh-sah)*
knee	**la rodilla** *(lah roh-'dee-yah)*
leg	**la pierna** *(lah pee-'ehr-nah)*
mouth	**la boca** *(lah 'boh-kah)*
muscle	**el músculo** *(ehl 'moos-koo-loh)*
neck	**el cuello** *(ehl 'kweh-yoh)*
nerve	**el nervio** *(ehl 'nehr-bee-oh)*
nose	**la nariz** *(lah nah-'rees)*
shoulder	**el hombro** *(ehl 'ohm-broh)*
skin	**la piel** *(lah pee-'ehl)*
stomach	**el estómago** *(ehl eh-'stoh-mah-goh)*
toe	**el dedo del pie** *(ehl 'deh-doh dehl pee-'eh)*
tooth	**el diente** *(ehl dee-'ehn-teh)*

IMPORTANT: Learn these phrases as soon as you can.

Does it hurt?	**¿Le duele?** *(leh 'dweh-leh)*
Do they hurt?	**¿Le duelen?** *(leh 'dweh-lehn)*
It hurts!	**¡Me duele!** *(me 'dweh-leh)*
They hurt!	**¡Me duelen!** *(me 'dweh-lehn)*

(7) ¿CUÁNTO APRENDIÓ?

Can you translate these sentences?

Me duele la cabeza.	Son los brazos.
¿Le duelen los pies?	La nariz está en la cara.
¿Qué le duele?	Hay muchos dientes en la boca.
No me duelen los ojos.	No tiene diez dedos.

Who is it?

¿Quién es? *(kee-'ehn ehs)*

Now that you know what hurts, let's find out who needs your assistance. Some of the first words you'll hear as a beginner are those that designate the "who" of a sentence.

I **yo** *(yoh)*	We **nosotros** *(noh-'soh-trohs)*
You **usted** *(oo-'stehd)*	You, plural **ustedes** *(oo-'steh-dehs)*
She **ella** *('eh-yah)*	He **él** *(ehl)*
They, feminine **ellas** *('eh-yahs)*	They, masculine **ellos** *('eh-yohs)*

This is how they might appear in conversation:

He has big feet. **Él tiene pies grandes.**
(ehl tee-'eh-neh 'pee-ehs 'grahn-dehs)

How are you? **¿Cómo está usted?** *('koh-moh eh-'stah oo-'stehd)*

I have blue eyes. **Yo tengo ojos azules.**
(yoh 'tehn-goh 'oh-hohs ah-'soo-lehs)

They are the patients. **Ellos son los pacientes.**
('eh-yohs sohn lohs pah-see-'ehn-tehs)

We are doctors. **Nosotros somos doctores.**
(noh-'soh-trohs 'soh-mohs dohk-'toh-rehs)

Where is she? **¿Dónde está ella?** *('dohn-deh eh-'stah 'eh-yah)*

¡No Se Olvide!

• **Nosotras** *(noh-'soh-trahs)* is "We" feminine: We are female doctors **Nosotras somos doctoras** *(noh-'soh-trahs 'soh-mohs dohk-'toh-rahs)*.

• You don't have to use the subject pronouns in every sentence. It's usually understood who's involved: **Nosotros somos** *(noh-'soh-trohs 'soh-mohs)* and **Somos** *('soh-mohs)* both mean "We are."

• **¿Y usted?** *(ee oo-'stehd)* "And you?" is a great expression.
¿Cómo está? *('koh-moh eh-'stah)* "How are you?"
Bien. ¿Y usted? *(bee-'ehn ee oo-'stehd)* "Fine. And you?"

Whose is it?

¿De quién es? *(deh kee-'ehn ehs)*

"**¿De quién es?**" *(deh kee-'ehn ehs)* means "Whose is it?" To answer this question in Spanish, you're going to need three new words. Look closely how each one functions:

It's my doctor.	**Es mi doctor.** *(ehs mee dohk-'tohr)*
It's your, his, her, or their doctor.	**Es su doctor.** *(ehs soo dohk-'tohr)*
It's our doctor.	**Es nuestro doctor.**
	(ehs noo-'ehs-troh dohk-'tohr)

Notice at happens when you talk about more than one.

mi doctor *(mee dohk-'tohr)*   **mis doctores** *(mees dohk-'toh-rehs)*
su doctor *(soo dohk-'tohr)*   **sus doctores** *(soos dohk-'toh-rehs)*
nuestro doctor *(noo-'ehs-troh dohk-'tohr)*
nuestros doctores *(noo-'ehs-trohs dohk-'toh-rehs)*

And don't forget the change when you refer to the feminine.

Our female friend   **nuestra amiga** *(noo-'ehs-trah ah-'mee-gah)*

Now try these other possessive words:

mine	**mío** *('mee-oh)*
yours, his, hers, or theirs.	**suyo** *('soo-yoh)*

If something "belongs to" someone else, use **de**:

It's Mary's.	**Es de María.** *(ehs deh mah-'ree-ah)*
It's the hospital's.	**Es del hospital.** *(ehs dehl ohs-pee-'tahl)*
It's his.	**Es de él.** *(ehs deh ehl)*

(8) ¿CUÁNTO APRENDIÓ?

Fill in the missing word.

Yo tengo mi papel.
Sr. Pérez tiene _____ papel.
Los niños tienen _____ papel.
Nosotros tenemos _____ papel.

A description, please

Una descripción, por favor.

('oo-nah dehs-kreep-see-'ohn, pohr fah-'bohr)

As you begin to describe people, places, and things in Spanish, it is important to add these words to your vocabulary. As you read this list, think of all the comments you can make about your patients.

alive	**vivo** *('bee-boh)*
asleep	**dormido** *(dohr-'mee-doh)*
available	**disponible** *(dees-poh-'neeb-leh)*
awake	**despierto** *(dehs-pee-'ehr-toh)*
bad	**malo** *('mah-loh)*
better	**mejor** *(meh-'hohr)*
big	**grande** *('grahn-deh)*
clean	**limpio** *('leem-pee-oh)*
cold	**frío** *('free-oh)*
correct	**correcto** *(koh-'rrehk-toh)*
crazy	**loco** *('loh-koh)*
dangerous	**peligroso** *(peh-lee-'groh-soh)*
dead	**muerto** *('mwehr-toh)*
deep	**profundo** *(proh-'foon-doh)*
difficult	**difícil** *(dee-'fee-seel)*
dirty	**sucio** *('soo-see·oh)*
dry	**seco** *('seh-koh)*
dull (edge)	**romo** *('roh-moh)*
dull (sound)	**sordo** *('sohr-doh)*
easy	**fácil** *('fah-seel)*
empty	**vacío** *(bah-'see-oh)*
fast	**rápido** *('rah-pee-doh)*
fat	**gordo** *('gohr-doh)*
full	**lleno** *('yeh-noh)*
good	**bueno** *('bweh-noh)*
hard	**duro** *('doo-roh)*
hot	**caliente** *(kah-lee-'ehn-teh)*
new	**nuevo** *(noo-eh-boh)*

old	**viejo** *(bee-'eh-hoh)*
older	**mayor** *(mah-'yohr)*
poor	**pobre** *('poh-breh)*
pretty	**bonito** *(boh-'nee-toh)*
quiet	**tranquilo** *(trahn-'kee-loh)*
restless	**inquieto** *(een-kee-'eh-toh)*
rich	**rico** *('ree-koh)*
safe	**seguro** *(seh-'goo-roh)*
sane	**cuerdo** *('kwehr-doh)*
severe	**severo** *(seh-'beh-roh)*
sharp (edge)	**afilado** *(ah-fee-'lah-doh)*
sharp (sound)	**agudo** *(ah-'goo-doh)*
short in height	**bajo** *('bah-hoh)*, in length **corto** *('kohr-toh)*
sick	**enfermo** *(ehn-'fehr-moh)*
slow	**lento** *('lehn-toh)*
small	**chico** *('chee-koh)*
soft	**blando** *('blahn-doh)*
strong	**fuerte** *('fwehr-teh)*
tall	**alto** *('ahl-toh)*
thick	**grueso** *(groo-'eh-soh)*
thin	**delgado** *(dehl-'gah-doh)*
ugly	**feo** *('feh-oh)*
weak	**débil** *(deh-'beel)*
well	**bien** *(bee-'ehn)*
wet	**mojado** *(moh-'hah-doh)*
worse	**peor** *(peh-'ohr)*
wrong	**equivocado** *(eh-kee-boh-'kah-doh)*
young	**joven** *('hoh-behn)*
younger	**menor** *(meh-'nohr)*

Notice how many descriptive words end in the same letters.

bent	**doblado** *(doh-'blah-doh)*
busy	**ocupado** *(oh-koo-'pah-doh)*
closed	**cerrado** *(seh-'rrah-doh)*

comfortable	**cómodo** *('koh-moh-doh)*
private	**privado** *(pree-'bah-doh)*
prohibited	**prohibido** *(proh-ee-'bee-doh)*
watery	**aguado** *(ah-'gwah-doh)*

To describe your actions in Spanish, try some of these:

completely	**completamente** *(kohm-pleh-tah-'mehn-teh)*
immediately	**inmediatamente** *(een-meh-dee-ah-tah-'mehn-teh)*
normally	**normalmente** *(nohr-mahl-'mehn-teh)*
quickly	**rápidamente** *(rah-pee-dah-'mehn-teh)*
slowly	**lentamente** *(lehn-tah-'mehn-teh)*

Don't forget the **o** at the end of a word has to change to **a** when you're referring to the feminine.

El muchacho es alto. *(ehl moo-'chah-choh ehs 'ahl-toh)*
La muchacha es alta. *(lah moo-'chah-chah ehs 'ahl-tah)*
El cuarto está lleno. *(ehl 'kwahr-toh eh-'stah 'yeh-noh)*
La oficina está llena. *(lah oh-fee-'see-nah eh-'stah 'yeh-nah)*

Also, remember to combine your words in reverse order:

| It's a new house. | **Es una casa nueva.** |
| | *(ehs 'oo-nah 'kah-sah noo-'eh-bah)* |

Finally, notice what you can do with these little words: I'm—**Estoy** *(eh-'stoh-ee)*

I'm sick	estoy **enfermo** *(ehn-'fehr-moh)*
I'm sicker	estoy **más enfermo** *(mahs ehn-'fehr-moh)*
I'm as sick as	estoy **tan enfermo como**
	(tahn ehn-'fehr-moh 'koh-moh)

These descriptions are easy to recall (but check out the stresses):

general *(heh-neh-'rahl)*
gradual *(grah-doo-'ahl)*
local *(loh-'kahl)*
normal *(nohr-'mahl)*
simple *('seem-pleh)*

⑨ ¿Cuánto Aprendió?

• Practice using your new vocabulary by reading and translating these sentences:

Ella es alta y él es bajo.
('eh-yah ehs 'ahl-tah ee ehl ehs 'bah-ho)

Los niños están dormidos.
(lohs 'nee-nyohs eh-'stahn dohr-'mee-dohs)

No somos muy ricos. *(noh 'soh-mohs 'moo-ee 'ree-kohs)*

El doctor es viejo y delgado.
(ehl dohk-'tohr ehs bee-'eh-hoh ee dehl-'gah-doh)

¿Dónde está el agua caliente?
('dohn-deh eh-'stah ehl 'ah-gwah cah-lee-'ehn-teh)

• Complete these sentences with the words you just learned.

María es . . . *(mah-'ree-ah ehs)*

as sick as her brother _____

sick _____

sicker _____

El paciente es muy . . . *(ehl pah-see-'ehn-teh ehs 'moo-ee)*

fat _____

weak _____

young _____

Ustedes son . . . *(oo-'steh-dehs sohn)*

older _____

pretty _____

thin _____

More important words
Más palabras importantes
(mahs pah-'lah-brahs eem-pohr-'tahn-tehs)

Let's learn some more practical terms that can be used as single-word responses. Add some of these to your vocabulary, and you'll begin to communicate:

all	**todo** *('toh-doh)*
almost	**casi** *('kah-see)*
alone	**solo** *('soh-loh)*
also	**también** *(tahm-bee-'ehn)*
different	**diferente** *(dee-feh-'rehn-teh)*
enough	**bastante** *(bah-'stahn-teh)*
few	**pocos** *(poh-kohs)*
first	**primero** *(pree-'meh-roh)*
last	**último** *('ool-tee-moh)*
less	**menos** *('meh-nohs)*
many	**muchos** *('moo-chohs)*
more	**más** *(mahs)*
next	**siguiente** *(see-gee-'ehn-teh)*
none	**ninguno** *(neen-'goo-noh)*
nothing	**nada** *('nah-dah)*
same	**mismo** *('mees-moh)*
some	**algunos** *(ahl-'goo-nohs)*
something	**algo** *('ahl-goh)*
too much	**demasiado** *(deh-mah-see-'ah-doh)*
very	**muy** *('moo·ee)*

They aren't the same patients.
No son los mismos pacientes.
(noh 'soh-mohs lohs 'mees-mohs pah-see-'ehn-tehs)

Something is in the stomach.
Algo está en el estómago.
('ahl-goh eh-'stah ehn ehl ehs-'toh-mah-goh)

There's enough medicine, too.

Hay bastante medicina, también.

('ah·ee bah-'stahn-teh meh-dee-'see-nah, tahm-bee-'ehn)

More action
Más acción *(mahs ahk-see·'ohn)*

Are you ready to expand your list of action words? Warm up by reviewing the following pattern.

Tengo que <u>comer</u> y <u>dormir</u> en el cuarto.

('tehn-goh keh koh-'mehr ee dohr-'meer ehn ehl 'kwahr-toh)

Tiene que <u>escribir</u> y <u>leer</u> en la mesa.

(tee-'eh-neh keh ehs-kree-'beer ee leh-'ehr ehn lah 'meh-sah)

Tienen que <u>ir</u> a la cita. *(tee-'eh-'nehn keh eer ah lah 'see-tah)*

Tenemos que <u>hablar</u> más español en el hospital.

(teh-'neh-mohs keh ah-'blahr mahs ehs-pah-'nyohl ehn ehl ohs-pee-'tahl)

Now take a look at more survival action words.

to answer	**contestar** *(kohn-tehs-'tahr)*
to ask	**preguntar** *(preh-goon-'tahr)*
to come	**venir** *(beh-'neer)*
to do/make	**hacer** *(ah-'sehr)*
to leave	**salir** *(sah-'leer)*
to return	**regresar** *(reh-greh-'sahr)*
to say	**decir** *(deh-'seer)*
to understand	**entender** *(ehn-tehn-'dehr)*
to walk	**caminar** *(kah-mee-'nahr)*

The following verb is very important in helping a patient. Learn it and then combine it with a different set of words to create another pattern.

TO NEED	**NECESITAR** *(neh-seh-see-'tahr)*
I need	**necesito** *(neh-seh-'see-toh)*
I need to ask	**necesito preguntar** *(neh-seh-'see-toh preh-goon-'tahr)*
you need,	
he/she needs	**necesita** *(neh-seh-'see-tah)*

you/need, he/she needs to walk	**necesita caminar** *(neh-seh-'see-tah kah-mee-'nahr)*
you (plural) or they need	**necesitan** *(neh-seh-'see-tahn)*
you (plural), they need to return	**necesitan regresar** *(neh-seh-'see-tahn reh-greh-'sahr)*
we need	**necesitamos** *(neh-seh-see-'tah-mohs)*
we need to leave	**necesitamos salir** *(neh-seh-see-'tah-mohs sah-'leer)*

The verb **volver** *(bohl-'behr)* also means "to return." As in most languages, there is always more than one way to say the same thing.

By putting "No" in front of your verbs, you can tell "not to do" something.

no returning	**no regresar, no volver**
	(noh reh-greh-'sahr, noh bohl-'behr)
no running	**no correr** *(noh koh-'rrehr)*
no leaving	**no salir** *(noh sah-'leer)*

These words mean almost the same as **necesita.** Learn them:

necessary	**necesario** *(neh-seh-'sah-ree·oh)*
	Es necesario preguntar.
	(ehs neh-seh-'sah-ree·oh preh-goon-'tahr)
must	**debe** *('deh-beh)*
	Debe regresar. *('deh-beh reh-greh-'sahr)*

⑩ ¿ C U Á N T O   A P R E N D I Ó ?

Practice **necesitar** with your new vocabulary. Read the following aloud and translate the sentences.

Necesito una cita. *(neh-seh-'see-tah 'oo-nah 'see-tah)*
¿Necesita usted la medicina?
(neh-seh-'see-tah oo-'stehd lah meh-dee-'see-nah)
Margarita y yo necesitamos camas.
(mahr-gah-'ree-tah ee yoh neh-seh-see-'tah-mohs 'kah-mahs)

Family

La familia *(lah fah-'mee-lee-ah)*

As you build conversations with your Latino patients, be aware of family and friends who lend their support and encouragement. Many of them will be relatives, **parientes** *(pah-ree-'ehn-tehs)*, who need to be greeted and kept informed. The names for family members in Spanish can be memorized easily by reading aloud the following words:

It's my	Es mi *(ehs mee)* . . .
aunt	**tía** *('tee-ah)*
boyfriend	**novio** *('noh-bee·oh)*
brother	**hermano** *(ehr-'mah-noh)*
brother-in-law	**cuñado** *(koo-'nyah-doh)*
cousin	**primo** *('pree-moh)*
daughter	**hija** *('ee-hah)*
daughter-in-law	**nuera** *('nweh-rah)*
father	**padre** *('pah-dreh)*
father-in-law	**suegro** *('sweh-groh)*
girlfriend	**novia** *(noh-'bee·ah)*
granddaughter	**nieta** *(nee-'eh-tah)*
grandfather	**abuelo** *(ah-'bweh-loh)*
grandmother	**abuela** *(ah-'bweh-lah)*
grandson	**nieto** *(nee-'eh-toh)*
husband	**esposo** *(ehs-'poh-soh)*
mother	**madre** *('mah-dreh)*
mother-in-law	**suegra** *('sweh-grah)*
nephew	**sobrino** *(soh-'bree-noh)*
niece	**sobrina** *(soh-'bree-nah)*
sister	**hermana** *(ehr-'mah-nah)*
sister-in-law	**cuñada** *(koo-'nyah-dah)*
son	**hijo** *('ee-hoh)*
son-in-law	**yerno** *('yehr-noh)*
uncle	**tío** *('tee-oh)*
wife	**esposa** *(ehs-'poh-sah)*

For affection, add **-ito** and **-ita** to your words:

grandmother	**abuela** *(ah-'bweh-lah)*
granny	**abuelita** *(ah-bweh-'lee-tah)*
brother	**hermano** *(ehr-'mah-noh)*
little brother	**hermanito** *(ehr-mah-'nee-toh)*
baby	**bebé** *(beh-'beh)*
tiny baby	**bebito** *(beh-'bee-toh)*

DOS CULTURAS

In-laws and godparents, **padrinos** *(pah-'dree-nohs)*, are considered important family members and often assist in decision-making.

The extended family may include friends or neighbors who have lent their support to family members in the past. They may also want to be involved in hospital visits or procedures.

Latino families respect the elderly. Older children, too, are given more responsibilities and are treated differently. When dealing with a large family, it is usually a good idea to find out who is in charge.

Now, you're going to need more vocabulary and a few more Spanish skills before you can effectively communicate with non-English speakers.

Begin with these:

youth	**joven** *('hoh-behn)*
elderly person	**anciano** *(ahn-see-'ah-noh)*
buddy	**compañero** *(kohm-pah-nee-'eh-roh)*
couple	**pareja** *(pah-'reh-hah)*
partner	**socio** *('soh-see-oh)*

¿CUÁNTO APRENDIÓ?

Start practicing today by making comments abouts various family members.

Do you have grandchildren?
¿Tiene usted nietos? *(tee-'eh-neh oos-'tehd nee-eh-tohs)*

Her son-in-law has to drive.
Su yerno tiene que manejar.
(soo 'yehr-noh tee-'eh-neh keh mah-neh-'har)

His sisters are nurses.
Sus hermanas son enfermeras.
(soos ehr-'mah-nahs sohn ehn-fehr-'meh-rahs)

My son is in his room.
Mi hijo está en su cuarto.
(mee 'ee-hoh ehs-'tah ehn soo 'kwahr-toh)

Point to your girlfriend.
Señale a su novia.
(seh 'nyah loh ah soo 'noh boo ah)

Our grandmother needs to return.
Nuestra abuela necesita regresar.
(noo-'ehs-trah ah-'bweh-lah neh-seh-'see-tah)

Who is your father?
¿Quién es su padre? *(kee-'ehn ehs soo 'pah-dreh)*

Chapter Three

Capítulo Tres
(kah-'pee-too-loh trehs)

Admissions
Admisiones
(ahd-mee-see·'oh-nehs)

The Espinozas have been in this country for less than a year and they've suddenly required the services of a medical facility. There are six members of the Espinoza family. Juan Espinoza and his wife María are the parents of two young children, Margarita and Miguel. Juan's father, Carlos, lives next door, and María's grandmother, Guadalupe, is in a skilled nursing home nearby.

Each family member has a unique problem and needs to be followed from admissions through release. All of the words and expressions used to handle these cases have either already been introduced or will appear in the remaining text. Begin by greeting the Espinozas as they walk through the front doors of your medical facility.

Greetings
Saludos *(sah-'loo-dohs)*

Do you speak English?	**¿Habla inglés?** *('ah-blah een-'glehs)*
Good afternoon. What's going on?	**Buenas tardes. ¿Qué pasa?** *('bweh-nahs 'tahr-dehs keh 'pah-sah)*
Good evening. How's it going?	**Buenas noches. ¿Qué tal?** *('bweh-nahs 'noh-chehs keh tahl)*
Good morning. How are you?	**Buenos días. ¿Cómo está?** *('bweh-nohs 'dee-ahs 'koh-moh eh-'stah)*
Come.	**Venga.** *('behn-gah)*

Go with the nurse.	**Vaya con la enfermera.**
	('bah-yah kohn lah ehn-fehr-'meh-rah)
Sit on the chair.	**Siéntese en la silla.**
	(see-'ehn-teh-seh ehn lah 'see-yah)
Wait in the room.	**Espere en el cuarto.**
	(ehs-'peh-reh ehn ehl 'kwahr-toh)

As long as we're telling the Espinoza family what to do, let's add a few more commands to your vocabulary.

Bring	**traiga** *('trah-ee-gah)*
Bring the water	**Traiga el agua.** *('trah-ee-gah ehl 'ah-gwah)*
Call	**llame** *('yah-meh)*
Call the doctor.	**Llame al doctor.** *('yah-meh ahl dohk-'tohr)*
Carry	**lleve** *('yeh-beh)*
Carry the baby.	**Lleve el bebé.** *('yeh-beh ehl beh-'beh)*
Get up	**súbase** *('soo-bah-seh)*
Get up on the table.	**Súbase a la mesa.** *('soo-bah-seh ah lah 'meh-sah)*
Sign	**firme** *('feer-meh)*
Sign your name.	**Firme su nombre.** *('feer-meh soo 'nohm-breh)*
Take	**tome** *('toh-meh)*
Take the medicine.	**Tome la medicina.**
	('toh-meh lah meh-dee-'see- nah)
Turn	**dese vuelta** *('deh-seh 'bwehl-tah)*
Turn, please.	**Dese vuelta, por favor.**
	('deh-seh 'bwehl-tah pohr fah-'bohr)

The information

La información *(lah een-fohr-mah-see·'ohn)*

This is the Espinoza's first trip to an American hospital. They're nervous, and they don't speak much English. You're the only one available to walk them through the registration process. Be patient, friendly, and courteous because it's going to take time. Use the expression ¿**Cuál es su . . .?** (What is your . . .?) for virtually every question on the registration forms.

What is your . . .?	**¿Cuál es su . . .?** *(kwahl ehs soo)*
address	**dirección** *(dee-rehk-see-'ohn)*
age	**edad** *(eh-'dahd)*
beeper number	**número de bíper** *('noo-meh-roh deh 'bee-pehr)*
blood type	**tipo de sangre** *('tee-poh deh 'sahn-greh)*
cell phone number	**número de teléfono celular** *('noo-meh-roh deh teh-'leh-foh-noh seh-loo-'lahr)*
date of birth	**fecha de nacimiento** *('feh-chah deh nah-see-mee-'ehn-toh)*
email number	**número de correo electrónico** *('noo-meh-roh deh kohr-'reh-oh eh-lehk-'troh-nee-koh)*
first language	**primer lenguaje** *(pree-'mehr lehn-'gwah-heh)*
first name	**primer nombre** *(pree-'mehr 'nohm-breh)*
full name	**nombre completo** *('nohm-breh kohm-'pleh-toh)*
group number	**número del grupo** *('noo-meh-roh dehl 'groo-poh)*
height	**altura** *(ahl-'too-rah)*
insurance company	**compañía de seguros** *(kohm-pah-'nyee-ah deh seh-'goo-rohs)*
last name	**apellido** *(ah-peh-'yee-doh)*
maiden name	**nombre de soltera** *('nohm-breh deh sohl-'teh-rah)*
marital status	**estado civil** *(eh-'stah-doh see-'beel)*
middle initial	**segunda inicial** *(seh-'goon-dah ee-nee-see-'ahl)*
nationality	**nacionalidad** *(nah-see-oh-nah-lee-'dahd)*
place of birth	**lugar de nacimiento** *(loo-'gahr deh nah-see-mee-'ehn-toh)*
place of employment	**lugar de empleo** *(loo-'gahr deh ehm-'pleh-oh)*
policy number	**número de póliza** *('noo-meh-roh deh 'poh-lee-sah)*

race	**raza** *('rah-sah)*
relationship	**parentezco** *(pah-rehn-'tehs-koh)*
religion	**religión** *(reh-lee-'gee-'ohn)*
sex	**sexo** *('sehk-soh)*
social security number	**número de seguro social**
	('noo-meh-roh deh seh-'goo-roh soh-see-'ahl)
telephone number	**número de teléfono**
	('noo-meh-roh deh teh-'leh-foh-noh)
weight	**peso** *('peh-soh)*
zip code	**zona postal** *('soh-nah poh-'stahl)*

Perhaps the easiest way to learn more personal information about the Espinoza family is to ask simple questions that they can answer with **sí** or **no**.

Do you smoke?	**¿Fuma usted?** *('foo-mah oos-'tehd)*
Do you drink alcohol?	**¿Toma alcohol usted?**
	('toh-mah ahl-koh-'ohl oos-'tehd)
Do you use drugs?	**¿Usa drogas usted?**
	('oo-sah 'droh-gahs oos-'tehd)

Are you . . .?	**¿Es . . . ?** *(ehs)*
divorced	**divorciado** *(dee-bohr-see-'ah-doh)*
married	**casado** *(kah-'sah-doh)*
single	**soltero** *(sohl-'teh-roh)*

Do you have . . .?	**¿Tiene . . .?** *(tee-'eh-neh)*
allergies	**alergias** *(ah-'lehr-hee·ahs)*
documents	**los documentos** *(lohs doh-koo-'mehn-tohs)*
a driver's license	**una licencia de manejar**
	('oo-nah lee-'sehn-see·ah deh mah-neh-'hahr)
the forms	**los formularios** *(lohs fohr-moo-'lah-ree·ohs)*
high blood pressure	**alta presión sanguínea**
	('ahl-tah preh-see-'ohn sahn-'gee-neh-ah)
identification	**identificación** *(ee-dehn-tee-fee-kah-see-'ohn)*

a lot of pain	**mucho dolor** *('moo-choh doh-'lohr)*
medical insurance	**seguro médico** *(seh-'goo-roh 'meh-dee-koh)*
a question	**una pregunta** *('oo-nah preh-'goon-tah)*
the receipt	**el recibo** *(ehl reh-'see-boh)*
the results	**los resultados** *(lohs reh-sool-'tah-dohs)*
seizures	**ataques** *(ah-'tah-kehs)*
high temperature	**fiebre** *(fee-'eh-breh)*

Do you need . . .?	**¿Necesita . . . ?** *(neh-seh-'see-tah)*
an appointment	**una cita** *('oo-nah 'see-tah)*
a class	**una clase** *('oo-nah 'klah-seh)*
a consultation	**una consulta** *('oo-nah kohn-'sool-tah)*
a counselor	**un consejero** *(oon kohn-seh-'heh-roh)*
an exam	**un examen** *(oon ehk-'sah-mehn)*
an interpreter	**un intérprete** *(oon een-'tehr-preh-teh)*
a schedule	**un horario** *(oon oh-'rah-ree·oh)*

Are there . . .?	**¿Hay . . .?** *('ah-ee)*
problems with your heart	**problemas con su corazón?** *(proh-'bleh-mahs kohn soo koh-rah-'sohn)*
problems with your hearing	**problemas con sus oídos** *(proh-'bleh-mahs kohn soos oh-'ee-dohs)*
problems with your kidneys	**problemas con sus riñones** *(proh-'bleh-mahs kohn soos reen-'yoh-nehs)*
problems with your respiration	**problemas con su respiración** *(proh-'bleh-mahs kohn soo rehs-pee-rah-see-'ohn)*
problems with your stomach	**problemas con su estómago** *(proh-'bleh-mahs kohn soo ehs-'toh-mah-goh)*
problems with your vision	**problemas con su visión** *(proh-'bleh-mahs kohn soo bee-see-'ohn)*

(11) ¿ C U Á N T O   A P R E N D I Ó ?

Translate the English to form a complete sentence.

¿Cuál es su . . .? *(kwahl ehs soo)*
   (first name, father's last name, address)
¿Quién . . .? *(kee-'ehn)* (is the doctor, is sick)
¿Tiene. . .? *(tee-'eh-neh)* (medical insurance, the receipt)

A lot of work
Mucho trabajo *('moo-choh trah-'bah-hoh)*

While you're taking the patient's personal information, you will occasionally pose questions related to his or her current occupation and employment status. Although this list is not complete, do a "job" on all of these:

carpenter	**el carpintero** *(ehl kahr-peen-'teh-roh)*
cashier	**el cajero** *(ohl kah-'heh-roh)*
cook	**el cocinero** *(ehl koh-see-'neh-roh)*
employee	**el empleado** *(ehl ehm-pleh-'ah-doh)*
farmer	**el campesino** *(ehl kahm-peh-'see-noh)*
fireman	**el bombero** *(ehl bohm-'beh-roh)*
gardener	**el jardinero** *(ehl hahr-dee-'neh-roh)*
laborer	**el obrero** *(ehl oh-'breh-roh)*
lawyer	**el abogado** *(ehl ah-boh-'gah-doh)*
manager	**el gerente** *(ehl heh-'rehn-teh)*
mechanic	**el mecánico** *(ehl meh-'kah-nee-koh)*
painter	**el pintor** *(ehl peen-'tohr)*
plumber	**el plomero** *(ehl ploh-'meh-roh)*
police officer	**el policía** *(ehl poh-lee-'see-ah)*
priest	**el cura** *(ehl 'koo-rah)*
salesman	**el vendedor** *(ehl behn-deh-'dohr)*
secretary	**el secretario** *(ehl seh-kreh-'tah-ree-oh)*
servant	**el criado** *(ehl kree-'ah-doh)*

student	**el estudiante** *(ehl ehs-too-dee-'ahn-teh)*
teacher	**el maestro** *(ehl mah-'ehs-troh)*
truck driver	**el camionero** *(ehl kah-mee-'oh-neh-roh)*
waiter	**el mesero** *(ehl meh-'seh-roh)*

¡ No Se Olvide !

• Don't forget to change the ending of the nouns when you are referring to females: Anne is the cook. **Ana es la cocinera.**

• **Jefe** means "boss." Who's your boss? **¿Quién es su jefe?** *(kee-'ehn ehs soo 'heh-feh)*

You may also need other work-related vocabulary words. These tell us where most people are employed:

I work in	Trabajo en . . . .
agency	**la agencia** *(lah ah-'hehn-see·ah)*
airport	**el aeropuerto** *(ehl ah·eh-roh-'pwehr-toh)*
bank	**el banco** *(ehl 'bahn-koh)*
building	**el edificio** *(ehl eh-dee-'fee-see·oh)*
business	**el negocio** *(ehl neh-'goh-see·oh)*
church	**la iglesia** *(lah ee-'gleh-see·ah)*
company	**la compañía** *(lah kohm-pah-'nyee-ah)*
factory	**la fábrica** *(lah 'fah-bree-kah)*
movie theater	**el cine** *(ehl 'see-neh)*
park	**el parque** *(ehl 'pahr-keh)*
restaurant	**el restaurante** *(oon rehs-tah·oo-'rahn-teh)*
school	**la escuela** *(lah ehs-'kweh-lah)*
station	**la estación** *(lah ehs-tah-see-'ohn)*
store	**la tienda** *(lah tee-'ehn-dah)*
warehouse	**el almacén** *(ehl ahl-mah-'sehn)*

¡No Se Olvide!

Just a reminder—while chatting about occupations, use **es** *(ehs)* instead of **está** *(eh-'stah):* Frank is a chef. **Francisco es un cocinero.** *(frahn-'sees-koh ehs oon koh-see-'neh-roh).* And use **está** *(eh-'stah)* to state where a person is located: He is at the restaurant. **Está en el restaurante.** *(eh-'stah ehn oon rehs-tah-oo-'rahn-teh).*

Which illnesses?
¿Cuáles enfermedades?
('kwah-lehs ehn-fehr-meh-'dah-dehs)

As you continue to complete the registration forms, use the terms you need from the list below to learn the medical history of the Espinoza family. Again, have them answer with **sí** or **no**.

AIDS	**SIDA** *('see-dah)*
anemia	**anemia** *(ah-'neh-mee-ah)*
asthma	**asma** *('ahs-mah)*
cancer	**cáncer** *('kahn-sehr)*
chicken pox	**varicela** *(bah-ree-'seh-lah)*
cholera	**cólera** *('koh-leh-rah)*
diabetes	**diabetes** *(de-ah-'beh-tehs)*
diphtheria	**difteria** *(deef-'teh-ree-ah)*
epilepsy	**epilepsia** *(eh-pee-'lehp-see-ah)*
German measles	**rubéola** *(roo-'beh-oh-lah)*
HIV	**VIH** *(beh-ee-'ah-cheh)*
heart disease	**enfermedad del corazón** *(ehn-fehr-meh-'dahd dehl koh-rah-'sohn)*
hepatitis	**hepatitis** *(ehp-ah-'tee-tees)*
leukemia	**leucemia** *(leh-oo-'seh-mee-ah)*
measles	**sarampión** *(sah-rahm-pee-'ohn)*
meningitis	**meningitis** *(meh-neen-'hee-tees)*
mumps	**paperas** *(pah-'peh-rahs)*
pneumonia	**pulmonía** *(pool-moh-'nee-ah)*

polio	**polio** *('poh-lee·oh)*
rheumatic fever	**fiebre reumática** *(fee-'eh-breh reh-oo-'mah-tee-kah)*
scarlet fever	**escarlatina** *(ehs-kahr-lah-'tee-nah)*
smallpox	**viruela** *(bee-roo-'eh-lah)*
tetanus	**tétano** *('teh-tah-noh)*
tuberculosis	**tuberculosis** *(too-behr-koo-'loh-sees)*
typhoid	**tifoidea** *(tee-foh·ee-'deh-ah)*
whooping cough	**tos ferina, tos convulsiva**
	(tohs feh-'ree-nah, tohs kohn-bool-'see-bah)

The Consent Form
El formulario de consentimiento
(ehl fohr-moo-'lah-ree-oh deh kohn-sehn-tee-mee-'ehn-toh)

Do you have a consent form?

¿Tiene usted un formulario de consentimiento?

(tee-'eh-neh oos-'tehd oon fohr-moo-'lah-ree-oh deh kohn-sehn-tee-mee-'ehn-toh)

Would you like one?

¿Quisiera tener uno?

(kee-see-'eh-rah teh-'nehr 'oo-noh)

Who will bring me a copy of the form?

¿Quién me va a traer una copia del formulario?

(kee-'ehn meh bah ah trah-'ehr 'oo-nah 'koh-pee-ah dehl fohr-moo-'lah-ree-oh)

Do you have any special requests?

¿Tiene usted algunos pedidos adicionales?

(tee-'eh-neh oos-'tehd ahl-'goo-nohs peh-'dee-dohs ah-dee-see-oh-'nah-lehs)

Who is your legal healthcare agent?

¿Quién es su agente legal para el cuidado de la salud?

(kee-'ehn ehs soo ah-'hehn-teh leh-'gahl 'pah-rah ehl kwee-'dah-doh deh lah sah-'lood)

We need your permission.

Necesitamos su permiso.

(neh-seh-see-'tah-mohs soo pehr-'mee-soh)

Do you have insurance?

¿Tiene seguro? *(tee-'eh-neh seh-'goo-roh)*

Questions related to admitting often lead to health insurance coverage. As you read the following sentences, pay particular attention to those words you may already know.

Do you have insurance?

¿Tiene seguro? *(tee-'eh-neh seh-'goo-roh)*

Which is your insurance company?

¿Cuál es su compañía de seguros?
(kwahl ehs soo koh-pah-'nyee-ah deh seh-'goo-rohs)

What's your policy and group number?

¿Cuál es su número de póliza y grupo?
(kwahl ehs soo 'noo-meh-roh deh 'poh-lee-sah ee 'groo-poh)

If you need more information, learn these words and expressions:

employer	**empresario** *(ehm-preh-'sah-ree-oh)*
employment	**empleo** *(ehm-'pleh-oh)*
workman's compensation	**compensación de obrero**
	(kohm-pehn-sah-see-'ohn deh oh-'breh-roh)

What kind?	**¿Qué tipo?** *(keh 'tee-poh)*
An insurance for . . .	**Un seguro de . . .** *(oon seh-'goo-roh deh)*
accidents	**accidentes** *(ahk-see-'dehn-tehs)*
automobile	**automóvil** *(ow-toh-'moh-beel)*
Blue Cross	**Cruz Azul** *('kroos ah-'sool)*
Blue Shield	**Escudo Azul** *(ehs-'koo-doh ah-'sool)*
disability	**incapacidad** *(in-kah-pah-see-'dahd)*
family	**familia** *(fah-'mee-lee-ah)*
health	**salud** *(sah-'lood)*
hospital	**hospital** *(ohs-pee-'tahl)*
life	**vida** *('bee-dah)*
personal	**personal** *(pehr-soh-'nahl)*

Keep going:

federal grant	**beca federal** *('beh-kah feh-deh-'rahl)*
HMO	**Organización para el Mantenimiento de la Salud** *(ohr-gah-nee-sah-see-'ohn 'pah-rah ehl mahn-teh-nee-mee-'ehn-toh deh lah sah-'lood)*
PPO	**Organización de Proveedores Preferentes** *(ohr-gah-nee-sah-see-'ohn deh proh-beh-eh-'doh-rehs preh-feh-'rehn-tehs)*
special programs	**programas especiales** *(proh-'grah-mahs ehs-peh-see-'ah-lehs)*
state aid	**ayuda estatal** *(ah-'yoo-dah ehs-tah-'tahl)*

Dos Culturas

Many immigrants aren't familiar with health insurance procedures in the United States. Don't be surprised if some patients attempt to pay cash for hospital services.

Once you've filled out the registration and insurance forms, your next concern is why the Espinoza family has come to your hospital. Here are some questions you can use to acquire more basic information.

Do you have a doctor?	**¿Tiene un doctor?** *('tee-'eh-neh oon dohk-'tohr)*
Who is sick?	**¿Quién está enfermo?** *(kee-'ehn eh-'stah ehn-'fehr-moh)*
Who is your doctor?	**¿Quién es su doctor?** *(kee-'ehn ehs soo dohk-'tohr)*
Whose child is it?	**¿De quién es el niño?** *(deh kee-'ehn ehs ehl 'nee-nyoh)*

More key words:

benefits	**beneficios** *(beh-neh-'fee-see-ohs)*
cash	**efectivo** *(eh-fehk-'tee-boh)*

charge	**cargo** *('kahr-goh)*
check	**cheque** *('cheh-keh)*
cost	**costo** *('kohs-toh)*
deductible	**deducible** *(deh-doo-'seeb-leh)*
deposit	**depósito** *(deh-'poh-see-toh)*
discount	**descuento** *(dehs-'kwehn-toh)*
expenses	**gastos** *('gahs-tohs)*
free	**gratis** *('grah-tees)*
group	**grupo** *('groo-poh)*
income	**ingreso** *(een-'greh-soh)*
loan	**préstamo** *('prehs-tah-moh)*
member	**miembro** *(mee-'ehm-broh)*
plan	**plan** *(plahn)*
provider	**proveedor** *(proh-beh-eh-'dohr)*
resources	**recursos** *(reh-'koor-sohs)*

(12) ¿CUÁNTO APRENDIÓ?

Try to translate these sentences without using a dictionary.

¿Qué tipo de seguro tiene?
(keh 'tee-poh deh seh-'goo-roh tee-'eh-neh)

¿Cuál es la dirección de su empresario?
(kwahl ehs lah dee-rehk-see-'ohn deh soo ehm-preh-'sah-ree-oh)

Necesita seguro para accidentes.
('neh-seh-'see-etah seh-'goo-roh 'pah-rah ahk-see-'dehn-tehs)

Parts of the hospital
Las partes del hospital
(lahs 'pahr-tehs dehl ohs-pee-'tahl)

Once the Espinoza family has been interviewed, you'll want to send the patient to the appropriate department, or at least give the family general directions to different parts of the hospital. Pointing helps, but it only sends them so far. Here's some beginning vocabulary for everyone who works in Admissions. To practice the names of any objects or locations, try labeling them in Spanish with removable stickers. For daily practice, begin your phrases with one of the most valuable phrases in medicine:

Do you need . . . ?	**¿Necesita . . . ?** *(neh-seh-'see-tah)*
Administration	**La administración**
	(lah ahd-mee-nee-strah-see-'ohn)
Cashier	**El cajero** *(ehl kah-'heh-roh)*
Chapel	**La capilla** *(lah kah-'pee-yah)*
Conference Room	**La sala de conferencias**
	(lah 'sah-lah deh kohn-feh-'rehn-see-ahs)
Delivery Room	**La sala de partos**
	(lah 'sah-lah deh 'pahr-tohs)
Emergency Room	**la sala de emergencia**
	(lah 'sah-lah deh eh-mehr-'hehn-see-ah)
Intensive Care	**la sala de cuidados intensivos**
	(lah 'sah-lah deh kwee-'dah-dohs een-tehn-'see-bohs)
Laboratory	**El laboratorio** *(ehl lah-boh-rah-'toh-ree-oh)*
Maternity Ward	**la sala de maternidad**
	(lah 'sah-lah deh mah-tehr-nee-'dahd)
Meditation Room	**La sala de meditación**
	(lah 'sah-lah deh meh-dee-tah-see-'ohn)
Nursery	**La guardería** *(lah gwahr-deh-'ree-ah)*
Operating Room	**la sala de operaciones**
	(lah 'sah-lah deh oh-peh-rah-see·'oh-nehs)
Radiology	**Radiología** *(rah-dee-oh-loh-'hee-ah)*
Recovery Room	**la sala de recuperación**
	(lah 'sah-lah deh reh-koo-peh-rah-see·'ohn)
Waiting Room	**la sala de espera**
	(lah 'sah-lah deh ehs-'peh-rah)

And when it comes to centers . . .

Blood Donor Center	**Centro de donación de sangre** *('sehn-troh deh doh-nah-see-'ohn deh 'sahn-greh)*
Cancer Center	**Centro de cáncer** *('sehn-troh deh 'kahn-sehr)*
Dialysis Center	**Centro de diálisis** *('sehn-troh deh dee-'ah-lee-sees)*
Neuropsychiatric Center	**Centro neurosiquiátrico** *('sehn-troh neh-oo-roh-see-kee-'ah-tree-koh)*
Orthopedic Center	**Centro ortopédico** *('sehn-troh ohr-toh-'peh-dee-koh)*

Let's see the inside of the building . . .

ATM machine	**El cajero automático** *(ehl kah-'heh-roh ow-toh-'mah-tee-koh)*

basement	**el sótano** *(ehl 'soh-tah-noh)*
cafeteria	**la cafetería** *(lah kah-feh-teh-'ree-ah)*
department	**el departamento** *(ehl deh-pahr-tah-'mehn-toh)*
elevator	**el ascensor** *(ehl ah-sehn-'sohr)*
entrance	**la entrada** *(lah ehn-'trah-dah)*
exit	**la salida** *(lah sah-'lee-dah)*
gift shop	**la tienda de regalos** *(lah tee-'ehn-dah deh reh-'gah-lohs)*
hallway	**el corredor** *(ehl koh-rreh-'dohr)*
main lobby	**el salón principal** *(ehl sah-'lohn preen-see-'pahl)*
mailbox	**el buzón** *(ehl boo-'sohn)*
parking lot	**el estacionamiento** *(ehl eh-stah-see-oh-nah-mee-'ehn-toh)*
stairs	**las escaleras** *(lahs eh-skah-'leh-rahs)*
telephone	**el teléfono** *(ehl teh-'leh-foh-noh)*
toilet	**el excusado** *(ehl ehks-koo-'sah-doh)*
water fountain	**la fuente de agua** *(lah 'fwehn-teh deh 'ah-gwah)*

Directions

Las direcciones *(lahs dee-rehk-see·'ohn-nehs)*

If you're at a loss for words while giving directions to someone, try using these expressions:

Where is it/he/she?	**¿Dónde está?** *('dohn-deh eh-'stah)*
above	**encima** *(ehn-'see-mah)*
straight ahead	**adelante** *(ah-deh-'lahn-teh)*
behind	**detrás** *(deh-'trahs)*
down	**abajo** *(ah-'bah-hoh)*
first floor	**primer piso** *(pree-'mehr 'pee-soh)*
second floor	**segundo piso** *(seh-'goon-doh 'pee-soh)*
in front of	**en frente de** *(ehn 'frehn-teh deh)*
here	**aquí** *(ah-'kee)*
inside	**adentro** *(ah-'dehn-troh)*
to the left	**a la izquierda** *(ah lah ees-kee-'ehr-dah)*
near	**cerca** *('sehr-kah)*
next to	**al lado de** *(ahl 'lah-doh deh)*
outside	**afuera** *(ah-foo-'eh-rah)*
to the right	**a la derecha** *(ah lah deh-'reh-chah)*
there	**allí** *(ah-'yee)*
over there	**allá** *(ah-'yah)*
up	**arriba** *(ah-'rree-bah)*

north **norte** *('nohr-teh)*

west **oeste** *(oh-'eh-steh)* ◄┼► east **este** *('eh-steh)*

south **sur** *(soor)*

Remember that **en** *(ehn)* (in, on, at) is one of the most commonly used words in Spanish: She's at the hospital, on the third floor, in the bed. **Está en el hospital** *(eh-'stah ehn ehl ohs-pee-'tahl),* **en el tercer piso** *(ehn ehl tehr-'sehr 'pee-soh),* **en la cama** *(ehn lah 'kah-mah).*

Always use **estar** *(eh-'stahr)* instead of **ser** *(sehr)* to tell where someone is located. The doctor is here. **El doctor está aquí.**

Be familiar with as many location words as you can:

face down	**boca abajo** *('boh-kah ah-'bah-hoh)*
face up	**boca arriba** *('boh-kah ah-'rree-bah)*

| on its way | **en camino** *(ehn kah-'mee-noh)* |
| toward the back | **hacia atrás** *('ah-see-ah ah-'trahs)* |

(13) ¿CUÁNTO APRENDIÓ?

• Practice your location words by completing the following sentences. If you find this exercise difficult, refer back to the previous section.

Vaya . . . *('bah-yah)*   in front of the lobby:

over there:

outside:

straight ahead:

• Translate the following sentence:

Suba en el ascensor y dé vuelta a la derecha. *('soo-bah ehn ehl ah-sehn-'sohr ee deh 'bwehl-tah ah lah deh-'reh-chah)*

Time

La hora *(lah 'oh-rah)*

While you're sending the Espinoza family this way and that way, be on the lookout for the common expression for "What time is it?" **¿Qué hora es?** *(keh 'oh-rah ehs)*. Luckily, all that is needed to respond to this question is the hour, followed by the word **y** *(ee)* (and), and the minutes. For example, 7:15 is **siete y quince** *(see-'eh-teh ee 'keen-seh)*. To say "It's . . .", use **Son las . . .** *(sohn lahs)* For example, "It's 7:15" **Son las siete y quince** *(sohn lahs see-'eh-teh ee 'keen-seh)*. You may want to go back and review your numbers in Spanish on page 12 before you try this. Here are a few more examples.

It's 12:30 A.M.	**Son las doce y trienta de la mañana.** *(sohn lahs 'doh-seh ee 'treh-een-tah deh lah mah-'nyah-nah)*
At 6:00 P.M.	**A las seis de la tarde.** *(ah lahs 'seh-ees deh lah 'tahr-deh)*
It's 3:45	**Son las tres y cuarenta y cinco.** *(sohn lahs trehs ee 'kwah-'rehn-tah ee 'seen-koh)*

¡No Se Olvide!

- **A las** *(ah lahs)* refers to "At." At 7:15. **A las siete y quince.** *(ah lahs see-'eh-teh ee 'keen-seh).* At what time? **¿A qué hora?**

- A.M. is **de la mañana** *(deh lah mah-'nyah-nah).* P.M. is **de la tarde.** *(deh lah 'tahr-deh).*

- For 1:00–1:59, use **Es la** *(ehs lah)* instead of **Son las.** *(sohn lahs).* For example, It's one o'clock. **Es la una.** *(ehs lah 'oo-nah).* It's one-thirty. **Es la una y treinta.** *(ehs lah 'oo-nah ee 'treh-een-tah).*

- Listen for the word, **¿Cuándo?** *('kwahn-doh)* ("When?"). You will definitely need your time-telling skills to answer this question.

The calendar
El calendario *(kah-lehn-'dah-ree·oh)*

You can't fill out all that paperwork without a calendar. Regardless of the forms you use, sooner or later the Espinozas will ask you questions about a specific day or date. Spend a few minutes looking over the following words and one-liners. These won't take you long to learn.

The days of the week
Los días de la semana
(lohs 'dee-ahs deh lah seh-'mah-nah)

Monday	**lunes** *('loo-nehs)*
Tuesday	**martes** *('mahr-tehs)*
Wednesday	**miércoles** *(mee-'ehr-koh-lehs)*
Thursday	**jueves** *('hoo·eh-behs)*
Friday	**viernes** *(bee-'ehr-nehs)*
Saturday	**sábado** *('sah-bah-doh)*
Sunday	**domingo** *(doh-'meen-goh)*
today	**hoy** *('oh·ee)*
tomorrow	**mañana** *(mah-'nyah-nah)*
yesterday	**ayer** *(ah-'yehr)*

Now practice some of the new expressions:

Today is Wednesday.	**Hoy es miércoles.**
	('oh·ee ehsmee-'ehr-koh-lehs)
Tomorrow is Thursday.	**Mañana es jueves.**
	(mah-'nyah-nah ehs 'hoo·eh-behs)
I have to work on Sunday.	**Tengo que trabajar el domingo.**
	('tehn-goh keh trah-bah-'hahr ehl doh-'meen-goh)

What is the date?

¿Cuál es la fecha? *(kwahl ehs lah 'feh-chah)*

Answering questions in Spanish concerning upcoming events, appointments, birthdays, and holidays can often be handled by pointing to dates on the calendar. However, it does help if you know the following. Notice how many of these look and sound like English:

The months of the year

Los meses del año *(lohs 'meh-sehs dehl 'ah-nyoh)*

January	**enero** *(eh-'neh-roh)*
February	**febrero** *(feh-'breh-roh)*
March	**marzo** *('mahr-soh)*
April	**abril** *(ah-'breel)*
May	**mayo** *('mah-yoh)*
June	**junio** *('hoo-nee·oh)*
July	**julio** *(hoo-lee·oh)*
August	**agosto** *(ah-'goh-stoh)*
September	**septiembre** *(sehp-tee-'ehm-breh)*
October	**octubre** *(ohk-'too-breh)*
November	**noviembre** *(noh-vee-'ehm-breh)*
December	**diciembre** *(dee-see-'ehm-breh)*

• To give the date, reverse the order of your words. For example, February 2nd is **El dos de febrero** *(ehl dohs deh feh-'breh-roh)*.

This is how you say "the first" in Spanish: **el primero.** *(ehl pree-'meh-roh)*

January 1st	**El primero de enero**
	(ehl pree-'meh-roh deh eh-'neh-roh)

• Several different **preguntas** *(preh-'goon-tahs)* can be used to ask "when." Learn the following:

How long ago?	**¿Hace cuánto?** *('ah-seh 'kwahn-toh)*
What day, month, year?	**¿Qué día, mes, año?**
	(keh 'dee-ah, mehs, 'ah-'nyoh)
When is it?	**¿Cuándo es?** *('kwahn-doh ehs)*

• The year is built the same as in English:

2002	**dos mil dos** *(dohs meel dohs)*

• "On Friday" is **el viernes** *(ehl bee-'ehr-nehs)* but "on Fridays" is **los viernes.** *(lohs bee-'ehr-nehs)*

If you want, you can interject the following expressions:

the next one	**el próximo** *(ehl 'prohk-see-moh)*
the past one	**el pasado** *(ehl pah-'sah-doh)*
the weekend	**el fin de semana** *(ehl feen deh seh-'mah-nah)*

• How is the year divided in nature?

spring	**la primavera** *(lah pree-mah-'beh-rah)*
summer	**el verano** *(ehl beh-'rah-noh)*
fall	**el otoño** *(ehl oh-'tohn-yoh)*
winter	**el invierno** *(ehl een-bee-'ehr-noh)*

(14) ¿CUÁNTO APRENDIÓ?

Fill in the missing words.

lunes, martes, _____ , jueves,
viernes, _____ , domingo.

enero, febrero, marzo, _____, mayo, junio,
julio, _____ .

Specialists

Los **especialistas** *(lohs eh-speh-see-ah-'lee-stahs)*

The Espinozas will probably need a variety of medical services. Choose what you need from the following list. Notice how many **especialistas** words look just like their English equivalents.

You need . . .	Necesita un (una) . . .
anesthetist	**anestesista** *(ah-nehs-teh-'sees-tah)*
bacteriologist	**bacteriólogo** *(bahk-teh-ree-'oh-loh-goh)*
cardiologist	**cardiólogo** *(kahr-dee-'oh-loh-goh)*
chiropractor	**quiropráctico** *(kee-roh-'prahk-tee-koh)*
dermatologist	**dermatólogo** *(dehr-mah-'toh-loh-goh)*
gastroenterologist	**gastroenterólogo** *(gahs-troh-ehn-teh-'roh-loh-goh)*
gynecologist	**ginecólogo** *(hee-neh-'koh-loh-goh)*
neurologist	**neurólogo** *(neh-oo-'roh-loh-goh)*
obstetrician	**obstetriz** *(ohb-steh-'trees)*
ophthalmologist	**oftalmólogo** *(of-tahl-'moh-loh-goh)*
optometrist	**optometrista** *(ohp-toh-meh-'trees-tah)*
orthodontist	**ortodoncista** *(ohr-toh dohn-'sees-tah)*
orthopedist	**ortopédico** *(ohr-toh-'peh-dee-koh)*
pathologist	**patólogo** *(pah-'toh-loh-goh)*
pediatrician	**pediatra** *(peh-dee-'ah-trah)*
podiatrist	**podiatra** *(poh-dee-'ah-trah)*
proctologist	**proctólogo** *(prohk-'toh-loh-goh)*
psychiatrist	**psiquiatra** *(see-kee-'ah-trah)*
psychologist	**psicólogo** *(see-'koh-loh-goh)*
radiologist	**radiólogo** *(rah-dee-'oh-loh-goh)*
surgeon	**cirujano** *(see-roo-'hah-noh)*
urologist	**urólogo** *(oo-'roh-loh-goh)*

Some other hospital staff members are:

assistant	**ayudante** *(ah-yoo-'dahn-teh)*
dietician	**dietista** *(dee-eh-'tees-tah)*
nurse	**enfermera** *(enh-fehr-'meh-rah)*
orderly	**practicante** *(prahk-tee-'kahn-teh)*

pharmacist	**farmacéutico** *(fahr-mah-'seh·oo-tee-koh)*
technician	**técnico** *('tehk-nee-koh)*
therapist	**terapeuta** *(teh-rah-peh-'oo-tah)*

REMEMBER: Use **el** for males, and **la** for females: **Bob es el dietista, Betty es la dietista.** *(B. ehs ehl dee-eh-'tees-tah, B. ehs lah dee-eh-'tees-tah)*

(15) ¿CUÁNTO APRENDIÓ?

Translate the following:

¿Necesita. . .?

water fountain _____

mailbox _____

stairs _____

emergency room _____

pediatrician _____

gynecologist _____

therapist _____

More action!
¡Más acción! *(mahs ahk-see·'ohn)*

In order to communicate more effectively with the Espinoza family and other patients, you'll need to increase your list of action words. Read each word and sample sentence. Then see if you can translate their meanings.

to change	**cambiar** *(kahm-bee-'ahr)*
	No necesitan cambiar doctores.
	(noh neh-seh-'see-tahn kahm-bee-'ahr dohk-'toh-rehs)

to fill	llenar *(yeh-'nahr)*
	Necesita llenar el formulario.
	(neh-seh-'see tah yeh-'nahr ehl fohr-moo-'lah-ree·oh)
to learn	**aprender** *(ah-prehn-'dehr)*
	Necesitamos aprender inglés.
	(neh-seh-see-'tah-mohs ah-prehn-'dehr een-'glehs)
to look for	**buscar** *(boos-'kahr)*
	Tienen que buscar los libros.
	(tee-'eh-nehn keh boos-'kahr lohs 'lee-brohs)
to pay	**pagar** *(pah-'gahr)*
	Tengo que pagar el hospital.
	('tehn-goh keh pah-'gahr ehl ohs-pee-'tahl)
to register	**registrar** *(reh-hee-'strahr)*
	Tiene que registrarse el lunes.
	(tee-'eh-neh keh reh-hee-'strahr-seh ehl 'loo-nehs)
to smoke	**fumar** *(foo-'mahr)*
	No fumar en el cuarto.
	(no foo-'mahr ehn ehl 'kwahr-toh)
to study	**estudiar** *(eh-stoo-doo 'ahr)*
	¿Tiene que estudiar?
	(tee-'eh-neh keh eh-stoo-dee-'ahr)
to use	**usar** *(oo-'sahr)*
	Necesito usar el baño.
	(neh-seh-'see-toh oo-'sahr ehl 'bah-nyoh)
to verify	**verificar** *(beh-ree-fee-'kahr)*
	Tenemos que verificar la información.
	(teh-'neh-mohs keh beh-ree-fee-'kahr lah een-fohr-mah-see-'ohn)

What do you want?

¿Qué quiere? *(keh kee-'eh-reh)*

Ready to learn a new pattern? Earlier you learned **tener que** *(teh-'nehr keh)* (to have to) and **necesitar** *(neh-seh-see-'tahr)* (to need). Now practice the four forms of the verb **QUERER** *(keh-'rehr)* (TO WANT).

I want	**quiero** (kee-'eh-roh)
	Quiero hablar con el doctor.
	(kee-'eh-roh ah-'blahr kohn ehl dohk-'tohr)
you want,	
he/she wants	**quiere** *(kee-'eh-reh)*
	¿Quiere usar el teléfono?
	(kee-'eh-reh oo-'sahr ehl teh-'leh-foh-noh)
you (plural)	
want/they want	**quieren** *(kee-'eh-rehn)*
	Quieren trabajar en la oficina.
	(kee-'eh-rehn trah-bah-'hahr ehn lah oh-fee-'see-nah)
we want	**queremos**
	Queremos verificar la información.
	(keh-'reh-mohs beh-ree-fee-'kahr lah een-fohr-mah-see·'ohn)

Notice how action words change form according to who completes the action. The pattern is the same for most words:

HABLAR *(ah-'blahr)*	TO SPEAK
hablo *('ah-bloh)*	I speak
habla *('ah-blah)*	you, he, she speaks
hablamos *(ah-'blah-mohs)*	we speak
hablan *('ah-blahn)*	you (plural), they speak

COMER *(koh-'mehr)*	TO EAT
como *('koh-moh)*	I eat
come *('koh-meh)*	you, he, she eats
comemos *(koh-'meh-mohs)*	we eat
comen *('koh-mehn)*	you (plural) they eat

ESCRIBIR *(ehs-kree-'beer)*	TO WRITE
escribo *(ehs-'kree-boh)*	I write
escribe *(ehs-'kree-beh)*	you, he, she writes
escribimos *(ehs-kree-'bee-mohs)*	we write
escriben *(ehs-'kree-behn)*	you (plural), they write

¡No se Olvide!

These words can be used in the same way as **quiere.**

desire	**desea** *(deh-'seh-ah)*
	¿Desea el doctor? *(deh-'seh-ah ehl dohk-'tohr)*
prefer	**prefiere** *(pre-fee-'eh-reh)*
	¿Prefiere el doctor?
	(preh-fee-'eh-reh ehl dohk-'tohr)
would like	**quisiera** *(kee-see-'eh-rah)*
	Quisiera el doctor. *(kee-see-'eh-rah ehl dohk-'tohr)*

Chapter Four

Capítulo Cuatro
(kah-'pee-too-loh 'kwah-troh)

The Accident
El Accidente
(ehl ahk-see-'dehn-teh)

Juan Carlos Espinoza, age 34, has been in an automobile accident. He arrives at your hospital with a probable broken arm and bruises on his forehead. As the medical attendant, you need to evaluate his condition. Unfortunately, he doesn't speak English. It's probably best to begin with a few simple questions to make Juan feel relaxed. **¿Cómo está?** *('koh-moh eh-'stah)* (How are you?) will work. Juan could answer with almost anything. The key is to get him to keep it to one word. Let him know you speak only a little Spanish—**"Hablo poquito español"** *('ah-bloh poh-'kee-toh ehs-pah-'nyohl)*. If he speaks too quickly, get him to slow it down with **"Más despacio, por favor"** *(mahs dehs-'pah-see·oh, pohr fah-'bohr)*. Once he understands that communication is limited, his possible answers to your question may include the following:

How are you?

¿Cómo está usted? *('koh-moh eh-'stah oo-'stehd)*

I am. . .	**Estoy** . . . *(eh-'stoh·ee)*
dizzy	**mareado** *(mah-reh-'ah-doh)*
exhausted	**agotado** *(ah-goh-'tah-doh)*
nervous	**nervioso** *(nehr-bee-'oh-soh)*
sore	**dolorido** *(doh-loh-'ree-doh)*
sweaty	**sudoroso** *(soo-doh-'roh-soh)*
tired	**cansado** *(kahn-'sah-doh)*

| uncomfortable | **incómodo** *(een-'koh-moh-doh)* |
| weak | **débil** *('deh-beel)* |

Still More Emotions
Más emociones aún
(mahs eh-moh-see-'oh-nehs ah-'oon)

angry	**enojado** *(eh-noh-'hah-doh)*
bad	**mal** *(mahl)*
bored	**aburrido** *(ah-boor-'ree-doh)*
calm	**calmado** *(kahl-'mah-doh)*
confused	**confundido** *(kohn-foon-'dee-doh)*
excited	**emocionado** *(eh-moh-see-oh-'nah-doh)*
happy	**feliz** *(feh-'lees)*
relaxed	**relajado** *(reh-lah-'hah-doh)*
sad	**triste** *('trees-teh)*
scared	**espantado** *(ehs-pahn-'tah-doh)*
sleepy	**soñoliento** *(soh-nyoh-lee-'ehn-toh)*
surprised	**sorprendido** *(sohr-prehn-'dee-doh)*
worried	**preocupado** *(preh-oh-koo-'pah-doh)*

¡No Se Olvide!

• Instead of "How are you?" another popular expression that you can use is **¿Cómo se siente?** *('koh-moh seh see-'ehn-teh)* (How do you feel?).

• Another important question to ask a patient when you first see him is "What are your symptoms?" **¿Cuáles son sus síntomas?** *('kwah-lehs sohn soos 'seen-toh-mahs)*. Or, if you believe that his educational level is not very high, "What's happening to you?" **¿Qué le pasa?** *(keh leh 'pah-sah)* will always elicit a response.

More parts of the body
Más partes del cuerpo
(mahs 'pahr-tehs dehl 'kwehr-poh)

Once you know how Juan feels, try to get him to tell you where it hurts. Pointing to a body part and asking "Does it hurt?" **¿Le duele?** is one approach, if your vocabulary is limited. You could also instruct the patient to "Point to where it hurts"—**Señale dónde le duele**—and let the patient point at the painful area. Although you have already learned several major parts of the body, there are others you may need to know.

ankle	**el tobillo** *(ehl toh-'bee-yoh)*
armpit	**la axila** *(lah ahk-'see-lah)*
breasts	**los senos** *(lohs 'seh-nohs)*
buttock	**la nalga** *(lah 'nahl-gah)*
calf	**la pantorrilla** *(lah pahn-toh-'rree-yah)*
collarbone	**la clavícula** *(lah klah-'bee-koo-lah)*
diaphragm	**el diafragma** *(ehl dee-ah-'frahg-mah)*
forearm	**el antebrazo** *(ehl ahn-teh-'brah-soh)*
groin	**la ingle** *(lah 'een-gleh)*
heel	**el talón** *(ehl tah-'lohn)*
hip	**la cadera** *(lah kah-'deh-rah)*
kneecap	**la rótula** *(lah 'roh-too-lah)*
nail	**la uña** *(lah 'oon-yah)*
palm	**la palma de la mano** *(lah 'pahl-mah deh lah 'mah-noh)*
pelvis	**la pelvis** *(lah 'pehl-bees)*
rectum	**el recto** *(ehl 'rehk-toh)*
rib	**la costilla** *(lah koh-'stee-yah)*
sole	**la planta del pie** *(lah 'plahn-tah dehl pee-'eh)*
spine	**el espinazo** *(ehl ehs-pee-'nah-soh)*
thigh	**el muslo** *(ehl 'moos-loh)*
throat	**la garganta** *(lah gahr-'gahn-tah)*
tongue	**la lengua** *(lah 'lehn-gwah)*
waist	**la cintura** *(lah seen-'too-rah)*
wrist	**la muñeca** *(lah moo-'nyeh-kah)*

The organs
Los órganos *(lohs 'ohr-gah-nohs)*

appendix	**el apéndice** *(ehl ah-'pehn-dee-seh)*
bladder	**la vejiga** *(lah beh-'hee-gah)*
brain	**el cerebro** *(ehl seh-'reh-broh)*
colon	**el colon** *(ehl 'koh-lohn)*
esophagus	**el esófago** *(ehl eh-'soh-fah-goh)*
gallbladder	**la vesícula** *(lah beh-'see-koo-lah)*
genitals	**los genitales** *(lohs heh-nee-'tah-lehs)*
heart	**el corazón** *(ehl koh-rah-'sohn)*
kidney	**el riñón** *(ehl ree-'nyohn)*
large intestine	**el intestino grueso** *(ehl een-tehs-'tee-noh groo-'eh-soh)*
liver	**el hígado** *(ehl 'ee-gah-doh)*
lungs	**los pulmones** *(lohs pool 'moh nehs)*
pancreas	**el páncreas** *(ehl 'pahn-kreh-ahs)*
small intestine	**el intestino delgado** *(ehl een-tehs-'tee-noh dehl-'gah-doh)*
spleen	**el bazo** *(ehl 'bah-soh)*
thyroid gland	**la tiroides** *(lah tee-'roh-ee-dehs)*
tonsils	**las amígdalas** *(lahs ah-'meeg-dah-lahs)*
uterus	**el útero** *(ehl 'oo-teh-roh)*

More important parts of the body
¡Más partes importantes del cuerpo!
(mahs 'pahr-tehs eem-pohr-'tahn-tehs dehl 'kwehr-poh)

Learn to ask the following important question:

Do you have problems with . . .	**Tiene problemas con . . .** *(tee-'eh-neh proh-'bleh-mahs kohn)*
artery	**la arteria** *(lah ahr-'teh-ree-ah)*
cartilage	**el cartílago** *(ehl kahr-'tee-lah-goh)*
ligament	**el ligamento** *(ehl lee-gah-'mehn-toh)*
spinal column	**la columna vertebral** *(lah koh-'loom-nah behr-teh-'brahl)*
tendon	**el tendón** *(ehl tehn-'dohn)*

| thyroid | **la tiroides** *(lah tee-'roh-ee-dehs)* |
| vein | **la vena** *(lah 'beh-nah)* |

The face
La cara *(lah 'kah-rah)*

cheek	**la mejilla** *(lah meh-'hee-yah)*
cheekbone	**el pómulo** *(ehl 'poh-moo-loh)*
chin	**la barbilla** *(lah bahr-'bee-yah)*
eyebrow	**la ceja** *(lah 'seh-hah)*
eyelash	**la pestaña** *(lah peh-'stah-nyah)*
eyelid	**el párpado** *(ehl 'pahr-pah-doh)*
facial skin	**el cutis** *(ehl 'koo-tees)*
forehead	**la frente** *(lah 'frehn-teh)*
gum	**la encía** *(lah ehn-'see-ah)*
inner ear	**el oído** *(ehl oh-'ee-doh)*
jaw	**la mandíbula** *(lah mahn-'dee-boo-lah)*
lip	**el labio** *(ehl 'lah-bee-oh)*
nostril	**la fosa nasal** *(lah 'foh-sah nah-'sahl)*
temple	**la sien** *(lah 'see-ehn)*

What happened?
¿Qué pasó? *(keh pah-'soh)*

Just naming body parts is not enough to handle every emergency that'll come your way. You need to also know phrases that will accomplish a lot more. Listen for the "yes" and "no"— **sí** and **no**.

Are you cut?	**¿Está cortado?** *(eh-'stah kohr-'tah-doh)*
Are you injured?	**¿Está herido?** *(eh-'stah eh-'ree-doh)*
Are you in pain?	**¿Tiene dolor?** *(tee-'eh-neh doh-'lohr)*
Are you pregnant?	**¿Está embarazada?**
	(eh-'stah ehm-bah-rah-'sah-dah)
Is it broken?	**¿Está roto?** *(eh-'stah 'roh-toh)*
Is it burned?	**¿Está quemado?** *(eh-'stah keh-'mah-doh)*
Is it infected?	**¿Está infectado?** *(eh-'stah een-fehk-'tah-doh)*
Is it inflamed?	**¿Está inflamado?** *(eh-'stah een-flah-'mah-doh)*
Is it irritated?	**¿Está irritado?** *(eh-'stah eer-ree-'tah-doh)*

Is it twisted?	**¿Está torcido?** *(eh-'stah tohr-'see-doh)*
Is it swollen?	**¿Está hinchado?** *(eh-'stah een-'chah-doh)*

Once you have examined Juan, you'll want to let him and the rest of the Espinoza family know what is wrong. Combine the word **tiene** *(tee-'eh-neh)* with the following vocabulary for a more extensive diagnosis.

He has . . .	**Tiene . . .** *(tee-'eh-neh)*
bruises	**contusiones** *(kohn-too-see·'oh-nehs)*
burns	**quemaduras** *(keh-mah-'doo-rahs)*
cuts	**cortadas** *(kohr-'tah-dahs)*
a dislocation	**una dislocación** *('oo-nah dees-loh-kah-see·'ohn)*
a fracture	**una fractura** *('oo-nah frahk-'too-rah)*
hemorrhage	**hemorragia** *(heh-mohr-'rah-hee-ah)*
lacerations	**laceraciones** *(lah-seh-rah-see·'oh-nehs)*
punctures	**perforaciones** *(pehr-foh-rah-see·'oh-nehs)*
scrapes	**rasguños** *(rahs-'goo-nyohs)*
a sprain	**una torcedura** *('oo-nah tohr-seh-'doo-rah)*

Is he conscious or unconscious?
¿Está él consciente o inconsciente?
(eh-'stah ehl kohn-see-'ehn-teh oh een-kohn-see-'ehn-teh)
Is she in a coma?
¿Está ella en estado de coma?
(eh-'stah 'eh-yah ehn ehs-'tah-doh deh 'koh-mah)

The emergency room
La sala de emergencias
(lah 'sah-lah deh eh-mehr-'hehn-see·ahs)

While emergency treatment is being applied, invaluable personal information can be collected. Ask the following questions of Juan or his family to further diagnose his condition.

How severe is the pain?	**¿Cuán fuerte es el dolor?**
	(kwahn foo-'ehr-teh ehs ehl do-'lohr)
Can you move?	**¿Puede moverse?** *(poo-'eh-deh moh-'behr-seh)*

Is your pain . . .	¿Tiene un dolor . . . ? *(tee-'eh-neh oon doh-'lohr)*
burning	**quemante** *(keh-'mahn-teh)*
constant	**constante** *(kohn-'stahn-teh)*
deep	**profundo** *(proh-'foon-doh)*
dull	**sordo** *('sohr-doh)*
intermittent	**intermitente** *(een-tehr-mee-'tehn-teh)*
mild	**moderado** *(moh-deh-'rah-doh)*
severe	**muy fuerte** *('moo·ee 'fwehr-teh)*
sharp	**agudo** *(ah-'goo-doh)*
stable	**estable** *(ehs-'tahb-leh)*
throbbing	**pulsante** *(pool-'sahn-teh)*
worse	**peor** *(peh-'ohr)*

Keep talking, but this time say: You need . . . he needs . . . **Necesita . . .** *(neh-seh-'see-tah)*.

a bandage	**un vendaje** *(oon behn-'dah-heh)*
a blood transfusion	**una transfusión de sangre** *('oo-nah trahns-foo-see-'ohn deh 'sahn-greh)*
a cast	**una armadura de yeso** *('oo-nah ahr-mah-'doo-rah deh 'yeh-soh)*
CPR	**la resucitación cardiopulmonar** *(lah reh-soo-see-tah-see-'ohn kahr-dee-oh-pool-moh-'nahr)*
first aid	**los primeros auxilios** *(lohs pree-'meh-rohs owk-'see-lee-ohs)*
gauze	**la gasa** *(lah 'gah-sah)*
intensive care	**el cuidado intensivo** *(ehl kwee-'dah-doh een-tehn-'see-boh)*
intravenous fluids	**los líquidos intravenosos** *(lohs 'lee-kee-dohs een-trah-beh-'noh-sohs)*
an operation	**una operación** *('oo-nah oh-peh-rah-see-'ohn)*
oxygen	**el oxígeno** *(ehl ohk-'see-heh-noh)*
physical therapy	**la terapia física** *(lah teh-'rah-pee·ah 'fee-see-kah)*
serum	**el suero** *(ehl 'sweh-roh)*
a shot	**una inyección** *('oo-nah een-yehk-see-'ohn)*

a sling	**un cabestrillo** *(oon kah-behs-'tree-yoh)*
stitches	**las puntadas** *(lahs poon-'tah-dahs)*
a stretcher	**un camilla** *('oo-nah kah-'mee-yah)*
a tourniquet	**un torniquete** *(oon tohr-nee-'keh-teh)*
X rays	**los rayos equis** *(lohs 'rah-yohs 'eh-kees)*

More orders

Más mandatos *(mahs mahn-'dah-tohs)*

You definitely will need to give Juan a few commands. Try using these phrases:

breathe	**respire** *(rehs-'pee-reh)*
Breathe more slowly.	**Respire más despacio.** *(rehs-pee-'reh mahs dehs-'pah-see·oh)*
follow	**siga** *('see-gah)*
Follow instructions.	**Siga las instrucciones.** *('see-gah lahs een-strook-see·'oh-nehs)*
grab	**agarre** *(ah-'gah-rreh)*
Grab my hand.	**Agarre mi mano.** *(ah-'gah-rreh mee 'mah-noh)*
listen	**escuche** *(ehs-'koo-cheh)*
Listen to the doctor.	**Escuche al doctor.** *(ehs-'koo-cheh ahl dohk-'tohr)*
look	**mire** *('mee-reh)*
Look here.	**Mire aquí.** *('mee-reh ah-'kee)*
lower	**baje** *('bah-heh)*
Lower your head.	**Baje la cabeza.** *('bah-heh lah kah-'beh-sah)*
raise	**levante** *(leh-'bahn-teh)*
Raise your leg.	**Levante la pierna.** *(leh-'bahn-teh lah pee-'ehr-nah)*
tell	**diga** *('dee-gah)*
Tell everything to the nurse.	**Diga todo a la enfermera.** *('dee-gah 'toh-doh ah lah ehn-fehr-'meh-rah)*

Emergencies

Las emergencias *(lahs eh-mehr-'henh-see·ahs)*

Unfortunately, certain dramatic situations may result in a patient being brought to the hospital. Become familiar with these expressions:

a bad fall	**una mala caída** *('oo-nah 'mah-lah kah-'ee-dah)*
a bee sting	**una picadura de abeja**
	('oo-nah pee-kah-'doo-rah deh ah-'beh-hah)
a convulsion	**una convulsión** *('oo-nah kohn-bool-see-'ohn)*
dehydration	**deshidratación** *(dehs-ee-drah-tah-see-'ohn)*
a dog bite	**una mordedura de perro**
	('oo-nah mohr-deh-'doo-rah deh 'peh-rroh)
fatigue	**fatiga** *(fah-'tee-gah)*
frostbite	**congelamiento** *(kohn-heh-lah-mee-'ehn-toh)*
a gunshot wound	**una herida de bala**
	('oo-nah eh-'ree-dah deh 'bah-lah)
a heart attack	**un ataque al corazón**
	(oon ah-'tah-keh ahl koh-rah-'sohn)
heat stroke	**postración** *(pohs-trah-see-'ohn)*
an insect bite	**una mordedura de insecto**
	('oo-nah mohr-deh-'doo-rah deh een-'sehk-toh)
intoxication	**intoxicación** *(een-tohk-see-kah-see-'ohn)*
an overdose	**una dosis excesiva**
	('oo-nah 'doh-sees ehk-seh-'see-bah)
shock	**postración nerviosa**
	(pohs-trah-see-'ohn nehr-bee-'oh-sah)
a snake bite	**una mordedura de culebra**
	('oo-nah mohr-deh-'doo-rah deh koo-'leh-brah)
a spasm	**un espasmo** *(oon ehs-'pahs-moh)*
a stabbing	**una puñalada** *('oo-nah poo-nyah-'lah-dah)*
strangulation	**estrangulamiento** *(ehs-trah-goo-lah-mee-'ehn-toh)*
a stroke	**un ataque fulminante**
	(oon ah-'tah-keh fool-mee-'nahn-teh)
sun stroke	**insolación** *(een-soh-lah-see-'ohn)*

suffocation	**sofocación** *(soh-foh-kah-see·'ohn)*
trauma	**traumatismo** *(traw-mah-'tees-moh)*

On many of your commands, you can add the word **me** to direct the action toward yourself.

call me	**llámeme** *('yah-meh-meh)*
follow me	**sígame** *('see-gah-meh)*
help me	**ayúdeme** *(ah-'yoo-deh-meh)*
look at me	**míreme** *('mee-reh-meh)*
tell me	**dígame** *('dee-gah-meh)*

D O S   C U L T U R A S

Fear and apprehension may cause some accident victims to leave the scene prior to receiving medical treatment. Many non-English speaking Hispanics do not trust facilities where only English is spoken. If possible, ask a translator to assist you during such an emergency. Patients need to be assured that their lives are in good hands.

More action!
¡Más acción! *(mahs ahk-see·'ohn)*

Once again, you may find yourself limited by what you can say. However, before you learn new action words, take a moment to review some of the verbs and patterns that already have been introduced.

I have to work at 8:00.	**Tengo que trabajar a las ocho.** *('tehn-goh keh trah-bah-'hahr ah lahs 'oh-choh)*
You have to work at 8:00.	**Tiene que trabajar a las ocho.** *(tee-'eh-neh keh trah-bah-'hahr ah lahs 'oh-choh)*
I need to fill out my form.	**Necesito llenar mi formulario.** *(neh-seh-'see-toh yeh-'nahr ehl fohr-moo-'lah-ree-oh)*
You need to fill out your form.	**Necesita llenar su formulario.** *(neh-seh-'see-tah yeh-'nahr soo fohr-moo-'lah-ree-oh)*

I want to return on Friday.	**Quiero regresar el viernes.** *(kee-'eh-roh reh-greh-'sahr ehl bee-'ehr-nehs)*
You want to return on Friday.	**Quiere regresar el viernes.** *(kee-'eh-reh reh-greh-'sahr ehl bee-'ehr-nehs)*

Now, using what you've already learned, think of ways to apply the following action words in real-life emergency situations. Change the endings of these when it's appropriate.

to help	**ayudar** *(ah-yoo-'dahr)*
They help a lot.	**Ayudan mucho.** *(ah-'yoo-dahn 'moo-choh)*
to examine	**examinar** *(ehk-sah-mee-'nahr)*
I examine the patient.	**Examino al paciente.** *(ehk-sah-'mee-noh ahl pah-see-'ehn-teh)*
to send	**mandar** *(mahn-'dahr)*
We send the papers.	**Mandamos los papeles.** *(mahn-'dah-mohs lohs pah-'peh-lehs)*
to drive	**manejar** *(mah-neh-'hahr)*
Do you drive?	**¿Maneja usted?** *(mah-'neh-hah oo-'stehd)*
to put	**poner** *(poh-'nehr)*
Put the forms there.	**Pongan los formularios allí.** *('pohn-gahn lohs fohr-moo-'lah-ree·ohs ah-'yee)*
to receive	**recibir** *(reh-see-'beer)*
We receive the medicine.	**Recibimos la medicina.** *(reh-see-'bee-mohs lah meh-dee-'see-nah)*
to suffer	**sufrir** *(soo-'freer)*
He isn't suffering.	**El no sufre.** *(ehl noh 'soo-freh)*
to live	**vivir** *(bee-'beer)*
We live in California.	**Vivimos en California.** *(bee-'bee-mohs ehn Kah-lee-'fohr-nee·ah)*

¿Cuánto Aprendió?

Have you attempted to create any present tense verb forms on your own? By now, you should be able to understand them:

I don't walk much. **No camino mucho.**
   (noh kah-'mee-noh 'moo-choh)

Tony doesn't smoke. **Tony no fuma.** *(T. noh 'foo-mah)*

We run in the park. **Corremos en el parque.**
   (koh-'rreh-mohs ehn ehl 'pahr-keh)

What are you going to do?
¿Qué va a hacer? *(keh bah ah ah-'sehr)*

Every health care professional needs to know this pattern, and it's easy to use. To tell Juan what's going to happen next, add your action words to one of these phrases:

I'm going to . . .   **voy a . . .** *('boh·ee ah)*

you/he/she is going to . . . **va a . . .** *(bah ah)*

they're going to . . .   **van a . . .** *(bahn ah)*

we're going to . . .   **vamos a . . .** *('bah-mohs ah)*

We're going to help the patient.
Vamos a ayudar al paciente.
   ('bah-mohs ah ah-yoo-'dahr ahl pah-see-'ehn-teh)

I'm going to examine your leg.
Voy a examinar su pierna.
   ('boh·ee ah ehk-sah-mee-'nahr soo pee-'ehr-nah)

Everything is going to be fine.
Todo va a estar bien. *('toh-doh bah a eh-'stahr 'bee·ehn)*

¡No Se Olvide!

• These words are forms of the verb, **ir** *(eer)* (to go). They're usually spoken in reference to location. Observe:

I'm going to my house.	**Voy a mi casa.** *('boh-ee ah mee 'kah-sah)*
Peter is going to his room.	**Pedro va a su cuarto.** *('peh-droh bah ah soo 'kwahr-toh)*
They're going to the right.	**Van a la derecha.** *('bahn ah lah deh-'reh-chah)*
We're going to the clinic.	**Vamos a la clínica.** *('bah-mohs ah lah 'klee-nee-kah)*

• **Le** *(leh)* is another popular part of Spanish sentences. It simply refers to "you", "him", or "her." Notice its position in the following phrases.

It hurts you.	**Le duele.** *(leh 'dweh-leh)*
We're going to call him.	**Vamos a llamarle.** *('bah-mohs ah yah-'mahr-leh)*
Tell her.	**Dígale.** *('dee-gah-leh)*

• **Lo** *(loh)* and **la** *(lah)* are also active parts of Spanish sentences. However, they're used to refer to objects instead of people.

We're going to examine it.	**Lo vamos a examinar.** *(loh 'bah-mohs ah ehk-sah-mee'nahr)*

More emergencies

Más emergencias *('mahs eh-mehr-'hehn-see·ahs)*

Juan or another member of the Espinoza family may come into your facility for some other kind of emergency. Naturally, you can't learn every word in a Spanish/English dictionary. But you can focus on areas that are common. Here are lists of vocabulary for more emergencies, including burns and poisonings.

Burns

Las quemaduras *(lahs keh-mah-'doo-rahs)*

acid	**el ácido** *(ehl 'ah-see-doh)*
chemicals	**los productos químicos** *(lohs proh-'dook-tohs 'kee-mee-kohs)*
fire	**el fuego** *(ehl 'fweh-goh)*
flames	**las llamas** *(lahs 'yah-mahs)*
gas	**el gas** *(ehl gahs)*
grease	**la grasa** *(lah 'grah-sah)*
hot water	**el agua caliente** *(ehl 'ah-gwah kah-lee-'ehn-teh)*
oil	**el aceite** *(ehl ah-'seh-ee-teh)*
smoke	**el humo** *(ehl 'oo-moh)*

Poisonings

Envenenamientos *(ehn-beh-neh-nah-mee-'ehn-tohs)*

alcohol	**el alcohol** *(ehl ahl-koh-'ohl)*
ammonia	**amoníaco** *(ah-moh-'nee-ah-koh)*
bleach	**el cloro** *(ehl 'kloh-roh)*
cyanide	**el cianuro** *(ehl see-ah-'noo-roh)*
detergent	**el detergente** *(ehl deeh-tehr-'hehn-teh)*
food	**la comida** *(lah koh-'mee-dah)*
insecticide	**el insecticida** *(ehl een-sehk-tee-'see-dah)*
liquor	**el licor** *(ehl lee-'kohr)*
lye	**la lejía** *(lah leh-'hee-ah)*
mushrooms	**los hongos** *(lohs 'ohn-gohs)*
paint	**la pintura** *(lah peen-'too-rah)*
poison	**el veneno** *(ehl beh-'neh-noh)*
sleeping pills	**los tranquilizantes** *(lohs trahn-kee-lee-'sahn-tehs)*

Drug abuse

El abuso de las drogas
(ehl ah-'boo-soh deh lahs 'droh-gahs)

amphetamines	**las anfetaminas** *(lahs ahn-feh-tah-'mee-nahs)*
barbiturates	**los barbitúricos** *(lohs bahr-bee-'too-ree-kohs)*
capsules	**las cápsulas** *(lahs 'kahp-soo-lahs)*

cigar	**el puro** *(ehl 'poo-roh)*
cigarette	**el cigarrillo** *(ehl see-gah-'rree-yoh)*
cocaine	**la cocaína, la coca**
	(lah koh-kah-'ee-nah, lah 'koh-kah)
crack	**el crack** *(ehl krahk)*
glue	**la goma, la cola** *(lah 'goh-mah, lah 'koh-lah)*
hashish	**el hachich** *(ah-'cheech)*
heroin	**la heroína** *(lah eh-roh-'ee-nah)*
marijuana	**la marijuana, la mota, la hierba**
	(lah mah-ree-'wah-nah, lah 'moh-tah, lah 'yehr-bah)
morphine	**la morfina** *(lah mohr-'fee-nah)*
pills	**las píldoras** *(lahs 'peel-doh-rahs)*
pipe	**la pipa** *(lah 'pee-pah)*
speed	**la metadrina** *(lah meh-tah-'dree-nah)*
tablets	**las tabletas** *(lahs tah-'bleh-tahs)*

When conversations get serious, these phrases may help:

It seems that . . .
Parece que . . . *(pah-'reh-seh keh)*
It seems that he is taking cocaine.
Parece que está tomando cocaína.
   (pah-'reh-seh keh eh-'stah toh-'mahn-doh koh-kah-'ee-nah)
I believe that . . .
Creo que . . . *('kreh-oh keh)*
I believe that these tablets are very strong.
Creo que estas tabletas son muy fuertes.
   ('kreh-oh keh 'eh-stahs tah-'bleh-tahs sohn 'moo-ee 'fwehr-tehs)

Now make your own sentences with this vocabulary:

So . . .	**Así que . . .** *(ah-'see keh)*
Therefore . . .	**Por eso . . .** *(pohr 'eh-soh)*
However . . .	**Sin embargo . . .** *(seen ehm-'bahr-goh)*

16 ¿Cuánto Aprendió?

Translate the following terms. They're a lot like English:

convulsiones *(kohn-bool-see-'oh-nehs)*
náusea *('now-seh-ah)*
vómitos *('boh-mee-tohs)*
dilatación de las pupilas
 (dee-lah-tah-see-'ohn deh lahs poo-'pee-lahs)
pupilas reducidas *(poo-'pee-lahs reh-doo-'see-dahs)*
temperatura *(tehm-peh-rah-'too-rah)*
nerviosidad *(nehr-bee-oh-see-'dahd)*
depresión *(deh-preh-see-'ohn)*
tensión *(tehn-see-'ohn)*
ilusiones paranoicas *(ee-loo-see-'oh-nehs pah-rah-'noh-ee-kahs)*
alucinaciones *(ah-loo-see-nah-see-'oh-nehs)*
agresividad *(ah-greh-see-bee-'dahd)*
confusión *(kohn-foo-see-'ohn)*
dificultad respiratoria
 (dee-fee-kool-'tahd rehs-pee-rah-'toh-ree-ah)
irritabilidad *(ee-ree-tah-bee-lee-'dahd)*
insomnio *(een-'sohm-nee-oh)*

There may come a time when you are confronted with a natural disaster. Learn the following vocabulary for dealing with it:

Natural disasters
Los desastres naturales
(lohs deh-'sahs-trehs nah-too-'rah-lehs)

drought	**sequía** *(seh-'kee-ah)*
earthquake	**terremoto** *(teh-rreh-'moh-toh)*
epidemic	**epidemia** *(eh-pee-'deh-mee-ah)*
flood	**inundación** *(een-oon-dah-see-'ohn)*
hurricane	**huracán** *(oo-rah-'kahn)*
plague	**plaga** *('plah-gah)*
tornado	**tornado** *(tohr-'nah-doh)*

Become familiar with these expressions:

Danger!	**¡Peligro!** *(peh-'lee-groh)*
Fire!	**¡Fuego!** *('fweh-goh)*
Help!	**¡Socorro!** *(soh-'koh-rroh)*

Here are some additional words you may need to know:

to beat **golpear** *(gohl-peh-'ahr)*
They want to beat my neighbor.
Quieren golpear a mi vecino.
 (keh-'rehn gohl-peh-'ahr ah mee beh-'see-noh)

to fight **pelear** *(peh-leh-'ahr)*
They fight a lot.
Ellos pelean mucho. *('eh-yohs peh-'leh-ahn 'moo-choh)*

to kick **patear** *(pah-teh-'ahr)*
He does not kick the door.
El no patea la puerta. *(ehl noh pah-'teh-ah lah 'pwehr-tah)*

to kill **matar** *(mah-'tahr)*
Drugs kill.
Las drogas matan. *(lahs 'droh-gahs 'mah-tahn)*

to rape **violar** *(bee-oh-'lahr)*
She was raped.
Ella fue violada. *('eh-yah foo-'eh bee-oh-'lah-dah)*

to shoot **disparar** *(dees-pah-'rahr)*
The police shoot.
La policía dispara. *(lah poh-lee-'see-ah dees-'pah-rah)*

DOS CULTURAS

In many cultures, violence and tragedy are not uncommon. Do not be surprised by people's reaction to emergency situations. Also remember that families and friends will undoubtedly arrive to lend their support. Be aware that groups in the ER can be quite large, and that everyone will want to spend time with the patient.

X rays

Rayos equis *('rah-yohs 'eh-kees)*

It may become necessary to take x-rays of Juan's injuries. To help alleviate some of his fear, you'll want to explain all this to Juan. Use the following sentences in Spanish to convey the appropriate information.

Calm down and breathe slowly.

Cálmese y respire más despacio.

('kahl-meh-seh ee rehs-'pee-reh mahs dehs-'pah-see·oh)

Follow my directions.

Siga mis instrucciones. *('see-gah mees een-strook-see·'oh-nehs)*

Go to that room and wait.

Vaya a ese cuarto y espere. *('bah-yah ah 'eh-seh 'kwahr-toh ee ehs-'peh-reh)*

I will send the information to your doctor.

Voy a mandar la información a su doctor.

('boh·ee ah mahn-'dahr lah een-fohr-mah-see·'ohn ah soo dohk-'tohr)

Move your leg closer and higher.

Mueva la pierna más cerca y más alto.

('mweh-bah lah pee-'ehr-nah mahs 'sehr-kah ee mahs 'ahl-toh)

Sit down on the table and turn around.

Siéntese en la mesa y voltéese.

(see-'ehn-teh-seh ehn lah 'meh-sah ee bohl-'teh-ee-seh)

Thanks for your cooperation.

Gracias por su cooperación. *('grah-see-ahs pohr soo koo-peh-rah-see·'ohn)*

Take a deep breath and hold it.

Inspire profundamente y espere.

(een-'spee-reh proh-foon-dah-'mehn-teh ee ehs-'peh-reh)

The results are negative.

Los resultados son negativos.

(lohs reh-sool-'tah-dohs sohn neh-gah-'tee-bohs)

Chapter Five

Capítulo Cinco
(kah-'pee-too-loh 'seen-koh)

The Pregnancy
El Embarazo
(ehl ehm-bah-'rah-soh)

María Espinoza, Juan's wife, thinks she's pregnant with her third child. She has never received medical attention in this country, but her family has encouraged her to see an obstetrician. María needs to be informed about everything from family planning to the care of a newborn. She needs to know what services are available to her, and she needs to have some of her own questions answered. María, like her husband, speaks little or no English. Perhaps some of these Spanish words and phrases will get you started.

Important expressions
Expresiones importantes
(ehks-preh-see·'oh-nehs eem-pohr-'tahn-tehs)

Do you have . . .?	¿Tiene . . .?(tee-'eh-neh)
allergies	**alergias** (ah-'lehr-hee·ahs)
bleeding	**sangramiento** (sahn-grah-mee-'ehn-toh)
blisters	**ampollas** (ahm-'poh-yahs)
chills	**escalofríos** (ehs-kah-loh-'free-ohs)
constipation	**estreñimiento** (ehs-treh-nyee-mee-'ehn-toh)
contractions	**contracciones** (kohn-trahk-see·'oh-nehs)
convulsions	**convulsiones** (kohn-bool-see·'oh-nehs)
cramps	**calambres** (kah-'lahm-brehs)
cravings	**antojos** (ahn-'toh-hohs)

diarrhea	**diarrea** *(dee-ah-'rreh-ah)*
discharge	**flujo** *('floo-hoh)*
dizziness	**mareos** *(mah-'reh-ohs)*
emotional problems	**problemas emocionales** *(proh-'bleh-mahs eh-moh-see·oh-'nah-lehs)*
exhaustion	**agotamiento** *(ah-goh-tah-mee-'ehn-toh)*
fever	**fiebre** *(fee-'eh-breh)*
hair loss	**pérdida de cabello** *('pehr-dee-dah deh kah 'beh-yoh)*
hemorrhoids	**hemorroides** *(eh-moh-'rroh·ee-dehs)*
high blood pressure	**presión alta** *(preh-see-'ohn 'ahl-tah)*
indigestion	**indigestión** *(een-dee-hehs-tee-'ohn)*
itching	**picazón** *(pee-kah-'sohn)*
labor pains	**dolores de parto** *(doh-'loh-rehs deh 'pahr-toh)*
lesions	**lesiones** *(leh-see-'oh-nehs)*
mucus	**mucosidad** *(moo-koh-see-'dahd)*
nausea	**náusea** *('now-seh-ah)*
palpitations	**palpitaciones** *(pahl-pee-tah-see·'oh-nehs)*
your period	**su regla** *(soo 'reh-glah)*
rash	**erupción** *(eh-roop-see·'ohn)*
severe pain	**dolores fuertes** *(doh-'loh-rehs 'fwehr-tehs)*
sexually transmitted disease	**enfermedad transmitida por relaciones sexuales** *(ehn-fehr-meh-'dahd trahns-mee-'tee-dah pohr reh-lah-see-'oh-nehs sehk-soo-'ah-lehs)*
swelling	**hinchazón** *(een-chah-'sohn)*
vaginal discharge	**descarga vaginal** *(dehs-'kahr-gah bah-hee-'nahl)*
varicose veins	**venas varicosas** *('beh-nahs bah-ree-'koh-sahs)*
venereal disease	**enfermedad venérea** *(ehn-fehr-meh-'dahd beh-'neh-reh-ah)*
visual problems	**problemas de visión** *(proh-'bleh-mahs deh bee-see·'ohn)*
weight gain	**aumento de peso** *(ow-'mehn-toh deh 'peh-soh)*

A very important question: When was your last period? **¿Cuándo fue su última regla?** *('kwahn-doh fweh soo 'ool-tee-mah 'reh-glah)*

Do you want to talk?

¿Quiere hablar? *(kee-'eh-reh ah-'blahr)*

María has received most of her medical advice concerning pregnancy from family and friends. When it comes to proper family planning, however, it may be best to bring in a professional. You can offer her counseling with the following information.

Do you want to talk about . . . ?	**¿Quiere hablar de . . . ?** *(kee-'eh-reh ah-'blahr deh)*
abortion	**el aborto** *(ehl ah-'bohr-toh)*
adoption	**adopción** *(ah-dohp-see-'ohn)*
AIDS	**el SIDA** *(ehl 'see-dah)*
cleanliness	**la limpieza** *(lah leem-pee-'eh-sah)*
your clothing	**su ropa** *(soo 'roh-pah)*
depression	**la depresión** *(lah deh-preh-see-'ohn)*
your diet	**su dieta** *(soo dee-'eh-tah)*
drug use	**el uso de drogas** *(ehl 'oo-soh deh 'droh-gahs)*
exercise	**el ejercicio** *(ehl eh-hehr-'see-see-oh)*
family planning	**planificación familiar** *(plah-nee-fee-kah-see-'ohn fah-mee-lee-'ahr)*
your job	**su trabajo** *(soo trah-'bah-hoh)*
Lamaze Method	**el método de Lamaze** *(ehl 'meh-toh-doh deh lah-'mah-seh)*
natural childbirth	**el parto natural** *(ehl 'pahr-toh nah-too-'rahl)*
prenatal care	**la atención prenatal** *(lah ah-tehn-see-'ohn preh-nah-'tahl)*
your sexual relations	**sus relaciones sexuales** *(soos reh-lah-see-'oh-nehs sehk-soo-'ah-lehs)*

Birth control methods
Los métodos de anticoncepción
(lohs 'meh-toh-dohs deh ahn-tee-kohn-seh-psee·'ohn)

birth control pills	**las píldoras anticonceptivas**
	(lahs 'peel-doh-rahs ahn-tee-kohn-seh-'ptee-bahs)
coitus interruptus	**la interrupción del coito**
	(lah een-teh-rroop-see·'ohn dehl koh-'ee-toh)
condoms	**los condones** *(lohs kohn-'doh-nehs)*
creams	**las cremas** *(lahs 'kreh-mahs)*
diaphragm	**el diafragma** *(ehl dee-ah-'frahg-mah)*
douching	**el baño de asiento**
	(ehl 'bah-nyoh deh ah-see-'ehn-toh)
foams	**las espumas** *(lahs ehs-'poo-mahs)*
IUD	**el aparato intrauterino**
	(ehl ah-pah-'rah-toh een-trah-oo-teh-'ree-noh)
rhythm method	**el método del ritmo**
	(ehl 'meh-toh-doh dehl 'reet-moh)
tubal ligation	**la ligadura de los tubos**
	(lah lee-gah-'doo-rah deh lohs 'too-bohs)
vasectomy	**la vasectomía** *(lah bah-sehk-toh-'mee-ah)*

The reproductive system
El sistema reproductivo
(ehl sees-'teh-mah reh-proh-dook-'tee-boh)

María wants more details, but explaining the reproductive system in Spanish will require a rather extensive vocabulary. Use this selection as a guide:

amniotic sac	**la bolsa amniótica**
	(lah 'bohl-sah ahm-nee-'oh-tee-kah)
anus	**el ano** *('ehl 'ah-noh)*
breasts	**los senos** *(lohs 'seh-nohs)*
cervical canal	**el canal cervical** *(ehl kah-'nahl sehr-bee-'kahl)*
cervix	**el cuello uterino** *(ehl 'kweh-yoh oo-teh-'ree-noh)*
embryo	**el embrión** *(ehl ehm-bree-'ohn)*

erection	**la erección** *(lah eh-rehk-see-'ohn)*
Fallopian tubes	**las trompas de Falopio**
	(lahs 'trohm-pahs deh fah-'loh-pee·oh)
fetus	**el feto** *(ehl 'feh-toh)*
navel	**el ombligo** *(ehl ohm-'blee-goh)*
nipple	**el pezón** *(ehl peh-'sohn)*
ovary	**el ovario** *(ehl oh-'bah-ree·oh)*
ovum	**el óvulo** *(ehl 'oh-boo-loh)*
penis	**el pene** *(ehl 'peh-neh)*
placenta	**la placenta** *(lah plah-'sehn-tah)*
scrotum	**el escroto** *(ehl ehs-'kroh-toh)*
semen	**el semen** *(ehl 'seh-mehn)*
sperm	**la esperma** *(lah ehs-'pehr-mah)*
testicles	**los testículos** *(lohs tehs-'tee-koo-lohs)*
umbilical cord	**el cordón umbilical**
	(ehl kohr-'dohn oom-bee-lee-'kahl)
urethra	**la uretra** *(lah oo-'reht-rah)*
uterus	**el útero, la matriz** *(ehl 'oo-teh-roh, lah mah-'trees)*
vagina	**la vagina** *(lah bah-'hee-nah)*
vulva	**la vulva** *(lah 'vool-vah)*

Additional relevant terms:

fertilization	**la fertilización** *(lah fehr-tee-lee-sah-see·'ohn)*
genes	**los genes** *(lohs 'heh-nehs)*
hormones	**las hormonas** *(lahs ohr-'moh-nahs)*
intercourse	**el coito** *(ehl 'koh·ee-toh)*
menstrual cycle	**el ciclo menstrual** *(ehl 'seek-loh mehn-stroo-'ahl)*

You are pregnant

Está embarazada *(eh-'stah ehm-bah-rah-'sah-dah)*

María will need to undergo several tests. The results from those tests must be made available to her in clear instructions. Use the following patterns to communicate this information.

Let's Check the . . .

Verifiquemos . . . *(beh-ree-fee-'keh-mohs)*

area	**el área** *(ehl 'ah-reh-ah)*
liquid	**el líquido** *(ehl 'lee-kee-doh)*
organ	**el órgano** *(ehl 'ohr-gah-noh)*
pulse	**el pulso** *(ehl 'pool-soh)*
size	**el tamaño** *(ehl tah-'mahn-yoh)*

You need a . . .

Necesita un . . . *(neh-seh-'see-tah oon)*

AIDS test	**examen de SIDA** *(ehk-'sah-mehn deh 'see-dah)*
blood test	**examen de sangre** *(ehk-'sah-mehn deh 'sahn-greh)*
enema	**enema** *(eh-'neh-mah)*
pap smear	**examen de Papanicolao**
	(ehk-'sah-mehn deh pah-pah-nee-koh-'lah-oh)
pelvic exam	**examen pélvico** *(ehk-'sah-mehn 'pehl-bee-koh)*
pregnancy test	**examen de embarazo**
	(ehk-'sah-mehn deh ehm-bah-'rah-soh)
rectal exam	**examen del recto** *(ehk-'sah-mehn dehl 'rehk-toh)*
Rh factor test	**examen del factor Rhesus**
	(ehk-'sah-mehn dehl fahk-'tohr 'Reh-soos)
urine test	**examen de orina** *(ehk-'sah-mehn deh oh-'ree-nah)*

Use all the Spanish you've learned to conduct the following interview with María.

Did you ever have a miscarriage?

¿Perdió el bebé alguna vez? *(perh-dee-'oh ehl beh-'beh ahl-'goo-nah behs)*

Do you have other children?

¿Tiene otros hijos? *('tee-'eh-neh 'oh-trohs 'ee-hohs)*

What are you going to need?

¿Qué va a necesitar? *(keh bah a neh-seh-see-'tahr)*

When is the date of birth?

¿Cuándo es la fecha de nacimiento?
('kwahn-doh ehs lah 'feh-chah deh nah-see-mee-'ehn-toh)

Who is the father?

¿Quién es el padre? *(kee-'ehn ehs ehl 'pah-dreh)*

There isn't time!
¡No hay tiempo! *(noh 'ah·ee tee-'ehm-poh)*

While you're handling María's pregnancy, time may become important to the conversation. Spend a few **momentos** scanning this next vocabulary list. These words are invaluable to health care professionals.

When?
¿Cuándo? *('kwahn-doh)*

after	**después** *(dehs-'pwehs)*
already	**ya** *(yah)*
always	**siempre** *(see-'ehm-preh)*
before	**antes** *('ahn-tehs)*
early	**temprano** *(tehm-'prah-noh)*
frequently	**con frecuencia** *(kohn freh-'kwehn-see-ah)*
late	**tarde** *('tahr-deh)*
later	**luego** *(loo-'eh-goh)*
many times	**muchas veces** *('moo-chahs 'beh-sehs)*
never	**nunca** *('noon-kah)*
now	**ahora** *(ah-'oh-rah)*
once	**una vez** *('oo-nah behs)*
right now	**ahorita** *(ah-oh-'ree-tah)*
sometimes	**a veces** *(ah 'beh-sehs)*
soon	**pronto** *('prohn-toh)*
then	**entonces** *(ehn-'tohn-sehs)*
yet	**todavía** *(toh-dah-'bee-ah)*

Learn as many "time" words as you can:

day after tomorrow	**pasado mañana** *(pah-'sah-doh mah-'nyah-nah)*
day before yesterday	**anteayer** *(ahn-teh-ah-'yehr)*
last night	**anoche** *(ah-'noh-cheh)*

tomorrow	**mañana** *(mah-'nyah-nah)*
tonight	**esta noche** *('eh-stah 'noh-cheh)*

(17) ¿CUÁNTO APRENDIÓ?

Are you able to interpret the sample phrases below?

ago	**hace** *('ah-seh)*
	hace una semana *('ah-seh 'oo-nah seh-'mah-nah)*
between	**entre** *('ehn-treh)*
	entre las tres y las cuatro
	('ehn-treh lahs trehs ee lahs 'kwah-troh)
the following	**el siguiente** *(ehl see-gee-'ehn-teh)*
	el siguiente día *(ehl see-gee-'ehn-teh 'dee-ah)*
last	**el pasado** *(ehl pah-'sah-doh)*
	el pasado año *(ehl pah-'sah-doh 'ah-nyoh)*
the next	**el próximo** *(ehl 'prohk-see-moh)*
	el próximo mes *(ehl 'prohk-see-moh mehs)*
until	**hasta** *('ah-stah)*
	hasta mañana *('ah-stah mah-'nyah-nah)*
within	**dentro de** *('dehn-troh deh)*
	dentro de dos horas *('dehn-troh deh dohs 'oh-rahs)*

Match the words on the left with their opposites.

temprano *(tehm-'prah-noh)*	**muchas veces** *('moo-chahs 'beh-sehs)*
mañana *(mah-'nyah-nah)*	**siempre** *(see-'ehm-preh)*
el próximo *(ehl 'prohk-see-moh)*	**tarde** *('tahr-deh)*
una vez *('oo-nah behs)*	**después** *(dehs-'pwehs)*
nunca *('noon-kah)*	**ayer** *(ah-'yehr)*
antes *('ahn-tehs)*	**el pasado** *(ehl pah-'sah-doh)*

We need answers
Necesitamos respuestas
(neh-seh-see-'tah-mohs rehs-'pwehs-tahs)

Never give up on your standard **preguntas**. Use the basic question words to gather more information.

How much . . .?	**¿Cuánto . . .?** *('kwahn-toh)*
do you weigh	**pesa** *('peh-sah)*
did you gain	**subió** *(soo-bee-'oh)*
time	**tiempo** *(tee-'ehm-poh)*
How often?	**¿Cada cuánto tiempo?**
	('kah-dah 'kwahn-toh tee-'ehm-poh)
How long ago?	**¿Hace cuánto tiempo?**
	('ah-seh 'kwahn-toh tee-'ehm-poh)
How many . . .?	**¿Cuántos? ¿Cuántas . . .?**
	('kwahn-tohs, 'kwahn-tahs)
days	**días** *('dee-ahs)*
hours	**horas** *('oh-rahs)*
minutes	**minutos** *(mee-'noo-tohs)*
months	**meses** *('meh-sehs)*
seconds	**segundos** *(seh-'goon-dohs)*
weeks	**semanas** *(seh-'mah-nahs)*
years	**años** *('ah-nyohs)*

The past
El pasado *(ehl pah-'sah-doh)*

Gathering data on María's past requires working knowledge of Spanish verbs. Try to recall the changes that take place to most verb endings when we refer to <u>present</u> action.

to speak	**hablar** *(ah-'blahr)*
I speak a little Spanish.	**Hablo poquito español.**
	('ah-bloh poh-'kee-toh ehs-pah-'nyohl)
to live	**vivir** *(vee-'veer)*
Where do you live?	**¿Dónde vive usted?**
	('dohn-deh 'vee-veh oo-'stehd)
to eat	**comer** *(koh-'mehr)*
We eat at 6:00.	**Comemos a las seis.**
	(koh-'meh-mohs ah lahs 'seh·ees)

Although there are a variety of ways to state a <u>past</u> tense in Spanish, you need to start by learning the more commonly used form. Read the following examples and, just as you did with <u>present</u> actions, make the changes in your verbs. You won't be perfect at first, but María will know what you're trying to say.

- **ar** ending verbs—**HABLAR** *(ah-'blahr)* TO SPEAK

I spoke with the doctor.	**Hablé con el doctor.**
	(ah-'bleh kohn ehl dohk-'tohr)
You/he/she spoke a lot.	**Habló mucho.** *(ah-'bloh 'moo-choh)*
They spoke in English.	**Hablaron en inglés.**
	(ah-'blah-rohn ehn een-'glehs)
We spoke afterwards.	**Hablamos después.**
	(ah-'blah-mohs dehs-'pwehs)

- **er/ir** ending verbs—**BEBER** *(beh-'behr)* TO DRINK
  SALIR *(sah-'leer)* TO LEAVE

I left at eight.	**Salí a las ocho.**
	(sah-'lee ah lahs 'oh-choh)
I drank the medicine.	**Bebí la medicina.**
	(beh-'bee lah meh-dee-'see-nah)
You/he/she left late.	**Salió tarde.** *(sah-lee-'oh 'tahr-deh)*
You/he/she drank	**Bebió el café.** *(beh-bee-'oh ehl kah-'feh)*
the coffee.	

They left happy.	**Salieron contentos.**
	(sah-lee-'eh-rohn kohn-'tehn-tohs)
They drank water last night.	**Bebieron agua anoche.**
	(beh-bee-'eh-rohn 'ah-gwah ah-'noh-cheh)
We left in a car.	**Salimos en el carro.**
	(sah-'lee-mohs ehn ehl 'kah-rroh)
We drank the day before yesterday.	**Bebimos anteayer.**
	(beh-'bee-mohs ahn-teh-ah-'yehr)

Build your commands
Construya sus órdenes
(kohns-'troo-yah soos 'or-deh-nehs)

A simple approach to forming a command in Spanish requires knowledge of the three different action word (verb) endings. As we stated above, the endings are:

ar as in **hablar**—to speak

er as in **comer**—to eat

ir as in **escribir**—to write

To make a command, drop the last two letters of the infinitive form and replace them as follows.

ar	**e**	
hablar *(ah-'blahr)*	**hable** *('ah-bleh)*	speak
er	**a**	
comer *(koh-'mehr)*	**coma** *('koh-mah)*	eat
ir	**a**	
escribir *(ehs-kree-'beer)*	**escriba** *(ehs-'kree-bah)*	write

But beware. Some verbs are strange and simply have to be memorized.

ir *(eer)*	**vaya** *('bah-yah)*	go
venir *(beh-'neer)*	**venga** *('behn-gah)*	come
decir *(deh-'seer)*	**diga** *('dee-gah)*	speak

Some common verbs have irregular past tenses, so be on the lookout.

To be—**Ser** *(sehr)* or To go—**Ir** *(eer)*

I was or went	**fui** *(fwee)*
you were or went	**fue** *(fweh)*
he/she was or went	**fue** *(fweh)*
you (plural)/they were or went	**fueron** *('fweh-rohn)*
we were or went	**fuimos** *('fwee-mohs)*

To have—**Tener** *(teh'nehr)*

I had	**tuve** *('too-beh)*
you/he/she had	**tuvo** *('too-boh)*
you (plural)/they had	**tuvieron** *(too-bee-'eh-rohn)*
we had	**tuvimos** *(too-'bee-mohs)*

<u>Past</u> tense isn't the only verb form you're going to need. Although these won't be discussed in detail, check out the spellings and meanings of these examples below:

I used to have	**tenía** *(teh-'nee-ah)*
I would have	**tendría** *(tehn-'dree-ah)*
I will have	**tendré** *(tehn-'dreh)*

(18) ¿CuÁnto Aprendió?

Translate the following messages.

¿Qué comió? *(keh koh-mee-'oh)*

¿Tomó medicina? *(toh-'moh meh-dee-'see-nah)*

¿Fumó? *(foo-'moh)*

¿Se enfermó? *(seh ehn-fehr-'moh)*

¿Tuvo problemas? *('too-boh proh-'bleh-mahs)*

More action!

¡Más acción! *(mahs ahk-see-see·'ohn)*

Add these action words to your list. They specifically target the needs of patients like María.

to be born	**nacer**
When were you born?	**¿Cuándo nació?** *('kwahn-doh nah-see-'oh)*
to begin	**comenzar** *(koh-mehn-'sahr)*
When did the pains begin?	**¿Cuándo comenzaron los dolores?** *('kwahn-doh koh-mehn-'sah-rohn lohs doh-'loh-rehs)*
to defecate	**defecar** *(deh-feh-'kahr)*
Did you defecate?	**¿Defecó?** *(deh-feh-'koh)*
to end	**terminar** *(tehr-mee-'nahr)*
Did the pains stop?	**¿Terminaron los dolores?** *(tehr-mee-'nah-rohn lohs doh-'loh-rehs)*
to grow	**crecer** *(kreh-'sehr)*
He grew very fast.	**Creció muy rápido.** *(kreh-see-'oh 'moo·ee 'rah-pee-doh)*
to menstruate	**menstruar** *(mehn-stroo-'ahr)*
When did you menstruate?	**¿Cuándo menstruó?** *('kwahn-doh mehn-stroo-'oh)*
to rest	**descansar** *(dehs-kahn-'sahr)*
Are you going to rest?	**¿Va a descansar?** *(bah ah dehs-kahn-'sahr)*
to urinate	**orinar** *(oh-ree-'nahr)*
Do you urinate a lot?	**¿Orina mucho?** *(oh-ree-'nah 'moo-choh)*
to visit	**visitar** *(bee-see-'tahr)*
I need to visit María.	**Necesito visitar a María.** *(neh-seh-'see-toh bee-see-'tahr ah mah-'ree-ah)*

Can I help you?

¿Puedo ayudarle? *('pweh-doh ah-yoo-'dahr-leh)*

Here's still another one of those incredible verb patterns that makes speaking Spanish so much easier. Combine your verbs with the forms of the word **poder**, which means "can."

I can	**puedo** *('pweh-doh)*
I can begin.	**Puedo comenzar.** *('pweh-doh koh-mehn-'sahr)*
You, she/he can	**puede** *('pweh-deh)*
She can visit.	**Puede visitar.** *('pweh-deh hee-see-'tahr)*
you (plural)/ they can	**pueden** *('pweh-dehn)*
They can rest.	**Pueden descansar.** *('pweh-dehn dehs-kahn-'sahr)*
we can	**podemos** *(poh-'deh-mohs)*
We can finish.	**Podemos terminar.** *(poh-'deh-mohs tehr-mee-'nahr)*

María feels comfortable with her physician, and decides to visit the clinic at least once a month. As her time draws near, your questions may grow in intensity. Use your newly-acquired skill of using past tense to help you with these questions.

At what age did you begin to menstruate?
¿A qué edad comenzó a menstruar?
(ah keh eh-'dahd koh-mehn-'soh ah mehn-stroo-'ahr)

Do you have a hereditary disease?
¿Tiene una enfermedad hereditaria?
(tee-'eh-neh 'oo-nah ehn-fehr-meh-'dahd eh-reh-dee-'tah-ree-ah)

Do you have shortness of breath?
¿Respira con dificultad? *(rehs-'pee-rah kohn dee-fee-kool-'tahd)*

Do your breasts hurt?
¿Le duelen los senos? *(leh 'dweh-lehn lohs 'seh-nohs)*

Is there blood or water?
¿Hay sangre o agua? *('ah-ee 'sahn-greh oh 'ah-gwah)*

Were all your pregnancies normal?

¿Fueron todos sus embarazos normales?

('fweh-rohn 'toh-dohs soos ehm-bah-'rah-sohs nohr-'mah-lehs)

When it comes to multiple births, you should also learn these words:

second	**segundo** *(seh-'goon-doh)*
third	**tercero** *(tehr-'seh-roh)*
fourth	**cuarto** *('kwahr-toh)*
fifth	**quinto** *('keen-toh)*
sixth	**sexto** *('sehks-toh)*
seventh	**séptimo** *('sehp-tee-moh)*
eighth	**octavo** (ohk-'tah-boh)

Commands
Ordenes *('ohr-deh-nehs)*

The weeks are going by quickly. Check to see if María is following your instructions. Review your command words.

Bring the urine.	**Traiga la orina.** *('trah-ee-gah la oh-'ree-nah)*
Call the gynecologist.	**Llame al ginecólogo.** *('yah-meh ahl hee-neh-'koh-loh-goh)*
Come with your husband.	**Venga con su esposo.** *('behn-gah kohn soo ehs-'poh-soh)*
Follow the diet.	**Siga la dieta.** *('see-gah lah dee-'eh-tah)*
Take the medicine.	**Tome la medicina.** *('toh-meh lah meh-dee-'see-nah)*

Add a few more commands and create your own sentences.

pull	**jale** *('hah-leh)*
push	**empuje** *(ehm-'poo-heh)*
bend	**doble** *('doh-bleh)*
open	**abra** *('ah-brah)*
close	**cierre** *(see-'eh-rreh)*
eat	**coma** *('koh-mah)*

María is ready to deliver, and it's time for action. You probably won't have the opportunity to read these expressions at the time of the birth, so you may want to memorize them before it's too late.

Breathe deeply.	**Respire profundamente.**
	(rehs-'pee-reh proh-foon-dah-'mehn-teh)
Grab my hand.	**Agarre mi mano.** *(ah 'gah rreh mee 'mah-noh)*
Move your leg.	**Mueva la pierna.**
	('moo-ee-bah lah pee-'ehr-nah)
Raise your head.	**Levante la cabeza.**
	(leh-'bahn-teh lah kah 'beh sah)
Rest.	**Descanse.** *(dehs-'kahn-seh)*
This is for the pain.	**Esto es para el dolor.**
	('ehs-toh ehs 'pah-rah ehl doh-'lohr)
You need anesthesia.	**Necesita anestesia.**
	(neh-seh-'see-tah ah-nehs-'teh-see-ah)
You need a Cesarean section.	**Necesita una operación cesárea.**
	(neh-seh-'see-tah 'oo-nah oh-peh-rah-see-'ohn seh-'sah-reh-ah)

While giving orders to María, use the word **así,** *(ah-'see)* which means "like this." Breathe like this. **Respire así.** *(rehs-'pee-reh ah-'see)*

Remember to always say **por favor** *(pohr fah-'bohr)* (please) and **gracias** *('grah-see-ahs)* (thanks) with your commands. They help!

Note: Many Hispanics use the expression **dar a luz** *(dahr ah loos)* when referring to childbirth: María gave birth. **María dio a luz.** *(mah-'ree-ah dee-'oh ah loos)*

DOS CULTURAS

Babies are sacred creatures in most cultures. In many Hispanic homes, the traditions and rituals of childbearing are not easily changed. Some family customs are centuries old, even though they may contradict modern science. Keep these things in mind as you give advice to expectant mothers.

The Newborn

El recién nacido *(ehl reh-see-'ehn nah-'see-doh)*

Congratulations! It's a girl! ¡una niña! *('oo-nah 'nee-nyah)* The delivery went well, the baby is healthy, and mother is doing fine. After she rests, María is going to need some information about proper care of the newborn. Although this is her third child, she needs to know what is best for her new baby girl. By the way, her name is Angelina.

Do you want to go home?

¿Quiere ir a la casa? *(kee-'eh-reh eer ah lah 'kah-sah)*

She must eat a lot every day.

Tiene que comer mucho todos los días.

(tee'eh-neh keh koh-'mehr 'moo-choh 'toh-dohs lohs 'dee-ahs)

They eat every 3 or 4 hours.

Comen cada tres o cuatro horas.

('koh-mehn 'kah-dah trehs oh 'kwah-troh 'oh-rahs)

You must prepare the formula.

Tiene que preparar la fórmula.

(tee-'eh-neh keh preh-pah-'rahr lah 'fohr-moo-lah)

You will need a pediatrician.

Va a necesitar un pediatra.

(bah a neh-seh-see-'tahr oon peh-dee-'ah-trah)

Will you be breast feeding?

Va a amamantar? *(bah ah ah-mah-mahn-'tahr)*

Describe her!

Descríbala *(dehs-'kree-bah-lah)*

Some of the first words you'll want to express to María will be descriptive words relating to her new baby, Angelina. Try these:

She is . . .	**Es . . .** *(ehs)*
baldy	**calvita** *(kahl-'bee-tah)*
blond	**rubia** *('roo-bee-ah)*

brunette	**morena** *(moh-'reh-nah)*
dark-skinned	**prieta** *(pree-'eh-tah)*
redhead	**pelirroja** *(peh-lee-'roh-hah)*
a twin	**una gemela** *('oo-nah heh-'meh-lah)*

How much does the baby weigh? **¿Cuánto pesa el bebé?** *('kwahn-toh 'peh-sah ehl beh-'beh)* Study these terms:

grams	**gramos** *('grah-mohs)*
inches	**pulgadas** *(pool-'gah-dahs)*
liters	**litros** *('leet-rohs)*
meters	**metros** *('meht-rohs)*
ounces	**onzas** *('ohn-sahs)*
pounds	**libras** *('lee-brahs)*

Bad news

¡Malas noticias! *('mah-lahs noh-'tee-see·ahs)*

Not all news is good news. Sometimes patients are not as fortunate as María when it comes to the health of their baby.

It is . . .	**Es** *(ehs)* . . .
or It has . . .	**Tiene** *('tee-'eh-neh)* . . .
a birth defect	**un defecto de nacimiento** *(oon deh-'fehk-toh deh nah-see-mee'-ehn-toh)*
blind	**ciego** *(see-'eh-goh)*
deaf	**sordo** *('sohr-doh)*
fetal alcohol syndrome	**el síndrome de alcohol fetal** *(ehl 'seen-droh-meh deh ahl-koh-'ohl feh-'tahl)*
jaundice	**ictericia** *(eek-teh-'ree-see·ah)*
a miscarriage	**una pérdida** *(oo-nah 'pehr-dee-dah)*
premature	**prematuro** *(preh-mah-'too-roh)*
stillborn	**nacido muerto** *(nah-'see-doh 'mwehr-toh)*

¡NO SE OLVIDE!

Remember how the words change based upon the child's sex:

The girl baby is premature.	**La bebé es prematura.**
	(lah beh-'beh ehs preh-mah-'too-rah)
The boy baby is premature.	**El bebé es prematuro.**
	(ehl beh-'beh ehs preh-mah-'too-roh)

Visiting hours

Las horas de visita *(lahs 'oh-rahs deh bee-'see-tah)*

Family and friends will no doubt want to come visit María and her new child. Prepare yourself by learning the phrase for "I'm sorry, but . . ." **"Lo siento, pero . . ."** *(loh see-'ehn-toh 'peh-roh)*

Children do not visit patients.
Los niños no visitan a los pacientes.
(lohs 'nee-nyohs noh bee-'see-tahn ah lohs pah-see-'ehn-tehs)

She needs rest.
Ella necesita descansar. *('eh-yah neh-seh-'see-tah dehs-kahn-'sahr)*

The patient isn't seeing any visitors.
El paciente no recibe visitantes.
(ehl pah-see-'ehn-teh noh reh-'see-beh bee-see-'tahn-tehs)

There are too many visitors in the room.
Hay demasiados visitantes en el cuarto.
('ae-ee deh-'mah-see-ah-dohs bee-see-'tahn-tehs ehn ehl 'kwahr-toh)

Visitors only during visiting hours, please.
Visitantes solamente durante las horas de visita, por favor.
(bee-see-'tahn-tehs soh-lah-'mehn-teh doo-'rahn-teh lahs 'oh-rahs deh bee-'see-tah, pohr fah-'vohr)

Visiting hours are over.
Las horas de visita terminaron.
(lahs 'oh-rahs de bee-'see-tah tehr-mee-'nah-rohn)

Infants

¡Los infantes! *(lohs een-'fahn-tehs)*

Care to know more about babies? These words will definitely get it done.

bottle nipple or pacifier
el chupete *(ehl choo-'peh-teh)*

The bottle nipple was very big.
El chupete es muy grande.
(ehl choo-'peh-teh ehs 'moo·eeh 'grahn-deh)

colic
el cólico *(ehl 'koh-lee-koh)*

The baby has colic.
El bebé tiene cólico.
(ehl beh-'beh lee-'eh-neh 'koh-lee-koh)

diaper
el pañal *(ehl pah-'nyahl)*

He urinated in the diaper.
Orinó en el pañal.
(oh-ree-'noh ehn ehl pah-'nyahl)

formula
la fórmula *(lah 'fohr-moo-lah)*

We have the formula.
Tenemos la fórmula.
(teh-'neh-mohs lah 'fohr-moo-lah)

milk
la leche *(lah 'leh-cheh)*

Do you want more milk?
¿Quiere más leche?
(kee-'eh-reh mahs 'leh-cheh)

nap
la siesta *(lah see-'ehs-tah)*

She nees a nap.
Necesita una siesta.
(neh-seh-'see-tah 'oo-nah see-'ehs-tah)

nursing bottle
el biberón *(ehl bee-beh-'rohn)*

Use the nursing bottle.
Use el biberón.
('oo-seh ehl bee-beh-'rohn)

rash
la erupción *(lah eh-roop-see-'ohn)*

I am going to examine the rash.
Voy a examinar la erupción.
('boh·ee ah ehk-sah-mee-'nahr lah eh-roohp-see-'ohn)

talcum powder   **el talco** *(ehl 'tahl-koh)*

Where is the talcum powder?   **¿Dónde está el talco?**

                 ('dohn-deh eh-'stah ehl 'tahl-koh)

And don't forget: Hugs and kisses! **¡Abrazos y besos!** *(ah-'brah-sohs ee 'beh-sohs)*

D O S   C U L T U R A S

Jewish religion requires the rite of circumcision—**circuncisión** *(seehr-coon-see-see.'ohn)*—and this practice also has become common among non-Jews in the United States. The opposite is true for Latin people. They often are surprised and shocked when the hospital nurse or physician asks them, as a matter of fact, about performing the procedure. Be aware that the overwhelming majority of Latin people are neither circumcised nor do they wish their babies to be circumcised.

At home
En casa *(ehn 'kah-sah)*

María is grateful for all your efforts, and can't wait to tell all her friends about the outstanding care she received. Here are some phrases you can use to let her know about some of your other programs.

There are ...   **Hay** *('ah-ee)* ...

   classes for mothers   **clases para las madres**

                 ('klah-sehs 'pah-rah lahs 'mah-drehs)

   exercise classes   **clases para ejercicios**

                 ('klah-sehs 'pah-rah eh-hehr-'see-see·ohs)

   free vaccination   **vacunación gratuita**

                 (bah-koo-nah-see-'ohn grah-too-'ee-tah)

   services for teen-age   **servicios para adolescentes**

     pregnancies   **embarazadas**

                 (sehr-'bee-see·ohs 'pah-rah ah-doh-leh-
                 'sehn-tehs ehm-bah-rah-'sah-dahs)

Chapter Six

Margarita Espinoza, Age Six

Little Margarita has had a chest cold for several days. Home remedies have been tried, but her condition has only gotten worse. She now has acute bronchitis and needs a physician's care. A pediatrician has recently opened a small office in the neighborhood and everyone says she is great with children—**los niños.** Juan and María have just made an appointment for their ailing daughter.

Young children require special care and, in order to communicate properly, lots of special Spanish vocabulary is required. Let's observe what goes on in the pediatrician's office, and discover what is being used to nurse the little ones back to good health.

The visit
La visita *(lah vee-'see-tah)*

Margarita cannot get proper care until you have more answers about her past history. As usual, everything is divided into similar patterns.

Begin by asking the parents to respond to your questions about the patient with a simple **sí** *(see)* or **no** *(noh).*

Does she have pain?	**¿Tiene dolor?** *(tee-'eh-neh doh-'lohr)*
Is it an injury?	**¿Es una herida?** *(ehs oonah eh-'ree-dah)*
Is she sick?	**¿Está enferma?** *(eh-'stah ehn-'fehr-mah)*

Remember the *present* tense verb form? It works great during office visits.

It burns...	**Me quema** *(meh 'keh-mah)*
It hurts...	**Me duele** *(meh doo-'eh-leh)*
It itches...	**Me pica** *(meh 'pee-kah)*

Does he/she breathe well?	**¿Respira bien?**
	(reh-'spee-rah bee·'ehn)
Does he/she drink milk?	**¿Toma leche?** *('toh-mah 'leh-cheh)*
Does he/she eat well?	**¿Come bien?** *('koh-meh bee·'ehn)*
Does he/she talk?	**¿Habla?** *('ah-blah)*
Does he/she walk?	**¿Camina?** *(kah-'mee-nah)*

More action
Más acción *(mahs ahk-see·'ohn)*

Eventually, you are going to run out of things to say. As you have already discovered, certain verbs target the language needs in specific areas of medicine. The following list and sample sentences will help you get children's background information:

to be constipated	**estar estreñido** *(ehs-'tahr ehs-treh-'nyee-doh)*
Is she constipated?	**¿Está estreñida?** *(eh-'stah ehs-treh-'nyee-dah)*
to burp	**eructar** *(eh-roohk-'tahr)*
Does she burp?	**¿Eructa?** *(eh-'rook-tah)*
to cough	**toser** *(toh-'sehr)*
Does she cough?	**¿Tose?** *('toh-seh)*
to cry	**llorar** *('yoh-'rahr)*
Does she cry?	**¿Llora?** *('yoh-rah)*
to feed	**alimentar** *(ah-lee-mehn-'tahr)*
When do you feed the child?	**¿Cuándo alimenta al niño?**
	('kwahn-doh ah-lee-'mehn-tah ahl 'nee-nyoh)
to sneeze	**estornudar** *(ehs-tohr-noo-'dahr)*
Does she sneeze?	**¿Estornuda?** *(ehs-tohr-'noo-dah)*

to swallow	**tragar** *(trah-'gahr)*
Does she swallow her food?	**¿Traga la comida?**
	('trah-gah lah koh-'mee-dah)
to vomit	**vomitar** *(boh-mee-'tahr)*
Does she vomit?	**¿Vomita?** *(boh-'mee-tah)*

The verb form is the same for most actions. A few words change slightly. Review these examples:

to play	**jugar** *(hoo-'gahr)*
Does she play much?	**¿Juega mucho?** *('hweh-gah 'moo-choh)*
to understand	**entender** *(ehn-tehn-'dehr)*
Does she understand?	**¿Entiende?** *(ehn-tee-'ehn-deh)*

Use **es** *(ehs)* to refer to the child's nature. **Está** *(eh-'stah)* only refers to her present condition.

She is sick (has a chronic illness).
Ella es enferma. *('eh-yah ehs ehn-'fehr-mah)*

She's feeling sick.
Ella está enferma. *('eh yah eh-'stah ehn-'fehr-mah)*

Beber *(beh-'behr)* and **tomar** *(toh-'mahr)* may both be used to mean "to drink," although **beber** *(beh-'behr)* is more specific.

Here's another suggestion: Stick some of your base action forms (**ar, er, ir**) next to one of these:

Is he/she going to . . .?	**¿Va a . . .?** *(bah ah)*
Does he/she want to . . .?	**¿Quiere . . .?** *(kee-'eh-reh)*
Does he/she need to . . .?	**¿Necesita . . .?** *(neh-seh-'see-tah)*
Does he/she have to . . .?	**¿Tiene que . . .?** *(tee-'eh-neh keh)*
Can you . . .?	**¿Puede . . .?** *('pweh-deh)*
defecate	**defecar** *(deh-feh-'kahr)*
drink	**beber** *(beh-'behr)*
get up	**levantarse** *(leh-bahn-'tahr-seh)*
sit down	**sentarse** *(sehn-'tahr-seh)*

stand	**pararse** *(pah-'rahr-seh)*
swallow	**tragar** *(trah-'gahr)*
urinate	**orinar** *(oh-ree-'nahr)*

Continue to search for action words that you need. In the world of pediatrics, these verbs are always useful:

to bite	**morder** *(mohr-'dehr)*
to chew	**masticar** *(mah-stee-'kahr)*
to crawl	**gatear** *(gah-teh-'ahr)*
to nurse	**lactar** *(lahk-'tahr)*
to suck	**chupar** *(choo-'pahr)*

Symptoms
Los síntomas *(lohs 'seen-toh-mahs)*

Keep focusing on the "yes-no" questions. Feel free to mix in a few expressions with **tiene:**

Does he/she have . . .?	**¿Tiene . . .?** *(tee-'eh-neh)*
blisters	**ampollas** *(ahm-poh-yahs)*
bumps	**protuberancias** *(proh-too-beh-'rahn-see-ahs)*
calluses	**callos** *('kah-yohs)*
constipation	**estreñimiento** *(ehs-treh-nyee-mee-'ehn-toh)*
convulsions	**convulsiones** *(kohn-boohl-see-'oh-nehs)*
a cough	**tos** *(tohs)*
diarrhea	**diarrea** *(dee-ah-'rreh-ah)*
fever	**fiebre** *(fee-'eh-breh)*
fleas	**pulgas** *('pool-gahs)*
hiccups	**hipo** *('ee-poh)*
infection	**infección** *(een-fehk-see-'ohn)*
lice	**piojos** *(pee-'oh-hohs)*
loss of appetite	**falta de apetito** *('fahl-tah deh ah-peh-'tee-toh)*
phlegm	**flema** *('fleh-mah)*
pimples	**granos** *('grah-nohs)*
pus	**pus** *(poohs)*

a rash	**erupción** *(eh-roop-see-'ohn)*
scabs	**costras** *('koh-strahs)*
a splinter	**una astilla** *('oo-nah ahs-'tee-yah)*
stuffy nose	**la nariz tapada** *(lah nah-'rees tah-'pah-dah)*
sweating	**sudor** *(soo-'dohr)*
swelling	**hinchazones** *(een-chah-'soh-nehs)*
temperature	**temperatura** *(tehm-peh-rah-'too-rah)*
ticks	**garrapatas** *(gahr-rah-'pah-tahs)*
warts	**verrugas** *(beh-'rroo-gahs)*

Does he/she have problems . . .?

¿Tiene dificultades para . . .? *(tee-'eh-neh dee-fee-kool-'tah-dehs 'pah-rah)*

breathing	**respirar** *(rehs-pee-'rahr)*
chewing	**masticar** *(mah-stee-'kahr)*
crawling	**gatear** *(gah-teh-'ahr)*
defecating	**defecar** *(deh-feh-'kahr)*
eating	**comer** *(koh-'mehr)*
sleeping	**dormir** *(dohr-'meer)*
swallowing	**tragar** *(trah-'gahr)*
walking	**caminar** *(kah-mee-'nahr)*
urinating	**orinar** *(oh-ree-'nahr)*

To get all the details, you will probably have to throw in a few verbs that refer to *past* action. Use your question words to find out what caused Margarita's condition. And see how much vocabulary you can string together:

When did he/she get sick?

¿Cuándo se enfermó? *('kwahn-doh seh ehn-fehr-'moh)*

When was the last doctor's visit?

¿Cuándo fue la última visita al doctor?
('kwahn-doh fweh lah 'ool-tee-mah bee-'see-tah ahl dohk-'tohr)

What color was his/her stool?

¿De qué color fue su excremento?
(deh keh koh-'lohr fweh soo ehks-kreh-'mehn-toh)

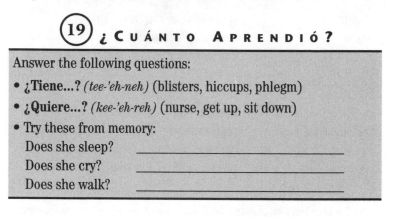

(19) ¿CUÁNTO APRENDIÓ?

Answer the following questions:

• **¿Tiene...?** *(tee-'eh-neh)* (blisters, hiccups, phlegm)

• **¿Quiere...?** *(kee-'eh-reh)* (nurse, get up, sit down)

• Try these from memory:

Does she sleep? _____

Does she cry? _____

Does she walk? _____

The appointment
La cita *(lah 'see-tah)*

Are you learning all the new vocabulary? Here is only a sample of the many new words you'll need as you handle cases such as this one. These items will work well with your commands:

Bring...	Traiga...
bottle	**la botella** *(lah boh-'teh-yah)*
catheter	**el catéter** *(ehl kah-'teh-ter)*
chart	**el gráfico** *(ehl 'grah-fee-koh)*
cup	**la copa** *(lah 'koh-pah)*
instrument	**el instrumento** *(ehl eens-troo-'mehn-toh)*
light	**la luz** *(lah loos)*
needle	**la aguja** *(lah ah-'goo-hah)*
pan	**el bacín** *(ehl bah-'seen)*
scale	**la báscula** *(lah 'bahs-koo-lah)*
stethoscope	**el estetoscopio** *(ehl ehs-teh-tohs-'koh-pee-oh)*
syringe	**la jeringa** *(lah heh-'reen-gah)*
thermometer	**el termómetro** *(ehl tehr-'moh-meh-troh)*
tongue depressor	**la pisa-lengua** *(lah pee-sah-'lehn-gwah)*
tube	**el tubo** *(ehl 'too-boh)*

Dos Culturas

A healer or **curandero** *(koo-rahn-'deh-roh)* is believed to have magic powers to heal the sick. In some neighborhoods, families prefer to send their ailing children to a healer first. You may want to check on where your patients are receiving their medical advice.

The history
La historia *(lah ees-'toh-ree·ah)*

Perhaps there's something **en la familia** that is part of Margarita's problem. Dig deeper into the past. Most of these words you should already know:

What did the . . . die of? **¿De qué se murió . . .?**

(deh keh seh-moo-ree-'oh)

father	**el padre** *(ehl 'pah-dreh)*
mother	**la madre** *(lah 'mah-dreh)*
grandfather	**el abuelo** *(ehl ah 'bweh-loh)*
grandmother	**la abuela** *(lah ah-'bweh-lah)*

As long as you're doing family research, see if you can remember any of the following diseases in Spanish. They were introduced in **Capítulo Tres** when the Espinoza family first came to the hospital:

Did they have . . .   **¿Tuvieron . . .?** *(too-bee-'eh-rohn)*

> **difteria** *(deef-'teh-ree·ah)*
> **fiebre escarlatina**
>   *(fee-'eh-breh ehs-kahr-lah-'tee-nah)*
> **fiebre reumática** *(fee-'eh-breh reh-oo-'mah-tee-kah)*
> **fiebre tifoidea** *(fee-'eh-breh tee-foo·ee-'deh-ah)*
> **hipoglicemia** *(ee-poh-glee-'seh-mee-ah)*
> **paperas** *(pah-'peh-rahs)*
> **sarampión** *(sah-rahm-pee-'ohn)*
> **varicela** *(bah-ree-seh-lah)*

Here are a few that you may not know:

another major illness	**otra enfermedad grave**
	('oht-rah ehn-fehr-meh-'dah 'grah-beh)
contagious diseases	**enfermedades contagiosas**
	(ehn-fehr-meh-'dah-dehs kohn-tah-hee-'oh-sahs)
emotional problems	**dificultades emocionales**
	(dee-fee-kool-'tah-dehs eh-moh-see·oh-'nah-lehs)
heart disease	**enfermedades del corazón**
	(ehn-fehr-meh-'dah-dehs dehl koh-rah-'sohn)
high blood pressure	**presión alta** *(preh-see-'ohn 'ahl-tah)*
low blood pressure	**presión baja** *(preh-see-'ohn 'bah-hah)*
mental problems	**dificultades mentales**
	(dee-fee-kool-'tah-dehs mehn-'tah-lehs)
respiratory problems	**problemas respiratorios**
	(proh-'bleh-mahs rehs-pee-rah-'toh-ree·ohs
venereal disease	**enfermedades venéreas**
	(ehn-fehr-meh-'dah-dehs beh-'neh-reh-ahs)

Don't forget the common cold. Here are three ways to say "Does she have a cold?" In some Spanish-speaking countries, the words differ slightly:

¿**Tiene resfrío?** *(tee-'eh-neh rehs-'free-oh)*

¿**Tiene catarro?** *(tee-'eh-neh kah-'tah-rroh)*

¿**Está resfriado?** *(eh-'stah rehs-free-'ah-doh)*

¿ C U Á N T O   A P R E N D I Ó ?

Guess the meanings of these terms:

diabetes *(dee-ah-'beh-tehs)*
cáncer *('kahn-sehr)*
anemia *(ah-'neh-mee·ah)*
laringitis *(lah-reen-'hee-tees)*
tuberculosis *(too-behr-koo-'loh-sees)*
sinusitis *(see-noos-'ee-tees)*
influenza *(een-floo-'ehn-sah)*
angina *(ahn-'hee-nah)*
pancreatitis *(pahn-kreh-ah-'tee-tees)*
mononucleosis *(moh-noh-noo-kleh-'oh-sees)*
hepatitis *(eh-pah-'tee-tees)*
polio *('poh-lee·oh)*
glaucoma *(glah·oo-'koh-mah)*
indigestión *(een-dee-hehs-tee·'ohn)*

More illnesses
¡Más enfermedades!
(mahs ehn-fehr-meh-'dah-dehs)

The words for some illnesses are harder to figure out because they don't look like English. Ask Juan and María if anyone has ever suffered from these. You may even want to prepare a written list so they can simply check them off:

gallstones	**cálculos en la vesícula**
	('kahl-koo-lohs ehn lah beh-'see-koo-lah)
hay fever	**fiebre de heno** *(fee-'eh-breh deh 'eh-noh)*
hives	**urticaria** *(oor-tee-'kah-ree·ah)*
jaundice	**ictericia** *(eek-teh-'ree-see·ah)*
kidney stones	**cálculos en los riñones**
	('kahl-koo-lohs ehn lohs ree-'nyoh-nehs)

pneumonia   **pulmonía** *(pool-moh-'nee-ah)*
whooping cough   **tosferina** *(tohs-feh-'ree-nah)*

Try your hand at translating the following. And don't forget to pronounce them in Spanish first!

apendicitis *(ah-pehn-dee-'see-tees)*
arteriosclerosis
  (ahr-teh-ree-oh-ehs-kleh-'roh-sees)
artritis *(ahr-'tree-tees)*
asma *('ahs-mah)*
bronquitis *(brohn-'kee-tees)*
cirrosis *(see-'rroh-sees)*
cólera *(koh-'leh-rah)*
colon espástico
  ('koh-lohn ehs-'pahs-tee-koh)
disentería *(dee-sehn-teh-'ree-ah)*
enfisema *(ehn-fee-'seh-mah)*
epilepsia *(eh-pee-'lehp-see·ah)*

gonorrea *(goh-noh-'rreh-ah)*
halitosis *(ah-lee-'toh-sees)*
hemorroides
  (eh-moh-'rroh·ee-dehs)
herpes *('ehr-pehs)*
leucemia *(lee-oo-'seh-mee·ah)*
nefritis *(neh-'free-tees)*
parálisis *(pah-'rah-lee-sees)*
pleuresía *(pleh-oo-ree-'see-ah)*
reumatismo *(reh-oo-mah-'tees-moh)*
sífilis *('see-fee-lees)*
tétanos *('teh-tah-nohs)*
úlceras *('ool-seh-rahs)*

Have you had problems?
¿Ha tenido problemas?
(ah teh-'nee-doh proh-'bleh-mahs)

Bear in mind that all of the verb forms you have learned so far work wonders throughout the medical facility. Yet, you cannot communicate properly until a few more verb changes are made. For example, to ask the Espinozas if anyone in the family "has had" a certain disease before, you must use the phrase, **"Ha tenido,"** which translates "Have you...?" or "Has he or she had...". Try it:

Have you had a cough?
¿Ha tenido tos? *(ah teh-'nee-doh tohs)*

Have you had the illness?
¿Ha tenido la enfermedad? *(ah teh-'nee-doh lah ehn-fehr-meh-'dahd)*

Have you had mumps?

¿Ha tenido paperas? *(ah teh-'nee-doh pah-'peh-rahs)*

Study this two-part verb pattern. It's important in health care because it refers to actions that have already taken place. Practice these examples:

Have you had this pain before?

¿Ha tenido este dolor antes? *(ah teh-'nee-doh 'eh-steh doh-'lohr 'ahn-tehs)*

Have you spoken with the doctor?

¿Ha hablado con el doctor? *(ah ah-'blah-doh kohn ehl dohk-'tohr)*

Notice that in Spanish, you need both parts of the verb. Here is all you need to get started:

I have . . .	**he** . . . *(eh)*	had . . .	**tenido** *(teh-'nee-doh)*
you, he, or she has . . .	**ha** . . . *(ah)*	eaten	**comido** *(koh-'mee-doh)*
they or you (plural) have . . .	**han** . . . *(ahn)*	drunk	**tomado** *(toh-'mah-doh)*
we have . . .	**hemos** . . . *('eh-mohs)*	gone	**ido** *('ee-doh)*

This next series is an overview of actions that "have happened." Read them aloud:

Has he/she had an accident?

¿Ha tenido un accidente? *(ah teh-'nee-doh oon ahk-see-'dehn-teh)*

Has he/she taken any medicines?

¿Ha tomado alguna medicina?

(ah toh-'mah-doh ahl-'goo-nah meh-dee-'see-nah)

Has he/she vomited?

¿Ha vomitado? *(ah boh-mee-'tah-doh)*

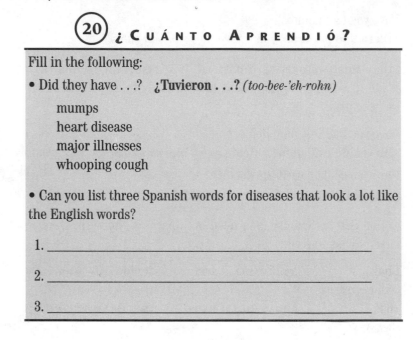

20 ¿CUÁNTO APRENDIÓ?

Fill in the following:

• Did they have . . .? ¿Tuvieron . . .? *(too-bee-'eh-rohn)*

mumps
heart disease
major illnesses
whooping cough

• Can you list three Spanish words for diseases that look a lot like the English words?

1. _____

2. _____

3. _____

Allergies
Las alergias *(lahs ah-'lehr-hee·ahs)*

One of the most common ailments is a simple allergic reaction to the world around us. Find out from Mr. and Mrs. Espinoza if these things are of any concern:

Are you allergic to . . .?	¿Tiene alergia a . . .?
	(tee-'eh-neh ah-'lehr-hee·ah ah)
dust	**el polvo** *(ehl -pohl-boh)*
flowers	**las flores** *(lahs flohr-ehs)*
any food	**alguna comida** *(ahl-'goo-nah koh-'mee-dah)*
grass	**la hierba** *(lah 'yehr-bah)*
insect bites	**las picaduras de insectos**
	(lahs pee-kah-'doo-rahs deh een-'sehk-tohs)
any medicine	**alguna medicina**
	(ahl-'goo-nah meh-dee-'see-nah)

penicillin	**la penicilina** *(lah peh-nee-see-'lee-nah)*
poison ivy	**la hiedra venenosa**
	(lah 'yeh-drah beh-neh-'noh-sah)
poison oak	**la encina venenosa**
	(lah ehn-'see-nah beh-neh-'noh-sah)
pollen	**el polen** *(ehl 'poh-lehn)*
shots	**las inyecciones** *(lahs een-yehk-see·'oh-nehs)*
trees	**los árboles** *(lohs 'ahr-bohl-ehs)*

Some people may be allergic to animals or may have been bitten by one. Learn the following vocabulary:

The animals	**Los animales** *(lohs ah-nee-'mah-lehs)*
ant	**la hormiga** *(lah ohr-'mee-gah)*
bee	**la abeja** *(lah ah-'beh-hah)*
bird	**el pájaro** *(ehl 'pah-hah-roh)*
cat	**el gato** *(ehl 'gah-toh)*
dog	**el perro** *(ehl 'peh-rroh)*
lizard	**el lagarto** *(ehl lah-'gahr-toh)*
mosquito	**el zancudo** *(ehl sahn-'koo-doh)*
mouse	**el ratón** *(ehl rah-'tohn)*
rat	**la rata** *(lah 'rah-tah)*
scorpion	**el escorpión** *(ehl ehs-kohr-pee-'ohn)*
snake	**la víbora** *(lah 'bee-boh-rah)*
spider	**la araña** *(lah ah-'rah-nyah)*
squirrel	**la ardilla** *(lah ahr-'dee-yah)*

How's the weather?
¿Cómo está el tiempo?
('koh-moh eh-'stah ehl tee·'ehm-poh)

There are some things in life we can't control. Unfortunately, they are often the cause of our physical problems. Here's how we comment on the current weather conditions:

| It's . . . | **Hace . . .** *('ah-seh)* |
| cold | **frío** *('free-oh)* |

hot	**calor** *(kah-'lohr)*
nice weather	**buen tiempo** *('bwehn tee-'ehm-poh)*
sunny	**sol** *(sohl)*
windy	**viento** *(bee-'ehn-toh)*

It's ...	Está ...
clear	**despejado** *(dehs-peh-'hah-doh)*
cloudy	**nublado** *(noo-'blah-doh)*
drizzling	**lloviznando** *(yoh-bees-'nahn-doh)*
raining	**lloviendo** *(yoh-bee-'ehn-doh)*
snowing	**nevando** *(neh-'bahn-doh)*

What is bothering you?
¿Qué le molesta? *(keh leh moh-'leh-stah)*

Margarita is old enough to tell you what is bothering her. Listen for **tengo:**

I have ...	Tengo ... *('tehn-goh)*
backaches	**dolores de espalda** *(doh-loh-rehs deh ehs-'pahl-dah)*
a bunion	**un juanete** *(oon wah-'neh-teh)*
chest pains	**dolores en el pecho** *(doh-'loh-rehs ehn ehl 'peh-choh)*
a corn	**un callo** *(oon 'kah-yoh)*
a dislocated shoulder	**un hombro dislocado** *(oon 'ohm-broh dees-loh-'kah-doh)*
earache	**dolor de oído** *(doh-lohr deh oh-'ee-doh)*
a hangnail	**un padrastro** *(oon pah-'drah-stroh)*
headache	**dolor de cabeza** *(doh-lohr deh kah-'beh-sah)*
an ingrown toenail	**una uña encarnada** *(oo-nah 'oo-nyah ehn-kahr-'nah-dah)*
a pulled muscle	**un músculo rasgado** *(oon 'moos-koo-loh rahs-'gah-doh)*
a sore throat	**dolor de garganta** *(doh-'lohr deh gahr-'gahn-tah)*

a sprained ankle	**un tobillo torcido** *(oon toh-'bee-yoh tohr-'see-doh)*
stomachache	**dolor de estómago** *(doh-lohr deh eh-'stoh-mah-goh)*
a toothache	**dolor de muela** *(doh-'lohr deh 'mweh-lah)*

I have problems . . .	**Tengo problemas . . .** *('tehn-goh proh-'bleh-mahs)*
after eating	**después de comer** *(dehs-'pwehs deh koh-'mehr)*
in this weather	**en este clima** *(ehn 'eh-steh 'klee-mah)*
when I urinate	**cuando orino** *('kwahn-doh oh-'ree-noh)*

The pain is . . .	**El dolor es . . .** *(ehl doh-'lohr ehs)*
burning	**quemante** *(keh-'mahn-teh)*
deep	**profundo** *(proh-'foon-doh)*
dull	**sordo** *('sohr-doh)*
sharp	**agudo** *(ah-'goo-doh)*

¡N o S e O l v i d e !

Keep in mind that the action words directed at "you" may also refer to "he" or "she." Study the translations below:

you drink; he or she drinks	**toma** *('toh-mah)*
you, he or she drank	**tomó** *(toh-'moh)*
you have drunk, he or she has drunk	**ha tomado** *(ah toh-'mah-doh)*

The physical exam
El examen físico *(ehl ehk-'sah-mehn 'fee-see-koh)*

Margarita needs to be examined thoroughly. Most physical exams do not require much communication but it might be in your best interest to look over the following. Begin by informing the patient about the procedures:

I'm going to . . .	**Voy a . . .** *('boh·ee ah)*
listen to your chest	**escuchar su pecho**
	(ehs-koo-'chahr soo 'peh-choh)
make a diagnosis	**hacer un diagnóstico**
	(ah-'sehr oon dee-ahg-'nohs-tee-koh)
read your chart	**leer su gráfico** *(leh-'ehr soo 'grah-fee-koh)*
roll up your sleeve	**levantarle la manga**
	(leh-bahn-'tahr-leh lah 'mahn-gah)
take your temperature	**tomar su temperatura**
	(toh-'mahr soo tehm-peh-rah-'too-rah)

Now let the patient know that the exam is quite painless. Create your own comments utilizing the Spanish you already know:

Are you comfortable?	**¿Está cómodo?** *(eh-'stah 'koh-moh-doh)*
Everything will be OK.	**Todo va a estar bien.**
	('toh-doh bah ah eh-'stahr bee·'ehn)
It doesn't hurt.	**No duele.** *(noh 'dweh-leh)*

More commands!
¡Más ordenes! *(mahs 'ohr-deh-nehs)*

How can you give an exam without telling the patient what to do? As you instruct Margarita, try putting several Spanish words in a row:

Bring a sample in this cup.
Traiga una muestra en este vaso.
('trah·ee-gah 'oo-nah 'mweh-strah ehn 'eh-steh 'bah-soh)

Go to the scale.
Vaya a la báscula. *('bah-yah ah lah 'bahs-koo-lah)*

Put the thermometer in your mouth.
Ponga el termómetro en la boca.
('pohn-gah ehl tehr-'moh-meh-troh ehn lah 'boh-kah)

Take a deep breath.
Aspire profundo. *(ahs-'pee-reh proh-'foon-doh)*

Remember these? They send messages all by themselves:

move	**muévase** *(moo-'eh-bah-seh)*
relax	**relájese** *(reh-'lah-heh-seh)*
sit down	**siéntese** *(see-'ehn-teh-seh)*
turn	**voltéese** *(bohl-'teh-eh-seh)*
stand up	**levántese** *(leh-'bahn-teh-seh)*

Now combine your command words with some body parts:

Bend your arm.	**Doble el brazo.** *('doh-bleh ehl 'brah-soh)*
Close your mouth.	**Cierre la boca.** *(see-'eh-reh lah 'boh-kah)*
Lie on your back.	**Acuéstese de espalda.**
	(ah-'kweh-steh-seh deh eh-'spahl-dah)
Open your hand.	**Abra la mano.** *(ah-'brah lah 'mah-noh)*
Touch your head.	**Tóquese la cabeza.** *('toh-keh-seh lah kah-'beh-sah)*

You can never have enough of the "command words." Review this new list carefully, repeat them aloud, and experiment with a few during your next exam:

cross	**cruce** *('kroo-seh)*	_____
describe	**describa** *(dehs-'kree-bah)*	_____
exhale	**expire** *(ehk-'spee-reh)*	_____
extend	**estire** *(ehks-'tee-reh)*	_____
inhale	**aspire** *(ah-'spee-reh)*	_____
say	**diga** *('dee-gah)*	_____
try	**trate** *('trah-teh)*	_____

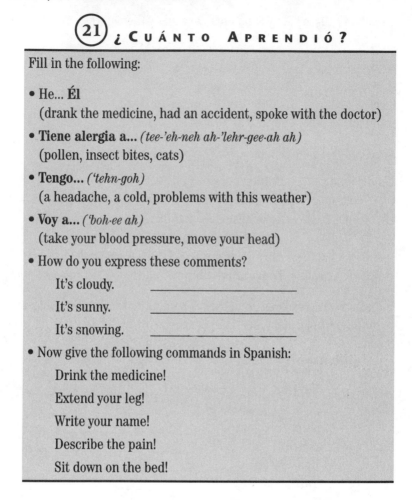

(21) ¿CUÁNTO APRENDIÓ?

Fill in the following:

- He... **Él**
  (drank the medicine, had an accident, spoke with the doctor)
- **Tiene alergia a...** *(tee-'eh-neh ah-'lehr-gee-ah ah)*
  (pollen, insect bites, cats)
- **Tengo...** *('tehn-goh)*
  (a headache, a cold, problems with this weather)
- **Voy a...** *('boh-ee ah)*
  (take your blood pressure, move your head)
- How do you express these comments?

  It's cloudy. _____

  It's sunny. _____

  It's snowing. _____

- Now give the following commands in Spanish:

  Drink the medicine!

  Extend your leg!

  Write your name!

  Describe the pain!

  Sit down on the bed!

Analysis, examination, and test!
¡Análisis, examen y prueba!
(ah-'nah-lee-sees, ehk-'sah-mehn ee proo-'eh-bah)

Special tests are needed for the young patient. Try to determine what the physician has decided to do:

I need . . .	Necesito . . . *(neh-seh-'see-toh)*
a blood sample	**una muestra de sangre**
	('oo-nah 'mweh-strah deh 'sahn-greh)
a count	**un recuento** *(oon reh-'kwehn-toh)*
a smear	**un frotis** *(oon 'froh tees)*
a sputum sample	**una muestra de esputo**
	('oo-nah 'mweh-strah deh ehs-'poo-toh)
a stool sample	**una muestra de excremento**
	('oo-nah 'mweh-strah deh ehks-kreh-'mehn-toh)
a urine sample	**una muestra de orina**
	('oo nah 'mweh-strah deh oh-'ree-nah)
an X ray	**una radiografía** *('oo-nah rah-dee-oh-grah-'fee-ah)*

Fortunately, many of the words that surface in your discussions about the test results sound a lot like English.

albúmina *(ahl-boo-'mee-nah)*
bacteria *(bahk-'teh-ree-ah)*
coagulación *(koh-ah-goo-lah-see-'ohn)*
defensas *(deh-'fehn-sahs)*
globular *(gloh-boo-'lahr)*
laboratorio *(lah-boh-rah-'toh-ree-oh)*
metabolismo *(meh-tah-boh-'lees-moh)*
microscopio *(mee-kro-'skoh-pee-oh)*
negativo *(neh-gah-'tee-boh)*
positivo *(poh-see-'tee-boh)*
saliva *(sah-'lee bah)*

The results
Los resultados
(lohs reh-sool-'tah-dohs)

Results indicate there is an infection, but Margarita's health can be restored easily through medication, rest, and appropriate care. Take note of what the doctor has to say:

She needs...	Necesita...
an antibiotic	**un antibiótico** *(oon ahn-tee-bee-'oh-tee-koh)*
cough medicine	**medicina para la tos**
	(meh-dee-'see-nah 'pah-rah lah tohs)
a good diet	**una buena dieta** *('oo-nah 'bweh-nah dee-'eh-tah)*
more liquids	**más líquidos** *(mahs 'lee-kee-dohs)*
a specialist	**un especialista** *(oon eh-speh-see-ah-'lee-stah)*
vitamins	**las vitaminas** *(lahs bee-tah-'mee-nahs)*

Kids!
¡Los niños! *(lohs 'nee-nyohs)*

Margarita is feeling much better. Chances are, the pediatrician will see her again in the future. The following questions, comments, and commands are designed for conversations with younger children. This relationship is an informal one, where friendly conversation and humor are blended with your job-related language skills. As you have learned, you can accomplish a great deal with very little language.

These phrases all mean "How cute!"

¡Qué bonito! *(keh boh-'nee-toh)*
¡Qué precioso! *(keh preh-see-'oh-soh)*
¡Qué lindo! *(keh 'leen-doh)*

Remember that the above phrases are for male subjects. Change to "a" endings when talking about female subjects.

And, they can be added to any item:

What a cute . . .	¡Qué bonita . . .! *(keh boh-'nee-toh)*
face	**cara** *('kah-rah)*
haircut	**corte de pelo** *('kohr-teh deh 'peh-loh)*
outfit	**ropa** *('roh-pah)*
smile	**sonrisa** *(sohn-'ree-sah)*
voice	**voz** *(vohs)*

Now, learn some vocabulary for a baby's or young child's personal belongings:

Where is the . . .?	¿Dónde está . . .? *('dohn-deh eh-'stah)*
ball	**la pelota** *(lah peh-'loh-tah)*
bassinet	**el bacinete** *(ehl bah-see-'neh-teh)*
blanket	**la cobija** *(lah koh-'bee-hah)*
crib	**la cuna** *(lah 'koo-nah)*
doll	**la muñeca** *(lah moo-'nyeh-kah)*
game	**el juego** *(ehl 'hweh-goh)*
infant car seat	**el asiento para infantes** *(ehl ah-see-'ehn-toh 'pah-rah een-'fahn-tehs)*
storybook	**el librito de cuentos** *(ehl lee-'bree-toh deh 'kwehn-tohs)*
stroller	**el cochecillo** *(ehl koh-cheh-'see-yoh)*
toy	**el juguete** *(ehl hoo-'geh-teh)*

¡No Se Olvide!

- The word **tú** is the informal way of saying "you" or "your" in Spanish. The "informal" form is also exchanged between family and friends. Here are some examples.

You are my friend.
Tú eres mi amigo. *(too 'eh-rehs mee ah-'mee-goh)*

You must move.
Tú debes moverte. *(too 'dee-behs moh-'behr-teh)*

It's your hand.
Es tu mano. *(ehs too 'mah-noh)*

Your heart is all right.
Tu corazón está bien. *(too koh-rah-'sohn eh-'stah 'bee-ehn)*

Did you notice that "your" is **tu**, but without the accent?

- The command words take on a slightly different form when you address children. Memorize these examples:

Say "ah."	**Di "ah."** *(dee ah)*
Open your mouth.	**Abre la boca.** *('ah-breh lah 'boh-kah)*
Go to sleep.	**Duérmete.** *('dwehr-meh-teh)*
Stand up.	**Levántate.** *(leh-'bahn-tah-teh)*

Don't . . .	No . . .
be afraid	**tengas miedo** *('tehn-gahs me-'eh-doh)*
be naughty	**seas malcriado** *('seh-ahs mahl-kree-'ah-doh)*
cry	**llores** *('yoh-rehs)*
move	**te muevas** *(teh 'mweh-bahs)*

- All verb forms require changes when you talk to kids. Most can be recognized because they end in the letter "s."

Do you have . . . ?	**¿Tienes . . . ?** *(tee-'eh-nehs)*
Do you want . . . ?	**¿Quieres . . . ?** *(kee-'eh-rehs)*
Do you need . . . ?	**¿Necesitas . . . ?** *(neh-seh-'see-tahs)*

DOS CULTURAS

Don't be afraid to touch the baby! In some Spanish-speaking countries, people believe that children can get sick if you stare at them without making physical contact. A brief stroke, hug, or light caress will make everyone feel more comfortable.

Remedies

Los remedios *(lohs reh-'meh-dee·ohs)*

As Margarita and her parents prepare to leave for home, you will have to write a prescription and then provide them with instructions. To do so, you will need the proper Spanish terminology and phrases. Fortunately, most medicines are spelled similarly in both languages:

Just as you did with previous lists, try to guess at the meanings of these:

antiácido *(ahn-tee-'ah-see-doh)*
antibiótico *(ahn-tee-bee-'oh-tee-koh)*
antídoto *(ahn-'tee-doh-toh)*
antihistamínicos *(ahn-tee-ees-tah-'mee-nee-kohs)*
antiséptico *(ahn-tee-'sehp-tee-koh)*
aspirina *(ah-spee-'ree-nah)*
astringente *(ahs-treen-'hehn-teh)*
codeína *(koh-deh-'ee-nah)*
cortisona *(kohr-tee-'soh-nah)*
demerol *(deh-meh-'rohl)*
desinfectante *(dehs-een-fehk-'tahn-teh)*
insulina *(een-soo-'lee-nah)*
morfina *(mohr-'fee-nah)*
nitroglicerina *(nee-troh-glee-seh-'ree-nah)*
penicilina *(peh-nee-see-'lee-nah)*
tranquilizantes *(trahn-kee-lee-'sahn-tehs)*
vitaminas *(bee-tah-'mee-nahs)*

These key words should be learned quickly. To make it easy on yourself, practice first with those words that you use most often:

capsules	**las cápsulas** *(lahs 'kahp-soo-lahs)*
lozenges	**las pastillas** *(lahs pah-'stee-yahs)*
pills	**las píldoras** *(lahs 'peel-doh-rahs)*
tablets	**las tabletas** *(lahs tah-'bleh-tahs)*

Try them out:

Pills for . . .	**Las píldoras para . . .** *(lahs 'peel-doh-rahs 'pah-rah)*
birth control	**anticoncepción** *(ahn-tee-kohn-sehp-see-'ohn)*
sleeping	**dormir** *(dohr-'meer)*

How about a few over-the-counter remedies? Some of them will be very easy to remember. As a matter of fact, if you mention a drug in English, they will probably understand what you are saying:

adhesive tape	**cinta adhesiva** *('seen-tah ah-deh-'see-bah)*
bandage	**venda** *('behn-dah)*
Band-Aid®	**curita** *(koo-'ree-tah)*
cough syrup	**el jarabe para la tos** *(ehl hah-'rah-beh 'pah-rah lah tohs)*
decongestant	**descongestionante** *(dehs-kohn-hehs-tee-oh-'nahn-teh)*
Epsom salt	**la sal de Epsom** *(lah sahl deh ehp-sohm)*
gauze	**gasa** *('gah-sah)*
ice pack	**bolsa de hielo** *('bohl-sah deh ee-'eh-loh)*
iodine	**yodo** *('yoh-doh)*
laxative	**laxante** *(lahk-'sahn-teh)*
hydrogen peroxide	**agua oxigenada** *('ah-gwah ohk-see-heh-'nah-dah)*
sedative	**sedante** *(seh-'dahn-teh)*
stimulant	**estimulante** *(ehs-tee-moo-'lahn-teh)*
vaseline	**vaselina** *(bah-seh-'lee-nah)*

These words allow you to explain the medication in detail:

drops	**las gotas** *(lahs 'goh-tahs)*
They are drops for the eyes.	**Son gotas para los ojos.** *(sohn 'goh-tahs 'pah-rah lohs 'oh-hohs)*
mixture	**la mezcla** *(lah 'mehs-klah)*
It is an aspirin and tranquilizer mixture.	**Es una mezcla de aspirina y sedante.** *(ehs 'oo-nah 'mehs-klah deh ahs-pee-'ree-nah ee seh-'dahn-teh)*
solution	**la solución** *(lah soh-loo-see-'ohn)*
The white solution is for the hair.	**La solución blanca es para el pelo.** *(lah soh-loo-see-'ohn 'flahn-kah ehs 'pah-rah ehl 'peh-loh)*

Now, it's your turn. Use the following words in sentences:

creams	**las cremas** *(lahs 'kreh-mahs)*
jelly	**la jalea** *(lah 'hah-'leh-ah)*
liniment	**el linimento** *(ehl lee-nee-'mehn-toh)*
lotion	**la loción** *(lah loh-see-'ohn)*
powder	**el talco** *(ehl 'tahl-koh)*
soap	**el jabón** *(ehl hah-'bohn)*
suppositories	**los supositorios** *(lohs soo-poh-see-'toh-ree-ohs)*

DOS CULTURAS

Millions of people in the United States do not believe in pharmaceutical drugs. Many Hispanics still rely on **medicinas caseras** or home remedies. Certain **especias** *(eh-'speh-see-ahs)* (spices), for example, are taken to cure everything from a headache to heart disease. You may want to read up on such methods, not only to learn more about their culture, but also to find out if what they are taking at home has any real medicinal value.

The gift shop
La tienda de regalos
(lah tee-'ehn-dah deh reh-'gah-lohs)

Hospital gift shops play a significant role in recovery. Juan and María decide to do a little shopping to make Margarita happy and, also, to get a few things for home use.

I need . . .	**Necesito** . . . *(neh-seh-'see-toh)*
candy	**dulces** *('dool-sehs)*
a comb	**un peine** *(oon 'peh-ee-neh)*
cosmetics	**cosméticos** *(kohs-'meh-tee-kohs)*
a deodorant	**un desodorante** *(oon dehs-oh-doh-'rahn-teh)*
envelopes	**sobres** *('soh-brehs)*
feminine napkins	**paños** *('pah-nyohs)*
flowers	**flores** *('floh-rehs)*
gifts	**regalos** *(reh-'gah-lohs)*
greeting cards	**tarjetas de saludo**
	(tahr-'heh-tahs deh sah-'loo-doh)
a hairbrush	**un cepillo de pelo**
	(oon seh-'pee-yoh deh deh 'peh-loh)
magazines	**revistas** *(reh-'bee-stahs)*
a needle	**una aguja** *('oo-nah ah-'goo-hah)*
newspapers	**periódicos** *(peh-ree-'oh-dee-kohs)*
a pin	**un alfiler** *(oon ahl-fee-'lehr)*
postcards	**tarjetas postales** *(tahr-'heh-tahs poh-'stah-lehs)*
razor blades	**navajas para afeitar**
	(nah-'bah-hahs 'pah-rah ah-'feh-ee-tahr)
rolls of film	**rollos de foto** *('roh-yohs deh 'foh-toh)*
scissors	**tijeras** *(tee-'heh-rahs)*
stamps	**estampillas** *(ehs-tahm-'pee-yahs)*
tape	**una cinta** *('oo-nah 'seen-tah)*
thread	**hilo** *('ee-loh)*
a toothbrush	**un cepillo de dientes**
	(oon seh-'pee-yoh deh dee-'ehn-tehs)
toothpaste	**pasta de dientes** *('pah-stah deh dee-'ehn-tehs)*

Margarita cries out when she sees one of these! Juan rewards his exhausted little girl with her favorite toy.

Stuffed animals	**Animales de peluche**
	(ah-nee-'mah-lehs deh peh-'loo-cheh)
bear	**el oso** *(ehl 'oh-soh)*
cat	**el gato** *(ehl 'gah toh)*
dog	**el perro** *(ehl 'peh-rroh)*
duck	**el pato** *(ehl 'pah-toh)*
elephant	**el elefante** *(ehl eh-leh-'fahn-teh)*
giraffe	**la jirafa** *(lah hee 'rah-fah)*
monkey	**el mono** *(ehl 'moh-noh)*
mouse	**el ratón** *(ehl rah-'tohn)*
pig	**el puerco** *(ehl poo-'ehr-koh)*
rabbit	**el conejo** *(ehl koh-'neh-hoh)*
sheep	**la oveja** *(lah oh-'beh-hah)*
zebra	**la cebra** *(lah 'seh-brah)*

(22) ¿CUÁNTO APRENDIÓ?

Fill in the following:

• **Necesito . . .** *(neh-seh-'see-toh)*
(aspirin, scissors, flowers, greeting cards, a comb)

_____

_____

_____

_____

The prescription
La receta médica *(lah reh-'seh-tah 'meh-dee-kah)*

Telling the Espinozas what medication they need to buy isn't enough. In order to administer the drug properly, clear and concise instructions must be given. Always begin by telling them what they have to do:

You have to...	**Tiene que...** *(tee-'eh-neh keh)*
bathe	**bañarse** *(bah-'nyahr-seh)*
gargle	**hacer gárgaras** *(ah-sehr 'gahr-gah-rahs)*
measure carefully	**medir con cuidado**
	(meh-'deer kohn kwee-'dah-doh)
read the label	**leer la etiqueta**
	(leh-'ehr lah eh-tee-'keh-tah)
refrigerate it	**refrigerarlo** *(reh-free-heh-'rahr-loh)*
take the medicine	**tomar la medicina**
	(toh-'mahr lah meh-dee-'see-nah)
wash	**lavarse** *(lah-'bahr-seh)*

Use **tome** *('toh-meh)* (take) with all of your new vocabulary!

Take the medicine...	**Tome la medicina...**
	(toh-meh lah meh-dee-'see-nah)
after meals	**después de las comidas**
	(dehs-'pwehs deh lahs koh-'mee-dahs)
before meals	**antes de las comidas**
	('ahn-tehs deh lahs koh-'mee-dahs)
between meals	**entre las comidas**
	('ehn-treh lahs koh-'mee-dahs)
when you have pain	**cuando tiene dolor**
	('kwahn-doh tee-'eh-neh doh-'lohr)
with water	**con agua** *(kohn 'ah-gwah)*
___ times every ___	**___veces cada ___** *('beh-sehs 'kah-dah)*

Make sure the patient takes the correct amount of medication. Review these words used for measurement:

Take ...   **Tome ...** *('toh-meh)*
  a cup   **una copa** *('oo-nah 'koh-pah)*
  a glass   **un vaso** *(oon 'bah-soh)*
  half   **la mitad** *(lah mee-tahd)*
  one tablespoon   **una cucharada** *('oo-nah koo-chah-'rah-dah)*
  one teaspoon   **una cucharadita** *('oo-nah koo-chah-rah-'dee-tah)*

¡ N o   S e   O l v i d e !

- Keep in mind that **no** means "don't." Be sure to tell the Espinozas what *not* to do:

Don't take the capsules.   **No tome las cápsulas.**
             (noh 'toh-meh lahs 'kahp-soo-lahs)

Don't drink alcohol with this.   **No tome alcohol con esto.**
             (noh 'toh-meh ahl-koh-'ohl kohn
             'eh-stoh)

It isn't for children.   **No es para niños.**
             (noh ehs 'pah-rah 'nee-nyohs)

Get well soon!
¡Qué se alivie pronto!
(keh seh ah-'lee-bee-eh 'prohn-toh)

As the family heads for the pharmacy on their way home, make sure all the instructions are clear. Please add your own comments to the ones below:

Do you need something stronger?
¿Necesita algo más fuerte? *(neh-seh-'see-tah 'ahl-goh mahs 'fwehr-teh)*

Have you had a bad reaction to the medicine?
¿Ha tenido una mala reacción a la medicina?
  (ah teh-'nee-doh 'oo-nah 'mah-lah reh-ahk-see-'ohn ah lah meh-deh-'see-nah)

I need to explain the prescription.

Necesito explicar la receta.

(neh-seh-'see-toh ehks-plee-'kahr lah reh-'seh-tah)

Let's lower the dosage.

Vamos a bajar la dosis. *('bah-mohs ah bah-'hahr lah 'doh-sees)*

Take this prescription to the pharmacy.

Lleve la receta a la farmacia.

('yeh-beh lah reh-'seh-tah ah lah fahr-'mah-see-ah)

You have to talk to the pharmacist.

Tiene que hablar con el farmacéutico.

(tee-'eh-neh keh ah-'blahr kohn ehl fahr-mah-'seh-oo-tee-koh)

You need to return in one week.

Necesita regresar en una semana.

(neh-seh-'see-tah reh-greh-'sahr ehn 'oo-nah seh-'mah-nah)

23 ¿**C**UÁNTO **A**PRENDIÓ?

Finish the following:

• **Necesita . . .** *(neh-seh-'see-tah)*
  (a blood sample, a test, more liquids)

_____

_____

_____

• **Tiene que . . .** *(tee-'eh-neh keh)*
  (read the label, drink half)

_____

_____

• Translate: Take the pills with water.

  Take two tablespoons three times every day.

  You need to bathe in hot water.

  We are going to lower the dosage.

Chapter Seven

Miguel Espinoza,
Age 12

Early one morning, young Miguel cries out in great pain and is immediately rushed to the hospital by his father. Upon further examination, the doctor determines that Miguel has appendicitis. With no time to lose, an operation is scheduled. Although his admission forms have already been completed, there are a variety of other questions that need to be answered prior to Miguel's surgery. Since his English is not good and he will be staying in the hospital for awhile, specialized words and phrases are going to be needed in order to exchange information and communicate requests.

The operation
La operación *(lah oh-peh-rah-see·'ohn)*

The Espinoza family needs to be informed of Miguel's condition as soon as possible. Here are some terms you'll need to communicate information about the appendicitis, as well as some other areas of surgery:

It's very . . .	**Es muy . . .** *(ehs 'moo·ee)*
common	**común** *(koh-'moon)*
complicated	**complicada** *(kohm-plee-'kah-dah)*
dangerous	**peligrosa** *(peh-lee-'groh-sah)*
necessary	**necesaria** *(neh-seh-'sah-ree·ah)*
risky	**arriesgado** *(ahr-ree-ehs-'gah-doh)*
serious	**grave** *('grah-beh)*
simple	**sencilla** *(sehn-'see-yah)*

He needs . . .	**Necesita** . . . *(neh-seh-'see-tah)*
an appendectomy	**una apendectomía**
	(ah-pehn-dehk-'to-mee·ah)
a biopsy	**una biopsia** *('oo-nah bee-'ohp-see·ah)*
a blood transfusion	**una transfusión de sangre**
	('oo-nah trahs-foo-see-'ohn deh 'sahn-greh)
an exploratory	**una operación exploratoria** *('oo-nah oh-*
operation	*peh-rah-see-'ohn ehks-ploh-rah-'toh-ree·ah)*

Although they don't pertain to Miguel's condition, here are some other operations you may some day need to discuss in Spanish:

an amputation	**una amputación** *('oo-nah ahm-poo-tah-see-'ohn)*
a hysterectomy	**una histerectomía**
	('oo-nah ees-teh-rehk-'tom-mee·ah)
a mastectomy	**una mastectomía** *('oo-nah mahs-tehk-'tom-mee·ah)*
a plastic surgery	**una cirugía plástica**
	('oo-nah see-roo-'hee-ah 'plahs-tee-kah)
a tonsillectomy	**una tonsilectomía**
	(oo-nah tohn-see-lehk-toh-'mee·ah)

More action
Más acción *(mahs ahk-see·'ohn)*

The families of patients in surgery have questions, and you need to be as honest and informative as you can. The following list of action words provides you with much of the language that you'll need. Use them with the patterns you are familiar with:

We need to	**Necesitamos** *(neh-seh-see-'tah-mohs)*
We have to	**Tenemos que** *(teh-'neh-mohs keh)*
We're going to . . .	**Vamos a** . . . *('bah-mohs ah)*
to cover	**tapar** *(tah-'pahr)*
cover you	. . . **taparle** *(tah-'pahr-leh)*
to give	**dar** *(dahr)*

give you the anesthesia	**. . . darle anestesia** *('dahr-leh ah-nehs-'teh- see-ah)*
to operate	**operar** *(oh-peh-'rahr)*
operate on you right now	**. . . operarle ahorita** *(oh-peh-'rahr-leh ah-oh-'ree-tah)*
to prepare	**preparar** *(preh-pah-'rahr)*
prepare you for the operation	**. . . prepararle para la operación** *(preh-pah-'rahr-leh 'pah-rah lah oh-peh-rah-see-'ohn)*
to remove	**sacar** *('sah-'kahr)*
take out your appendix	**. . . sacarle el apéndice** *(sah-'kahr-leh ehl ah-'pehn-dee-seh)*
to repair	**reparar** *(reh-pah-'rahr)*
repair the damage (done to you)	**. . . repararle el daño** *(reh-pah-'rahr-leh ehl 'dah-nyoh)*
to sew	**coser** *(koh-'sehr)*
sew up your wound	**. . . coserle la herida** *(koh-'sehr-leh luh eh-'ree-dah)*
to shave	**afeitar** *(ah-feh-ee-'tahr)*
shave the area (on your body)	**. . . afeitarle el área** *(ah-feh-ee-'tahr-leh ehl 'ah-reh-ah)*
to transplant	**trasplantar** *(trahs-plahn-'tahr)*
transplant the organ	**trasplantar el órgano** *(trahs-plahn-'tahr ehl 'ohr-gah-noh)*

¡No Se Olvide!

• To remove **sacar** *(sah-'kahr)* should be practiced with specific body parts. Some of this vocabulary may be new to you.

We are going to	Vamos a sacarle . . .
remove . . .	*('bah-mohs ah sah-'kahr-leh)*
appendix	**el apéndice** *(ehl ah-'pehn-dee-seh)*
cataracts	**las cataratas** *(lah kah-tah-'rah-tahs)*
cyst	**el quiste** *(ehl 'kees-teh)*
gallbladder	**la vesícula biliar**
	(lah beh-'see-koo-lah bee-lee-'ahr)
gallstones	**los cálculos biliares**
	(lohs 'kahl-koo-lohs bee-lee-'ah-rehs)
kidney stones	**los cálculos renales**
	(lohs 'kahl-koo-lohs reh-'nah-lehs)
tonsils	**las amígdalas** *(lahs ah-'meeg-dah-lahs)*

• Keep using **le** *(leh)* after the verb when addressing someone. This personal pronoun means either "him/her/you," or "to him/to her/to you," and therefore switches the sentence from a general to a personal level.

The surgery
La cirugía *(lah see-roo-'hee-ah)*

Keep talking to the Espinozas about the upcoming surgery. Let Miguel and his family know what's going to happen next. Use the forms of **ir a** (to go to) as you discuss future procedures:

He's going to be fine.

Va a estar bien. *(bah ah eh-'stahr bee·ehn)*

I'm going to go to the operating room with him.

Voy a ir a la sala de operaciones con él.

('boh·ee ah eer ah lah 'sah-lah deh oh-peh-rah-see·'oh-nehs kohn ehl)

The doctor is going to explain everything.
El doctor le va a explicar todo.
 (ehl dohk-'tohr leh bah ah ehks-plee-'kahr 'toh-doh)

The surgery is going to be at . . .
La cirugía va a ser a las . . . *(lah see-roo-'hee-ah bah a sehr ah lahs)*

We're going to need your signature.
Vamos a necesitar su firma.
 ('bah-mohs ah neh-seh-see-'tahr soo 'feer-mah)

Don't forget to talk to Miguel personally. Prior to operating on older children and adults, you may need to exchange information with them directly. Use the various verb forms that you've learned to communicate.

Do you take medication?
¿Toma medicina? *('toh-mah meh-dee-'see-nah)*

Do you want another opinion?
¿Quiere otra opinión? *(kee-'eh-reh 'oh-trah oh-pee-nee-'ohn)*

Do you want to call someone?
¿Quiere llamar a alguien? *(kee-'eh-reh yah-'mahr ah 'ahl-gee-ehn)*

Have you had an operation before?
¿Ha tenido alguna operación antes?
 (ah teh-'nee-doh ahl-'goo-nah oh-peh-rah-see-'ohn 'ahn-tehs)

Your family is outside.
Su familia está afuera. *(soo fah-'mee-lee-ah eh-'stah ah-'fweh-rah)*

As you prepare Miguel for surgery, it's important that he follows directions carefully. Note that all the command words on this page are for addressing a child and therefore follow **tú** instead of **usted** rules. (Go to page 121 to review **tú, usted,** and the commands for children.)

Please . . .	**Por favor . . .** *(pohr fah-'bohr)*
Don't touch.	**No toques.** *(noh 'toh-kehs)*
Drink this.	**Toma esto.** *('toh-mah 'eh-stoh)*
Lie down.	**Acuéstate.** *(ah-'kwehs-tah-teh)*
Look here.	**Mira aquí.** *('mee-rah ah-'kee)*
Turn around.	**Voltéate.** *(bohl-'teh-ah-teh)*

Here are some more words that will help you out in pre-op. Not all of these commands are easy to pronounce, so practice before you direct them at patients. Follow the example and be creative:

bathe	**báñate** *(bah-'nyah-teh)*
drink	**bebe** *('beh-beh)*
keep	**guarda** *('gwarh-dah)*
press	**aprieta** *(ah-pree-'eh-tah)*
put on	**ponte** *('pohn-teh)*
take off	**quítate** *('kee-tah-teh)*
turn off	**apaga** *(ah-'pah-gah)*
turn on	**prende** *('prehn-deh)*
wash	**lávate** *('lah-bah-teh)*
Wash your hands.	**Lávate las manos.** *('lah-bah-teh lahs 'mah-nohs)*

Instruments

Los instrumentos *(lohs eens-troo-'mehn-tohs)*

Here are some words you may need to elaborate on the surgical specifics.

catheter	**el catéter** *(ehl kah-'teh-tehr)*
forceps	**las tenazas** *(lahs teh-'nah-sahs)*
gloves	**los guantes** *(lohs 'gwahn-tehs)*
knife	**el cuchillo** *(ehl koo-'chee-yoh)*
mask	**la máscara** *(lah 'mahs-kah-rah)*
monitor	**el monitor** *(ehl moh-nee-'tohr)*
pincers	**las pinzas** *(lahs 'peen-sahs)*
probe	**la sonda** *(lah 'bohm-bah)*
pump	**la bomba** *(lah 'bohm-bah)*
respirator	**el respirador** *(ehl rehs-pee-rah-'dohr)*
retractor	**el retractor** *(ehl reh-trahk-'tohr)*
scissors	**las tijeras** *(lahs tee-'heh-rahs)*
sponge	**la esponja** *(lah ehs-'pohn-hah)*
stethoscope	**el estetoscopio** *(ehl eh-steh-toh-'skoh-pee·oh)*
suture	**la sutura** *(lah soo-'too-rah)*
thermometer	**el termómetro** *(ehl tehr-'moh-meh-troh)*

| tongue depressor | la pisa-lengua *(lah 'pee-sah 'lehn-gwah)* |
| tube | el tubo *(ehl 'too-boh)* |

Clothing
La ropa *(lah 'roh-pah)*

Why not put your new skills into immediate action? In order to prep patients for surgery, you most get them into the proper attire. To do so, apply the commands, **quítese** *('kee-teh-seh)* and **póngase** *('pohn-gah-seh)*, along with the following items of clothing:

Take off . . .	**Quítese** . . . *('kee-teh-seh)*
Put on . . .	**Póngase** . . . *('pohn-gah-seh)*
brassiere	**el sostén** *(ehl sohs-'tehn)*
belt	**el cinturón** *(ehl seen-too-'rohn)*
blouse	**la blusa** *(lah 'bloo-sah)*
boots	**las botas** *(lahs 'boh-tahs)*
dress	**el vestido** *(ehl behs-'tee-doh)*
jacket	**la chaqueta** *(lah chah-'keh-tah)*
pajamas	**los piyamas** *(lohs pee-'yah-mahs)*
panties	**las bragas** *(lahs 'brah gahs)*
pants	**los pantalones** *(lohs pahn-tah-'loh-nehs)*
robe	**la bata** *(lah 'bah-tah)*
shirt	**la camisa** *(lah kah-'mee-sah)*
shoes	**los zapatos** *(lohs sah-'pah-tohs)*
shorts	**los calzoncillos** *(lohs kahl-sohn-'see-yohs)*
skirt	**la falda** *(lah 'fahl-dah)*
slippers	**las pantuflas** *(lahs pahn-'too-flahs)*
sport jacket	**el saco** *(ehl 'sah-koh)*
socks	**los calcetines** *(lohs kahl-seh-'tee-nehs)*
stockings	**las medias** *(lahs 'meh-dee-ahs)*
suit	**el traje** *(ehl 'trah-heh)*
sweater	**el suéter** *(ehl 'sweh-tehr)*
tie	**la corbata** *(lah kohr-'bah-tah)*
t-shirt	**la camiseta** *(lah kah-mee-'seh-tah)*
underwear	**la ropa interior** *(lah 'roh-pah een-teh-ree-'ohr)*

Clothing isn't the only thing that needs to be set aside. Here are some more personal possessions that you should know. Practice them by saying their names as each one is removed. As you have discovered, the most effective method for learning the names for objects in Spanish is to physically interact with them:

barrettes	**las hebillas** *(lahs eh-'bee-yahs)*
billfold	**la billetera** *(lah bee-yeh-'teh-rah)*
bobby pins	**los ganchos** *(lohs 'gahn-chohs)*
bracelet	**el brazalete** *(ehl brah-sah-'leh-teh)*
checkbook	**la chequera** *(lah cheh-'keh-rah)*
contact lenses	**los lentes de contacto**
	(lohs 'lehn-tehs deh kohn-'tahk-toh)
credit card	**la tarjeta de crédito**
	(lah tahr-'heh-tah deh 'kreh-dee-toh)
earrings	**los aretes** *(lohs ah-'reh-tehs)*
glasses	**los anteojos** *(lohs ahn-teh-'oh-hohs)*
gloves	**los guantes** *(lohs 'gwahn-tehs)*
handbag	**la bolsa, la cartera** *(lah 'bohl-sah, lah kahr-'teh-rah)*
hearing aids	**los audífonos** *(lohs ow-'dee-foh-nohs)*
jewelry	**las joyas** *(lahs 'hoh-yahs)*
make-up	**el maquillaje** *(ehl mah-kee-'yah-heh)*
money	**el dinero** *(ehl dee-'neh-roh)*
necklace	**el collar** *(ehl koh-'yahr)*
ring	**el anillo** *(ehl ah-'nee-yoh)*
scarf	**la bufanda** *(lah boo-'fahn-dah)*
watch	**el reloj** *(ehl reh-'loh)*

The anesthesia
La anestesia *(lah ah-nehs-'teh-see·ah)*

Although Miguel is sedated, he still feels pain. It's time to discuss the anesthesia. Bring in his parents and give them the details:

She's the anesthesiologist.

Ella es la anestesista. *('eh-yah ehs lah ah-nehs-teh-'sees-tah)*

She's going to give him an injection.

Va a ponerle una inyección.

(bah ah poh-'nehr-leh 'oo-nah een-yehk-see·'ohn)

It hurts a little.

Le duele un poco. *(leh 'dweh-leh oon 'poh-koh)*

He will sleep soon.

Va a dormir muy pronto. *(bah ah dohr-'meer moo·ee 'prohn-toh)*

¡No Se Olvide!

• Intravenous—**Intravenoso**—is an important word when talking about surgery. In fact, you'll need that word throughout the hospital: **Vamos a darle un tubo intravenoso.** *('bah-mohs ah 'dahr-leh ehl 'too-boh een-trah-beh-'noh-soh)*

• Notice how many words related to **anestesia** are a lot like English. It should make things easier.

gas	**gas** *(gahs)*
local	**local** *(loh-'kahl)*
general	**general** *(heh-neh-'rahl)*
partial	**parcial** *(pahr-see·'ahl)*
spinal	**espinal** *(ehs-pee-'nahl)*
sodium pentothal	**pentotal de sodio** *(pehn-toh-'tahl deh 'soh-dee·oh)*

Post-op
Después de la operación
(dehs-'pwehs deh lah oh-peh-rah-see·'ohn)

The operation was a success, and there were no **complicaciones** *(kohm-plee-kah-see·'oh-nehs)*. Young Miguel, however, has been through quite an ordeal and is feeling pretty groggy. His parents never left the hospital, and have just been cleared to visit their son in Recovery. Specific instructions and questions cannot be avoided. The Espinozas must be informed immediately of Miguel's situation. Take what you need from the list below.

The operation went well.

La operación salió bien. *(lah oh-peh-rah-see·'ohn sah-lee-'oh bee·ehn)*

The tube in his arm is for I.V. fluids.

El tubo en su brazo es para líquidos intravenosos.

(ehl 'too-boh ehn soo 'brah-soh ehs 'pah-rah 'lee-kee-dohs een-trah-beh-'noh-sohs)

The tube in his bladder is for urinating.

El tubo que tiene en su vejiga es para orinar.

(ehl 'too-boh keh tee-'eh-neh ehn soo beh-'hee-gah ehs 'pah-rah oh-ree-'nahr)

The tube in his stomach is for the food.

El tubo que tiene en su estómago es para la comida.

(ehl 'too-boh keh tee-'eh-neh ehn soo ehs-'toh-mah-goh ehs 'pah-rah lah koh-'mee-dah)

The tube in his throat is for breathing.

El tubo que tiene en su garganta es para respirar.

(ehl 'too-boh keh tee-'eh-neh ehn soo gahr-'gahn-tah ehs 'pah-rah rehs-pee-'rahr)

Use this familiar pattern to tell Miguel what's going to happen next:

We're going to . . .	**Vamos a . . .** *('bah-mohs ah)*
change the bandage	**cambiarle el vendaje** *(kahm-bee-'ahr-leh ehl behn-'dah-heh)*
give you a bath	**darle un baño** *('dahr-leh oon 'bah-nyoh)*
take out the I.V.	**sacarle el tubo intravenoso** *(sah-'kahr-leh ehl 'too-boh een-trah-veh-'noh-soh)*
take you to your room	**llevarle a su cuarto** *(yeh-'bahr-leh ah soo 'kwahr-toh)*

¡No Se Olvide!

• The word "stitches" is **las puntadas** in Spanish, and the word "scar" is **cicatriz**. Most patients seem to ask about them first.

We're going to remove the stitches.

Vamos a sacarle las puntadas
('bah-mohs ah sah-'kahr-leh lahs poon 'tah-dahs)

You're going to have a scar.

Va a tener una cicatriz *('bah ah teh-'nehr 'oo-nah see-kah-'trees)*

Miguel has been rolled into his room where he'll have to spend the night. A number of standard hospital procedures need to be discussed, along with several important questions and requests. These patterns were presented earlier. Can you translate everything?

Do you want . . .?	**¿Quiere . . .?** *(kee 'eh reh)*
	sentarse *(sehn-'tahr-seh)*
	dormir *(dohr-'meer)*
	orinar *(oh-ree-'nahr)*
	descansar *(dehs-kahn-'sahr)*
	agua *('ah-gwah)*
	comida *(koh-'mee-dah)*
	medicina *(meh-dee-'see-nah)*
	la silla de ruedas *(lah 'see-yah deh roo-'eh-dahs)*
	las muletas *(lahs moo-'leh-tahs)*
	ayuda *(ah-'yoo-dah)*
	un sedante *(oon seh-'dahn-teh)*
It's . . .	**Es . . .** *(ehs)*
codeine	**codeína** *(koh-deh-'ee-nah)*
morphine	**morfina** *(mohr-'fee-nah)*
penicillin	**penicilina** *(peh-nee-see-'lee-nah)*

Controls
Los controles *(lohs kohn-'troh-lehs)*

The room is full of equipment and furniture. Many pieces can be manipulated electrically. Learn their names as you explain their function to Miguel.

It's for controlling the . . .	**Es para controlar . . .**
	(ehs 'pah-rah kohn-troh-'lahr)
bedrails	**las barandas de la cama**
	(lahs bah-'rahn-dahs deh lah 'kah-mah)
bell	**el timbre** *(ehl 'teem-breh)*
the head of the bed	**la cabecera de la cama**
	(lah kah-beh-'seh-rah deh lah 'kah-mah)
light	**la luz** *(lah loos)*
thermostat	**el termostato** *(ehl tehr-moh-'stah-toh)*
TV	**la televisión** *(lah teh-leh-bee-see-'ohn)*

When we say "to check," they use "to verify" **(verificar)** *(beh-ree-fee-'kahr)*. Therefore . . .

We check your . . .	**Verificamos su . . .**
	(beh-ree-fee-'kah-mohs soo)
blood pressure	**presión de sangre**
	(preh-see-'ohn deh 'sahn-greh)
breathing	**respiración** *(rehs-pee-rah-see-'ohn)*
pulse	**pulso** *('pool-soh)*
temperature	**temperatura** *(tehm-peh-rah-'too-rah)*
vital signs	**signos vitales** *('seeg-nohs bee-'tah-lehs)*

Doctor's orders!
¡Las órdenes del doctor!
(lahs 'ohr-deh-nehs dehl dohk-'tohr)

Miguel must follow a few simple instructions. Following are words that you should be using every day. Take time to check up on what you've already learned.

Call the technician.
Llame al técnico. *('yah-meh ahl 'tehk-nee-koh)*

Do not touch the I.V.
No toque el tubo intravenoso.
(noh 'toh-keh ehl 'too-boh een-trah-beh-'noh-soh)

Follow your diet.
Siga su dieta. *('see-gah soo dee-'eh-tah)*

Go to the bathroom.
Vaya al baño. *('bah-yah ahl 'bah-nyoh)*

Stay in bed.
Quédese en la cama. *('keh-deh-seh ehn lah 'kah-mah)*

Tell the nurse.
Dígale a la enfermera. *('dee-gah-leh ah lah ehn-fehr-'meh-rah)*

Try to sleep.
Trate de dormir. *('trah-teh deh dohr-'meer)*

Turn off the radio.
Apague la radio. *(ah-'pah-geh lah 'rah-dee·oh)*

Bad news

Malas noticias *('mah-lahs noh-'tee-see·ahs)*

Not all surgeries are a complete success. The medical staff is responsible for sharing the bad news as well as the good. Unfortunately, you may need to use the following expressions:

There are complications.
Hay complicaciones. *('ah-ee kohm-plee-kah-see-'oh-nehs)*

He/she is not going to live.
No va a vivir. *(noh bah ah bee-'beer)*

He/she is going to die.
Se va a morir. *(seh bah ah moh-'reer)*

He/she died.
Se murió. *(seh moo-ree-'oh)*

I'm very sorry.
Lo siento mucho. *(loh see-'ehn-toh 'moo-choh)*

(24) ¿ C U Á N T O   A P R E N D I Ó ?

Can you translate these?

¿Quiere . . . ? *(kee-'eh-reh)*
gloves, shirt, underwear,
earrings, belt, shoes,
tube, diet.

Voy a . . . *(boy·ee ah)*
control the light, have a scar,
turn on the TV, live,
call your family, remove your stitches.

Furniture and equipment
Los muebles y el equipo
(lohs 'mweh-blehs ee ehl eh-'kee-poh)

Practice the vocabulary for all the parts of the hospital room by adding them to your commands. You can acquire most of these at home.

Point to . . .	**Señale . . .** *(seh-'nyah-leh)*
Touch . . .	**Toque . . .** *('toh-keh)*
ceiling	**el techo** *(ehl 'teh-choh)*
floor	**el piso** *(ehl 'pee-soh)*
wall	**la pared** *(lah pah-'rehd)*

Open/Close the . . .	**Abra/Cierre . . .** *('ah-brah/see-'eh-reh)*
cabinet	**el gabinete** *(ehl gah-bee-'neh-teh)*
closet	**el ropero** *(ehl roh-'peh-roh)*
curtains	**las cortinas** *(lahs kohr-'tee-nahs)*
door	**la puerta** *(lah 'pwehr-tah)*

drawer	**el cajón** *(ehl kah-'hohn)*
window	**la ventana** *(lah 'behn-tah-nah)*

A few of these words may be new to you. Are you still putting removable labels on everything?

ashtray	**el cenicero** *(ehl seh-nee-'seh-roh)*
bandage	**la venda** *(lah 'vehn-dah)*
bedpan	**la chata** *(lah 'chah-tah)*
blanket	**la frazada** *(lah frah-'sah-dah)*
cup	**la taza** *(lah 'tah-sah)*
flower vase	**el florero** *(ehl floh-'reh-roh)*
fork	**el tenedor** *(ehl teh-neh-'dohr)*
glass	**el vaso** *(ehl 'bah-soh)*
knife	**el cuchillo** *(ehl koo-'chee-yoh)*
mattress	**el colchón** *(ehl kohl-'chohn)*
napkin	**la servilleta** *(lah sehr-bee-'yeh-tah)*
nightstand	**la mesa de noche** *(lah 'meh-sah deh 'noh-cheh)*
pillow	**la almohada** *(lah ahl-moh-'ah-dah)*
pillowcase	**la funda** *(lah 'foon-dah)*
pitcher	**la jarra** *(lah 'har-rah)*
plate	**el plato** *(ehl 'plah-toh)*
sheet	**la sábana** *(lah 'sah-bah-nah)*
soap	**el jabón** *(ehl hah-'bohn)*
spoon	**la cuchara** *(lah koo-'chah-rah)*
step	**el escalón** *(ehl ehs-kah-'lohn)*
towel	**la toalla** *(lah toh-'ah-yah)*
trashcan	**el cesto de basura** *(ehl 'sehs-toh deh bah-'soo-rah)*
tray	**la bandeja** *(lah bahn-'deh-hah)*

Here's another one of those phrases that makes learning easier. To ask patients if they like something, use **¿Le gusta . . .?** *(leh 'goos-tah)*

Do you like the bed?	**¿Le gusta la cama?**
	(leh 'goos-tah lah 'kah-mah)
Do you like the food?	**¿Le gusta la comida?**
	(leh 'goos-tah lah koh-'mee-dah)

Do you like the light? **¿Le gusta la luz?** *(leh 'goos-tah lah loos)*

Do you like the soap? **¿Le gusta el jabón?**

(leh 'goos-tah ehl hah-'bohn)

Chances are they'll answer with a "yes." Here's what you'll hear:

¡Sí, me gusta! *(see meh 'goos-tah)*

¿ C u á n t o   A p r e n d i ó ?

How's your pronunciation? Read these sentences aloud:

Press here.	**Apriete aquí.** *(ah-pree-'eh-teh ah-'kee)*
Turn on the light.	**Prenda la luz.** *('prehn-dah lah loos)*
Turn off the TV.	**Apague la televisión.**
	(ah-'pah-geh lah teh-leh-bee-see-'ohn)
Dial the phone.	**Marque el teléfono.**
	('mahr-keh ehl teh-'leh-foh-noh).
Take a nap.	**Tome una siesta.**
	('toh-meh 'oo-nah see-'ehs-tah)

The bathroom
El cuarto de baño
(ehl 'kwahr-toh deh 'bah-nyoh)

Miguel has questions about the facility. Prepare yourself for the proper response.

Where is the . . .	**¿Donde está . . .?** *('dohn-deh eh-'stah)*
bathtub	**la bañera** *(lah bah-'nyeh-rah)*
mirror	**el espejo** *(ehl ehs-'peh-hoh)*
shower	**la ducha** *(lah 'doo-chah)*
sink	**el lavamanos** *(ehl lah-bah-'mah-nohs)*
toilet	**el excusado** *(ehl ehs-koo-'sah-doh)*
toilet paper	**el papel higiénico** *(ehl pah-'pehl ee-hee-'eh-nee-koh)*
urinal	**el orinal** *(ehl oh-ree-'nahl)*
washcloth	**la toallita** *(lah toh-ah-'yee-tah)*

Special vocabulary
El vocabulario especial
(ehl boh-kah-boo-'lah-ree·oh ehs-peh-see-'ahl)

Miguel should be made aware of everything around him. Use the following pattern along with special hospital vocabulary to familiarize Miguel and others with items found in a hospital room.

Here is (the) . . .	**Aquí está . . .** *(ah-'kee ehs-'tah)*
air conditioning	**el aire acondicionado**
	(ehl 'ah·ee-reh ah-kohn-dee-see-oh-'nah-doh)
alarm	**la alarma** *(lah ah 'lahr-mah)*
electric fan	**el ventilador** *(ehl behn-tee-lah-'dohr)*
electricity	**la electricidad** *(lah eh-lehk-tree-see-'dahd)*
heating	**la calefacción** *(lah kah-leh-fahk-see-'ohn)*
light switch	**el interruptor** *(ehl een-teh-rroop-'tohr)*
machine	**la máquina** *(lah 'mah-kee-nah)*
outlet	**el enchufe** *(ehl ehn-'choo-feh)*
radio	**el radio** *(ehl 'rah-dee-oh)*
refrigerator	**el refrigerador** *(ehl reh-free-heh-rah-'dohr)*
remote control	**el control remoto** *(ehl kohn-'trohl reh-'moh-toh)*
wire	**el cable** *(ehl 'kah-bleh)*

The recovery
La recuperación
(lah reh-koo-peh-rah-see·'ohn)

While Miguel rests in his hospital bed, you will be busy with a number of routine duties. As you treat the recovering patient, make up general comments and questions using the Spanish that you know. Notice that none of these are translated:

Necesita . . . *(neh-seh-'see-tah)*
 un examen. *(oon ehk-'sah-mehn)*
 dormir. *(dohr-'meer)*
 comer. *(koh-'mehr)*

¿**Tiene** . . . *(tee-'eh-neh)*
sueño? *('sweh-nyoh)*
dolores? *(doh-'loh-rehs)*

Voy a . . . *(boh·ee ah)*
hacer la cama. *(ah-'sehr lah 'kah-mah)*
tomar el pulso. *(toh-'mahr ehl 'pool-soh)*

¿**Está cómodo?** *(eh-'stah 'koh-moh-doh)*

Su dieta es muy importante.
(soo dee-'eh-tah ehs moo·ee eem-pohr-'tahn-teh)

Es necesario descansar. *(ehs neh-seh-'sah-ree·oh dehs-kahn-'sahr)*

He terminado. *(eh tehr-mee-'nah-doh)*

It is imperative that Miguel is given all the correct information. He will be released soon and wants to know what the doctors are saying.

Doctor's orders.
Órdenes del médico. *('ohr-deh-nehs dehl 'meh-dee-koh)*

The doctor says no.
El médico dice que no. *(ehl 'meh-dee-koh 'dee-seh keh noh)*

Don't try to do too much.
No trate de hacer demasiado.
(noh 'trah-teh deh ah-'sehr deh-mah-see-'ah-doh)

We have to talk with your doctor first.
Tenemos que hablar con su doctor primero.
(teh-'neh-mohs keh ah-'blahr kohn soo dohk-'tohr pree-'meh-roh)

You are not well enough.
No está completamente bien.
(noh-eh-'stah kohm-pleh-tah-'mehn-teh bee·'ehn)

Miguel is ready to be released to his family. Make a few final comments to him and his family.

You are going to be discharged today.
Le van a dar de alta hoy. *(leh bahn ah dahr deh 'ahl-tah 'oh·ee)*

You have to sign the release.

Tiene que firmar el permiso.

(tee-'eh-neh keh feer-'mahr ehl pehr-'mee-soh)

You need to return in one week.

Necesita regresar en una semana.

(neh-seh-'see-tah reh-greh-'sahr ehn 'oo-nah seh-'mah-nah)

(25) ¿CUÁNTO APRENDIÓ?

Translate the following sentences:

Mueva . . . *('mweh-bah)*
(the cabinet, the mirror, the tray)

Traiga . . . *('trah-ee-gah)*
(the plate, the fan, the soap, the spoon, the blanket)

Necesita . . . *(neh-seh-'see-tah)*
(shower, nap)

Chapter Eight

Capítulo Ocho
(kah-'pee-too-loh 'oh-choh)

Carlos Espinoza,
Age 65

Carlos has just finished dinner and his favorite cigar when he feels a tightness in his chest and pains down his left arm. He realizes immediately what is happening, and is able to remain calm. Within minutes, the pains subside. He decides to call his son, Juan, to let him know what has happened but instead of waiting for assistance, he stubbornly climbs into his pickup truck and drives three blocks to the local Medical Center.

Once admitted, a series of test results including an electrocardiogram, **el electrocardiograma** *(ehl eh-lehk-troh-kahr-dee-oh-'grah-mah)*, confirm his fears—he has suffered a heart attack. But that's not all. A routine chest X ray reveals a possible mass at the base of his right lung. More tests are needed, in addition to a variety of treatments and medications. Follow along as we explore the Spanish that is required in various fields of specialized medicine.

First, use the familiar commands to get Carlos to relax. He has begun to panic:

¡Siéntese! *(see-'ehn-teh-seh)*
¡Cálmese! *('kahl-meh-seh)*
¡No se preocupe! *(noh seh preh-oh-'koo-peh)*

Now, help him breathe. These words allow you to be very specific:

Breathe . . .	**Respire . . .** *(rehs-'pee-reh)*
again	**otra vez** *('oh-trah behs)*
deeply	**profundamente** *(proh-foon-dah-'mehn-teh)*

in	**hacia adentro** *('ah-see·ah ah-'dehn-troh)*
normally	**normalmente** *(nohr-mahl-'mehn-teh)*
out	**hacia afuera** *('ah-see·ah ah-'fweh-rah)*

Ask him some questions related to his physical condition.

Was it a sharp or dull pain?	**¿Fue un dolor agudo o sordo?** *(fweh oon doh-'lohr ah-'goo-doh oh 'sohr-doh)*
In what part?	**¿En qué parte?** *(ehn keh 'pahr-teh)*
How long ago?	**¿Hace cuánto tiempo?** *('hah-seh 'kwahn-toh tee-'ehm-poh)*
How often?	**¿Con qué frecuencia?** *(kohn keh freh-'kwehn-see·ah)*
What were you doing at the time?	**¿Qué estaba usted haciendo entonces?** *(keh ehs-'tah-bah oo-'stehd ah-see 'ehn-doh ehn-'tohn-sehs)*

These two questions may help to locate his pain. Don't forget that the word **se** is frequently part of an action word:

to stay	**Quedarse** *(keh-'dahr-seh)*
Does it stay?	**¿Se queda?** *(seh 'keh-dah)*
to spread	**Extenderse** *(ehks-tehn-'dehr-seh)*
Does it spread?	**¿Se extiende?** *(seh ehks-tee'ehn-deh)*

Now ask the patient:

Do you have . . .?	**¿Tiene . . .?** *(tee-'eh-neh)*
burning	**ardor** *(ahr-'dohr)*
chest pains	**dolores en el pecho** *(doh-'loh-rehs ehn ehl 'peh-choh)*
heart murmurs	**murmullos en el corazón** *(moor-'moo-yohs ehn ehl koh-rah-'sohn)*
irregular heartbeats	**latidos de corazón irregulares** *(lah-'tee-dohs deh koh-rah-'sohn ee-rreh-goo-'lah-rehs)*

shortness of breath	**falta de aliento**
	(fahl-tah deh ah-lee-'ehn-toh)
tingling	**hormigueo**
	(ohr-mee-'geh-oh)

Heart attack!
¡El ataque cardíaco!
(ehl ah-'tah-keh kahr-'dee-ah-koh)

You need as much information as possible. Look at all the verb forms that you know!

Do you cough up blood?

¿Escupe sangre? *(ehs-'koo-peh 'sahn-greh)*

Do you get short of breath upon exertion?

¿Se queda sin aliento después de hacer un esfuerzo?
(seh 'keh-dah seen ah-lee-'ehn-toh dehs-'pwehs deh ah-'sehr oon ehs-'fwehr-soh)

Do you feel pressure?

¿Siente presión? *(see-'ehn-teh preh-see-'ohn)*

Do your legs swell?

¿Se le hinchan las piernas? *(seh leh 'een-chahn lahs pee-'ehr-nahs)*

Do you sleep well?

¿Duerme bien? *('dwehr-meh bee-'ehn)*

Do you take medication?

¿Toma medicinas? *('toh-mah meh-dee-'see-nahs)*

Do you wake up at night with shortness of breath and perspiring.

¿Despierta por la noche con la respiración corta y sudando?
(dehs-pee-'ehr-tah pohr lah 'noh-cheh kohn lah rehs-pee-rah-see-'ohn 'kohr-tah ee soo-'dahn-doh)

Have you ever had a heart attack?

¿Ha tenido alguna vez un ataque cardíaco?
(ah teh-'nee-doh ahl-'goo-nah behs oon ah-'tah-keh kahr-'dee-ah-koh)

How many pillows do you sleep on?

¿Con cuántas almohadas duerme?

(kohn 'kwahn-tahs ahl-moh-'ah-dahs 'dwehr-meh)

When did the problem begin?

¿Cuándo empezó el problema?

('kwahn-doh ehm-peh-'soh ehl proh-'bleh-mah)

Here are some more key words related to heart attacks. These will not only help you form specific questions, but they will help you understand the patient's responses:

aorta	**la aorta** *(lah ah-'ohr-tah)*
atrium	**la cámara** *(lah 'kah-mah-rah)*
blocked artery	**la arteria obstruida**
	(lah ahr-'teh-ree-ah ohb-stroo-'ee-dah)
brain	**el cerebro** *(ehl seh-'reh-broh)*
graft	**el injerto** *(ehl een-'hehr-toh)*
hardening	**el endurecimiento** *(ehl ehn-doo-reh-see mee-'ehn-toh)*
heartbeat	**el ritmo cardíaco** *(ehl 'reet-moh kahr-'dee-ah-koh)*
hypertension	**la hipertensión arterial**
	(lah ee-pehr-tehn-see-'ohn ahr-teh-ree-'ahl)
overweight	**el sobrepeso** *(ehl soh-breh-'peh-soh)*
oxygen level	**el nivel de oxígeno** *(ehl nee-'behl deh ohk-'see-heh-noh)*
pacemaker	**el marcapasos** *(ehl mahr-kah-'pah-sohs)*
strained muscle	**el músculo forzado** *(ehl 'moos-koo-loh fohr-'sah-doh)*
stroke	**el ataque** *(ehl ah-'tah-keh)*
valve	**la válvula** *(lah 'bahl-boo-lah)*
vein	**la vena** *(lah 'beh-nah)*
ventricle	**el ventrículo** *(ehl behn-'tree-koo-loh)*

Now take a few minutes to translate the following. They are so similar to English that you shouldn't have to look them up.

aneurisma *(ah-neh-oo-'rees-mah)*
angina *(ahn-'hee-nah)*
angiografía *(ahn-hee-oh-grah-'fee-ah)*

angioplastia *(ahn-hee-oh-'plahs-tee-ah)*

arteriosclerosis *(ahr-teh-ree-oh-skleh-'roh-sees)*

cardiología *(kahr-dee-oh-loh-'hee-ah)*

cardiovascular *(kahr-dee-oh-bahs-koo-'lahr)*

circulación *(seer-koo-lah-see-'ohn)*

colesterol *(koh-leh-steh-'rohl)*

enfisema *(ehn-fee-'seh-mah)*

hematócrito *(eh-mah-toh-'kree-toh)*

hipertensión *(ee-pehr-tehn-see-'ohn)*

nitroglicerina *(nee-troh-glee-seh-'ree-nah)*

taquicardia *(tah-kee-'kahr-dee-ah)*

triglicéridos *(tree-glee-'seh-ree-dahs)*

Results

Los resultados

(lohs reh-sool-'tah-dohs)

After the physical examination and tests, give Carlos all the data that you have. When he and his family ask, "What is happening?" **¿Qué está pasando?** *(keh eh-'stah pah-'sahn-doh)* let him know what is wrong:

Your blood pressure is very high.

Su presión es muy alta. *(soo preh-see-'ohn ehs 'moo-ee 'ahl-tah)*

The artery is blocked.

La arteria está obstruida.

(lah ahr-'teh-ree-ah eh-'stah ohb-stroo-'ee-dah)

The heart muscles are strained.

Los músculos del corazón están forzados.

(lohs 'moos-koo-lohs dehl koh-rah-'sohn eh-'stahn fohr-'sah-dohs)

There is some hardening of the coronary arteries.

Tiene algo de endurecimiento de las arterias coronarias.

(tee-'eh-neh 'ahl-goh deh ehn-doo-reh-see-mee-'ehn-toh deh lahs ahr-'teh-ree-ahs koh-roh-'nah-ree-ahs)

You are overweight.

Tiene sobrepeso. *(tee-'eh-neh soh-breh-'peh-soh)*

Your case is (not) serious.

Su caso (no) es grave. *(soo 'kah-soh [noh] ehs 'grah-beh)*

Your pulse is very fast.

Su pulso es muy rápido. *(soo 'pool-soh ehs 'moo·ee 'rah-pee-doh)*

Your color is good.

Tiene buen color. *(tee-'eh-neh boo-'ehn koh-'lohr)*

Therapy and treatment
Terapia y tratamiento
(teh-'rah-pee-ah ee 'trah-tah-mee-ehn-toh)

After telling the patient and his family what is wrong with him, learn some of the following sentences to explain the next step:

I want to explain the equipment in this room.

Quiero explicarle el equipo de este cuarto.

(kee-'eh-roh ehks-plee-'kahr-leh ehl eh-'kee-poh deh 'eh-steh 'kwahr-toh)

We are going to draw a little blood from your vein.

Vamos a sacar un poco de sangre de su vena.

('bah-mohs ah sah-'kahr-leh oon 'poh-koh deh 'sahn-greh deh soo 'beh-nah)

We are going to check the cardiovascular function.

Vamos a verificar el funcionamiento cardiovascular.

('bah-mohs ah beh-ree-fee-'kahr ehl foon-see-oh-nah-mee-'ehn-toh kahr-dee-oh-bahs-koo-'lahr)

We are going to give you medications.

Vamos a darle medicamentos.

('bah-mohs ah 'dahr-leh meh-dee-kah-'mehn-tohs)

You need complete bed rest for now.

Por ahora, necesita completo descanso en cama.

(pohr ah-'oh-rah neh-seh-'see-tah kohm-'pleh-toh dehs-'kahn-soh ehn 'kah-mah)

You need to keep your legs straight.

Necesita tener sus piernas en posición recta.

(neh-seh-'see-tah teh-'nehr soos pee-'ehr-nahs ehn poh-see-see-'ohn 'rehk-tah)

We are going to put the catheter in the artery.

Vamos a poner el catéter en la arteria.

('bah-mohs ah poh-'nehr ehl kah-'teh-tehr ehn lah ahr-'teh-ree-ah)

The balloon will open the blocked artery.

El globito va a abrir la arteria obstruída.

(ehl gloh-'bee-toh vah ah ahb-'reer lah ahr-'teh-ree-ah ohbs-troo-'ee-dah)

Dos Culturas

When conversing with Hispanics about foods, stress both the good as well as the bad, and remember that their basic meals may differ from those eaten by most Americans.

The dietician

El dietista *(ehl dee-eh-'tees-tah)*

Because Carlos Espinoza is overweight and has poor eating habits, a dietician is contacted to help counsel him. As a matter of fact, all of the Espinozas could use some sound advice. It's visiting hours and they're all gathered around the patient's bed. Now is a good time to get the background information you need. At this stage of language development, most of these basic survival verb forms and vocabulary have been introduced:

Are you allergic to any food?

¿Tiene alergias a alguna comida?

(tee-'eh-neh ah-'lehr-hee-ahs ah ahl-'goo-nah koh-'mee-dah)

Do you have problems swallowing?

¿Tiene problemas al tragar?

(tee-'eh-neh proh-'bleh-mahs ahl trah-'gahr)

Have you gained or lost weight?

¿Ha ganado o perdido peso?

(ah gah-'nah-doh oh pehr-'dee-doh 'peh-soh)

How is your appetite?

¿Cómo está su apetito? *('koh-moh eh-'stah soo ah-peh-'tee-toh)*

Have you had any operation on your digestive system?

¿Ha tenido alguna operación en el sistema digestivo? *(ah teh-'nee-doh ahl-'goo-nah oh-peh-rah-see-'ohn ehn ehl sees-'teh-mah dee-hehs-'tee-boh)*

What do you eat?

¿Qué come? *('keh 'koh-meh)*

Give Carlos and his family a few practical suggestions:

You have to follow a diet.

Tiene que seguir una dieta. *(tee-'eh-neh keh seh-'geer 'oo-nah dee-'eh-tah)*

You need to eat three meals a day.

Necesita comer tres comidas al día.
(neh-seh-'see-tah koh-'mehr trehs koh-'mee-dahs ahl 'dee-ah)

Do not eat between meals.

No coma entre comidas. *(noh 'koh-mah 'ehn-treh koh-'mee-dahs)*

When it comes to good health, you can never have enough vocabulary:

You cannot eat . . .	**No puede comer . . .** *(noh 'pweh-deh koh-'mehr)*
. baking soda	**bicarbonato** *(bee-kahr-boh-'nah-toh)*
dairy products	**productos lácteos** *(proh-'dook-tohs 'lahk-teh-ohs)*
fried foods	**comida frita** *(koh-'mee-dah 'free-tah)*
margarine	**margarina** *(mahr-gah-'ree-nah)*
red meat	**carne roja** *('kahr-neh 'roh-hah)*
salt	**sal** *(sahl)*
seasonings	**condimentos** *(kohn-dee-'mehn-tohs)*
snacks	**meriendas** *(meh-ree-'ehn-dahs)*
spices	**especias** *(eh-'speh-see-ahs)*
sugar	**azúcar** *(ah-'soo-kahr)*
sweets	**dulces** *('dool-sehs)*
raw vegetables	**legumbres crudas** *(leh-'goom-brehs 'kroo-dahs)*

The diet
La dieta *(lah dee-'eh-tah)*

Now you need to talk to Carlos and his family. Use this menu to select the items that are to be allowed or forbidden in his diet.

Eat . . .	**Coma . . .** *('koh-mah)*
Do not eat . . .	**No coma . . .** *(noh 'koh-mah)*
breakfast	**el desayuno** *(ehl deh-sah-'yoo-noh)*
lunch	**el almuerzo** *(ehl ahl-moo-'ehr-soh)*
dinner	**la cena** *(lah 'seh-nah)*
apple	**la manzana** *(lah mahn-'sah-nah)*
avocado	**el aguacate, la palta**
	(ehl ah-gwah-'kah-teh, lah 'pahl-tah)
banana	**el plátano** *(ehl 'plah-tah-noh)*
bread	**el pan** *(ehl pahn)*
butter	**la mantequilla** *(lah 'mahn-teh-'kee-yah)*
cabbage	**el repollo** *(ehl reh-'poh-yoh)*
cake	**la torta** *(lah 'tohr-tah)*
candy	**el dulce** *(ehl 'dool-seh)*
carrot	**la zanahoria** *(lah sah-nah-'oh-ree·ah)*
cereal	**el cereal** *(ehl seh-reh-'ahl)*
cheese	**el queso** *(ehl 'keh-soh)*
cherry	**las cerezas** *(lahs seh-'reh-sahs)*
chicken	**el pollo** *(ehl 'poh-yoh)*
cookie	**la galleta** *(lah gah-'yeh-tah)*
corn	**el maíz** *(ehl mah-'ees)*
cream	**la crema** *(lah 'kreh-mah)*
dessert	**el postre** *(ehl poh-'streh)*
egg	**el huevo** *(ehl 'weh-bohs)*
fish	**el pescado** *(ehl pehs-'kah-doh)*
flour	**la harina** *(lah ah-'ree-nah)*
garlic	**el ajo** *(ehl 'ah-hoh)*
grape	**las uvas** *(lahs 'oo-bahs)*
grapefruit	**la toronja** *(lah toh-'rohn-hah)*

green bean	**el ejote** *(ehl eh-'hoh-teh)*
gum	**el chicle** *(ehl 'chee-kleh)*
ice cream	**el helado** *(ehl eh-'lah-doh)*
jelly	**la jalea** *(lah hah-'leh-ah)*
lamb	**el carnero** *(ehl kahr-'neh-roh)*
lard	**la manteca** *(lah mahn-'teh-kah)*
lemon	**el limón** *(ehl lee-'mohn)*
lettuce	**la lechuga** *(lah leh-'choo-gah)*
milk	**la leche** *(lah 'leh-cheh)*
noodles	**los fideos** *(lohs fee 'deh-ohs)*
nuts	**las nueces** *(lahs noo-'eh-sehs)*
oil	**el aceite** *(ehl ah-'seh-ee-teh)*
onion	**la cebolla** *(lah seh-'boh-yah)*
orange	**la naranja** *(lah nah-'rahn-hah)*
peas	**los chícharos** *(lohs 'chi-chah-rrohs)*
pepper	**la pimienta** *(lah pee-mee-'ehn-tah)*
pie	**el pastel** *(ehl pah-'stehl)*
pineapple	**la piña** *(lah 'pee-nyah)*
pork	**el cerdo** *(ehl 'sehr-doh)*
potato	**la papa** *(lah 'pah-pah)*
rice	**el arroz** *(ehl ah-'rrohs)*
salad	**la ensalada** *(lah ehn-sah-'lah-dah)*
salt	**la sal** *(lah sahl)*
sauce	**la salsa** *(lah 'sahl-sah)*
shellfish	**los mariscos** *(lohs mah-'rees-kohs)*
soup	**la sopa** *(lah 'soh-pah)*
steak	**el bistec** *(ehl bees-'tehk)*
strawberry	**las fresas** *(lahs 'freh-sahs)*
sugar	**el azúcar** *(ehl ah-'soo-kahr)*
tomato	**el tomate** *(ehl toh-'mah-teh)*
turkey	**el pavo** *(ehl 'pah-boh)*
yogurt	**el yogur** *(ehl yoh-'goor)*
Drink . . .	**Tome . . .** *('toh-meh)*
Do not drink . . .	**No tome . . .** *(noh 'toh-meh)*

beer	**la cerveza** *(lah sehr-'beh-sah)*
coffee	**el café** *(ehl 'kah-feh)*
decaffeinated coffee	**el café descafeinado**
	(ehl kah-'feh dehs-kah-feh·ee-'nah-doh)
juice	**el jugo** *(ehl 'hoo-goh)*
liquor	**el licor** *(ehl lee-'kohr)*
milk	**la leche** *(lah 'leh-cheh)*
soft drink	**el refresco** *(ehl reh-'frehs-koh)*
tea	**el té** *(ehl teh)*
water	**el agua** *(ehl 'ah-gwah)*
wine	**el vino** *(ehl 'bee-noh)*

By the way, the word for "ice" is **hielo** *(ee-'eh-loh)*. **Traiga el hielo.** *('trah-ee-gah ehl ee-'eh-loh)*

(26) ¿CUÁNTO APRENDIÓ?

Fill in the following:

- **No coma** . . . *(Noh 'koh-mah)*
  (butter, salt, candy, cheese, steak, cookies)

- **Tome** . . . *('toh-meh)*
  *(*tea, milk, juice)

- **Voy a** . . . *('boh·ee ah)*
  (give you medication)
  (explain the equipment)
  (draw a little blood)
  (listen to your chest)

Now you must give the family some sound advice.

You need . . .   **Necesita** . . .
                        (neh-seh-'see-tah)

a bland diet

una dieta blanda
('oo-nah dee-'eh-tah 'blahn-dah)

a calorie-
controlled diet

una dieta controlada en calorías
('oo-nah dee-'eh-tah kohn-troh-'lah-dah ehn
kah-loh-'ree-ahs)

cooked foods

las comidas cocidas
(lahs koh-'mee-dahs koh-'see-dahs)

decaffeinated coffee

café descafeinado
(kah-'feh dehs-kah-feh-ee-'nah-doh)

a diabetic diet

una dieta para diabéticos
('oo-nah dee-'eh-tah 'pah-rah dee-ah-'beh-tee-
kohs)

more fiber

más fibra *(mahs 'feeb-rah)*

more fruits and
vegetables

más frutas y legumbres
(mahs 'froo-tahs ee leh-'goom-brehs)

iron

hierro *(ee-'ehr-roh)*

less sodium and
potassium

menos sodio y potasio *('meh-nohs 'soh-dee·oh*
ee poh-'tah-see·oh)

to lower your
cholesterol level

bajar su nivel de colesterol *(bah-'hahr soo*
nee-'behl deh koh-lehs-teh-'rohl)

a low-fat diet

una dieta baja en grasa
('oo-nah dee-'eh-tah 'bah-hah ehn 'grah-sah)

magnesium

magnesia *(mahg-'neh-see-ah)*

minerals

minerales *(mee-neh-'rah-lehs)*

more exercise

más ejercicio *(mahs eh-hehr-'see-see·oh)*

more liquids

más líquidos
(mahs 'lee-kee-dohs)

more protein

más proteínas
(mahs proh-teh-'ee-nahs)

nutritional
supplement

un suplemento nutritivo
(oon soo-pleh-'mehn-toh noo-tree-'tee-boh)

a restricted diet	**una dieta limitada**
	('oo-nah dee-'eh-tah lee-mee-'tah-dah)
vitamins	**vitaminas** *(bee-tah-'mee-nahs)*

You can't!
¡No puede! *(noh 'pweh-deh)*

Carlos needs to be warned about the possible dangers of his heart condition:

Don't overeat.

No coma demasiado. *(noh 'koh-mah deh-mah-see-'ah-doh)*

For now, you can't drive a car.

Por ahora, no puede manejar un carro.

('pohr ah-'oh-rah noh 'pweh-deh mah-neh-'hahr oon 'kah-rroh)

You can't do strenuous exercise.

No puede hacer mucho ejercicio físico.

(noh 'pweh-deh ah-'sehr 'moo-choh eh-hehr-'see-see·oh 'fee-see-koh)

You can't have a lot of stress or tension.

No puede tener mucho estrés o tensión.

(noh 'pweh-deh teh-'nehr 'moo-choh ehs-'trehs oh tehn-see·'ohn)

The tests
Las pruebas *(lahs proo-'eh-bahs)*

Cardiac patients like Carlos have to be watched closely, even when they leave the hospital. The following tests are vital for monitoring a patient's progress in the doctor's office or in the hospital as an outpatient:

Holter monitor
La prueba de Holter *(lah proo-'eh-bah deh ohl-'tehr)*

This is a heart monitoring test.

Este es un monitor para controlar el corazón.

('eh-steh ehs oon moh-nee-'tohr 'pah-rah kohn-troh-'lahr ehl koh-rah-'sohn)

It lasts 24 hours.

Dura veinticuatro horas. *('doo-rah veh-een-tee-'kwah-troh 'oh-rahs)*

You need to wear the monitor at all times.

Necesita llevar el monitor constantemente.

(neh-seh-'see-tah yeh-'bahr ehl moh-nee-'tohr kohn-stahn-teh-'mehn-teh)

During the test, write down what you do and how you feel.

Durante la prueba, anote lo que hace y como se siente.

(doo-'rahn-teh lah proo-'eh-bah, ah-'noh-teh loh keh 'ah-seh ee 'koh-moh seh see-'ehn-teh)

Stress test

La prueba del estrés *(lah proo-'eh-bah dehl eh-'strehs)*

You cannot eat anything for twelve hours before the test.

No puede comer nada por doce horas antes de la prueba.

(noh 'pweh-deh koh-'mehr 'nah-dah pohr 'doh-seh 'oh-rahs 'ahn-tehs deh lah proo-'eh-bah)

During the test, you have to stay relaxed.

Durante la prueba, tiene que estar tranquilo.

(doo-'rahn-teh lah proo-'eh-bah, tee-'eh-neh keh eh-'stahr trahn-'kee-loh)

We are going to give you something to increase the heart rate.

Vamos a darle algo para acelerar el ritmo cardíaco.

('bah-mohs ah 'dahr-leh 'ahl-goh 'pah-rah ah-seh-leh-'rahr ehl 'reet-moh kahr-'dee-ah-koh)

You must wear comfortable clothes and sneakers.

Tiene que usar ropa cómoda y zapatillas.

(tee-'eh-neh keh oo-'sahr 'roh-pah 'koh-moh-dah ee sah-pah-'tee-yahs)

We are going to change the speed of the machine.

Vamos a cambiar la velocidad de la máquina.

('bah-mohs ah kahm-'bee-'ahr lah beh-loh-see-'dahd deh lah 'mah-kee-nah)

Pulmonary function test
Prueba de la función pulmonar
(proo-'eh-bah deh lah foon-see·'ohn pool-moo-'nahr)

It is a breathing test.
Es una prueba de respiración.
(ehs 'oo-nah proo-'eh-bah deh rehs-pee-rah-see·'ohn)

I am going to put medicine in your mouth.
Voy a poner medicina en su boca.
('boh·ee ah poh-'nehr meh-dee-'see-nah ehn soo 'boh-kah)

Breathe normally through the mouth.
Respire normalmente por la boca.
(reh-'spee-reh nohr-mahl-'mehn-teh pohr lah 'boh-kah)

You may swallow normally.
Puede tragar normalmente.
('pweh-deh trah-'gahr nohr-mahl-'mehn-teh)

Try to let out all of the air in your lungs.
Trate de sacar todo el aire de los pulmones.
('trah-teh deh sah-'kahr 'toh-doh ehl 'ah·ee-reh deh lohs pool-'moh-nehs)

Breathe deeply.
Respire profundamente. *(reh-'spee-reh proh-foon-dah-'mehn-teh)*

Gastrointestinal problems
Los problemas gastrointestinales
(lohs proh-'bleh-mahs gahs-troh-een-tehs-tee-'nah-lehs)

Now learn those lines in Spanish you'll need to discuss gastrointestinal problems. Open with questions about what Carlos likes to drink.

How many alcoholic beverages do you drink a day?
¿Cuántas bebidas alcohólicas toma cada día?
('kwahn-tahs beh-'bee-dahs ahl-koh-'oh-lee-kahs 'toh-mah 'kah-dah 'dee-ah)

How many bottles of soft drink?
¿Cuántas botellas de refresco?
('kwahn-tahs boh-'teh-yahs deh reh-'frehs-koh)

How many cups of coffee do you drink?
¿Cuántas tazas de café toma?
('kwahn-tahs 'tah-sahs deh kah-'feh 'toh-mah)

How many glasses of water?
¿Cuántos vasos de agua? *('kwahn-tohs 'bah-sohs deh 'ah-gwah)*

How much milk?
¿Cuánta leche? *('kwahn-tah 'leh-cheh)*

What do you like to drink?
¿Qué le gusta tomar? *(keh leh 'goos-tah toh-'mahr)*

Now ask about food:

Do you eat spicy, fried, or fatty foods?
¿Come comidas picantes, fritas o grasosas?
('koh-meh koh-'mee-dahs pee-'kahn-tehs, 'free-tahs, oh grah-'soh-sahs)

Is there any food you cannot eat?
¿Hay alguna comida que no puede comer?
('ah·ee ahl-'goo-nah koh-'mee-dah keh noh 'pweh-deh koh-'mehr)

Use this formula to find out about the patient's history:

Have you had . . .?	**¿Ha tenido . . . ?** *(ah teh-'nee-doh)*
a barium enema	**un enema de bario**
	(oon eh-'neh-mah deh 'bah-ree·oh)
constipation	**estreñimento** *(ehs-treh-nyee-mee-'ehn-toh)*
diarrhea	**diarrea** *(dee-ah-'rreh-ah)*
flatulence	**flatulencia** *(flah-too-'lehn-see·ah)*
a gastrointestinal	**alguna enfermedad gastrointestinal**
illness	*(ahl-'goo-nah ehn-fehr-meh-'dahd gahs-troh-een-tehs-tee-'nahl)*
heartburn	**ardor en el estómago**
	(ahr-'dohr ehn ehl ehs-'toh-mah-goh)
hemorrhoids	**hemorroides** *(eh-moh-'rroh·ee-dehs)*
hiccups	**hipo** *('ee-poh)*
parasites in	**parásitos en el excremento**
your stool	*(pah-'rah-see-tohs ehn ehl ehks-kreh-'mehn-toh)*

sour	**sabor ácido en la boca**
regurgitations	*(sah-'bohr 'ah-see-doh ehn lah 'boh-kah)*
a stroke	**un ataque** *(oon ah-'tah-keh)*
ulcers	**úlceras** *('ool-seh-rahs)*

(27) ¿CUÁNTO APRENDIÓ?

* Try to guess at these terms: (They are just like English.)

Tiene... *(tee-'eh-neh)*
anorexia *(ah-noh-'rehk-see-ah)*
botulismo *(boh-too-'lees-moh)*
bulimia *(boo-'lee-mee-ah)*
colitis *(koh-'lee-tees)*

Necesita... *(neh-seh-'see-tah)*
leche de magnesia *('leh-cheh deh mahg-'neh-see-ah)*
supositorios *(soo-poh-see-'toh-ree-ohs)*
aceite mineral *(ah-'seh-ee-teh mee-neh-'rahl)*

Now fill in the following:

* **¿Ha tenido...** *(ah teh-'nee-doh)*
(diarrhea, a barium enema, heartburn, alcoholic beverages)

* **Quiere ...** *(kee-'eh-reh)*
(decaffeinated coffee, to lose thirty pounds, to eat breakfast, a
fat-restricted diet, a laxative)

Oncology

La oncología *(lah ohn-koh-loh-'hee-ah)*

The doctors are discussing the mass in Carlos' lung. They need to be explicit as they explain the various details to their non-English speaking patient. Results from their tests could indicate a life-threatening situation. Use the new verb **encontrar** (to find) to express yourself:

We found . . .	**Encontramos . . .** *(ehn-kohn-'trah-mohs)*
an abnormality	**una anormalidad** *('oo-nah ah-nohr-mah-lee-'dahd)*
a bump	**una protuberancia** *('oo-nah proh-too-beh-'rahn-see·ah)*
a cyst	**un quiste** *(oon 'kees-teh)*
a lesion	**una llaga** *('oo-nah 'yah-gah)*
a lump	**un bulto** *(oon 'bool-toh)*
a spot	**una mancha** *('oo-nah 'mahn-chah)*
a tumor	**un tumor** *(oon too-'mohr)*

The biopsy

La biopsia *(lah bee-'ohp-see·ah)*

So far, all examinations have been preliminary. Obviously, specialists would like to look closely at a piece of the lung tissue. First, create general statements, and then specify in detail with further tests and treatment.

The doctor needs a biopsy from your _____ .
El médico necesita una biopsia de su _____ .
(ehl 'meh-dee-koh neh-seh-'see-tah 'oo-nah bee-'oh-psee·ah de soo)

He's going to give you an injection.
Va a darle una inyección. *(bah ah 'dahr-leh 'oo-nah een-yehk-see-'ohn)*

He's going to use a special needle.
Va a usar una aguja especial.
(bah ah oo-'sahr 'oo-nah ah-'goo-hah ehs-peh-see-'ahl)

He has to clean the area first.

Tiene que limpiar el área primero.

(tee-'eh-neh keh leem-pee-'ahr lah 'ah-reh-ah pree-'meh-roh)

He has to send the sample to the laboratory.

Tiene que mandar la muestra al laboratorio.

(tee-'eh-neh keh mahn-'dahr lah 'mwehs-trah ahl lah-boh-rah-'toh-ree-oh)

When we receive the results, we'll know what to do.

Cuando recibamos los resultados, sabremos qué hacer.

('kwahn-doh reh-see-'bah-mohs lohs reh-sool-'tah-dohs, sah-'breh-mohs keh ah-'sehr)

Keep your ears and eyes open for the following terms. They will undoubtedly surface during conversations with patients such as Carlos. Can you come up with something to say about each one? Write it?

bone marrow	**la médula** *(lah 'meh-doo-lah)*
tissue	**el tejido** *(ehl teh-'hee-doh)*
spinal fluid	**el líquido cefalorraquídeo** *(ehl 'lee-kee-doh seh-fah-loh-rrah-'kee-deh-oh)*
cells	**las células** *(lahs 'seh-loo-lahs)*
blood count	**el recuento de los glóbulos sanguíneos** *(ehl reh-'kwehn-toh deh lohs 'gloh-boo-lohs sahn-'gee-neh-ohs)*

¡No Se Olvide!

These procedures demand a command.

Lie on your side.

Acuéstese de lado. *(ah-'kwehs-teh-seh deh 'lah-doh)*

Relax and breathe through your mouth.

Relájese y respire por la boca.

(reh-'lah-heh-seh ee rehs-'pee-reh pohr lah 'boh-kah)

Stay very still.

Quédese muy quieto. *('keh-deh-seh moo-ee kee-'eh-toh)*

Call the doctor if you cough up blood.

Llame al doctor si tose y escupe sangre.

('yah-meh ahl dohk-'tohr see 'toh-seh ee ehs-'koo-peh 'sahn-greh)

Lumbar puncture

La punción lumbar *(lah poon-see·'ohn loom-'bahr)*

Here are some expressions you will need to know in order to explain these procedures:

The doctor needs a sample of your spinal fluid.

El doctor necesita una muestra de su líquido cefalorraquídeo.

(ehl dohk-'tohr neh-seh-'see-tah 'oo-nah 'mwehs-trah deh soo 'lee-kee-doh 'seh-fah-loh-rrah-'kee-deh-oh)

First you'll need local anesthesia.

Primero necesita anestesia local.

(pree-'meh-roh neh-seh-'see-tah ah-nehs-'teh-see-ah loh-'kahl)

He has to put a needle in your spine.

Tiene que poner una aguja en su columna.

(tee-'eh-neh keh poh-'nehr 'oo-nah ah-'goo-hah ehn soo koh-'loom-nah)

Lie on your back for one hour after the procedure.

Acuéstese de espalda por una hora después del procedimiento.

(ah-'kwehs-teh-seh deh ehs-'pahl-dah pohr 'oo-nah 'oh-rah dehs-'pwehs dehl proh-seh-dee-mee-'ehn-toh)

Proctoscopy
Proctoscopía *(prohk-toh-skoh-'pee·ah)*

This is a colon examination.

Este es un examen del colon.

('eh-steh ehs oon ehk-'sah-mehn dehl 'koh-lohn)

Take an enema one hour before the procedure.

Hágase un enema una hora antes del procedimiento.

('ah-gah-seh oon eh-'neh-mah oonah 'oh-rah 'ahn-tehs dehl proh-seh-dee-mee-'ehn-toh)

The doctor is inserting the instrument into your rectum.

El médico está introduciendo el instrumento en el recto.

(ehl 'meh-dee-koh eh-'stah een-troh-doo-see-'ehn-doh ehl eens-troo-'mehn-toh ehn ehl 'rehk-toh)

He is removing the instrument.

Está sacando el instrumento.

(eh-'stah sah-'kahn-doh ehl een-stroo-'mehn-toh)

More tests
Más pruebas *('mahs proo·'eh-bahs)*

Some additional tests you should know how to describe are:

MRI (Magnetic Resonance Imaging)

Imagen por resonancia magnética

(ee-'mah-hehn pohr reh-soh-'nahn-see·ah mahg-'neh-tee-kah)

Sonogram

Sonograma *(soh-noh-'grah-mah)*

Angiogram

Angiograma *(ahn-hee-oh-'grah-mah)*

EEG (Electroencephalogram)

Electroencefalograma *(eh-lehk-troh-ehn-seh-fah-loh-'grah-mah)*

¡No Se Olvide!

As you continue to acquire more Spanish, be aware once again of the similarities to English. Match each word below with its translation:

el mamograma *(ehl mah-moh 'grah-mah)*   CT

la tomografía computarizada   cystoscopy
(lah toh-moh-grah-'fee-ah kohm-poo-tah-ree-'sah-dah)

la prueba del sistema gastrointestinal   mammogram
(lah proo-'eh-bah dehl sees-'teh-mah gahs-troh-een-tehs-tee-'nahl)

la cistoscopía *(lah sees-toh-sko-'pee-ah)*   Upper GI

el electrocardiograma   ECG
(ehl eh-lehk-troh-kahr-dee-oh-'grah-mah)

Cancer

El cáncer *(ehl 'kahn-sehr)*

The examinations are completed, and there were no major communication problems between medical staff and patient. Carlos and his family wait nervously for his test results. They are frightened because they know very little about oncology. Finally, the doctor gives them the news. Here are the phrases that often describe cancer:

The cells...	**Las células ...** *(lahs 'seh-loo-lahs)*
are normal.	**son normales.** *(sohn nohr-'mah-lehs)*
are benign.	**son benignas.** *(sohn beh-'neeg-nahs)*
are malignant.	**son malignas.** *(sohn mah-'leeg-nahs)*
grow very fast.	**crecen rápidamente.** *('kreh-sehn rah-pee-dah-'mehn-teh)*
are abnormal.	**son anormales.** *(sohn ah-nohr-'mah-lehs)*

The family has many questions about cancer treatment.

Chemotherapy

La quimoterapia *(lah kee-moh-teh-'rah-pee·ah)*

He is going to ... **Va a ...** *(bah ah)*

feel tired and weak.

sentirse cansado y débil. *(sehn-'teer-seh kahn-'sah-doh ee 'deh-beel)*

have nausea, vomiting, diarrhea, and constipation.

tener náuseas, vómitos, diarrea y estreñimiento.
(teh-'nehr 'now-seh-ahs, 'boh-mee-tohs, dee-ah-'rreh-ah ee ehs-treh-'nyee-mee-'ehn-toh)

have some side effects.

tener algunos efectos secundarios.
(teh-'nehr ahl-'goo-nohs eh-'fehk-tohs seh-koon-'dah-ree·ohs)

lose bone marrow cells.

perder células de la médula de los huesos.
(pehr-'dehr 'seh-loo-lahs deh lah 'meh-doo-lah deh lohs 'weh-sohs)

need radiation treatment.

necesitar radioterapia.
(neh-seh-see-'tahr rah-dee-oh-teh-'rah-pee-ah)

lose his hair and skin color.

perder el pelo y el color de la piel.
(pehr-'der ehl 'peh-loh ee ehl koh-'lohr deh lah pee-'ehl)

Explain to the Espinozas that cancer patients are required to follow strict orders.

Come to the hospital tomorrow.

Venga al hospital mañana. *('behn-gah ahl ohs-pee-'tahl mah-'nyah-nah)*

Drink lots of liquids.

Tome muchos líquidos. *('toh-meh 'moo-chohs 'lee-kee-dohs)*

If the test results indicate that the cancer cells are benign the doctor will say "All is well!" **¡Todo está bien!** *('toh-doh eh-'stah 'bee·ehn)*

Types of cancer
Tipos de cáncer
('tee-pohs deh 'kahn-sehr)

Learn the following terms:

bone cancer	**cáncer del hueso** *('kahn-sehr dehl 'weh-soh)*
breast cancer	**cáncer del seno** *('kahn-sehr dehl 'seh-noh)*
cervical cancer	**cáncer cervical** *('kahn-sehr sehr-bee-'kahl)*
colon cancer	**cáncer del colon** *('kahn-sehr dehl 'koh-lohn)*
leukemia	**leucemia** *(leh-oo-'seh-mee-ah)*
lung cancer	**cáncer del pulmón** *('kahn-sehr dehl pool-'mohn)*
pancreatic cancer	**cáncer pancreático**
	('kahn-sehr pahn-kreh-'ah-tee-koh)
prostate cancer	**cáncer de la próstata**
	('kahn-sehr deh lah 'proh-stah-tah)
skin cancer	**cáncer de la piel** *('kahn-sehr deh lah pee-'ehl)*
stomach cancer	**cáncer del estómago**
	('kahn-sehr dehl ehs-'toh-mah-goh)
thyroid cancer	**cáncer de la tiroides**
	('kahn-sehr deh lah tee-'roh-ee-dehs)
uterine cancer	**cáncer uterino** *('kahn-sehr oo-tch-'ree-noh)*

¡NO SE OLVIDE!

- Work on these invaluable expressions:

You need to come.

Necesita venir. *(neh-seh-'see-tah beh-'neer)*

His condition is worse.

Su condición está peor. *(soo kohn-dee-see-'ohn eh-'stah peh-'ohr)*

He is asking for you.

Está preguntando por usted.

(eh-'stah preh-goon-'tahn-doh pohr oo-'stehd)

Chapter Nine

Capítulo Nueve
(kah-'pee-too-loh 'nweh-beh)

The Elderly
Los Ancianos
(lohs ahn-see-'ah-nohs)

Due to the need for constant medical attention, Guadalupe Lourdes Velásquez de Espinoza, age 90, was recently admitted to a skilled nursing home. Family and friends visit frequently, but her condition has worsened.

Throughout the hospital, senior patients are requiring the services of numerous specialists. Let's focus on those other major areas where Spanish is needed the most.

First of all, become familiar with these terms:

ambulatory care	**cuidado ambulatorio**
	(kwee-'dah-doh ahm-boo-lah-'toh-ree·oh)
intermediate care	**cuidado intermedio**
	(kwee-'dah-doh een-tehr-'meh-dee·oh)
nursing care	**cuidado con enfermera**
	(kwee-'dah-doh kohn ehn-fehr-'meh-roh)
total care	**cuidado total** *(kwee-'dah-doh toh-'tahl)*

Orthopedics
Ortopedia *(ohr-toh-'peh-dee-ah)*

Brittle bones abound in the nursing home, so orthopedic treatment and physical therapy are frequently in demand. If you work with the elderly, here are some of the terms you may need:

	Necesita . . . *(neh-seh-'see-tah)*
cane	**el bastón** *(ehl bahs-'tohn)*
continuous passive motion machine	**la máquina de movimiento continuo** *(lah 'máh-kee-nah deh moh-vee-mee-'ehn-toh kohn-'tee-noo-oh)*
exercises	**ejercicios** *(eh-hehr-'see-see·ohs)*
girdle	**la faja** *(lah 'fah-hah)*
sling	**el cabestrillo** *(ehl kah-behs-'tree-yoh)*
traction	**la tracción** *(lah trahk-see·'ohn)*
trapeze	**el trapecio** *(ehl trah-'peh-see·oh)*
ultrasound	**el ultrasonido** *(ool-trah-soh-'nee-doh)*
walker	**la caminadora** *(lah kah-mee-nah-'doh-rah)*
whirlpool bath	**el baño con agua circulante** *(ehl 'bah-nyoh kohn 'ah-gwah seer-koo-'lahn-teh)*

Bones

Los huesos *(lohs 'weh-sohs)*

The Espinozas are obviously concerned, and would like to know more specifics about **abuelita's** physical condition. She has been complaining of pain. To understand what she's saying, first review the parts of the skeleton—**esqueleto.**

I feel pain in . . .	**Me duele . . .** *(meh-'dweh-leh)*
breastbone	**el esternón** *(ehl ehs-tehr-'nohn)*
cranium	**el cráneo** *(ehl 'krah-neh-oh)*
hip	**la cadera** *(lah kah-'deh-rah)*
joint	**la coyuntura** *(lah koh-yoon-'too-rah)*
rib	**la costilla** *(lah kohs-'tee-yah)*
spine	**la columna vertebral** *(lah koh-'loohm-nah behr-teh-'brahl)*

Now, can you identify these?

la escápula *(lah ehs-'kah-poo-lah)*
el radio *(ehl 'rah-dee·oh)*

la ulna *(lah 'ool-nah)*
el fémur *(ehl 'feh-moor)*
la tibia *(lah 'tee-bee·ah)*
la fíbula *(lah 'fee-boo-lah)*
la clavícula *(lah klah-'bee-koo-lah)*
la vértebra *(lah 'fehr-teh·brah)*

Hip surgery
Cirugía de la cadera
(see-roo-'hee-ah deh lah kah-'deh-rah)

Do not cross your legs or ankles.
No cruce sus piernas ni sus tobillos.
(noh 'kroo-seh soos pee-'ehr-nahs nee soos toh-'bee-yohs)
Do not turn your hips.
No voltee sus caderas.
(noh bohl-'teh-eh soos kah-'deh-rahs)
This helps prevent a hip dislocation.
Esto ayuda a prevenir una dislocación de las caderas.
('ehs-toh ah-'yoo-dah ah preh-beh-'neer 'oo-nah dees-loh-kah-see-'ohn deh lahs kah-'deh-rahs)

Muscles
Los músculos *(lohs 'moos-koo-lohs)*

After discussing her bones—**huesos** *('weh-sohs)*—mention the muscles—**músculos** *('moos-koo-lohs)*. They are easy to remember:

biceps	**bíceps** *('bee-sehps)*
external oblique	**oblicuo mayor** *(oh-'blee-koo-oh mah-'yohr)*
peroneus	**peroneo largo** *(peh-roh-'neh-oh 'lahr-goh)*
pectoris major	**pectoral mayor** *(pehk-toh-'rahl mah-'yohr)*
rectus abdominis	**rector del abdomen** *(rehk-'tohr dehl ahb-'doh-mehn)*
sartorius	**sartorio** *(sahr-'toh-ree-oh)*
trapezius	**trapecio** *(trah-'peh-see·oh)*
triceps	**tríceps** *('tree-sehps)*

Genitourinary

Genitourinario *(heh-nee-toh-oo-ree-'nah-ree·oh)*

In addition to structural damage, Mrs. Lupe shows signs of internal problems.

In elderly patients, the genitourinary system often shows signs of functional change. Lupe has been having problems in this area for several years. She once met with specialists, and a number of sensitive topics were discussed. First, we'll discuss a few female concerns and then address typical male problems. All of these questions contain vocabulary that you should become familiar with:

Did you have a hysterectomy?

¿Tuvo una histerectomía? *('too-boh 'oo-nah ees-teh-rehk-toh-'mee-ah)*

Did you have menstrual problems when young?

¿Ha tenido problemas menstruales cuando joven?
(ah teh-'nee-doh proh-'bleh-mahs mehn-stroo-'ah-lehs 'kwahn-doh 'hoh-behn)

Did they remove your tubes?

¿Le sacaron los tubos? *(leh sah-'kah-rohn lohs 'too-bohs)*

Do you ever lose your urine?

¿Se orina sin querer a veces? *(seh oh-'ree-nah seen keh-'rehr ah 'beh-sehs)*

Do your ovaries or vagina hurt?

¿Le duelen los ovarios o la vagina?
(leh 'dweh-lehn lohs oh-'bah-ree·ohs oh lah bah-'hee-nah)

Have you used contraceptive methods in the past?

¿Ha usado métodos anticonceptivos en el pasado?
(ah oo-'sah-doh 'meh-toh-dohs ahn-tee-kohn-sehp-'tee-bohs ehn ehl pah-'sah-doh)

How many pregnancies have you had?

¿Cuántas veces quedó embarazada?
('kwahn-tahs 'beh-sehs keh-'doh ehm-bah-rah-'sah-dah)

When did your periods stop?

¿Cuándo se terminó su regla?
('kwahn-doh seh tehr-mee-'noh soo 'reh-glah)

Now learn some terms for discussing these problems with men—**los hombres** *(lohs 'ohm-brehs)*. This time, use the same pattern to pick up on any new vocabulary:

Have you had . . . ?	**¿Ha tenido . . . ?** *(ah teh-'nee-doh)*
operations on your penis	**operaciones en su pene** *(oh-per-rah-see·oh-nehs ehn soo 'peh-neh)*
pain in your scrotum	**dolor en su escroto** *(doh-'lohr ehn soo ehs-'kroh-toh)*
problems with your foreskin	**problemas con su prepucio** *(proh-'bleh-mahs kohn soo preh-'poo-see·oh)*
problems with the testicles	**problemas con los testículos** *(proh-'bleh-mahs kohn lohs tehs-'tee-koo-lohs)*
problems during urination	**problemas al orinar** *(proh-'bleh-mahs ahl oh-ree-'nahr)*
a semen examination	**un examen del semen** *(oon ehk-'sah-mehn dehl 'seh-mehn)*
sores on your penis	**llagas en su pene** *('yah-gahs ehn soo 'peh-neh)*

Now here are some questions that work with both sexes:

Have you ever had . . .?	**¿Ha tenido alguna vez . . .?** *(ah teh-'nee-doh ahl-'goo-nah behs)*
bleeding when urinating	**sangramiento al orinar** *(sahn-grah-mee-'ehn-toh ahl oh-ree-'nahr)*
a burning sensation	**una sensación de ardor** *('oo-nah sehn-sah-see-'ohn deh ahr-'dohr)*
a discharge	**un desecho** *(oon dehs-'eh-choh)*
itching	**picazón** *(pee-kah-'sohn)*
pain while urinating	**dolor al orinar** *(doh-'lohr ahl oh-ree-'nahr)*
pain during sexual relations	**dolor durante las relaciones sexuales** *(doh-'lohr doo-'rahn-teh lahs reh-lah-see·'oh-nehs sehk-soo-'ah-lehs)*

pus	**pus** *(poos)*
rashes	**sarpullidos** *(sahr-poo-'yee-dohs)*
sores	**llagas** *('yah-gahs)*
swelling	**hinchazón** *(een-chah-'sohn)*
urinary infection	**infección urinaria** *(een-fehk-see-'ohn oo-ree-'nah-ree-ah)*
venereal disease	**una enfermedad venérea** *('oo-nah ehn-fehr-meh-'dahd beh-'neh-reh-ah)*

Proctology
Proctología *(prohk-toh-loh-'hee-ah)*

As long as you are discussing bodily functions with Guadalupe, why not practice a few lines from **el examen proctológico** *(ehl ehk-'sah-mehn prohk-toh-'loh-hee-koh)*. Mix in phrases that you know along with any new vocabulary:

Have you had . . . ?	**¿Ha tenido . . . ?** *(ah teh-'nee-doh)*
blood in the stool	**sangre en el excremento** *('sahn-greh ehn ehl ehks-kreh-'mehn-toh)*
constipation	**estreñimiento** *(ehs-treh-'nyee-mee-'ehn-toh)*
diarrhea	**diarrea** *(dee-ah-'rreh-ah)*
an enema	**un enema** *(oon eh-'neh-mah)*
hemorrhoids	**hemorroides** *(eh-moh-'rroh-ee-dehs)*
pain when defecating	**dolor al defecar** *(doh-'lohr ahl deh-feh-'kahr)*
parasites	**parásitos** *(pah-'rah-see-tohs)*
rectal trouble	**problemas en el recto** *(proh-'bleh-mahs ehn ehl 'rehk-toh)*
swollen glands	**glándulas hinchadas** *('glahn-doo-lahs een-'chah-dahs)*

How are your translation skills? Say each of the following with the proper Spanish pronunciation:

impotencia *(eem-poh-'tehn-see-ah)*
esterilidad *(ehs-teh-ree-lee-'dahd)*

masturbación *(mahs-toor-bah-see-'ohn)*
secreción *(seh-kreh-see-'ohn)*
prostatitis *(proh-stah-'tee-tees)*
menopausia *(meh-noh-'pow-see-ah)*
menstruación *(mehn-stroo-ah-see-'ohn)*
inflamación *(een-flah-mah-see-'ohn)*
infección por HIV *(een-fehk-see-'ohn pohr 'ah-cheh ee 'beh 'chee-kah)*
estrógeno *(ehs-'troh-heh-noh)*
testosterona *(tehs-tohs-teh-'roh-nah)*

Continue to guess:

cirrosis *(seer-'roh-sees)*
esclerosis *(ehs-kleh-'roh-sees)*
hernia *('ehr-nee-ah)*
reumatismo *(reh-oo-mah-'tees-moh)*
vaginitis *(bah-gee-'nee-tees)*

(29) ¿CUÁNTO APRENDIÓ?

Try to make sentences out of the following terms:

- **Necesita . . .** *(neh-seh-'see-tah)*
  (ambulatory care, whirlpool bath, exercises)

- **Me duele...** *(meh 'dweh-leh)*
  (spine, joint, penis)

- **¿Ha tenido...?** *(ah teh-'nee-doh)*
  (menstrual problems, a semen exam, venereal disease, swollen glands, problems with your ovaries)

The nervous system
El sistema nervioso
(ehl sees-'teh-mah nehr-bee-'oh-soh)

In addition to all of her other problems, Guadalupe has recently shown signs of a nervous disorder. Look at the following questions and mix any previously learned vocabulary with these words you are unfamiliar with:

Have you had . . . ?	**¿Ha tenido . . .?** *(ah teh-'nee-doh)*
any paralysis	**algún tipo de parálisis** *(ahl-'goon 'tee-poh deh pah-'rah-lee-sees)*
convulsions	**convulsiones** *(kohn-'bool-see·'oh-nehs)*
discharge from your ears	**desecho de los oídos** *(dehs-'eh-choh deh lohs oh-'ee-dohs)*
dizziness	**mareos** *(mah-'reh-ohs)*
emotional problems	**problemas emocionales** *(proh-'bleh-mahs eh-moh-see-oh-'nah-lehs)*
fainting spells	**desmayos** *(dehs-'mah-yohs)*
headaches	**dolores de cabeza** *(doh-'loh-rehs deh kah-'beh-sah)*
problems with your balance	**problemas con su equilibrio** *(proh-'bleh-mahs kohn soo eh-kee-'lee-bree·oh)*
problems with your sight	**problemas con la vista** *(proh-'bleh-mahs kohn lah 'bees-tah)*

Ask a variety of questions about the nervous system in Spanish. Now create your own sentences using the vocabulary below:

Do you have . . .?	**¿Tiene . . .?** *(tee-'eh-neh)*
blurred vision	**visión borrosa** *(bee-see·'ohn boh-'rroh-sah)*
double vision	**doble visión** *('doh-bleh bee-see·'ohn)*
numbness	**adormecimiento** *(ah-dohr-meh-see-'mee·'ehn-toh)*
sensitivity	**sensibilidad** *(sehn-see-bee-lee-'dahd)*
tingling	**hormigueo** *(ohr-mee-'geh-oh)*
weakness	**debilidad** *(deh-bee-lee-'dahd)*

The neuropsychiatric unit
La unidad neurosiquiátrica
(lah oo-nee-'dahd neh-oo-roh-see-kee-'ah-tree-kah)

When abnormal behaviors are evident, it may be a good idea to check on the patient's mental or emotional condition. In Guadalupe's case, senility—la senilidad *(lah seh-nee-lee-'dahd)*—has set in, and lots of questions need to be answered, either by the patient or her family, to get to the source. Study the key terms below, and then develop phrases you can use:

Do you have . . .?	¿Tiene . . . ? *(tee-'eh-neh)*
anxiety	**ansiedad** *(ahn-see-'eh-dahd)*
bad dreams	**sueños malos** *('sweh-nyohs 'mah-lohs)*
confusion	**confusión** *(kohn-foo-see-'ohn)*
depression	**desánimo** *(dehs-'ah-nee-moh)*
fear	**miedo** *(mee-'eh-doh)*
hysteria attacks	**histerias** *(ees-'teh-ree-ahs)*
insomnia	**insomnio** *(een-'sohm-nee·oh)*
loss of memory	**falta de memoria** *('fahl-tah deh meh-'moh-ree·ah)*
seizures	**ataques** *(ah-'tah-kehs)*
visions	**visiones** *(bee-see-'oh-nehs)*

Feelings
Los sentimientos *(lohs sehn-tee-mee-'ehn-tohs)*

abused	**abusado** *(ah-boo-'sah-doh)*
ashamed	**avergonzado** *(ah-behr-gohn-'sah-doh)*
depressed	**deprimido** *(deh-pree-'mee-doh)*
frustrated	**frustrado** *(froos-'trah-doh)*
guilty	**culpable** *(kool-'pah-bleh)*
insecure	**inseguro** *(een-seh-'goo-roh)*
jealous	**celoso** *(seh-'loh-soh)*
restless	**inquieto** *(een-kee-'eh-toh)*
sensitive	**sensible** *(sehn-'see-bleh)*
strange	**raro** *('rah-roh)*

suicidal	**con tendencias suicidas**
	(kohn tehn-'dehn-see-ahs soo-ee-'see-dahs)
trapped	**atrapado** *(ah-trah-'pah-doh)*

More Problems

Más problemas *(mahs proh-'bleh-mahs)*

It's . . .	**Es . . .** *(ehs)*
a chronic behavior	**un comportamiento crónico**
	(oon kohm-pohr-tah mee-'ehn-toh 'kroh-nee-koh)
a disability	**una incapacidad**
	('oo-nah een-kah-pah-see-'dahd)
a disorder	**un trastorno** *(oon trahs-'tohr-noh)*
a symptom	**un síntoma** *(oon 'seen-toh-mah)*
a syndrome	**un síndrome** *(oon 'seen-droh-meh)*

It's called . . .	**Se llama . . .** *(seh 'yah-mah)*
Attention Deficit Disorder	**trastorno de deficiencia de concentración**
	(trahs-'tohr-noh deh deh-fee-see-'ehn-see-ah deh kohn-sehn-trah-see-'ohn)
autism	**autismo** *(ow-'tees-moh)*
bipolar disorder	**desorden bipolar**
	(deh-'sohr-dehn bee-poh-'lahr)
cerebral palsy	**parálisis cerebral**
	(pah-'rah-lee-sees seh-reh-'brahl)
cystic fibrosis	**fibrosis cística** *(fee-'broh-sees 'sees-tee-kah)*
Down syndrome	**síndrome de Down**
	('seen-droh-meh deh 'dah-oon)
epilepsy	**epilepsia** *(eh-pee-'lehp-see-ah)*
hyperactivity	**hiperactividad** *(ee-pehr-ahk-tee-vee-'dahd)*
multiple sclerosis	**esclerosis múltiple**
	(ehs-kleh-'roh-sees 'mool-tee-pleh)
muscular dystrophy	**distrofia muscular**
	(dees-'troh-fee-ah moos-koo-'lahr)

Obsessive	**trastorno de comportamiento compulsivo y**
Compulsive	**obsesivo** *(trahs-'tohr-noh deh kohm-pohr-tah-*
Disorder	*mee-'ehn-toh kohm-pool-'see-boh ee ohb-seh-*
	'see-boh)
retardation	**retraso** *(reh-trah-soh)*

Emotional Comments
Comentarios emocionales
(koh-mehn-'tah-ree-ohs eh-moh-see-oh-'nah-lehs)

I'm afraid of the operation.
Tengo miedo de la operación.
('tehn-goh mee-'eh-doh deh lah oh-peh-rah-see-'ohn)
Hospitals make me feel nervous.
Los hospitales me hacen sentir nervioso.
(lohs ohs-pee-'tah-lehs meh 'ah-sehn sehn-'teer nehr-bee-'oh-soh)
I'm angry at the nurse.
Estoy enojado con la enfermera.
(ehs-'toh-ee eh-noh-'hah-doh kohn lah ehn-fehr-'meh-rah)
I'm worried about the results.
Estoy preocupado acerca de los resultados.
(ehs-'toh-ee preh-oh-koo-'pah-doh ah-'sehr-kah deh lohs reh-sool-'tah-dohs)
I'm sad because I can't go home.
Estoy triste porque no puedo ir a mi casa.
(ehs-'toh-ee 'trees-teh 'pohr-keh noh poo-'eh-doh eer ah mee 'kah-sah)

Ask Guadalupe or her family about all her **problemas.** Get to the root of her troubles with questions like these:

Are you eating and sleeping OK?
¿Está comiendo y durmiendo bien?
(eh-'stah koh-mee-'ehn-doh ee door-mee-'ehn-doh 'bee-ehn)
Are you worried about anything?
Está preocupada por algo? *(Eh-'stah preh-oh-koo-'pah-dah pohr 'ahl-goh)*
Did you have problems when you were a child?
¿Tuvo problemas de niña? *('too-boh proh-'bleh-mahs deh 'nee-nyah)*

Do you have financial problems?

¿Tiene problemas económicos?

(tee-'eh-neh proh-'bleh-mahs eh-koh-'noh-mee-kohs)

Do you have good relations with your relatives and friends?

¿Tiene buenas relaciones con sus parientes y amigos? *(tee-'eh-neh*
'bweh-nahs reh-lah-see-'oh-nehs kohn soos pah-ree-'ehn-tehs ee ah-'mee-gohs)

Do you have many responsibilites?

¿Tiene muchas responsabilidades?

(tee-'eh-neh 'moo-chahs rehs-pohn-sah-bee-lee-'dah-dehs)

What illnesses and operations have you had?

¿Qué enfermedades y operaciones ha tenido?

('keh ehn-fehr-meh-'dah-dehs ee oh-peh-rah-see-'oh-nehs keh ah teh-'nee-doh)

When did the problem start?

¿Cuándo empezó el problema?

('kwahn-doh ehm-peh-'soh ehl proh-'bleh-mah)

A personal tragedy or traumatic experience could lead to mental or
nervous disorders. However, no two cases are exactly alike. Use these
words to find out what happened to your patient. Follow the example:

Do you want to talk about . . .?	**¿Quiere hablar de . . .?** *(kee-'eh-reh ah-'blahr deh)*
abandonment	**el abandono** *(ehl ah-bahn-'doh-noh)*
death	**la muerte** *(lah 'mwehr-teh)*
divorce	**el divorcio** *(ehl dee-'bohr-see-oh)*
failure	**el fracaso** *(ehl frah-'kah-soh)*
molestation	**los acosos sexuales** *(lohs ah-'koh-sohs sehk-soo-'ah-lehs)*
rape	**la violación** *(lah bee-oh-lah-see-'ohn)*
war	**la guerra** *(lah 'geh-rrah)*
It is . . .	**Es . . .** *(ehs)*
Alzheimer's	**la enfermedad de Alzheimer** *(lah ehn-fehr-meh-'dahd deh ahls-'hah-ee-mehr)*

a hereditary problem	**un problema hereditario** *(oon proh-'bleh-mah eh-reh-dee-'tah-ree-oh)*
a mental disorder	**un desorden mental** *(oon dehs-'ohr-dehn mehn-'tahl)*
neurosis	**una neurosis** *('oo-nah neh·oo-'roh-sees)*
paranoia	**una paranoia** *('oo-nah pah-rah-'noh·ee-ah)*
a physical abnormality	**una anormalidad física** *('oo-nah ah-nohr-mah-lee-'dahd 'fee-see-kah)*
senile dementia	**demencia senil** *(deh-'mehn-see·ah seh-'neel)*
schizophrenia	**esquizofrenia** *(ehs-keet-soh-'freh-nee·ah)*

The following terms can become parts of very important sentences. These simple samples will get you started:

She needs . . .	**Ella necesita . . .** *('eh-yah neh-seh-'see-tah)*
counseling	**consejería** *(kohn-seh-heh-'ree-ah)*
intensive therapy	**terapia intensiva** *(teh-'rah-pee·ah een-tehn-'see-bah)*
physical therapy	**fisioterapia** *(fee-see-oh-teh-'rah-pee-ah)*
a psychiatrist	**un siquiatra** *(oon see-kee-'ah-trah)*
a psychiatric hospital	**un hospital psiquiátrico** *(oon ohs-pee-'tahl see-kee-'ah-tree-koh)*
a psychologist	**un psicólogo** *(opon see-'koh-loh-goh)*
psychotherapy	**psicoterapia** *(see-koh-teh-'rah-pee-ah)*
rehabilitation	**rehabilitación** *(reh-hah-bee-lee-tah-see-'ohn)*
speech therapy	**terapia del habla** *(teh-'rah-pee-ah dehl 'ah-blah)*
She is . . .	**Ella es . . .** *('eh-yah ehs)*
an addict	**una adicta** *('oo-nah ah-'deek-tah)*
an alcoholic	**una alcohólica** *('oo-nah ahl-koh-'oh-lee-kah)*

depressed	**está** (do not use **es**) **deprimida** *(ehs-'tah deh-pree-'mee-dah)*
an epileptic	**una epiléptica** *('oo-nah eh-pee-'lehp-tee-kah)*
a manic depressive	**una maníacodepresiva** *('oo-nah mah-'nee-ah-koh-deh-preh-'see-bah)*
paranoid	**una paranoica** *('oo-nah pah-rah-'noh-ee-kah)*
a schizophrenic	**una esquizofrénica** *('oo-nah ehs-kee-soh-'freh-nee-kah)*
suicidal	**tiene** (do not use **es**) **tendencias** **suicidas** *(tee-'eh-neh tehn-'dehn-see-ahs* *soo-ee-'see-dahs)*

More action
Más acción *(mahs ahk-see·'ohn)*

Don't be content with simple patterns and vocabulary lists. As you develop more advanced skills in Spanish, it will become evident that you are always going to need more action words. Just keep in mind that the best way to memorize verbs is through regular practice in everyday situations. Here are a few that will help you to communicate better with Mrs. Lupe or other elderly patients:

to apply	**aplicar** *(ah-plee-'kahr)*
I have to apply traction to you.	**Tengo que aplicarle tracción.** *('tehn-goh keh ah-plee-'kahr-leh trahk-see·'ohn)*
to avoid	**evitar** *(eh-bee-'tahr)*
You must avoid coffee.	**Necesita evitar el café.** *(neh-seh-'see-tah eh-bee-'tahr ehl kah-'feh)*
to hear	**oír** *(oh-'eer)*
We don't hear anything.	**No oímos nada.** *(noh oh-'ee-mohs 'nah-dah)*

to pray	**rezar** *(reh-'sahr)*
They pray a lot.	**Ellos rezan mucho.**
	('eh-yohs 'reh-sahn 'moo-choh)
to relieve	**aliviar** *(ah-lee-bee-'ahr)*
I am going to relieve your pain.	**Voy a aliviarle el dolor.**
	('boh·ee ah ah-lee-bee-'ahr-leh ehl doh-'lohr)
to see	**ver** *(behr)*
I like to see the sky.	**Me gusta ver el cielo.**
	(meh 'goos-tah behr ehl see-'eh-loh)
to smell	**oler** *(oh-lehr)*
He can't smell the medicine.	**No puede oler la medicina.** *(noh 'pweh-deh oh-'lehr lah meh-dee-'see-nah)*
to spit	**escupir** *(ehs-koo-'peer)*
He spits in the bath.	**El escupe en el baño.**
	(ehl ehs-'koo-peh ehn ehl 'bah-nyoh)
to taste	**saborear** *(sah-boh-reh-'ahr)*
Do you want to taste the fruit?	**¿Quiere saborear la fruta?**
	(kee-'eh-reh sah-boh-reh-'ahr lah 'froo-tah)
to think	**pensar** *(pehn-'sahr)*
What are you thinking about?	**¿En qué piensa usted?**
	(ehn keh pee-'ehn-sah oo-'stehd)

More Verb Infinitives
Más infinitivos verbales
(mahs een-fee-nee-'tee-bohs behr-'bah-lehs)

to accumulate	**acumular** *(ah-koo-moo-'lahr)*
to assist	**atender** *(ah-tehn-'dehr)*
to avoid	**evitar** *(eh-bee-'tahr)*
to breast-feed	**lactar** *(lahk-'tahr)*
to burn	**quemar** *(keh-'mahr)*
to burp	**eructar** *(eh-rook-'tahr)*
to cause	**causar** *(kow-'sahr)*

to certify	**certificar** *(sehr-tee-fee-'kahr)*
to check	**verificar** *(beh-ree-fee-'kahr)*
to chew	**mascar** *('mahs-kahr)*
to cross	**cruzar** *(kroo-'sahr)*
to detect	**detectar** *(deh-tehk-'tahr)*
to improve	**mejorar** *(meh-hoh-'rahr)*
to itch	**picar** *(pee-'kahr)*
to lack	**faltar** *(fahl-'tahr)*
to last	**durar** *(doo-'rahr)*
to perspire	**sudar** *(soo-'dahr)*
to prevent	**prevenir** *(preh-beh-'neer)*
to proceed	**proceder** *(proh-seh-'dehr)*
to prohibit	**prohibir** *(proh-hee-'beer)*
to protect	**proteger** *(proh-teh-'hehr)*
to pull	**jalar** *(hah-'lahr)*
to pump	**bombear** *(bohm-beh-'ahr)*
to purify	**purificar** *(poo-ree-fee-'kahr)*
to push	**empujar** *(ehm-poo-'hahr)*
to readmit	**readmitir** *(reh-ahd-mee-'teer)*
to replace	**remplazar** *(rehm-plah-'sahr)*
to research	**investigar** *(een-behs-tee-'gahr)*
to resist	**resistir** *(reh-sees-'teer)*
to rinse	**enjuagar** *(ehn-hwah-'gahr)*
to scratch	**rascar** *('rahs-kahr)*
to shave	**afeitarse** *(ah-feh-ee-'tahr-seh)*
to shower	**ducharse** *(doo-'chahr-seh)*
to sneeze	**estornudar** *(ehs-tohr-noo-'dahr)*
to spit	**escupir** *(ehs-koo-'peer)*
to squeeze	**apretar** *(ah-preh-'tahr)*
to sterilize	**esterilizar** *(ehs-teh-ree-lee-'sahr)*
to swallow	**tragar** *(trah-'gahr)*
to try	**tratar** *(trah-'tahr)*
to turn oneself over	**voltearse** *(bohl-teh-'ahr-seh)*
to vaccinate	**vacunar** *(bah-koo-'nahr)*

| to weigh | **pesar** *(peh-'sahr)* |
| to worsen | **empeorar** *(ehm-peh-oh-'rahr)* |

(30) ¿CUÁNTO APRENDIÓ?

• Have you had...?   ¿Ha tenido...? *(ah teh-'nee-doh)*

fainting spells   _____

double vision   _____

loss of memory   _____

divorce   _____

visions   _____

fear   _____

money problems   _____

• **Tiene...** *(tee-'eh-neh)*
(insomnia, depression, fits)

Chapter Ten

Capítulo Diez
(kah-'pee-too-loh dee-'ehs)

Additional Health Care Services

Servicios de Salud Adicionales
(sehr-'bee-se·ohs deh sah-'lood ah-dee-see-oh-'nah-lehs)

The social worker
El trabajador social
(ehl trah-bah-hah-'dohr soh-see-'ahl)

Guadalupe is under the care of several fine physicians, and life for her today is much more bearable. She is grateful to all of them, and especially to the person who has been there from the beginning—the social worker.

When she was first brought to the nursing home, a social worker was involved. Before any decisions were made, trust had to be established between patient and medical facility. In the Hispanic culture, it is imperative that such professionals work closely with family members in order to do what's best for an ailing relative. Social workers handle a variety of cases. This is an overview of the kinds of questions they might ask the patient or family. Many of these terms were previously mentioned, so practicing should be no problem at all:

Do you need . . .?	¿**Necesita . . .?** *(neh-seh-'see-tah).*
advice	**consejo** *(kohn-'seh-hoh)*
an agency	**una agencia** *('oo-nah ah-'hehn-see·ah)*
an appointment	**una cita** *('oo-nah 'see-tah)*
assistance	**ayuda** *(ah-'yoo-dah)*
employment	**empleo** *(ehm-'pleh-oh)*
an exam	**una prueba** *('oo-nah proo-'eh-bah)*
food stamps	**cupones de alimentos**
	(koo-'poh-nehs deh ah-lee-'mehn-tohs)
insurance	**seguro** *(seh-'goo-roh)*
an interpreter	**un intérprete** *(oon een-'tehr-preh-teh)*
medication	**medicinas** *(meh-dee-'see-nahs)*
a priest	**un sacerdote** *(oon sah-sehr-'doh-teh)*
a private nurse	**una enfermera privada**
	('oo-nah ehn-fehr-'meh-rah pree-'bah-dah)
security	**la seguridad** *(lah seh-goo-ree-'dahd)*
services	**servicios** *(sehr-'bee-see-ohs)*
social security	**seguro social** *(seh-'goo-roh soh-see-'ahl)*
therapy	**terapia** *(teh-'rah-pee·ah)*
transportation	**transporte** *(trahns-'pohr-teh)*
vaccinations	**vacunas** *(bah-'koo-nahs)*
welfare	**ayuda del bienestar social**
	(ah-'you-dah dehl bee-ehn-eh-'stahr soh-see-'ahl)

If you are closely involved with a patient's well-being, these topics are designed for you. The Espinoza family was interviewed recently and this is what they wanted to talk about to the social worker:

I want to talk about . . .	**Quiero hablar de . . .** *(kee-'eh-roh ah-'blahr deh)*
child abuse	**el abuso de los niños**
	(ehl ah-'boo-soh deh lohs 'nee-nyohs)
child care	**el cuidado del niño**
	(ehl 'kwee-dah-doh dehl 'nee-nyoh
drug abuse	**el abuso de las drogas**
	(ehl ah-'boo-soh deh lahs 'droh-gahs)

family problems	**los problemas familiares**
	(lohs proh-'bleh-mahs fah-mee-lee-'ah-rehs)
financial problems	**los problemas económicos**
	(lohs proh-'bleh-mahs eh-koh-'noh-mee-kohs)
the law	**la ley** *(lah leh·ee)*
marriage	**el matrimonio** *(ehl mah-tree-'moh-nee·oh)*
sanitary conditions	**las condiciones sanitarias**
	(lahs kohn-dee-see·'oh-nehs sah-nee-'tah-ree·ahs)

(31) ¿CUÁNTO APRENDIÓ?

Finish the following sentences:

• **Necesita . . .** *(neh-seh-'see-tah)*
(welfare, child care, food stamps)

• **Quiero hablar de . . .** *(kee-'eh-roh ah-'blahr deh)*
(marriage, child abuse, family problems)

The dentist
El dentista *(ehl dehn-'tees-tah)*

Elderly patients often wear dentures and Mrs. Lupe is no exception. As a matter of fact, all of the Espinozas have had problems with their teeth and gums. Let's check up on some of the words and phrases that dentists need to use when communicating with their Spanish-speaking patients. Listen in as each family member shares a different concern:

I have a cavity.	**Tengo una carie.**
	('tehn-goh 'oo-nah 'kah-ree·eh)
I have a toothache.	**Tengo dolor de muelas.**
	('tehn-goh doh-'lohr deh 'mweh-lahs)
I need a filling.	**Necesito un empaste.**
	(neh-seh-'see-toh oon ehm-'pah-steh)

I want a cleaning.	**Quiero una limpieza.**
	(kee-'eh-roh 'oo-nah leem-pee-'eh-sah)
I would like a checkup.	**Quisiera un examen.**
	(kee-see-'eh-rah oon ehk-'sah-mehn)
My denture is bothering me.	**Mi dentadura postiza me molesta.**
	(mee dehn-'tah-'doo-rah pohs-'tee-sah meh moh-'lehs-tah)
My gums are bleeding.	**Mis encías están sangrando.**
	(mees ehn-'see-ahs eh-'stahn sahn-'grahn-doh)
This tooth hurts.	**Este diente me duele.**
	('ehn-steh dee-'ehn-teh meh 'dweh-leh)

Use all the expressions you know in Spanish to ask the patient about his or her problem. None of these words should be foreign to you:

Does it hurt to chew?
¿Le duele al masticar? *(leh 'dweh-leh ahl mah-stee-'kahr)*

Does it hurt in the front or in the back?
¿Le duele enfrente o detrás?
(leh 'dweh-leh ehn-'frehn-teh oh deh-'trahs)

Does it hurt more in the day or at night?
¿Le duele más en el día o en la noche?
(leh 'dweh-leh mahs ehn ehl 'dee-ah oh ehn lah 'noh-cheh)

Does it hurt in the upper or lower part?
¿Le duele en la parte de arriba o de abajo?
(leh 'dweh-leh ehn lah 'pahr-teh deh ah-'rree-bah oh deh ah-'bah-hoh)

Does it hurt when you drink or eat something cold or hot?
¿Le duele cuando toma o come algo frío o caliente? *(leh 'dweh-leh 'kwahn-doh 'toh-mah oh 'koh-meh 'ahl-goh 'free-oh oh kah-lee-'ehn-teh)*

To the right or to the left?
¿A la derecha o a la izquierda?
(ah lah deh-'reh-chah oh ah lah ees-kee-'ehr-dah)

Is it loose?
¿Está flojo? *(eh-'stah 'floh-hoh)*

Now discuss your findings with the patient:

You have . . .	**Tiene . . .** *(tee-'eh-neh)*
an abscess	**un absceso** *(oon ahb-'seh-soh)*
bad breath	**mal aliento** *(mahl ah-lee-'ehn-toh)*
a badly decayed tooth	**un diente muy cariado** *(oon dee-'ehn-teh 'moo-ee kah-ree-'ah-doh)*
a cavity	**una carie** *('oo-nah 'kah-ree-eh)*
gingivitis	**gingivitis** *(heen-hee-'bee-tees)*
an impaction	**una impacción** *('oo-nah eem-pahk-see-'ohn)*
an infection	**una infección** *('oo-nah een-fehk-see-'ohn)*
inflammation	**inflamación** *(een-flah-mah-see-'ohn)*
plaque	**placa** *('plah-kah)*
pyorrhea	**piorrea** *(pee-oh-'rreh-ah)*
a sore	**una ulceración** *('oo-nah ool-seh-rah-see-'ohn)*
a lot of tartar	**mucho sarro** *('moo-choh 'sah-rroh)*

And, don't forget to isolate the pain. Use **tiene problemas** *(tee-'eh-neh proh-'bleh-mahs)* for those:

You have problems with . . .	**Tiene problemas con . . .** *(tee-'eh-neh proh-'bleh-mahs kohn)*
the baby tooth	**el diente de leche** *(ehl dee-'ehn-teh de 'leh-cheh)*
the canine tooth	**el diente canino** *(ehl dee-'ehn-teh kah-'nee-noh)*
your denture	**su dentadura postiza** *(soo dehn-tah-'doo-rah poh-'stee-sah)*
the gums	**las encías** *(lahs ehn-'see-ahs)*
the jaw	**la quijada** *(lah kee-'hah-dah)*
the molar	**la muela** *(lah 'mweh-lah)*
the palate	**el paladar** *(ehl pah-lah-'dahr)*
the root	**la raíz** *(lah rah-'ees)*
the wisdom tooth	**la muela del juicio** *(lah 'mweh-lah dehl hoo-'ee-see-oh)*

Now look at what you can do with these important words! Combine them with the phrases you've mastered to communicate a variety of messages.

Discuss your recommendations with the family:

You need . . .	**Necesita . . .** *(neh-seh-'see-tah)*
anesthesia	**anestesia** *(ah-nehs-'teh-see·ah)*
another visit	**otra visita** *('oh-trah bee-'see-tah)*
braces	**frenillos** *(freh-'nee-yohs)*
a bridge	**un puente** *(oon 'pwehn-teh)*
a checkup	**un reconocimiento dental**
	(oon reh-koh-noh-see-mee-'ehn-toh dehn-'tahl)
a crown	**una corona** *('oo-nah koh-'roh-nah)*
dentures	**dentaduras postizas**
	(dehn-tah-'doo-rahs pohs-'tee-sahs)
an extraction	**una extracción**
	('oo-nah ehks-trahk-see·'ohn)
an inlay	**una incrustación**
	('oo-nah een-kroos-tah-see·'ohn)
a plate	**una plancha** *('oo-nah 'plahn-chah)*
root canal work	**un tratamiento del nervio**
	(oon trah-tah-mee-'ehn-toh dehl 'nehr-bee·oh)
periodontal surgery	**cirugía periodontal**
	(see-roo-'hee-ah peh-ree·oh-dohn-'tahl)
treatment	**tratamiento** *(trah-tah-mee-'ehn-toh)*
X rays	**rayos equis** *(rah-'yohs 'eh-kees)*

X rays indicate that there is plenty of work to be done. Tell the patient about the following dental procedures. Start with:

I'm going to . . .	**Voy a . . .** *('boh·ee ah)*
clean it	**limpiarlo** *(leem-pee-'ahr-loh)*
change it	**cambiarlo** *(kahm-bee-'ahr-loh)*
cure it	**curarlo** *(koo-'rahr-loh)*
fill it	**empastarlo** *(ehm-pahs-'tahr-loh)*
remove it	**sacarlo** *(sah-'kahr-loh)*

This selection of verbs describes the job in full detail:

I need...	Necesito... *(neh-seh-'see-toh)*
to cut	**cortar** *(kohr-'tahr)*
to drill	**perforar** *(pehr-foh-'rahr)*
to extract	**extraer** *(ehks-trah-'ehr)*
to file	**limar** *(lee-'mahr)*
to fill	**empastar** *(ehm-pah-'stahr)*
to make an impression	**hacer una impresión**
	(ah-'sehr 'oo-nah eem-preh-see-'ohn)
to numb	**adormecer** *(ah-dohr-meh-'sehr)*
to scrape	**raspar** *(rahs-'pahr)*
to straighten	**enderezar** *(ehn-deh-reh-'sahr)*
to use gas	**usar gas** *(oo-'sahr gahs)*
to use novocaine	**usar novocaína**
	(oo-'sahr noh-boh-kah-'ee-nah)
to wire	**poner alambre** *(poh-'nehr ah-'lahm-breh)*

If you need any assistance, call on the following specialists:

I'm going to speak with...	Voy a hablar con...
	('boh-ee ah ah-'blahr kohn)
endodontist	**el endodontista**
	(ehl ehn-doh-dohn-'tees-tah)
hygienist	**el higienista** *(ehl ee-hee-eh-'nees-tah)*
orthodontist	**el ortodoncista** *(ehl ohr-toh-dohn-'sees-tah)*
periodontist	**el periodontista**
	(ehl peh-ree-oh-dohn-'tees-tah)
surgeon	**el cirujano** *(ehl see-roo-'hah-noh)*

Here are some special commands you should become familiar with:

Bite.	**Muerda.** *('mwehr-dah)*
Brush.	**Cepíllese.** *(seh-'pee-yeh-seh)*
Gargle.	**Haga gárgaras.** *('ah-gah 'gahr-gah-rahs)*
Open your mouth.	**Abra la boca.** *('ah-brah lah 'boh-kah)*

Rinse.	**Enjuáguese.** *(ehn-'hwah-geh-seh)*
Spit.	**Escupa.** *(ehs-'koo-pah)*

Additional vocabulary may be required, so use this command technique to practice Spanish with coworkers. First review the names for each item. Then, instead of using English, ask for each one in your new language!

Bring . . .	**Traiga** . . . *('trah·ee-gah)*
clasp	**el gancho** *(ehl 'gahn-choh)*
cuspidor	**la escupidera** *(lah ehs-koo-pee-'deh-rah)*
dental floss	**el hilo dental** *(ehl 'ee-loh dehn-'tahl)*
drill	**el taladro** *(ehl tah-'lah-droh)*
file	**la lima** *(lah 'lee-mah)*
forceps	**las tenazas** *(lahs teh-'nah-sahs)*
headrest	**el apoyo** *(ehl ah-'poh-yoh)*
mirror	**el espejo** *(ehl ehs-'peh-hoh)*
mold	**el molde** *(ehl 'mohl-deh)*
toothbrush	**el cepillo de dientes**
	(ehl seh-'pee-yoh deh dee-'ehn-tehs)
toothpaste	**la pasta de dientes**
	(lah 'pah-stah deh dee-'ehn-tehs)
tweezers	**las pinzas** *(lahs 'peen-sahs)*
water pick	**el limpiador** *(ehl leem-pee-ah-'dohr)*

When the dental work is complete and you need to describe the dentures or fillings, use **es:**

It's . . .	**Es** . . . *(ehs)*
artificial	**artificial** *(ahr-tee-fee-see-'ahl)*
cement	**cemento** *(seh-'mehn-toh)*
enamel	**esmalte** *(ehs-'mahl-teh)*
false	**postiza** *(poh-'stee-sah)*
fixed	**fija** *('fee-hah)*
full	**completa** *(kohm-'pleh-tah)*
gold	**oro** *('oh-roh)*
partial	**parcial** *(pahr-see-'ahl)*

porcelain **porcelana** *(pohr-seh-'lah-nah)*
removable **sacable** *(sah-'kah-bleh)*
silver **plata** *('plah-tah)*

The optometrist

El optometrista *(ehl ohp-toh-meh-'trees-tah)*

Many patients require the services of an optometrist. Since qualified medical treatment includes the continuous exchange of valuable information, take a moment to focus on what's going on here. These are extremely helpful because they only require a **sí** or **no** answer. And, you should recognize all the vocabulary:

Are your glasses broken?
¿Están rotos los anteojos? *(eh-'stahn 'roh-tohs lohs ahn-teh-'oh-hohs)*

Can you read this?
¿Puede leer esto? *('pweh-deh leh-'ehr 'eh-stoh)*

Can you see very well?
¿Puede ver bien? *('pweh-deh behr 'bee·ehn)*

Do you have blurred vision?
¿Tiene visión borrosa? *(tee-'eh-neh bee-see·'ohn boh-'rroh-sah)*

Do you have difficulty reading?
¿Tiene dificultad al leer? *(tee-'eh-neh dee-fee-kool-'tahd ahl leh-'ehr)*

Do you have lots of headaches?
¿Tiene muchos dolores de cabeza?
(tee-'eh-neh 'moo-chohs doh-'loh-rehs deh kah-'beh-sah)

Do you have something in your eye?
¿Tiene algo en el ojo? *(tee-'eh-neh 'ahl-goh ehn ehl 'oh-hoh)*

Do you see double?
¿Ve doble? *(beh 'doh-bleh)*

Do you wear glasses or contact lenses?
¿Usa anteojos o lentes de contacto?
('oo-sah ahn-teh-'oh-hohs oh 'lehn-tehs deh kohn-'tahk-toh)

Mrs. Lupe is losing her sight rapidly, and she needs frequent examinations. The following expressions will help you communicate with her. Open with a few commands and then use familiar patterns to discuss your patient's unique needs. There's lots of new vocabulary, so choose only a few key phrases at a time:

Cover your eye.	**Tape el ojo.** *('tah-peh ehl 'oh-hoh)*
Look here.	**Mire aquí.** *('mee-reh ah-'kee)*
Look up and down.	**Mire hacia arriba y abajo.**
	('mee-reh 'ah-see·ah ah-'rree-bah ee ah-'bah-hoh)
Read this.	**Lea esto.** *('leh-ah 'eh-stoh)*

As you carry out the examination, these questions will be helpful:

Is it . . . ?	**¿Está . . . ?** *(eh-'stah)*
better	**mejor** *(meh-'hohr)*
clear	**claro** *('klah-roh)*
cloudy	**borroso** *(boh-'rroh-soh)*
dark	**oscuro** *(oh-'skoo-roh)*
double	**doble** *('doh-bleh)*
worse	**peor** *(peh-'ohr)*

To discuss her vision problems with her and her family, say:

She needs . . .	**Necesita . . .** *(neh-seh-'see-tah)*
bifocals	**bifocales** *(bee-foh-'kah-lehs)*
a cataract operation	**una operación de cataratas**
	('oo-nah oh-peh-rah-see·'ohn deh kah-tah-'rah-tahs)
disinfectant	**desinfectante** *(deh-seen-fehk-'tahn-teh)*
eye drops	**gotas para los ojos**
	('goh-tahs 'pah-rah lohs 'oh-hohs)
laser surgery	**cirugía con láser** *(see-roo-'hee-ah kohn 'lah-sehr)*
new frames	**marcos nuevos** *('mahr-kohs noo-'eh-bohs)*
new lenses	**lentes nuevos** *('lehn-tehs noo-'eh-bohs)*
a prescription	**una receta** *('oo-nah reh-'seh-tah)*
reading glasses	**lentes para leer** *('lehn-tehs 'pah-rah leh-'ehr)*

| saline solution | **solución salina** *(soh-loo-see-'ohn sah-'lee-nah)* |
| two pair | **dos pares** *(dohs 'pah-rehs)* |

She has . . .	**Tiene . . .** *(tee-'eh-neh)*
astigmatism	**astigmatismo** *(ahs-teeg-mah-'tees-moh)*
cataracts	**cataratas** *(kah-tah-'rah-tahs)*
double vision	**doble visión** *('doh-bleh bee-see·'ohn)*
dyslexia	**dislexia** *(dees-'lehk-see-ah)*
glaucoma	**glaucoma** *(glow-'koh mah)*

She is . . .	**Es . . .** *(ehs)*
blind	**ciega** *(see-'eh-gah)*
color-blind	**daltónica** *(dahl-'toh-nee-kah)*
farsighted	**présbita** *('prehs-bee-tah)*
nearsighted	**miope** *(mee-'oh-peh)*

(32) ¿CUÁNTO APRENDIÓ?

- Fill in the following:

  Necesita . . . *(neh-seh-'see-tah)*
  (a crown, dentures, braces)

  Tiene . . . *(tee-'eh-neh)*
  (bad breath, tartar, cavities, gum problems)

  Voy a . . . *('boh·ee ah)*
  (remove the root, drill, straighten the molars)

  Es . . . *(ehs)*
  (false, made of gold, removable, enamel)

  Translate: Rinse and spit!
    Look here.

- Fill in the following:

  Necesita . . . *(neh-seh-'see-tah)*
  (new frames, an optometrist, contact lenses)

  Translate: Lupe is farsighted and has astigmatism.

The Discharge
Dar de Alta
(dahr deh 'ahl-tah)

At the time of being discharged from the hospital, all members of the Espinoza family must follow similar procedures. The following expressions should help you with some of them.

Before leaving you must go to Administration.
Antes de irse debe ir a la Administración
> *('ahn-tehs deh 'eer-teh 'deh-beh eer ah lah ahd-mee-nee-strah-see·'ohn)*

You must pay what the insurance does not cover.
Usted debe pagar lo que el seguro no cubre.
> *(oo-'stehd 'deh-beh pah-'gahr loh keh ehl seh-'goo-roh noh 'koo-breh)*

They will send the bill to your home.
Le enviarán la cuenta a su casa.
> *(leh ehn-bee-ah-'rahn lah 'kwehn-tah ah soo 'kah-sah)*

The telephone and TV rental must be paid at once.
El arriendo del teléfono y televisor debe ser pagado de inmediato.
> *(ehl ah-rree-'ehn-doh dehl teh-'leh-foh-noh ee teh-leh-bee-'sohr 'deh-beh sehr pah-'gah-doh deh een-meh-dee-'ah-toh)*

You must talk to the social worker.
Debe hablar con el trabajador social.
> *('deh-beh ah-blahr kohn ehl trah-bah-hah-'dohr soh-see-'ahl)*

You should talk to the priest.

Debiera hablar con el sacerdote.

('deh-bee-'eh-rah ah-'blahr kohn ehl sah-sehr-'doh-teh)

Take these medicines with you.

Tome estas medicinas con usted.

('toh-meh 'ehs-tahs meh-dee-'see-nahs kohn oo-'stehd)

Here is the prescription to buy more medication.

Aquí tiene la receta para comprar más medicamentos.

(ah-'kee tee-'eh-neh lah reh-'seh-tah 'pah-rah kohm-'prahr mahs meh-dee-kah-'mehn-tohs)

A nurse will come every _____ days to your home.

Una enfermera vendrá cada _____ días a su casa.

('oo-nah ehn-fehr-'meh-rah vehn-'drah 'kah-dah _____ 'dee-ahs ah soo 'kah-sah)

Do not forget to return every _____ weeks (_____ days).

No olvide volver cada _____ semanas (_____ días).

(noh ohl-'bee-deh bohl-'behr 'kah-dah _____ seh-'mah-nahs (_____ 'dee-ahs)

Here are the names and telephone numbers of the physicians who took care of you.

Aquí están los nombres y teléfonos de los médicos que lo atendieron. *(ah-'kee eh-'stahn lohs 'nohm-brehs ee teh-'leh-foh-nohs deh lohs 'meh-dee-kohs keh loh ah-tehn-dee-'eh-rohn)*

Back to the city
De vuelta en la ciudad
(de 'bwehl-tah ehn lah see-oo-'dahd)

Aside from strict health care vocabulary, there are urban and rural words that you must know in order to communicate. Learn the following nouns and verify your progress by creating sentences with them.

ambulance	**la ambulancia**	*(lah ahm-boo-'lahn-see-ah)*
bicycle	**la bicicleta**	*(lah bee-see-'kleh-tah)*

boat	**el barco** *(ehl 'bahr-koh)*
bridge	**el puente** *(ehl 'pwehn-teh)*
bus	**el autobús** *(ehl ow-toh-'boos)*
car	**el carro** *(ehl 'kah-rroh)*
city block	**la cuadra** *(lah 'kwah-drah)*
corner	**la esquina** *(lah ehs-'kee-nah)*
curb	**la orilla** *(lah oh-'ree-yah)*
grass	**el césped** *(ehl 'sehs-pehd)*
helicopter	**el helicóptero** *(ehl eh-lee-'kohp-teh-roh)*
highway	**la carretera** *(lah kah-rreh-'teh-rah)*
lane	**el carril** *(ehl kah-'rreel)*
motorcycle	**la motocicleta** *(lah moh-toh-see-'kleh-tah)*
plane	**el avión** *(ehl ah-bee-'ohn)*
road	**el camino** *(ehl kah-'mee-noh)*
sidewalk	**la acera** *(lah ah-'seh-rah)*
street	**la calle** *(lah 'kah-yeh)*
subway	**el metro** *(ehl 'meh-troh)*
train	**el tren** *(ehl trehn)*
truck	**el camión** *(ehl kah-mee-'ohn)*

Outside the city
Fuera de la ciudad
('fweh-rah deh lah see-oo-'dahd)

For those incidents outside city limits, you may need these terms:

beach	**la playa** *(lah 'plah-yah)*
countryside	**el campo** *(ehl 'kahm-poh)*
desert	**el desierto** *(ehl deh-see-'ehr-toh)*
dirt	**la tierra** *(lah tee-'eh-rrah)*
dust	**el polvo** *(ehl 'pohl-boh)*
forest	**el bosque** *(ehl 'bohs-keh)*
jungle	**la selva** *(lah 'sehl-bah)*
lake	**el lago** *(ehl 'lah-goh)*

mountains	**las montañas** *(lahs mohn-'tah-nyahs)*
mud	**el lodo** *(ehl 'loh-doh)*
park	**el parque** *(ehl 'pahr-keh)*
river	**el río** *(ehl 'ree-oh)*
rock	**la piedra** *(lah pee-'eh-drah)*
sand	**la arena** *(lah ah-'reh-nah)*
sea	**el mar** *(ehl mahr)*

Good-bye everyone!
¡Adiós a todos!
(ah-dee-'ohs ah 'toh-dohs)

All of the Espinozas have been treated and released. Thanks to the hospital employees who tried out their new Spanish skills, everyone in the family is delighted with the facility. Juan and María have already told their friends about the care they received, and have praised the physicians, nurses, and other staff members.

The administration—**la administración**—is pleased. The use of a few Spanish words and phrases by hospital staff members has increased hospital admissions. The Hispanic community feels comfortable here. They have found a facility where they can truly communicate their health care needs:

Are you satisfied?   **¿Está satisfecho?** *(eh-'stah sah-tees-'feh-choh)*

Several of the administrators are determined to learn Spanish too, so they have decided to give the Espinozas a followup phone call. Follow along as one of the CEOs give his new skills a try. No doubt all of the answers to these questions will be **"sí."**

Are the employees good?
¿Son buenos los empleados?
  (sohn boo-'eh-nohs lohs ehm-pleh-'ah-dohs)

Are you satisfied with the care given?
¿Está satisfecho con el cuidado recibido?
  (eh-'stah sah-tees'feh-choh kohn ehl kwee-'dah-doh reh-see-'bee-doh)

Did you have any suggestions or criticism?

¿Tiene cualquier sugerencia o crítica?

(tee-'eh-neh kwahl-kee-'ehr soo-heh-'rehn-see·ah oh 'kree-tee-kah)

Did you like the food?

¿Le gustó la comida? *(leh goo-'stoh lah koh-'mee-dah)*

If necessary, would you return to this hospital?

Si fuese necesario, ¿volvería a este hospital?

(see 'fweh-seh neh-seh-'sah-ree·oh, bohl-beh-'ree-ah ah 'eh-steh ohs-pee-'tahl)

Was everything very clean?

¿Fue todo muy limpio? *(foo-'eh 'toh-doh 'moo·ee 'leem-pee·oh)*

(33) ¿Cuánto Aprendió?

Read aloud and translate these final comments.

Soy de la administración del hospital.

('soh·ee deh lah ahd-mee-nees-trah-see·'ohn dehl ohs-pee-'tahl)

Llame a la oficina si tiene algún problema.

('yah-meh ah lah oh-fee-'see-nah see tee-'eh-neh ahl-'goon proh-'bleh-mah)

Muchas gracias, buena suerte y adiós.

('moo-chahs 'grah-see·ahs, 'bweh-nah 'swehr-teh ee ah-dee-'ohs)

Now that you've finished reading this book, are you ready to put all your skills into practice? Why don't you start today! Good-bye and good luck! **¡Adios y buena suerte!**

Answers to
¿Cuánto Aprendió?

1 **Muy bien.** *('moo-ee bee-'ehn)*
   ¡De nada! *(deh 'nah-dah)*
   ¡Pase! *('pah-seh)*

2 **doscientos cuartos** *(dohs-see-'ehn-tohs 'kwahr-tohs)*
   ochenta mesas *(oh-'chehn-tah 'meh-sahs)*
   tres enfermeros *(trehs ehn-fehr-'meh-rohs)*
   setenta y cinco libros *(seh-'tehn-tah ee 'seen-koh 'lee-brohs)*
   diez pisos *(dee-'ehs 'pee-sohs)*
   trescientos sesenta y un bebés *(trehs-see-'ehn-tohs seh-'sehn-tah ee oon beh-'behs)*

3 A lot of pain
   Three forms
   Injury and sickness
   Two appointments
   More help

4 **¿Qué pasa? Nada.**
   ¿Cómo está? Muy bien.
   ¿Quién es la enfermera? Kathy.
   ¿Cuál color? Verde.
   ¿Cuántos visitantes? Seis.
   ¿Cuánta medicina? Mucha.

5 **¿Quiénes son? Somos enfermeros.**
   ¿Dónde está? Estoy en el cuarto.

¿Qué medicinas son blancas? Las aspirinas.

¿Cuánta agua hay el baño? Mucha.

¿Qué comida es buena? Pizza.

¿Cuántas camas hay en el hospital? Doscientas cincuenta.

6   I am Robert. I am in the hospital. I have a pain in my stomach. There is a nurse in the room. She has the white medicine.

7   My head hurts.   They are arms.

Do your feet hurt?   The nose is on the face.

What hurts you?   There are many teeth in the mouth.

My eyes don't hurt.   He doesn't have ten fingers.

8   **su** *(soo)*

su *(soo)*

nuestro *(noo-'ehs-troh)*

9   She is tall and he is short.

The children are asleep.

We are not very rich.

The doctor is old and thin.

Where is the hot water?

tan enferma como su hermano *(tahn ehn-'fehr-mah 'koh-moh soo ehr-'mah-noh)*

enferma *(ehn-'fehr-mah)*

más enferma *(mahs ehn-'fehr-mah)*

gordo *('gohr-doh)*

débil *('deh-beel)*

joven *('hoh-behn)*

mayores *(mah-'yoh-rehs)*

bonitas *(boh-'nee-tahs)*

delgadas *(dehl-'gah-dahs)*

10 I need an appointment.

Do you need medicine?

Margaret and I need beds.

11 **primer nombre** *(pree-'mehr 'nohm-breh)*, **apellido paterno** *(ah-peh-'yee-doh pah-'tehr-noh)*, **dirección** *(dee-rehk-see-'ohn)*

es el doctor *(ehs ehl dohk-'tohr)*, **está enfermo** *(eh-'stah ehn-'fehr-moh)*

seguro médico *(seh-'goo-roh 'meh-dee-koh)*, **el recibo** *(ehl reh-'see-boh)*

12 What kind of insurance do you have?

What is your employer's address?

You need accident insurance.

13 **en frente del salón** *(ehn 'frehn-teh dehl sah-'lohn)*

allí *(ah-'yee)*

afuera *(ah-foo-'eh-rah)*

adelante *(ah-deh-'lahn-teh)*

Go up the elevator and turn right.

14 **miércoles**

sábado

abril

agosto

15 **la fuente de agua** *(lah foo-'ehn-teh deh 'ah-gwah)*

el buzón *(ehl boo-'sohn)*

las escaleras *(lahs ehs-kah-'leh-rahs)*

la sala de emergencia *(lah 'sah-lah deh eh-mehr-'hehn-see-ah)*

el pediatra *(ehl peh-dee-'ah-trah)*

el ginecólogo *(ehl hee-neh-'koh-loh-goh)*

el terapeuta *(ehl teh-rah-'peh-oo-tah)*

16   convulsions
nausea
vomiting
dilated pupils
reduced pupils
temperature
nervousness
depression
tension
paranoid illusions
hallucinations
aggressiveness
confusion
respiratory difficulty
irritability
insomnia

17   a week ago
between three and four
the following day
last year
next month
until tomorrow
within two hours

18   What did you eat?
Did you take medicine?
Did you smoke?
Did you get sick?
Did you have problems?

19   **ampollas** *(ahm-'poh-yahs)*, **hipo** *('ee-poh)*, **flema** *('fleh-mah)*
la enfermera *(lah ehn-fehr-'meh-rah)*, **levantarse** *(leh-bahn-'tahr-seh)*,
sentarse *(sehn-'tahr-seh)*

¿Duerme ella?

¿Llora ella?

¿Camina ella?

20 **paperas** *(pah-'peh-rahs)*

enfermedad del corazón *(ehn-fehr-meh-'dahd dehl koh-rah-'sohn)*

enfermedades graves *(ehn-fehr-meh-'dah-dehs 'grah-behs)*

tosferina *(tohs-feh-'ree-nah)*

21 • **tomó la medicina** *(toh-'moh lah meh-dee-'see-nah)*, **tuvo un accidente** *('too-boh oon ahk-see-'dehn-teh)*, **habló con el doctor** *(ah-'bloh kohn ehl dohk-'tohr)*

• **el polen** *(ehl 'poh-lehn)*, **las picaduras de insectos** *(lahs pee-kah-'doo-rahs deh een-'sehk-tohs)*, **gatos** *('gah-tohs)*

• **un dolor de cabeza** *(oon doh-'lohr deh kah-'beh-sah)*, **un resfrío** *(oon rehs-'free-oh)*, **problemas con este tiempo** *(proh-'bleh-mahs kohn 'eh-steh tee-'ehm-poh)*

• **tomar su presión arterial** *(toh-'mahr soo preh-see-'ohn ahr-teh-ree-'ahl)*, **mover su cabeza** *(moh-'behr soo kah-'beh-sah)*

• **Está nublado.** *(eh-'stah noo-'blah-doh)*

Hace sol. *('ah-seh sohl)*

Está nevando. *(es 'stah neh 'bahn doh)*

• **¡Tome la medicina!** *('toh-meh lah meh-dee-'see-nah)*

¡Estire su pierna! *(ehs-'tee-reh soo pee-'ehr-nah)*

¡Escriba su nombre! *(ehs-'kree-bah soo 'nohm-breh)*

¡Describa el dolor! *(dehs-'kree-bah ehl doh-'lohr)*

¡Siéntese en la cama! *(see-'ehn-teh-seh ehn lah 'kah-mah)*

22 **la aspirina** *(lah ahs-pee-'ree-nah)*

las tijeras *(lahs tee-'heh-rahs)*

las flores *(lahs 'floh-rehs)*

las tarjetas de saludo *(lahs tahr-'heh-tahs deh sah-'loo-doh)*

un peine *(oon 'peh-ee-neh)*

23 • una **muestra** de **sangre** *(oo-nah moo-'ehs-trah deh 'sahn-greh)*, un **examen** *(oon ehk-'sah-mehn)*, más **líquidos** *(mahs 'lee-kee-dohs)*

• leer la etiqueta *(leh-'ehr lah eh-tee-'keh-tah)*, tomar la mitad *(toh-'mahr lah mee-'tahd)*

• Tome las píldoras con agua. *('toh-meh lahs 'peel-doh-rahs kohn 'ah-gwah)*

Tome dos cucharadas tres veces cada día. *('toh-meh dohs koo-chah-'rah-dahs trehs 'beh-sehs 'kah-dah 'dee-ah)*

Necesita bañarse en agua caliente. *(neh-seh-'see-tah bahn-'yahr-seh ehn 'ag-wah kah-lee-'ehn-teh)*

Vamos a bajar la dosis. *('bah-mohs ah bah-'hahr lah 'doh-sees)*

24 los **guantes** *(lohs 'gwahn-tehs)*, la **camisa** *(lah kah-'mee-sah)*, la **ropa interior** *(lah 'roh-pah een-teh-ree-'ohr)*, los **aretes** *(lohs ah-'reh-tehs)*, el **cinturón** *(ehl seen-too-'rohn)*, los **zapatos** *(lohs sah-'pah-tohs)*, el **tubo** *(ehl 'too-boh)*, la **dieta** *(lah dee-'eh-tah)*

controlar la luz *(kohn-troh-'lahr lah loos)*, tener una cicatriz *(teh-'nehr 'oo-nah see-kah-'trees)*, prender la televisión *(prehn-'dehr lah teh-leh-bee-see-'ohn)*, vivir *(bee-'beer)*, llamar a su familia *(yah-'mahr ah soo fah-'mee-lee-ah)*, sacarle las puntadas *(sah-'kahr-leh lahs poon-'tah-dahs)*

25 • el **gabinete** *(ehl gah-bee-'neh-teh)*, el **espejo** *(ehl ehs-'peh-hoh)*, la **bandeja** *(lah bahn-'deh-hah)*

• el plato *(ehl 'plah-toh)*, el ventilador *(ehl behn-tee-lah-'dohr)*, el jabón *(ehl hah-'bohn)*, la cuchara *(lah koo-'chah-rah)*, la frazada *(lah frah-'sah-dah)*

• una ducha *('oo-nah 'doo-chah)*, una siesta *('oo-nah see-'ehs-tah)*

26 • la **mantequilla** *(lah mahn-teh-'kee-yah)*, la **sal** *(lah sahl)*, el **dulce** *(ehl 'dool-seh)*, el **queso** *(ehl 'keh-soh)*, el **bistec** *(ehl bees-'tehk)*, las **galletas** *(lahs gah-'yeh-tahs)*

• el té *(ehl teh)*, la leche *(lah 'leh-cheh)*, el jugo *(ehl 'hoo-goh)*

• darle medicamentos *('dahr-leh meh-dee-kah-'mehn-tohs)*

explicar el equipo *(ehks-plee-'kahr ehl eh-'kee-poh)*

sacar un poco de sangre *(sah-'kahr oon 'poh-koh deh 'sahn-greh)*

escuchar su pecho *(ehs-koo-'chahr soo 'peh-choh)*

27 • anorexia, botulism, bulimia, colitis

milk of magnesia, suppositories, mineral oil

- **diarrea** *(dee-ahr-'reh-ah)*, **un enema de bario** *(oon eh-'neh-mah deh 'bah-ree-oh)*, **ardor en el estómago** *(ahr-'dohr ehn ehl ehs-'toh-mah-goh)*, **bebidas alcohólicas** *(beh-'bee-dahs ahl-koh-'oh-lee-kahs)*

- **café descafeinado** *(kah-'feh dehs-kah-feh-ee-'nah-doh)*, **perder treinta libras** *(pehr-'dehr 'treh-een-tah 'leeb-rahs)*, **comer desayuno** *(koh-'mehr deh-sah-'yoo-noh)*, **una dieta limitada** *('oo-nah dee-'eh-tah lee-mee-'tah-dah)* **un laxante** *(oon lahk-'sahn-teh)*

28 **el mamograma**—mammogram

la tomografía computarizada—CT

la prueba del sistema gastrointestinal—upper GI

la cistoscopía—cistoscopy

el electrocardiograma—ECG

29 - **cuidado ambulatorio** *(kwee-'dah-doh ahm-boo-lah-'toh-ree-oh)*, **el baño con agua circulante** *(ehl 'bahn-yoh kohn 'ah-gwah seer-koo-'lahn-teh)*, **ejercicios** *(eh-hehr-'see-see-ohs)*

- **la columna vertebral** *(lah koh-'loom-nah behr-teh-'brahl)*, **la coyuntura** *(lah koh-yoon-'too rah)*, **el pene** *(ehl 'peh-neh)*

- **problemas menstruales** *(proh-'bleh-mahs mehns-troo-'ah-lehs)*, **un examen del semen** *(oon ehk-'sah-mehn dehl 'seh-mehn)*, **una enfermedad venérea** *('oo-nah ehn-fehr-meh-'dahd beh-'neh-reh-ah)*, **glándulas hinchadas** *('glahn-doo-lahs een-'chah-dahs)*, **problemas con sus ovarios** *(proh-'bleh-mahs kohn soos oh-'bah-ree-ohs)*

30 - **desmayos** *(dehs-'mah-yohs)*

doble visión *('doh-bleh bee-see-'ohn)*

falta de memoria *('fahl-tah deh meh-'moh-ree-ah)*

divorcio *(dee-'bohr-see-oh)*

visiones *(bee see-'oh-nehs)*

miedo *(mee-'eh-doh)*

problemas económicos *(proh-'bleh-mahs eh-koh-'noh-mee-kohs)*

- **insomnio** *(een-'sohm-nee-oh)*, **depresión** *(deh-preh-see-'ohn)*, **ataques** *(ah-'tah-kehs)*

31 • **ayuda del bienestar social** *(ah-'yoo-dah dehl bee-eh-nehs-'tahr soh-see-'ahl)*, el **cuidado del niño** *(ehl 'kwee-dah-doh dehl 'neen-yoh)*, **cupones de alimentos** *(koo-'poh-nehs deh ah-lee-'mehn-tohs)*

• el **matrimonio** *(ehl mah-tree-'moh-nee-oh)*, el **abuso de menores** *(ehl ah-'boo-soh deh meh-'noh-rehs)*, los **problemas familiares** *(lohs proh-'bleh-mahs fah-mee-lee-'ah-rehs)*

32 • **una corona** *('oo-nah koh-'roh-nah)*, **dentaduras postizas** *(dehn-tah-'doo-rahs pohs-'tee-sahs)*, **frenillos** *(freh-'nee-yohs)*

• **mal aliento** *(mahl ah-lee-'ehn-toh)*, **sarro** *('sahr-roh)*, **caries** *('kah-ree-ehs)*, **problemas con las encías** *(proh-'bleh-mahs kohn lahs ehn-'see-ahs)*

• **sacar la raíz** *(sah-'kahr lah rah-'ees)*, **perforar** *(pehr-foh-'rahr)*, **enderezar las muelas** *(ehn-deh-reh-'sahr lahs moo-'eh-lahs)*

• **falso** *(fahl-soh)*, **hecho de oro** *('eh-choh deh 'oh-roh)*, **sacable** *(sah-'kah-bleh)*, **esmalte** *(ehs-'mahl-teh)*

• **¡Enjuáguese y escupa!** *(ehn-'hwah-geh-seh ee ehs-'koo-pah)*

Mire aquí. *('mee-reh ah-'kee)*

• **marcos nuevos** *('mahr-kohs noo-'eh-bohs)*, **un optometrista** *(oon ohp-toh-meh-'trees-tah)*, **lentes de contacto** *('lehn-tehs deh kohn-'tahk-toh)*

• **Lupe es présbita y tiene astigmatismo.** *('loo-peh ehs 'prehs-bee-tah ee tee-'eh-neh ahs-teeg-mah-'tees-moh)*

33 I'm from the hospital administration.

Call the office if you have a problem.

Thanks a lot, good luck, and good-bye.

Cognate Words

Thousands of health care vocabulary words are similar in their forms and meanings in both Spanish and English. Notice these common patterns:

appendicitis	**apendicitis** *(ah-pehn-dee-'see-tees)*
arthritis	**artritis** *(ahr-'tree-tees)*
bronchitis	**bronquitis** *(brohn-'kee-tees)*
laryngitis	**laringitis** *(lah-reen-'hee-tees)*
hepatitis	**hepatitis** *(eh-pah-'tee-tees)*
analysis	**análisis** *(ah-'nah-lee-sees)*
syphilis	**sífilis** *('see-fee-lees)*
psychosis	**psicosis** *(see-'koh-sees)*
sclerosis	**esclerosis** *(ehs kleh-'roh-sees)*
tuberculosis	**tuberculosis** *(too-behr-koo-'loh-sees)*
flexibility	**flexibilidad** *(flehk-see-bee-lee-'dahd)*
mobility	**movilidad** *(moh bee-lee-'dahd)*
maternity	**maternidad** *(mah-tehr-nee-'dahd)*
sterility	**esterilidad** *(ehs-teh-ree-lee-'dahd)*
abnormality	**anormalidad** *(ah-nohr-mah-lee-'dahd)*
possible	**posible** *(poh-'seeb-leh)*
controllable	**controlable** *(kohn-troh-'lahb-leh)*
unstable	**inestable** *(een-ehs-'tahb-leh)*
responsible	**responsable** *(rehs-pohn-'sahb-leh)*
operable	**operable** *(oh-peh-'rahb-leh)*

genetic	**genético** *(heh-'neh-tee-koh)*
antiseptic	**antiséptico** *(ahn-tee-'sehp-tee-koh)*
diabetic	**diabético** *(dee-ah-'beh-tee-koh)*
diagnostic	**diagnóstico** *(dee-ah-'gnohs-tee-koh)*
accident	**accidente** *(ahk-see-'dehn-teh)*
transparent	**transparente** *(trahns-pah-'rehn-teh)*
persistent	**persitente** *(pehr-sees-'tehn-teh)*
urgent	**urgente** *(oor-'hehn-teh)*
patient	**paciente** *(pah-see-'ehn-teh)*
cancerous	**canceroso** *(kahn-seh-'roh-soh)*
contagious	**contagioso** *(kohn-tah-ee-'oh-soh)*
intravenous	**intravenoso** *(een-trah-beh-'noh-soh)*
nervous	**nervioso** *(nehr-bee-'oh-soh)*
mucous	**mucoso** *(moo-'koh-soh)*
alcoholism	**alcoholismo** *(ahl-koh-oh-'lees-moh)*
aneurysm	**aneurismo** *(ah-neh-oo-'rees-moh)*
astigmatism	**astigmatismo** *(ahs-teeg-mah-'tees-moh)*
metabolism	**metabolismo** *(meh-tah-boh-'lees-moh)*
rheumatism	**reumatismo** *(reh-oo-mah-'tees-moh)*
radiologist	**radiólogo** *(rah-dee-'oh-loh-goh)*
dermatologist	**dermatólogo** *(dehr-mah-'toh-loh-goh)*
gynecologist	**ginecólogo** *(hee-neh-'koh-loh-goh)*
ophthalmologist	**oftalmólogo** *(ohf-tahl-'moh-loh-goh)*
proctologist	**proctólogo** *(prohk-'toh-loh-goh)*
allergy	**alergia** *(ah-'lehr-hee-ah)*
atrophy	**atrofia** *(ah-'troh-fee-ah)*
autopsy	**autopsia** *(ow-'tohp-see-ah)*
biopsy	**biopsia** *(bee-'ohp-see-ah)*
epilepsy	**epilepsia** *(eh-pee-'lehp-see-ah)*

respiratory	**respiratorio** *(rehs-pee-rah-'toh-ree-oh)*
ambulatory	**ambulatorio** *(ahm-boo-lah-'toh-ree-oh)*
laboratory	**laboratorio** *(lah-boh-rah-'toh-ree-oh)*
ovary	**ovario** *(oh-'bah-ree-oh)*
sanitary	**sanitario** *(sah-nee-'tah-ree-oh)*

medicine	**medicina** *(meh-dee-'see-nah)*
toxin	**toxina** *(tohk-'see-nah)*
penicillin	**penicilina** *(peh-nee-see-'lee-nah)*
urine	**orina** *(oh-'ree-nah)*
aspirin	**aspirina** *(ahs-pee-'ree-nah)*

biology	**biología** *(bee-oh-loh-'hee-ah)*
radiology	**radiología** *(rah-dee-oh-loh-'hee-ah)*
psychology	**psicología** *(see-koh-loh-'hee-ah)*
cardiology	**cardiología** *(kahr-dee-oh-loh-'hee-ah)*
urology	**urología** *(oo-roh-loh-'hee-ah)*

coagulation	**coagulación** *(koh-ah-goo-lah-see-'ohn)*
rehabilitation	**rehabilitación** *(reh-ah-bee-lee-tah-see-'ohn)*
hospitalization	**hospitalización** *(ohs-pee-tah-lee-sah-see-'ohn)*
evacuation	**evacuación** *(eh-bah-kwah-see-'ohn)*
condition	**condición** *(kohn-dee-see-'ohn)*
detection	**detección** *(deh-tehk-see-'ohn)*
infection	**infección** *(een-fehk-see-'ohn)*
amputation	**amputación** *(ahm-poo-tah-see-'ohn)*
inflammation	**inflamación** *(een-flah-mah-see-'ohn)*
hypertension	**hipertensión** *(ee-pehr-tehn-see-'ohn)*
contraction	**contracción** *(kohn-trahk-see-'ohn)*
sensation	**sensación** *(sehn-sah-see-'ohn)*
complication	**complicación** *(kohm-plee-kah-see-'ohn)*
decision	**decisión** *(deh-see-see-'ohn)*
depression	**depresión** *(deh-preh-see-'ohn)*
circulation	**circulación** *(seer-koo-lah-see-'ohn)*
nutrition	**nutrición** *(noo-tree-see-'ohn)*

transfusion	**transfusión** *(trahns-foo-see-'ohn)*
reconstruction	**reconstrucción** *(reh-kohns-trook-see-'ohn)*
solution	**solución** *(soh-loo-see-'ohn)*
palpitation	**palpitación** *(pahl-pee-tah-see-'ohn)*
prevention	**prevención** *(preh-behn-see-'ohn)*
respiration	**respiración** *(rehs-pee-rah-see-'ohn)*
resuscitation	**resucitación** *(reh-soo-see-tah-see-'ohn)*
ulceration	**ulceración** *(ool-seh-rah-see-'ohn)*

Cognate Verbs

to absorb	**absorber** *(ahb-sohr-'behr)*
to accept	**aceptar** *(ah-sehp-'tahr)*
to adjust	**ajustar** *(ah-hoos-'tahr)*
to alter	**alterar** *(ahl-teh-'rahr)*
to amputate	**amputar** *(ahm-poo-'tahr)*
to analyze	**analizar** *(ah-nah-lee-'sahr)*
to authorize	**autorizar** *(ow-toh-ree-'sahr)*
to balance	**balancear** *(bah-lahn-seh-'ahr)*
to calm	**calmar** *(kahl-'mahr)*
to cause	**causar** *(cow-'sahr)*
to circulate	**circular** *(seer-koo-'lahr)*
to coagulate	**coagular** *(koh-ah-goo-'lahr)*
to communicate	**comunicar** *(koh-moo-nee-'kahr)*
to concentrate	**concentrar** *(kohn-sehn-'trahr)*
to consider	**considerar** *(kohn-see-deh-'rahr)*
to consist	**consistir** *(kohn-sees-'teer)*
to constipate	**constipar** *(kohns-tee-'pahr)*
to consult	**consultar** *(kohn-sool-'tahr)*
to contaminate	**contaminar** *(kohn-tah-mee-'nahr)*
to contain	**contener** *(kohn-teh-'nehr)*
to control	**controlar** *(kohn-troh-'lahr)*
to converse	**conversar** *(kohn-behr-'sahr)*
to convert	**convertir** *(kohn-behr-'teer)*
to cost	**costar** *(kohs-'tahr)*
to cure	**curar** *(koo-'rahr)*
to cut	**cortar** *(kohr-'tahr)*
to debilitate	**debilitar** *(deh-bee-lee-'tahr)*
to decide	**decidir** *(deh-see-'deer)*
to declare	**declarar** *(deh-klah-'rahr)*

to depend	**depender** *(deh-pehn-'dehr)*
to describe	**describir** *(dehs-kree-'beehr)*
to discover	**descubrir** *(dehs-koob-'reer)*
to disinfect	**desinfectar** *(dehs-een-fehk-'tahr)*
to destroy	**destruir** *(dehs-troo-'eer)*
to determine	**determinar** *(deh-tehr-mee-'nahr)*
to diagnose	**diagnosticar** *(dee-ahg-nohs-tee-'kahr)*
to dilate	**dilatar** *(dee-lah-'tahr)*
to discuss	**discutir** *(dees-koo-'teer)*
to dissolve	**disolver** *(dee-sohl-'behr)*
to distribute	**distribuir** *(dees-tree-boo-'eer)*
to divide	**dividir** *(dee-bee-'deer)*
to eliminate	**eliminar** *(eh-lee-mee-'nahr)*
to evacuate	**evacuar** *(eh-bah-koo-'ahr)*
to evaluate	**evaluar** *(eh-bah-loo-'ahr)*
to examine	**examinar** *(ehk-sah-mee-'nahr)*
to exist	**existir** *(ehk-sees-'teer)*
to explore	**explorar** *(ehks-ploh-'rahr)*
to facilitate	**facilitar** *(fah-see-lee-'tahr)*
to form	**formar** *(fohr-'mahr)*
to fracture	**fracturar** *(frahk-too-'rahr)*
to function	**funcionar** *(foon-see-oh-'nahr)*
to include	**incluir** *(een-kloo-'eer)*
to indicate	**indicar** *(een-dee-'kahr)*
to infect	**infectar** *(een-fehk-'tahr)*
to inform	**informar** *(een-fohr-'mahr)*
to immunize	**inmunizar** *(een-moo-nee-'sahr)*
to inoculate	**inocular** *(ee-noh-koo'lahr)*
to inspect	**inspeccionar** *(eens-pehk-see-oh-'nahr)*
to interpret	**interpretar** *(een-tehr-preh-'tahr)*
to maintain	**mantener** *(mahn-teh-'nehr)*
to note	**notar** *(noh-'tahr)*
to observe	**observar** *(ohb-sehr-'bahr)*
to obstruct	**obstruir** *(ohbs-troo-'eer)*
to occur	**ocurrir** *(oh-koor-'reer)*

to operate on	**operar** *(oh-peh-'rahr)*
to penetrate	**penetrar** *(peh-neht-'rahr)*
to permit	**permitir** *(pehr-mee-'teer)*
to practice	**practicar** *(prahk-tee-'kahr)*
to prepare	**preparar** *(preh-pah-'rahr)*
to prevent	**prevenir** *(preh-beh-'neer)*
to proceed	**proceder** *(proh-seh-'dehr)*
to progress	**progresar** *(prohg-reh-'sahr)*
to prohibit	**prohibir** *(proh-ee-'beer)*
to prolong	**prolongar** *(proh-lohn-'gahr)*
to protect	**proteger** *(proh-teh-'hehr)*
to propose	**proponer** *(proh-poh-'nehr)*
to purify	**purificar** *(poo-ree-fee-'kahr)*
to recommend	**recomendar** *(reh-koh-mehn-'dahr)*
to recognize	**reconocer** *(reh-koh-noh-'sehr)*
to recuperate	**recuperar** *(reh-koo-peh-'rahr)*
to reduce	**reducir** *(reh-doo-'seer)*
to refer	**referir** *(reh-feh-'reer)*
to relate	**relatar** *(reh-lah-'tahr)*
to remedy	**remediar** *(reh-meh-dee-'ahr)*
to renovate	**renovar** *(reh-noh-'bahr)*
to repair	**reparar** *(reh-pah-'rahr)*
to repeat	**repetir** *(reh-peh-'teer)*
to resolve	**resolver** *(reh-sohl-'behr)*
to respect	**respetar** *(rehs-peh-'tahr)*
to restore	**restaurar** *(rehs-tah-oo-'rahr)*
to resuscitate	**resucitar** *(reh-soo-see-'tahr)*
to result	**resultar** *(reh-sool-'tahr)*
to resume	**resumir** *(reh-soo-'meer)*
to select	**seleccionar** *(seh-lehk-see-oh-'nahr)*
to separate	**separar** *(seh-pah-'rahr)*
to sterilize	**esterilizar** *(ehs-teh-ree-lee-'sahr)*
to suffer	**sufrir** *(soof-'reer)*
to transmit	**transmitir** *(trahns-mee-'teer)*
to ulcerate	**ulcerar** *(ool-seh-'rahr)*

to urinate	**orinar** *(oh-ree-'nahr)*
to use	**usar** *(oo-'sahr)*
to utilize	**utilizar** *(oo-tee-lee-'sahr)*
to ventilate	**ventilar** *(behn-tee-'lahr)*
to visit	**visitar** *(bee-see-'tahr)*
to vomit	**vomitar** *(boh-mee-'tahr)*

Word and Expression Finder

Do you need a translation in a hurry? Main entries, subentries, and useful questions and expressions are alphabetically listed in the English-Spanish Word and Expression Finder.

Feminine nouns are followed by the feminine article "the" (*la*) in parentheses, and the masculine nouns are followed by the masculine article "the" (*el*). The same happens with the plurals *las* and *los*. The gender of pronouns and adjectives is indicated by (m.) or (f.). Terms related to the main entry are indented once. Expressions and phrases related to the main entry are indented twice.

Does your Spanish patient wish to tell you something, but does not know the word? Show him or her the Spanish-English Word Finder, and let the patient point at the Spanish word. The English equivalent will appear in the right column.

English-Spanish Word Finder

a	un (m.); una (f.)	*(oon, 'oo-nah)*
a.m.	de la mañana	*(deh lah mah-'nyah-nah)*
abandonment	abandono *(el)*	*(ehl ah-bahn-'doh-noh)*
abnormal	anormal	*(ah-nohr-'mahl)*
abortion	aborto *(el)*	*(ehl ah-'bohr-toh)*
Did you have an abortion?	¿Tuvo usted un aborto?	*(too-boh oo-'stehd oon ah-'bohr-toh)*
Do you want an abortion?	¿Desea usted un aborto?	*(deh-'seh-ah oo-'stehd oon ah-'bohr-toh)*
How many abortions have you had?	¿Cuántos abortos ha tenido?	*('kwahn-tohs ah-'bohr-tohs ah teh-'nee-doh)*
about	sobre	*('soh-breh)*
above	encima de	*(ehn-'see-mah deh)*
abscess	absceso *(el)*	*(ehl ahb-'seh-soh)*
abuse	abuso *(el)*	*(ehl ah-'boo-soh)*

child abuse	abuso de los niños *(el)*	*(ehl ah-'boo-soh deh lohs nee-'nyohs)*
drug abuse	abuso de las drogas *(el)*	*(ehl ah-'boo-soh deh lahs 'droh-gahs)*
This boy has been abused.	Este niño ha sido abusado.	*('ehs-teh 'nee-nyoh ah 'see-doh ah-boo-'sah-doh)*
Who abused this girl?	¿Quién abusó a esta niña?	*(kee-'ehn ah-boo-'soh ah 'ehs-tah 'nee-nyah)*
accident	accidente *(el)*	*(ehl ahk-see-'dehn-teh)*
accumulate (to)	acumular	*(ah-koo-moo-'lahr)*
acid	ácido *(el)*	*(ehl 'ah-see-doh)*
acrylic	acrílico *(el)*	*(ehl ah-'kree-lee-koh)*
action	acción *(la)*	*(lah ahk-see-'ohn)*
addict	adicto *(el)*, adicta *(la)*	*(ehl ah-'deek-toh, lah ah-'deek-tah)*
address	dirección *(la)*	*(lah dee-rehk-see-'ohn)*
Give me your address.	Deme su dirección.	*(deh-meh soo dee-rehk-see-'ohn)*
This is my address.	Esta es mi dirección.	*(ehs-'tah ehs mee dee-rehk-see-'ohn)*
adhesive tape	cinta adhesiva *(la)*	*(lah 'seen-tah ah-deh-'see-bah)*
administration	administración *(la)*	*(lah ahd-mee-nee-stra-see-'ohn)*
Go to the administration office.	Vaya a la oficina de la administración.	*('bah-yah ah lah oh-fee-'see-nah deh lah ahd-mee-nees-trah-see-'ohn)*
adoption	adopción *(la)*	*(lah ah-dohp-see-'ohn)*
You need adoption papers.	Necesita papeles de adopción.	*(neh-seh-'see-tah pah-'peh-lehs deh ah-dohp-see-'ohn)*
Do you wish to adopt a child?	¿Desea adoptar un niño?	*(deh-'seh-ah ah-dohp-'tahr oon 'nee-nyoh)*
after	después	*(dehs-'pwehs)*
age	edad *(la)*	*(lah eh-'dahd)*
How old are you?	¿Qué edad tiene usted?	*(keh eh-'dahd tee-'eh-neh oo-'stehd)*
What is his/her age?	¿Cuál es su edad?	*('kwahl ehs soo eh-'dahd)*
agency	agencia *(la)*	*(lah ah-'hehn-see-ah)*
AIDS	SIDA *(el)*	*(ehl 'see-dah)*
You don't have AIDS.	Usted no tiene el SIDA.	*(oo-'stehd noh tee-'eh-neh ehl 'see-dah)*
You have AIDS.	Usted tiene el SIDA.	*(oo-'stehd tee-'eh-neh ehl 'see-dah)*
air conditioning	aire acondicionado *(el)*	*(ehl 'ah-ee-reh ah-kohn-dee-see-oh-'nah-doh)*
airport	aeropuerto *(el)*	*(ehl ah-ee-roh-'pwehr-toh)*
alarm	alarma *(la)*	*(lah ah-'lahr-mah)*

alcoholic	alcohólico *(el)*,	*(ehl ahl-koh-'oh-lee-koh,*
	alcohólica *(la)*	*lah ahl-koh-'oh-lee-kah)*
alive	vivo (m.); viva (f.)	*('bee-boh, 'bee-bah)*
He is alive.	El está vivo.	*(ehl ehs-'tah 'bee-boh)*
all	todo	*('toh-doh)*
allergies	alergias *(las)*	*(lahs ah-'lehr-hee-ahs)*
Are you allergic to any food?	¿Tiene alergias a alguna comida?	*(tee-'eh-neh ah-'lehr-hee-ahs ah ahl-'yoo-nah koh-'mee-dah)*
almost	casi	*('kah-see)*
alone	solo (m.); sola (f.)	*('soh-loh, 'soh-lah)*
already	ya	*(yah)*
also	también	*(tahm-'bee-ehn)*
always	siempre	*(see-'ehm-preh)*
ambulance	ambulancia *(la)*	*(lah ahm-boo-'lahn-see-ah)*
ambulatory care	cuidado ambulatorio *(el)*	*(ehl kwee-'dah-doh ahm-boo-lah-'toh-ree-oh)*
ammonia	amoníaco *(el)*	*(ehl ah-moh-'nee-ah-koh)*
amniotic sac	bolsa amniótica *(la)*	*(lah 'boh-lsah ahm-nee-'oh-tee-kah)*
amphetamines	anfetaminas *(las)*	*(lahs ahn-feh-tah-'mee-nahs)*
amputate (to)	amputar	*(ahm-poo-'tahr)*
amputation	amputación *(la)*	*(lah ahm-poo-tah-see 'ohn)*
and	y	*('ee)*
anemia	anemia *(la)*	*(lah ah-'neh-mee-ah)*
anesthesia	anestesia *(la)*	*(lah ah-nehs-'leh-see-ah)*
anger	cólera *(la)*	*(lah 'koh-leh-rah)*
angry	enojado (m.); enojada (f.)	*(eh-noh-'hah-doh, eh-noh-'hah-dah)*
angiogram	angiograma *(el)*	*(ehl ahn-gee-oh-'grah-mah)*
animal	animal *(el)*	*(ehl ah-nee-'mahl)*
stuffed animals	animales de peluche *(los)*	*(lohs ah-nee-'mah-lehs deh peh-'loo-cheh)*
ankle	tobillo *(el)*	*(ehl toh-'bee-yoh)*
sprained ankle	tobillo torcido *(el)*	*(ehl toh-'bee-yoh tohr-'see-doh)*
answer (to)	contestar	*(kohn-tehs-'tahr)*
Answer all the questions.	Conteste a todas las preguntas.	*(kohn-'tehs-teh ah 'toh-dahs lahs preh-'goon-tahs)*
antibiotic	antibiótico *(el)*	*(ehl ahn-tee-bee-'oh-tee-koh)*
anus	ano *(el)*	*(ehl 'ah-noh)*

anxiety	ansiedad *(la)*	*(lah ahn-see-eh-dahd)*
aorta	aorta *(la)*	*(lah ah-'ohr-tah)*
appendectomy	apendectomía *(la)*	*(lah ah-pehn-dehk-toh-'mee-ah)*
appendix	apéndice *(el)*	*(ehl ah-'pehn-dee-seh)*
Did they remove your appendix?	¿Le han sacado el apéndice?	*(leh ahn sah-'kah-doh ehl ah-'pehn-dee-seh)*
appetite	apetito *(el)*	*(ehl ah-peh-'tee-toh)*
How is your appetite?	¿Cómo está su apetito?	*('koh-moh ehs-'tah soo ah-peh-'tee-toh)*
apple	manzana *(la)*	*(lah mahn-'sah-nah)*
apply (to)	aplicar	*(ah-plee-'kahr)*
appointment	cita *(la)*	*(lah 'see-tah)*
April	abril	*(ah-'breel)*
area	área *(el)*	*(ehl 'ah-reh-ah)*
arm	brazo *(el)*	*(ehl 'brah-soh)*
armpit	axila *(la)*	*(lah ahk-'see-lah)*
artery	arteria *(la)*	*(lah ahr-'teh-ree-ah)*
arthritis	artritis *(la)*	*(lah ahr-'tree-tees)*
artificial	artificial	*(ahr-tee-fee-see-'ahl)*
ash tray	cenicero *(el)*	*(ehl seh-nee-'seh-roh)*
ask (to)	preguntar	*(preh-goon-'tahr)*
asleep	dormido (m.); dormida (f.)	*(dohr-'mee-doh), (dohr-'mee-dah)*
assist (to)	atender	*(ah-tehn-'dehr)*
assistant	ayudante *(el)*	*(ehl ah-yoo-'dahn-teh)*
asthma	asma *(el)*	*(ehl 'ahs-mah)*
astigmatism	astigmatismo *(el)*	*(ehl ahs-teeg-mah-'tees-moh)*
at	en	*(ehn)*
August	agosto	*(ah-'gohs-toh)*
aunt	tía *(la)*	*(lah 'tee-ah)*
auricle	aurícula *(la)*	*(lah ow-'ree-koo-lah)*
automobile	automóvil *(el)*	*(ehl ow-toh-moh-'beel)*
available	disponible	*(dees-poh-'neeb-leh)*
avocado	aguacate *(el)*	*(ehl ah-gwah-'kah-teh)*
avoid (to)	evitar	*(eh-bee-'tahr)*
Avoid eating nuts.	Evite comer nueces.	*(eh-'bee-teh koh-'mehr noo·'eh-sehs)*
awake	despierto (m.); despierta (f.)	*(dehs-pee-'ehr-toh, dehs-pee-'ehr-tah)*

baby	bebé *(el)*	*(ehl beh-'beh)*
back	espalda *(la)*	*(lah ehs-'pahl-dah)*
backaches	dolores de espalda *(los)*	*(lohs doh-'loh-rehs deh ehs-'pahl-dah)*
backbone	espinazo *(el)*	*(ehl ehs-pee-'nah-soh)*
bacteriologist	bacteriólogo *(el)*	*(ehl bahk-teh-ree-'oh-loh-goh)*
bad (n.)	mal (m. & f.)	*(mahl)*
bad (adj.)	malo	*('mah-loh)*
This is bad.	Esto está malo.	*(ehs-'toh eh-'stah 'mah-loh)*
baking soda	bicarbonato *(el)*	*(ehl bee-kahr-boh-'nah-toh)*
balance	equilibrio *(el)*	*(ehl eh-kee-'lee-bree-oh)*
Do you lose your balance?	¿Pierde el equilibrio?	*(pee-'ehr-deh ehl eh-kee-'lee-bree·oh)*
bald	calvo	*('kahl-boh)*
ball	pelota *(la)*	*(lah peh-'loh-tah)*
balloons	globos *(los)*	*(lohs 'gloh-bohs)*
banana	plátano *(el)*	*(ehl 'plah-tah-noh)*
bandage	vendaje *(el)*	*(ehl behn-'dah-heh)*
Band-Aid®	curita *(la)*	*(lah koo-'ree-tah)*
bank	banco *(el)*	*(ehl 'bahn-koh)*
baptism	bautismo *(el)*	*(ehl bow-'tees-moh)*
barbiturates	barbitúricos *(los)*	*(lohs bahr-bee-'too-ree-kohs)*
barrette	hebilla *(la)*	*(lah eh-'bee-yah)*
basement	sótano *(el)*	*(ehl 'soh-tah-noh)*
bassinet	bacinete *(el)*	*(ehl bah-see-'neh-teh)*
bathe (to)	bañarse	*(bah-'nyahr-seh)*
Bathe *(request to)*	Báñese.	*('bah-nyeh-seh)*
Do you need help to bathe?	¿Necesita ayuda para bañarse?	*(neh-seh-'see-tah ah-'yoo-dah 'pah-rah bah-'nyahr-seh)*
Do you prefer a sponge bath?	¿Prefiere un baño de esponja?	*(preh-fee-'eh-reh oon 'bah-nyoh dehehs-'pohn-hah)*
bathroom	baño *(el)*	*(ehl 'bah-nyoh)*
Do you need help to go to the bathroom?	¿Necesita ayuda para ir al baño?	*(neh-seh-'see-tah ah-'yoo-dah 'pah-rah eer ahl 'bah-nyoh)*
bathtub	bañera *(la)*	*(lah bah-'nyeh-rah)*
be able (to)	poder	*(poh-'dehr)*
Are you able to stand?	¿Puede pararse?	*('pweh-deh pah-'rahr-seh)*
be born (to)	nacer	*(nah-'sehr)*

She was born on April 5.	Ella nació el cinco de abril.	*('eh-yah nah-see-'oh ehl 'see-nkoh de hah-'breel)*
The baby will be born in May.	El bebé nacerá en mayo.	*(ehl beh-'beh nah-seh-'rah ehn 'mah-yoh)*
be (to)	estar, ser	*(ehs-'tahr, sehr)*
beach	playa *(la)*	*(lah 'plah-yah)*
beat (to)	golpear	*(gohl-peh-'ahr)*
because	porque	*('pohr-keh)*
bed	cama *(la)*	*(lah 'kah-mah)*
bedpan	chata *(la)*	*(lah 'chah-tah)*
Do you need a bedpan?	¿Necesita una chata?	*(neh-seh-'see-tah 'oo-nah 'chah-tah)*
bedrails	barandas de la cama *(las)*	*(lahs bah-'rahn-dahs deh lah 'kah-mah)*
bee	abeja *(la)*	*(lah ah-'beh-hah)*
bee sting	picadura de abeja *(la)*	*(lah pee-kah-'doo-rah deh ah-'beh-hah)*
beer	cerveza *(la)*	*(lah sehr-'beh-sah)*
before	antes	*('ahn-tehs)*
begin (to)	comenzar	*(koh-mehn-'sahr)*
behind	detrás de	*(deh-'trahs deh)*
bell	timbre *(el)*	*(ehl 'teem-breh)*
belt	cinturón *(el)*	*(ehl seen-too-'rohn)*
bend (to)	doblar	*(doh-'blahr)*
Bend *(request to)*	Doble.	*('doh-bleh)*
Bend your arm.	Doble el brazo.	*('doh-bleh ehl 'brah-soh)*
benefits	beneficios *(los)*	*(lohs beh-neh-'fee-see-ohs)*
benign	benigno	*(beh-'neeg-noh)*
bent	doblado (m.); doblada (f.)	*(doh-'blah-doh, doh-'blah-dah)*
better	mejor	*(meh-'hohr)*
between	entre	*('ehn-treh)*
between meals	entre comidas	*('ehn-treh koh-'mee-dahs)*
beverage	bebida *(la)*	*(lah beh-'bee-dah)*
bicycle	bicicleta *(la)*	*(lah bee-see-'keh-tah)*
bifocals	bifocales *(los)*	*(lohs bee-foh-'kah-lehs)*
big	grande	*('grahn-deh)*
billfold	billetera *(la)*	*(lah bee-yeh-'teh-rah)*
biopsy	biopsia *(la)*	*(lah bee-'ohp-see-ah)*
bird	pájaro *(el)*	*(ehl 'pah-hah-roh)*
birth	nacimiento *(el)*	*(ehl nah-see-mee-'ehn-toh)*

birth control	anticoncepción *(la)*	*(lah ahn-tee-kohn-sehp-see-'ohn)*
birth control pills	píldoras anticonceptivas *(las)*	*(lahs 'peel-doh-rahs ahn-tee-kohn-sehp-'tee-vahs)*
birth defect	defecto de nacimiento *(el)*	*(ehl deh-'fehk-toh deh nah-see-mee-'ehn-toh)*
birthdate	fecha de nacimiento *(la)*	*(lah 'feh-chah deh nah-see-mee-'ehn-toh)*
bite (to)	morder	*(mohr-'dehr)*
Bite *(request to)*	Muerda.	*('mwehr-dah)*
black	negro *(el)*; negra *(la)*	*(ehl 'neh-groh, lah 'neh-grah)*
black boy	niño negro *(el)*	*(ehl 'nee-nyoh 'neh-groh)*
black girl	niña negra *(la)*	*(lah 'nee-nyah 'neh-grah)*
black man	hombre negro *(el)*	*(ehl 'ohm-breh 'neh groh)*
black woman	mujer negra *(la)*	*(lah moo-'hehr 'neh-grah)*
blackout	pérdida de conocimiento *(la)*	*(lah 'pehr-dee-dah deh koh-noh-see-mee-'ehn-toh)*
bladder	vejiga *(la)*	*(lah beh-'hee-gah)*
bladder infection	infección de la vejiga *(la)*	*(lah een-fehk-see-'ohn deh lah beh-'hee-gah)*
blanket	cobija *(la)*, frazada *(la)*	*(lah koh-'bee-hah, lah frah-'sah-dah)*
bleeding	hemorragia *(la)*	*(lah eh-moh-'rrah-hee-ah)*
Bless you!	¡Salud!	*(sah-'lood)*
blind	ciego *(el)*, ciega *(la)*	*(ehl see-'eh goh, lah see-'eh-gah)*
blister	ampolla *(la)*	*(lah ahm-'poh-yah)*
blisters	ampollas *(las)*	*(lahs ahm-'poh-yahs)*
blond	rubio *(el)*; rubia *(la)*	*(ehl 'rroo-bee-oh, lah 'rroo-bee-ah)*
blood	sangre *(la)*	*(lah 'sahn-gre)*
blood count	recuento de la sangre *(el)*	*(eh reh-'kwehn-toh deh lah 'sahn-greh)*
blood pressure	presión de la sangre *(la)*	*(lah preh-see-'ohn deh lah 'sahn-greh)*
blood transfusion	transfusión de sangre *(la)*	*(lah trahns-foo-see-'ohn deh 'sahn-greh)*
blood type	tipo de sangre *(el)*	*(ehl 'tee-poh deh 'sahn-greh)*
blouse	blusa *(la)*	*(lah 'bloo-sah)*
blue	azul	*(ah-'sool)*
Blue Cross	Cruz Azul *(la)*	*(lah kroos ah-'sool)*
Blue Shield	Escudo Azul *(el)*	*(ehl ehs-'koo-doh ah-'sool)*
bobby pin	horquilla *(la)*	*(lah ohr-'kee-yah)*
body	cuerpo *(el)*	*(ehl 'kwehr-poh)*
bone	hueso *(el)*	*(ehl 'weh-soh)*
bone marrow	médula *(la)*	*(lah 'meh-doo-lah)*

broken bone	hueso roto *(el)*	*(ehl 'weh-soh 'roh-toh)*
book	libro *(el)*	*(ehl 'lee-broh)*
boots	botas *(las)*	*(lahs 'boh-tahs)*
bored	aburrido (m.); aburrida (f.)	*(ah-boor-'ree-doh, ah-boor-'ree-dah)*
bottle	botella *(la)*	*(lah boh-'teh-yah)*
bottle nipple	chupete *(el)*	*(ehl choo-'peh-teh)*
boyfriend	novio *(el)*	*(ehl 'noh-bee-oh)*
bracelet	brazalete *(el)*	*(ehl brah-sah-'leh-teh)*
braces	frenillos *(los)*	*(lohs freh-'nee-yohs)*
brain	cerebro *(el)*	*(ehl seh-'reh-broh)*
brassiere	sostén *(el)*	*(ehl sohs-'tehn)*
bread	pan *(el)*	*(ehl pahn)*
breakfast	desayuno *(el)*	*(ehl deh-sah-'yoo-noh)*
breast-feed (to)	lactar	*(lahk-'tahr)*
breast feeding	amamantamiento *(el)*	*(ehl ah-mah-mahn-tah-mee-'ehn-toh)*
breasts	senos *(los)*, pechos *(los)*	*(lohs 'seh-nohs; lohs 'peh-chohs)*
breath	aliento *(el)*	*(ehl ah-lee-'ehn-toh)*
breathe (to)	respirar	*(rehs-pee-'rahr)*
Breathe *(request to)*	Respire.	*(rehs-'pee-reh)*
breathing	respiración *(la)*	*(lah rehs-pee-rah-see-'ohn)*
bridge	puente *(el)*	*(ehl 'pwehn-teh)*
bring (to)	traer	*('trah-ehr)*
Bring a sample in this cup.	Traiga una muestra en este vaso.	*('trah-ee-gah 'oo-nah 'mwehs-trah ehn 'eh-steh 'bah-soh)*
Bring *(request to)*	Traiga.	*('trah-ee-gah)*
brother	hermano *(el)*	*(ehl ehr-'mah-noh)*
brother-in-law	cuñado *(el)*	*(ehl koo-'nyah-doh)*
brown	café	*(kah-'feh)*
brunette	morena	*(moh-'reh-nah)*
brush	cepillo *(el)*	*(ehl seh-'pee-yoh)*
Brush *(request to)*	Cepíllese.	*(seh-'pee-yeh-seh)*
buddy	compañero (m.); compañera (f.)	*(kohm-pah-nee-'eh-roh, kohm-pah-nee-'eh-rah)*
building	edificio *(el)*	*(ehl eh-dee-'fee-se-oh)*
bump	protuberancia *(la)*	*(lah proh-too-beh-'rahn-see-ah)*
bumps	protuberancias *(las)*	*(lahs proh-too-beh-'rahn-see-ahs)*

bunion	juanete *(el)*	*(ehl wah-'neh-teh)*
burn (to)	quemar	*(keh-'mahr)*
burning (n.)	ardor *(el)*	*(ehl ahr-'dohr)*
burning (adj.)	quemante	*(keh-'mahn-teh)*
burp (to)	eructar	*(eh-rook-'tahr)*
bus	autobús *(el)*	*(ehl ow-toh-'boos)*
bush	arbusto *(el)*	*(ehl ahr-'boos-toh)*
business	negocio *(el)*	*(ehl neh-goh-'see·oh)*
busy	ocupado (m.); ocupada (f.)	*(oh-koo-'pah-doh, oh-koo-'pah-dah)*
but	pero	*('peh-roh)*
butter	mantequilla *(la)*	*(lah mahn-teh-'kee yah)*
buttock	nalga *(la)*	*(lah 'nahl-gah)*
cabbage	repollo *(el)*	*(ehl reh-'poh-yoh)*
cabinet	gabinete *(el)*	*(ehl gah-bee-'neh-teh)*
cafeteria	cafetería *(la)*	*(lah kah-feh-teh-'ree-ah)*
cake	torta *(la)*, bizcocho *(el)*	*(lah 'tohr-tah; ehl bees-'koh-choh)*
calendar	calendario *(el)*	*(ehl kah-lehn-'dah-ree·oh)*
calf	pantorrilla *(la)*	*(lah pahn-toh-'rree-yah)*
call (to)	llamar	*(yah-'mahr)*
Call me.	Llámeme.	*('yah-meh-meh)*
Call ___ ___. *(request to)*	Llame a _____.	*('yah-meh ah ___.)*
Call the doctor.	Llame al doctor.	*('yah-meh ahl dohk-'tohr)*
calluses	callos *(los)*	*(lohs 'kah-yohs)*
calm	calmado (m.); calmada (f.)	*(kahl-'mah-doh, kahl-'mah-dah)*
Be at ease.	Esté tranquilo.	*(ehs-'teh trahn-'kee-loh)*
can (container)	lata *(la)*	*(lah 'lah-tah)*
cancer	cáncer *(el)*	*(ehl 'kahn-sehr)*
candy	dulce *(el)*	*(ehl 'dool-seh)*
cane	bastón *(el)*	*(ehl bahs-'tohn)*
CAP test	prueba de CAP *(la)*	*(lah 'proo-eh-bah deh KAHP)*
capsule	cápsula *(la)*	*(lah 'kahp-soo-lah)*
Don't take the capsules.	No tome las cápsulas.	*(noh 'toh-meh lahs 'kah-psoo-lahs)*
car	carro *(el)*	*(ehl 'kah-rroh)*
cardiologist	cardiólogo *(el)*	*(ehl kahr-dee-'oh-loh-goh)*

care	cuidado *(el)*	*(ehl kwee-'dah-doh)*
carpenter	carpintero *(el)*	*(ehl kahr-peen-'teh-roh)*
carrot	zanahoria *(la)*	*(lah sah-nah-'oh-ree-ah)*
carry (to)	llevar	*(yeh-'bahr)*
Carry *(request to)*	Lleve.	*('yeh-beh)*
cartilage	cartílago *(el)*	*(ehl kahr-'tee-lah-goh)*
cash	efectivo *(el)*	*(ehl eh-'fehk-'tee-boh)*
cashier	cajero *(el)*, cajera *(la)*	*(ehl kah-'heh-roh, lah kah-'heh-rah)*
cast	armadnra de yeso *(la)*	*(lah ahr-mah-'doo-rah deh 'yes-oh)*
cat	gato *(el)*, gata *(la)*	*(ehl 'gah-toh, lah 'gah-tah)*
cataract	catarata *(la)*	*(lah kah-tah-'rah-tah)*
catheter	catéter *(el)*	*(ehl kah-'teh-tehr)*
cause (to)	causar	*(kow-'sahr)*
cavity	carie *(la)*	*(lah 'kah-ree-eh)*
ceiling	cielo raso *(el)*	*(ehl see-'eh-loh 'rrah-soh)*
cell	célula *(la)*	*(lah 'seh-loo-lah)*
cement	cemento *(el)*	*(ehl seh-'mehn-toh)*
cereal	cereal *(el)*	*(ehl seh-reh-'ahl)*
cerebral palsy	parálisis cerebral *(la)*	*(lah pah-'rah-lee-sees seh-reh-'brahl)*
Certificate of Live Birth	partida de nacimiento vivo *(la)*	*(lah pahr-'tee-dah deh nah-see-mee-'ehn toh 'bee-boh)*
certify (to)	certificar	*(sehr-tee-fee-'kahr)*
cervical canal	canal cervical *(el)*	*(ehl kah-'nahl sehr-bee-'kahl)*
cervix	cuello uterino *(el)*	*(ehl 'kweh-yoh oo-teh-'ree-noh)*
cesarean section	operación cesárea *(la)*	*(lah oh-peh-rah-see-'ohn ceh-'sah-ree-ah)*
chair	silla *(la)*	*(lah 'see-yah)*
change (to)	cambiar	*(kahm-bee-'ahr)*
Change the baby.	Cambie al bebé.	*('kahm-bee-eh ahl beh-'beh)*
chapel	capilla *(la)*	*(lah kah-'pee-yah)*
charge	cargo *(el)*	*(ehl 'kahr-goh)*
chart	gráfico *(el)*	*(ehl 'grah-fee-koh)*
check	cheque *(el)*	*(ehl 'cheh-keh)*
check (to)	verificar	*(beh-ree-fee-'kahr)*
checkup	reconocimiento *(el)*	*(ehl reh-koh-noh-see-mee-'ehn-toh)*
Did you have a checkup?	¿Le hicieron un reconocimiento?	*(leh ee-see-'eh-rohn oon reh-koh-noh-see mee-'ehn-toh)*

You need a checkup.	Necesita un reconocimiento.	*(neh-seh-'see-tah oon reh-koh-noh-see-mee-'ehn-toh)*
cheek	mejilla *(la)*	*(lah meh-'hee-yah)*
cheekbone	pómulo *(el)*	*(ehl 'poh-moo-loh)*
cheese	queso *(el)*	*(ehl 'keh-soh)*
chemical	producto químico *(el)*	*(ehl proh-'dook-toh 'kee-mee-koh)*
cherry	cereza *(la)*	*(lah seh-'reh-sah)*
chest	pecho *(el)*	*(ehl 'peh-choh)*
chew (to)	mascar, masticar	*(mahs-'kahr, mahs-tee-'kahr)*
Chew *(request to)*	Mastique.	*(mahs-'tee-keh)*
chicken	pollo *(el)*	*(ehl 'poh-yoh)*
chicken pox	varicela *(la)*	*(lah bah-ree-'seh-lah)*
child	niño *(el)*, niña *(la)*	*(ehl 'neen-yoh, lah 'neen-yah)*
Is it your first child?	¿Es su primer niño?	*(ehs soo pree-'mehr 'nee-nyoh)*
childbirth	parto *(el)*	*(ehl 'pahr-toh)*
natural childbirth	parto natural *(el)*	*(ehl 'pahr-toh nah-too-'rahl)*
childcare	cuidado del niño *(el)*	*(ehl kwee-'dah-doh dehl 'neen-yoh)*
chills	escalofríos *(los)*	*(lohs ehs-kah-loh-'free-ohs)*
chin	barbilla *(la)*	*(lah bahr-'bee-yah)*
chiropractor	quiropráctico *(el)*	*(ehl kee-roh-'prahk-tee-koh)*
chocolate	chocolate *(el)*	*(ehl choh-koh-'lah-teh)*
cholera	cólera *(el)*	*(ehl 'koh-leh-rah)*
church	iglesia *(la)*	*(lah ee-'gleh-see-ah)*
cigar	puro *(el)*	*(ehl 'poo-roh)*
cigarette	cigarrillo *(el)*	*(ehl see-gah-'rree-yoh)*
circumcision	circuncisión *(la)*	*(lah seer-koon-see-see-'ohn)*
city	ciudad *(la)*	*(lah see-oo-'dahd)*
city block	cuadra *(la)*	*(lah 'kwah-drah)*
clasp	broche *(el)*	*(ehl 'broh-cheh)*
class	clase *(la)*	*(lah 'klah-seh)*
clean	limpio (m.); limpia (f.)	*('leem-pee-oh, 'leem-pee-ah)*
clean (to)	limpiar	*(leem-pee-'ahr)*
Is everything clean?	¿Está todo muy limpio?	*(eh-'stah 'toh-doh 'moo-ee 'leem-pee-oh)*
Clean *(request to)*	Limpie.	*('leem-pee-eh)*
cleaning	limpieza *(la)*	*(lah leem-pee-'eh-sah)*
cleanliness	limpieza *(la)*	*(lah leem-pee-'eh-sah)*

clear	despejado	*(dehs-peh-'hah-doh)*
close (to)	cerrar	*(seh-'rrahr)*
Close *(request to)*	Cierre	*(see-'eh-rreh)*
Close your mouth.	Cierre la boca.	*(see-'eh-rreh lah 'boh-kah)*
closed	cerrado (m.); cerrada (f.)	*(seh-'rrah-doh, seh-'rrah-dah)*
closer	más cerca	*(mahs 'sehr-kah)*
closet	ropero *(el)*	*(ehl roh-'peh-roh)*
clothing	ropa *(la)*	*(lah 'roh-pah)*
cloudy	nublado	*(noo-'blah-doh)*
cocaine	cocaína *(la)*	*(lah koh-kah-'ee-nah)*
codeine	codeína *(la)*	*(lah koh-deh-'ee-nah)*
coffee	café *(el)*	*(ehl kah-feh)*
cold	frío *(el)*	*('ehl free-oh)*
Are you cold?	¿Tiene frío?	*(tee-'eh-neh 'free-oh)*
cold (illness)	resfrío *(el)*	*(ehl rehs-'free-oh)*
Does he/she have a cold?	¿Tiene un resfrío?	*(ehl rehs-'free-oh tee-'eh-neh oon rehs 'free-oh)*
colic	cólico *(el)*	*(ehl 'koh-lee-koh)*
collarbone	clavícula *(la)*	*(lah klah-'bee-koo-lah)*
colon	colon *(el)*	*(ehl 'koh-lohn)*
color	color *(el)*	*(ehl koh-'lohr)*
color-blind	daltónico	*(dahl-'toh-nee-koh)*
comb	peine *(el)*	*(ehl 'peh-ee-neh)*
come (to)	venir	*(beh-'neer)*
Come *(request to)*	Venga.	*('behn-gah)*
comfortable	cómodo	*('koh-moh-doh)*
common	común	*(koh-'moon)*
company	compañía *(la)*	*(lah kohm-pah-'nyee-ah)*
complex	complejo	*(kohm-'pleh-hoh)*
condition	estado *(el)*	*(ehl ehs-'tah-doh)*
She is in bad condition.	Ella está en mal estado.	*('eh-yah eh-'stah ehn mahl eh-'stah-doh)*
He is in good condition.	El está en buen estado.	*(ehl eh-'stah ehn bwehn ehs-'tah-doh)*
condom	condón *(el)*	*(ehl kohn-'dohn)*
Always use condoms.	Siempre use condones.	*(see-'ehm-preh 'oo-seh kohn-'doh-nehs)*
conference room	sala de conferencias *(la)*	*(lah 'sah-lah deh kohn-feh-'rehn-see-ahs)*

confused	confuso (m.); confusa (f.)	*(kohn-'foo-soh, koh-'foo-sah)*
confusion	confusión *(la)*	*(lah kohn-foo-see-'ohn)*
conscious	consciente (m. & f.)	*(kohn-see-'ehn-teh)*
consent form	formulario de consentimiento *(el)*	*(ehl fohr-moo-'lah-ree-oh deh kohn-sehn-tee-mee-'ehn-toh)*
constant	constante	*(kohn-'stahn-teh)*
constipated	estreñido	*(ehs-treh-'nyee-doh)*
Are you constipated?	¿Está estreñido?	*(eh-'stah ehs-treh-'nyee-doh)*
constipation	estreñimiento *(el)*	*(ehl ehs-treh-nyee-mee-'ehn-toh)*
consult (to)	consultar	*(kohn-sool-'tahr)*
Consult with your doctor.	Consulte a su médico.	*(kohn-'sool-teh ah soo 'meh-dee-koh)*
contact lenses	lentes de contacto *(los)*	*(lohs 'lehn-tehs deh kohn-'tahk-toh)*
Do you wear contact lenses?	¿Usa lentes de contacto?	*('oo-sah 'lehn-tehs deh kohn-'tahk-toh)*
When were they prescribed?	¿Cuándo se los recetaron?	*('kwahn-doh se lohs reh-seh-'tah-rohn)*
continuous passive motion machine	máquina de movimiento continuo *(la)*	*(lah 'mah-kee-nah deh moh-bee-mee-'ehn-toh kohn-'tee-noo-oh)*
contractions	contracciones *(las)*	*(lahs kohn-trahk-see-'oh-nehs)*
How often are the contractions?	¿Cuán rápido vienen las contracciones?	*(kwahn 'rah-pee doh bee-'eh-nehn lahs kohn-trahk-see-'oh-nehs)*
control (to)	controlar	*(kohn-troh-'lahr)*
Control the child.	Controle al niño.	*(kohn-'troh-leh ahl 'nee-nyoh)*
convulsion	convulsión *(la)*	*(lah kohn-bool-see-'ohn)*
cook	cocinero (m.); cocinera (f.)	*(koh-see-'neh-roh, koh-see-'neh-rah)*
cook (to)	cocinar	*(koh-see-'nahr)*
Cook without salt.	Cocine sin sal.	*(koh-'see-neh seen sahl)*
cookie	galleta *(la)*	*(lah gah-'yeh-tah)*
corn	callo *(el)*	*(ehl 'kah-yoh)*
corn (food)	maíz *(el)*	*(ehl mah-'ees)*
corner	esquina *(la)*	*(lah ehs-'kee-nah)*
correct	correcto	*(koh-'rrehk-toh)*
cosmetics	cosméticos *(los)*	*(lohs kohs-'meh-tee-kohs)*
cost	costo *(el)*	*(ehl 'kohs-toh)*
cough	tos *(la)*	*(lah tohs)*

cough (to)	toser	*(toh-'sehr)*
painful cough	tos dolorosa *(la)*	*(lah tohs doh-loh-'roh-sah)*
Do you cough often?	¿Tose a menudo?	*('toh-seh ah meh-'noo-doh)*
Cough *(request to)*	Tosa.	*('toh-sah)*
cough syrup	jarabe para la tos *(el)*	*(ehl hah-'rah-beh 'pah-rah lah tohs)*
counsel	consejo *(el)*	*(ehl kohn-'seh-hoh)*
counseling	consejería *(la)*	*(lah kohn-seh-heh-'ree-ah)*
counselor	consejero *(el)*, consejera *(la)*	*(ehl kohn-seh-'heh-roh; lah kohn-seh 'heh-rah)*
Go to the counselor.	Vaya al consejero.	*('bah-yah ahl kohn-seh-'heh-roh)*
count	recuento *(el)*	*(ehl reh-'kwehn-toh)*
countryside	campo *(el)*	*(ehl 'kahm-poh)*
couple	pareja *(la)*	*(lah pah-'reh-hah)*
cousin	primo (m.); prima (f.)	*('pree-moh, 'pree-mah)*
cover (to)	tapar	*(tah-'pahr)*
Cover the baby.	Tape al bebé.	*('tah-peh ahl beh-'beh)*
Cover yourself.	Tápese.	*('tah-peh-seh)*
CPR	resucitación cardiopulmonar *(la)*	*(lah reh-soo-see-tah-see-'ohn kahr-dee-oh-pool-moh-'nahr)*
crack (drug)	crack	*(krahk)*
cramps	calambres *(los)*	*(lohs kah-'lahm-brehs)*
Do you have cramps often?	¿Tiene calambres a menudo?	*(tee-'eh-neh kah-'lahm-brehs ah meh-'noo-doh)*
cranium, skull	cráneo *(el)*	*(ehl 'krah-neh-oh)*
crash (to)	chocar	*(choh-'kahr)*
crawl (to)	gatear	*(gah-teh-'ahr)*
crazy	loco (m.); loca (f.)	*('loh-koh, 'loh-kah)*
cream	crema *(la)*	*(lah 'kreh-mah)*
credit card	tarjeta de crédito *(la)*	*(lah tahr-'heh-tah deh 'kreh-dee-toh)*
Do you have a credit card?	¿Tiene tarjeta de crédito?	*(tee-'eh-neh tahr-'heh-tah deh 'kreh-dee-toh)*
crib	cuna *(la)*	*(lah 'koo-nah)*
criminal	criminal (m. & f.)	*(ehl (lah) kree-mee-'nahl)*
cross (to)	cruzar	*('kroo-sahr)*
Cross *(request to)*	Cruce.	*('kroo-seh)*
Cross your arms.	Cruce los brazos.	*('kroo-seh lohs 'brah-sohs)*
crown	corona *(la)*	*(lah koh-'roh-nah)*
cry (to)	llorar	*(yoh-'rahr)*

Does the baby cry a lot?	¿Llora mucho el bebé?	('yoh-rah 'moo-choh ehl beh-'beh)
CT scan	tomografía computarizada (la)	(lah toh-moh-grah-'fee-ah kom-poo-tah-ree-'zah-dah)
cup	copa (la)	(lah 'koh-pah)
curb	orilla (la)	(lah oh-'ree-yah)
cure (to)	curar	(koo-'rahr)
You are cured.	Está usted curado.	(eh-'stah oo-'stehd koo-'rah-doh)
curtains	cortinas (las)	(lahs kohr-'tee-nahs)
cut	corte (el)	(ehl 'kohr-teh)
Are you cut?	¿Está cortado?	(eh-'stah kohr-'tah-doh)
He is cut.	El está cortado.	(ehl eh-'stah kohr-'tah-doh)
She cut herself.	Ella se cortó.	('eh-yah seh kohr-'toh)
cute	simpático	(seem-'pah-tee-koh)
How cute!	¡Qué simpático!	(keh seem-'pah-tee-koh)
cyanide	cianuro (el)	(ehl see-ah-'noo-roh)
cyst	quiste (el)	(ehl 'kees-teh)
cystic fibrosis	fibrosis cística (la)	(lah fee-'broh-sees 'sees-tee-kah)
cystoscopy	cistoscopía (la)	(lah sees-toh-skoh-'pee-ah)
dairy products	productos lácteos (los)	(lohs proh-'dook-toh 'lack-teh-ohs)
dangerous	peligroso	(peh-lee-'groh-soh)
It is dangerous.	Es peligroso.	(ehs peh-lee-'groh-soh)
It is not dangerous.	No es peligroso.	(noh ehs peh-lee-'groh-soh)
dark-skinned	prieto (coll.)	(pree-'eh-toh)
daughter	hija (la)	(lah 'ee-hah)
daughter-in-law	nuera (la)	(lah 'noo-eh-rah)
day	día (el)	(ehl 'dee-ah)
dead	muerto (m.); muerta (f.)	('mwehr-toh, 'mwehr-tah)
He is dead.	El está muerto.	(ehl eh-'stah 'mwehr-toh)
She is not dead.	Ella no está muerta.	('eh-yah noh eh-'stah 'mwehr-tah)
deaf	sordo (m.); sorda (f.)	('sohr-doh, 'sohr-dah)
death	muerte (la)	(lah 'mwehr-teh)
decaffeinated	descafeinado	(dehs-kah-feh-ee-'nah-doh)
December	diciembre	(dee-see-'ehm-breh)
decongestant	descongestionante (el)	(ehl dehs-kohn-hehs-tee-oh-'nahn-teh)
deductible	deducible (el)	(ehl deh-doo-'seeb-leh)
deep	profundo (m.); profunda (f.)	(proh-'foon-doh, proh-'foon-dah)

defecate (to)	defecar	*(deh-feh-'kahr)*
dehydration	deshidratación *(la)*	*(lah dehs-ee-drah-tah-see-'ohn)*
delivery room	sala de partos *(la)*	*(lah 'sah-lah deh 'pahr-tohs)*
dental floss	hilo dental *(el)*	*(ehl 'ee-loh dehn-'tahl)*
denture	dentadura postiza *(la)*	*(lah dehn-tah-'doo-rah pohs-'tee-sah)*
Do the dentures fit well?	¿Le calzan bien las dentaduras postizas?	*(leh 'kahl-sahn 'bee-ehn lahs dehn-tah-doo-rahs pohs-'tee-sahs)*
Do you have denture pain?	¿Tiene dolor de las dentaduras postizas?	*(tee-'eh-neh doh-'lohr deh lahs dehn-tah-'doo-rahs pohs-'tee-sahs)*
Do you wear dentures?	¿Tiene dentaduras postizas?	*(tee-'eh-neh dehn-tah-'doo-rahs pohs' tee-sahs)*
You need dentures.	Usted necesita dentaduras postizas.	*(oo-'stehd neh-seh-'see-tah dehn-tah-'doo-rahs pohs-'tee-sahs)*
deodorant	desodorante *(el)*	*(ehl dehs-oh-doh-'rahn-teh)*
department	departamento *(el)*	*(ehl deh-pahr-tah-'mehn-toh)*
deposit	depósito *(el)*	*(ehl deh-'poh-see-toh)*
depression	depresión *(la)*	*(lah deh-preh-see-'ohn)*
Do you feel depressed?	¿Se siente deprimido?	*(seh see-'ehn-teh deh-pree-'mee-doh)*
dermatologist	dermatólogo *(el)*	*(ehl dehr-mah-'toh-loh-goh)*
description	descripción *(la)*	*(lah dehs-'kreep-see-on)*
Describe *(request to)*	Describa.	*(dehs-'kree-bah)*
desert	desierto *(el)*	*(ehl deh-see-'ehr-toh)*
desire	deseo *(el)*	*(ehl deh-'seh-oh)*
desk	escritorio *(el)*	*(ehl ehs-kree-'toh-ree-oh)*
dessert	postre *(el)*	*(ehl 'pohs-treh)*
detect (to)	detectar	*(deh-tehk-'tahr)*
detergent	detergente *(el)*	*(ehl deh-tehr-'hehn-teh)*
diabetes	diabetes *(la)*	*(lah dee-ah-'beh-tehs)*
diagnosis	diagnóstico *(el)*	*(ehl dee-ahg-'nohs-tee-koh)*
dial (to)	marcar	*('mahr-kahr)*
Dial *(request to)*	Marque.	*('mahr-keh)*
diaper	pañal *(el)*	*(ehl pah-'nyahl)*
diaphragm	diafragma *(el)*	*(ehl dee-ah-'frahg-mah)*
Do you wear a diaphragm?	¿Tiene puesto un diafragma?	*(tee-'eh-neh 'pwehs-toh oon dee-ah-'frahg-mah)*
diarrhea	diarrea *(la)*	*(lah dee-ah-'rreh-ah)*

Do you have diarrhea?	¿Tiene diarrea?	*(tee-'eh-neh dee-ah-'rreh-ah)*
die (to)	morir	*(moh-'reer)*
What did he/she die of?	¿De qué se murió?	*(deh keh seh moo-ree-'oh)*
He/she is going to die.	Se va a morir.	*(seh bah ah moh-'reer)*
diet	dieta *(la)*	*(lah dee-'eh-tah)*
bland diet	dieta blanda *(una)*	*('oo-nah dee-'eh-tah 'blahn-dah)*
diabetic diet	dieta para diabéticos *(una)*	*('oo-nah dee-'eh-tah 'pah-rah dee-ah-'beh-tee-kohs)*
restricted diet	dieta limitada *(una)*	*('oo-nah dee-'eh-lah lee-mee-'tah dah)*
You have to follow the diet.	Tiene que seguir la dieta.	*(tee-'eh-neh keh seh-'geer lah dee-'eh-tah)*
dietician	dietista *(el)*, dietista *(la)*	*(ehl dee-eh-'tees-tah, lah dee-eh-'tees-tah)*
different	diferente	*(dee-feh-'rehn-teh)*
difficult	difícil	*(dee-'fee-seel)*
dinner	cena *(la)*	*(lah 'seh-nah)*
diphteria	difteria *(la)*	*(lah deef-'teh-ree-ah)*
directions	instrucciones *(las)*	*(lahs een-strook-see-'oh-nehs)*
dirt	tierra *(la)*	*(lah tee-'eh-rrah)*
dirty	sucio (m.); sucia (f.)	*('soo-see-oh, 'soo-see-ah)*
disability	incapacidad *(la)*	*(lah een-kah-pah-see-'dahd)*
discharge	flujo *(el)*	*(ehl 'floo-hoh)*
discharge (to)	dar de alta	*(dahr deh 'ahl-tah)*
You will be discharged tomorrow.	Mañana lo darán de alta.	*(mah-'nyah-nah loh dah 'rahn deh 'ahl-tah)*
discount	descuento *(el)*	*(ehl dehs-kwehn-toh)*
disease	enfermedad *(la)*	*(lah ehn-fehr-meh-'dahd)*
disinfect (to)	desinfectar	*(dehs-een-fehk-'tahr)*
disinfectant	desinfectante *(el)*	*(ehl deh-seen-fehk-'tahn-teh)*
disorder	trastorno *(el)*	*(ehl trahs-'tohr-noh)*
disturbance	disturbio *(el)*	*(ehl dees-'toor-bee-oh)*
divorce	divorcio *(el)*	*(ehl dee-'bohr-see-oh)*
dizziness	mareos *(los)*	*(lohs mah-'reh-ohs)*
dizzy	mareado (m.); mareada (f.)	*(mah-reh-'ah-doh, mah-reh-'ah-dah)*

do (to)	hacer	*(ah-'sehr)*
Did you feel . . .?	¿Sintió usted. . . ?	*(seen-tee-'oh oo-'stehd)*
Did you have. . .?	¿Tuvo usted . . .?	*('too-boh oo-'stehd)*
Did you want . . .?	¿Deseó usted . . .?	*(deh-seh-'oh oo-'stehd)*
Do you feel . . .?	¿Siente usted . . .?	*(see-'ehn-teh oo-'stehd)*
Do you have. . .?	¿Tiene usted . . .?	*(tee-'eh-neh oo-'stehd)*
Do you want . . .?	¿Desea usted. . . ?	*(deh-'seh-ah oo-'stehd)*
doctor	doctor *(el)*, doctora *(la)* or médico *(el)*; médica *(la)*	*(ehl dohk-tohr, lah dohk-'toh-rah* or *ehl 'meh-dee-koh, lah 'meh-dee-kah)*
dog	perro *(el)*	*(ehl 'peh-rroh)*
dog bite	mordedura de perro *(la)*	*(lah mohr-deh-'doo-rah deh 'peh-rroh)*
doll	muñeca *(la)*	*(lah moo-'nyeh-kah)*
door	puerta *(la)*	*(lah 'pwehr-tah)*
dosage	dosis *(la)*	*(lah 'doh-sees)*
high dosage	dosis alta *(la)*	*(lah 'doh-sees 'ahl-tah)*
low dosage	dosis baja *(la)*	*(lah 'doh-sees 'bah-hah)*
Let's lower the dosage.	Vamos a bajar la dosis.	*('bah-mohs ah bah-'hahr lah 'doh-sees)*
double	doble *(el)*	*(ehl 'doh-bleh)*
down	abajo de	*(ah-'bah-hoh deh)*
drawer	cajón *(el)*	*(ehl kah-'hohn)*
dreams	sueños *(los)*	*(lohs 'sweh-nyohs)*
dress	vestido *(el)*	*(ehl behs-'tee-doh)*
drill	taladro *(el)*	*(ehl tah-'lah-droh)*
drill (to)	perforar	*(pehr-foh-'rahr)*
drink (to)	beber	*(beh-'behr)*
Don't drink alcohol with this.	No beba alcohol con esto.	*(noh 'beh-bah ahl-koh-'ohl kohn 'eh-stoh)*
Drink *(request to)*	Beba.	*("beh-bah)*
drive (to)	manejar	*(mah-neh-'hahr)*
driver's license	licencia de manejar *(la)*	*(lah lee-'sehn-see-ah deh mah-neh-'hahr)*
drops	gotas *(las)*	*(lahs 'goh-tahs)*
drought	sequía *(la)*	*(lah seh-'kee-ah)*
drown oneself (to)	ahogarse	*(ah-oh-'gahr-seh)*
He/she drowned.	Se ahogó.	*(seh ah-oh-'goh)*
drugs	drogas *(las)*	*(lahs 'droh-gahs)*

drugs (legal)	remedios *(los)*	*(lohs reh-'meh-dee-ohs)*
drug addict	drogadicto *(el)*, drogadicta *(la)*	*(ehl droh-ah-'deek-toh, lah drohg-ah-'deek-tah)*
drug addiction	drogadicción *(la)*	*(lah drohg-ah-deek-see-'ohn)*
drug dealer	droguero *(el)*, traficante de drogas *(el)*	*(ehl droh-'geh-roh, ehl trah-fee-'kahn-teh deh 'droh-gahs)*
drug traffic	narcotráfico	*(nahr-koh-'trah-fee-koh*
drug use	uso de drogas *(el)*	*(ehl 'oo-soh deh 'droh-gahs)*
drug-related	relacionado con drogas	*(reh-lah-see-oh-'nah-doh kohn 'droh-gahs)*
Have you been drinking or taking drugs?	¿Ha tomado licor o drogas?	*(ah toh-'mah-doh lee-'kohr oh 'droh-gahs)*
drunk	borracho *(el)*, borracha *(la)*	*(ehl boh-'rrah-choh, lah boh-'rrah chah)*
dry	seco (m.); seca (f.)	*('seh-koh, 'seh-kah)*
dull (edge)	romo	*('roh-moh)*
dull (sound)	sordo	*('sohr-doh)*
dust	polvo *(el)*	*(ehl 'pohl boh)*
ear	oído *(el)*	*(ehl oh-'ee-doh)*
earache	dolor de oído	*(doh-'lohr deh oh-'ee-doh)*
Are you exposed to loud noise?	¿Está expuesto a ruidos fuertes?	*(eh-'stah ehks-'pwehs-toh uh roo-'ee-dohs 'fwehr-tehs)*
Are you losing your hearing?	¿Está poniéndose sordo?	*(eh-'stah poh-nee-'ehn-doh-seh 'sohr-doh)*
Did you have an ear injury?	¿Tuvo una lesión en el oído?	*(too-boh 'oo-nah leh-see-'ohn ehn ehl oh-'ee-doh)*
Do you hear ringing or buzzing?	¿Oye un campanilleo o un zumbido?	*('oh-yeh oon kahm-pah-nee-'yeh-oh oh oon soom-'bee-doh)*
Do you lose your balance easily?	¿Pierde el equilibrio fácilmente?	*(pee-'ehr-deh ehl eh-kee-'lee-bree-oh fah-seel-'mehn-teh)*
Do your ears itch?	¿Le pican los oídos?	*(leh 'pee-kahn lohs oh-'ee-dohs)*
Does your ear suppurate?	¿Le sale líquido del oído?	*(leh 'sah-leh 'lee-kee-doh dehl oh-'ee-doh)*
early	temprano	*(tehm-prah-noh)*
earrings	aretes *(los)*	*(lohs ah-'reh-tehs)*
earthquake	terremoto *(el)*	*(ehl teh-rreh-'moh-toh)*
easy	fácil	*('fah-seel)*
eat (to)	comer	*(koh-'mehr)*

Eat *(request to)*	Coma.	*('koh-mah)*
ECG	electrocardiograma *(el)*	*(ehl eh-lehk-troh-kahr-dee-oh-'grah-mah)*
EEG	electroencefalograma *(el)*	*(ehl eh-lehk-troh-ehn-seh-fah-loh-'grah-mah)*
egg	huevo *(el)*	*(ehl 'weh-boh)*
eight	ocho	*('oh-choh)*
eighth	octavo	*(ohk-'tah-boh)*
elbow	codo *(el)*	*(ehl 'koh-doh)*
elderly	ancianos *(los)*	*(lohs ahn-see-'ah-nohs)*
elderly person	anciano (m.); anciana (f.)	*(ahn-see-'ah-noh, ahn-see-'ah-nah)*
electric fan	ventilador *(el)*	*(ehl behn-tee-lah-'dohr)*
electricity	electricidad *(la)*	*(lah eh-lehk-tree-see-'dahd)*
elevator	ascensor *(el)*	*(ehl ah-sehn-'sohr)*
eleven	once	*('ohn-seh)*
embryo	embrión *(el)*	*(ehl ehm-bree-'ohnv)*
emergency	emergencia *(la)*	*(lah eh-mehr-'hehn-see-ah)*
emergency operation	operación de emergencia *(la)*	*(lah oh-peh-rah-see-'ohn deh eh-mehr-'hehn-see-ah)*
Emergency Room	sala de emergencia *(la)*	*(lah 'sah-lah deh eh-mehr-'hehn-see-ah)*
emotional problems	problemas emocionales *(los)*	*(lohs proh-'bleh-mahs eh-moh-see-oh-'nah-lehs)*
emphysema	enfisema *(la)*	*(lah ehn-fee-'seh-mah)*
employee	empleado *(el)*, empleada *(la)*	*(ehl ehm-pleh-'ah-doh, lah ehm-pleh-'ah-dah)*
employer	empresario *(el)*, patrón *(el)*, jefe *(el)*	*(ehl ehm-preh-'sah-ree-oh, ehl pah-'trohn, ehl 'heh-feh)*
Who is your employer?	¿Quién es su patrón (jefe)?	*(kee-'ehn ehs soo pah-'trohn 'heh-feh)*
employment	empleo *(el)*	*(ehl ehm-'pleh-oh)*
Are you employed now?	¿Tiene empleo ahora?	*(tee-'eh-neh ehm-'pleh-oh ah-'oh-rah)*
When did you stop working?	¿Cuándo dejó de trabajar?	*('kwahn-doh deh-'hoh deh trah-bah-'hahr)*
empty	vacío	*(bah-'see-oh)*
enamel	esmalte *(el)*	*(ehl ehs-'mahl-teh)*
end (to)	terminar	*(tehr-mee-'nahr)*
enema	enema *(el)*	*(ehl eh-'neh-mah)*
enough	bastante	*(bahs-'tahn-teh)*

entrance	entrada *(la)*	*(lah ehn-'trah-dah)*
envelope	sobre *(el)*	*(ehl 'soh-breh)*
epidemic	epidemia *(la)*	*(lah eh-pee-'deh-mee-ah)*
epilepsy	epilepsia *(la)*	*(lah ehppee-'lehp-see-ah)*
epileptic	epiléptico *(el)*, epiléptica *(la)*	*(ehl-eh-pee-'lehp-tee-koh, lah-eh-pee-'lehp-tee-kah)*
epsom salt	sal de epsom *(la)*	*(lah sahl deh ehp-'sohm)*
equipment	equipo *(el)*	*(chl eh-'kee-poh)*
esophagus	esófago *(el)*	*(ehl eh-'soh-fah-goh)*
evaluate (to)	evaluar	*(eh-bah-loo-'ahr)*
exam	examen *(el)*	*(ehl ehk-'sah mehn)*
The exam will take two hours.	El examen tomará dos horas.	*(ehl ehk-'sah-mehn toh-mah 'rah dohs 'oh-rahs)*
examine (to)	examinar	*(ehk-sah-mee-'nahr)*
I'm going to examine your leg.	Voy a examinar su pierna.	*('boh-ee ah ehk-sah-mee-'nahr soo pee-'ehr-nah)*
excited	emocionado (m.); emocionada (f.)	*(eh-moh-see-oh-'nah-doh, eh-moh-see-oh-'nah-dah)*
exercise	ejercicio *(el)*	*(ehl eh-hehr-'see-see-oh)*
Do you exercise often?	¿Hace ejercicios a menudo?	*('ah-seh eh-hehr-'see-see-ohs ah meh-'noo-doh)*
exhale (to)	exhalar	*(ehks-ah-'lahr)*
Exhale *(request to)*	Exhale.	*(ehks-'ah-leh)*
Exhale slowly.	Exhale lentamente.	*(ehks-'ah-leh lehn-tah-'mehn-teh)*
exhausted	agotado (m.); agotada (f.)	*(ah-goh-'tah-doh, ah-goh-'tah-dah)*
Are you exhausted?	¿Está agotado?	*(eh-'stah ah-goh-'tah-doh)*
exhaustion	cansancio *(el)*	*(ehl kahn-'sahn-see-oh)*
exit	salida *(la)*	*(lah sah-'lee-dah)*
expenses	gastos *(los)*	*(lohs 'gahs-tohs)*
explain (to)	explicar	*(ehks-plee-'kahr)*
extend	estirar	*(ehs-'tee-rahr)*
Extend *(request to)*	Estire.	*(ehs-'tee-reh)*
extract (to)	extraer	*(ehks-trah-'ehr)*
Do you want me to extract the tooth?	¿Desea que yo extraiga el diente?	*(deh-'seh-ah keh yoh ehks-'trah-ee-gah ehl dee-'ehn-teh)*
I will extract the tooth.	Voy a extraer el diente.	*('boh-ee ah ehks-trah-'ehr ehl dee-'ehn-teh)*
extraction	extracción *(la)*	*(lah ehks-trahk-see-'ohn)*

eye	ojo *(el)*	*(ehl 'oh-hoh)*
Are you color blind?	¿No ve usted los colores?	*(noh beh oo-'stehd lohs koh-'loh-rehs)*
Are you farsighted?	¿Tiene usted presbicia?	*(tee-'eh-neh oo-'stehd prehs-'bee-see·ah)*
Are you nearsighted?	¿Tiene usted miopía?	*(tee-'eh-neh oo-'stehd mee-oh-'pee-ah)*
Close your eyes.	Cierre los ojos.	*(see-'eh-rreh los 'oh-hohs)*
Do you have pain in the eyes?	¿Le duelen los ojos?	*(leh 'dweh-lehn lohs 'oh-hohs)*
Do you have something in your eye?	¿Tiene algo en el ojo?	*(tee-'eh-neh 'ahl-goh ehn ehl 'oh-hoh)*
Do you see double?	¿Lo ve todo doble?	*(loh beh 'toh-doh 'doh-bleh)*
Do you see spots?	¿Ve puntos delante de los ojos?	*(beh 'poon-tohs deh-'lahn-teh deh lohs 'oh-hohs)*
Do you wear glasses?	¿Usa usted anteojos?	*('oo-sah oo-'stehd ahn-teh-'oh-hohs)*
Do your eyes water?	¿Le lloran los ojos?	*(leh 'yoh-rahn lohs 'oh-hohs)*
Open your eyes.	Abra los ojos.	*('ah-brah lohs 'oh-hohs)*
eye drops	gotas para los ojos *(las)*	*(lahs 'goh-tahs 'pah-rah lohs 'oh-hohs)*
eyebrow	ceja *(la)*	*(lah 'seh-hah)*
eyelash	pestaña *(la)*	*(lah pehs-'tah-nyah)*
eyelid	párpado *(el)*	*(ehl 'pahr-pah-doh)*
face	cara *(la)*	*(lah 'kah-rah)*
factory	fábrica or factoría *(la)*	*(lah 'fah-bree-kah, fahk-toh-'ree-ah)*
failure	fracaso *(el)*	*(ehl frah-'kah-soh)*
faint (to)	desmayarse	*(dehs-mah-'yahr-seh)*
fall	otoño *(el)*	*(ehl oh-'tohn-yoh)*
Fallopian tubes	trompas de Falopio *(las)*	*(lahs 'trohm-pahs deh fah-'loh-pee·oh)*
false	postizo	*(pohs-'tee-soh)*
family	familia *(la)*	*(lah fah-'mee-lee-ah)*
farmer	campesino *(el)*	*(ehl kahm-peh-'see-noh)*
fast	rápido	*('rah-pee-doh)*
fat (food)	grasa *(la)*	*(lah 'grah-sah)*
fat (person)	gordo	*('gohr-doh)*
father	padre *(el)*	*(ehl 'pah-dreh)*
father-in-law	suegro *(el)*	*(ehl 'sweh-groh)*
fatigue	fatiga *(la)*	*(lah fah-'tee-gah)*
fear	miedo *(el)*	*(ehl mee-'eh-doh)*
February	febrero	*(feh-'breh-roh)*
feed (to)	alimentar	*(ah-lee-mehn-'tahr)*

feel (to)	sentir	*(sehn-'teer)*
feminine napkin	paño higiénico *(el)*	*(ehl 'pah-nyoh ee-hee-'eh-nee-koh)*
fertilization	fertilización *(la)*	*(lah fehr-tee-lee-sah-see-'ohn)*
fetal alcohol syndrome	síndrome del alcohol fetal *(el)*	*(ehl 'seen-droh-meh dehl ahl-koh-'ohl) (feh-'tahl)*
fetus	feto *(el)*	*(ehl 'feh-toh)*
fever	fiebre *(la)*	*(lah fee-'eh-breh)*
few	pocos	*('poh-kohs)*
fiber	fibra *(la)*	*(lah 'feeb-rah)*
fifth	quinto	*('keen-toh)*
fight (to)	pelear	*(peh-leh-'ahr)*
file (nailfile)	lima *(la)*	*(lah 'lee-mah)*
file (to)	limar	*(lee-'mahr)*
fill out (to)	llenar	*(yeh-'nahr)*
fill (teeth) (to)	empastar	*(ehm-pahs-'tahr)*
filling (for tooth)	empaste *(el)*	*(ehl ehm-'pahs-teh)*
find (to)	encontrar	*(ehn-kohn-'trahr)*
finger	dedo *(el)*	*(ehl 'deh-doh)*
fire	fuego *(el)*, incendio *(el)*	*(ehl 'fweh-goh, ehl een-'sehn-dee-oh)*
fireman	bombero *(el)*	*(ehl bohm-'beh-roh)*
first	primero	*(pree-'meh-roh)*
first aid	primeros auxilios *(los)*	*(lohs pree-'meh-rohs owk-'sve-lee-ohs)*
first floor	primer piso *(el)*	*(ohl pree-'mehr 'pee-soh)*
fish	pescado *(el)*	*(ehl pehs-'kah-doh)*
fits	ataques *(los)*	*(lohs ah-'tah-kehs)*
fixed	fijo	*('fee-hoh)*
flames	llamas *(las)*	*(lahs 'yah-mahs)*
flatulence	flatulencia *(la)*	*(lah flah-too-'lehn-see-ah)*
fleas	pulgas *(las)*	*(lahs 'pool-gahs)*
flood	inundación *(la)*	*(lah een-oon-dah-see-'ohn)*
floor	piso *(el)*	*(ehl 'pee-soh)*
flour	harina *(la)*	*(lah ah-'ree-nah)*
flower	flor *(la)*	*(lah flohr)*
flower vase	florero *(el)*	*(ehl floh-'reh-roh)*
foam	espuma *(la)*	*(lah ehs-'poo-mah)*
follow (to)	seguir	*(seh-'geer)*
Follow *(request to)*	Siga.	*('see-gah)*

Follow the diet.	Siga la dieta.	*('see-gah lah dee-'eh-tah)*
Follow the instructions.	Siga las instrucciones.	*('see-gah lahs een-strook-see-'oh-nehs)*
food	comida *(la)*	*(lah koh-'mee-dah)*
foot	pie *(el)*	*(ehl 'pee'eh)*
for	por, para	*(pohr, 'pah-rah)*
forceps	tenazas *(las)*	*(lahs teh-'nah-sahs)*
forearm	antebrazo *(el)*	*(ehl ahn-teh-'brah-soh)*
forehead	frente *(la)*	*(lah 'frehn-teh)*
forest	bosque *(el)*	*(ehl 'bohs-keh)*
fork	tenedor *(el)*	*(ehl teh-neh-'dohr)*
form	formulario *(el)*	*(ehl fohr-moo-'lah-ree-oh)*
Fill out this form.	Llene este formulario.	*('yeh-neh 'ehs-teh fohr-moo-'lah-ree-oh)*
formula	fórmula *(la)*	*(lah 'fohr-moo-lah)*
fourth	cuarto	*('kwahr-toh)*
free	gratis	*('grah-tees)*
frequency	frecuencia *(la)*	*(lah freh-'kwen-see-ah)*
frequently	con frecuencia	*(kohn freh-'kwehn-see-ah)*
Friday	viernes	*(bee-'ehr-nehs)*
front of	frente de	*('frehn-teh deh)*
frostbite	congelamiento *(el)*	*(ehl kohn-heh-lah-mee 'ehn-toh)*
fruit	fruta *(la)*	*(lah 'froo-tah)*
full	lleno	*('yeh-noh)*
function (to)	funcionar	*(foon-see-oh-'nahr)*
furniture	muebles *(los)*	*(lohs 'mweh-blehs)*
gain (weight) (to)	engordar	*(ehn-gohr-'dahr)*
They are gaining weight.	Están engordando.	*(Eh-'stahn ehn-gohr-'dahn-doh)*
gallstones	cálculos en la vesícula *(los)*	*(lohs 'kahl-koo-lohs ehn lah beh-'see-koo-lah)*
game	juego *(el)*	*(ehl 'hweh-goh)*
gardener	jardinero *(el)*	*(ehl hahr-dee-'neh-roh)*
gargle (to)	hacer gárgaras	*(ah-'sehr 'gahr-gah-rahs)*
garlic	ajo *(el)*	*(ehl 'ah-hoh)*
gas	gas *(el)*	*(ehl gahs)*
gastroenterologist	gastroenterólogo *(el)*	*(ehl gahs-troh-ehn-teh-'roh-loh-goh)*
gastroenterology	gastroenterología *(la)*	*(lah gahs-troh-ehn-teh-roh-loh-'gee-ah)*

gastrointestinal	gastrointestinal *(lo)*	*(loh gahs-troh-een-tehs-tee-'nahl)*
Are your stools black?	¿Son de color negro sus excrementos?*)*	*(sohn deh koh-'lohr 'neh-groh soos ehks-kreh-'mehn-tohs)*
Are your stools bloody?	¿Tienen sangre sus excrementos?	*(tee-'eh-nehn 'sahn-greh soos ehks-kreh-'mehn-tohs)*
Do you ever vomit blood?	¿Vomita sangre a veces?	*(boh-'mee-tah 'sahn-greh ah 'beh-sehs)*
Do you feel itching, pain, or burning in the rectum?	¿Siente picazón, dolor o quemazón en el recto?	*(see-'ehn-teh pee-kah-'sohn, doh-'lohr oh keh-mah-'sohn ehn ehl 'rehk-toh)*
Do you have a good appetite?	¿Tiene buen apetito?	*(tee-'eh-neh bwehn ah-peh-'tee-toh)*
Do you have frequent stomachaches?	¿Le duele el estómago a menudo?	*(leh 'dweh-leh ehl ehs-'toh-mah-goh ah meh-'noo-doh)*
Do you have indigestion and heartburn often?	¿Tiene indigestión y ardor de estómago a menudo?	*(tee-'eh-neh een-dee-hehs-tee-'ohn ee ahr-'dohr deh ehs-'toh-mah-goh ah meh-'noo-doh)*
Do you have nausea often?	¿Tiene náuseas con frecuencia?	*(tee-'eh-neh 'now-seh-ahs kohn freh-'kwehn-see-ah)*
gastritis	gastritis *(la)*	*(lah gahs-'tree-tees)*
gauze	gasa *(la)*	*(lah 'gah-sah)*
genes	genes *(los)*	*('lohs 'heh-nehs)*
genitals	genitales *(los)*	*(lohs heh-nee-'tah-lehs)*
genitourinary	genitourinario	*(heh-nee-toh-oo-ree-'nah-ree-oh)*
German measles	rubéola *(la)*	*(lah roo-'beh-oh-lah)*
get dressed (to)	vestirse	*(behs-'teer-seh)*
get sick (to)	enfermarse	*(ehn-fehr-'mahr-seh)*
gift	regalo *(el)*	*(ehl reh-'gah-loh)*
gift shop	tienda de regalos *(la)*	*(lah tee-'ehn-dah deh reh-'gah-lohs)*
girdle	faja *(la)*	*(lah 'fah-hah)*
girlfriend	novia *(la)*	*(lah 'noh-bee-ah)*
give (to)	dar	*(dahr)*
gland	glándula *(la)*	*(lah 'glahn-doo-lah)*
glass (drinking)	vaso *(el)*	*(ehl 'bah-soh)*
glasses (eyewear)	anteojos *(los)*	*(lohs ahn-teh-'oh-hohs)*
Do you wear glasses or contact lenses?	¿Usa anteojos o lentes de contacto?	*('oo-sah ahn-teh-'oh-hohs oh 'lehn-tehs deh kohn-'tahk-toh)*
glaucoma	glaucoma *(el)*	*(ehl glaw-'koh-mah)*

gloves	guantes *(los)*	*(lohs 'gwahn-tehs)*
glue	goma *(la)*	*(lah 'goh-mah)*
go to (to)	ir	*(eer)*
go up (to)	subir	*(soo-'beer)*
gold	oro *(el)*	*(ehl 'oh-roh)*
gonorrhea	gonorrea *(la)*	*(lah goh-noh-'rreh-ah)*
good	bueno	*('bweh-noh)*
gout	gota *(la)*	*(lah 'goh-tah)*
grab (to)	agarrar	*(ah-gah-'rrahr)*
Grab my hand.	Agarre mi mano.	*(ah-'gah-rreh mee 'mah-noh)*
graft	injerto *(el)*	*(ehl een-'hehr-toh)*
grams	gramos *(los)*	*(lohs 'grah-mohs)*
granddaughter	nieta *(la)*	*(lah nee-'eh-tah)*
grandfather	abuelo *(el)*	*(ehl ah-'bweh-loh)*
grandmother	abuela *(la)*	*(lah ah-'bweh-lah)*
grandson	nieto *(el)*	*(ehl nee-'eh-toh)*
grape	uva *(la)*	*(lah 'oo-bah)*
grapefruit	toronja *(la)*	*(lah toh-'rohn-hah)*
grass	hierba *(la)*	*(lah 'yehr-bah)*
gray	gris	*(grees)*
grease	grasa *(la)*	*(lah 'grah-sah)*
green	verde	*('behr-deh)*
green bean	ejote *(el)*	*(ehl eh-'hoh-teh)*
greeting card	tarjeta de saludo *(la)*	*(lah tahr-'heh-tah deh sah-'loo-doh)*
grief	tristeza *(la)*	*(lah trees-'teh-sah)*
groin	ingle *(la)*	*(lah 'een-gleh)*
group	grupo *(el)*	*(ehl 'groo-poh)*
grow (to)	crecer	*(kreh-'sehr)*
gum	chicle *(el)*	*(ehl 'chee-kleh)*
gums	encías *(las)*	*(lahs ehn-'see-ahs)*
gunshot wound	herida de bala *(la)*	*(lah eh-'ree-dah deh 'bah-lah)*
gynecologist	ginecólogo *(el)*	*(ehl hee-neh-'koh-loh-goh)*
hair	cabello *(el)*	*(ehl kah-'beh-yoh)*
haircut	corte de pelo *(el)*	*(ehl 'kohr-teh deh 'peh-loh)*
half	mitad *(la)*	*(lah mee-'tahd)*
hallway	corredor *(el)*	*(ehl koh-rreh-'dohr)*
hand	mano *(la)*	*(lah 'mah-noh)*

handbag	bolsa *(la)*	*(lah 'bohl-sah)*
hangnail	padrastro *(el)*	*(ehl pah-'drahs-troh)*
happy	feliz (m. & f.)	*(feh-'lees)*
hard	duro (m.); dura (f.)	*('doo-roh, 'doo-rah)*
hardening	endurecimiento *(el)*	*(ehl ehn-doo-reh-see-mee-'ehn-toh)*
have (to)	tener	*(teh-'nehr)*
Do you have problems with . . .?	¿Tiene problemas con . . .?	*(tee-'eh-neh proh-'bleh-mahs kohn)*
Have you had problems?	¿Ha tenido problemas?	*(ah teh-'nee-doh proh-'bleh-mahs)*
I have a lot of pain.	Tengo mucho dolor.	*('tehn-goh 'moo-choh doh-'lohr)*
hay fever	fiebre del heno *(la)*	*(lah fee-'eh-breh dehl 'eh-noh)*
he	él	*(ehl)*
head	cabeza *(la)*	*(lah kah-'beh-sah)*
headache	dolor de cabeza *(el)*	*(ehl doh-'lohr deh kah-'beh sah)*
headrest	apoyo *(el)*	*(ehl ah-'poh-yoh)*
health	salud *(la)*	*(lah sah-'lood)*
health care	servicios de salud *(los)*	*(lohs sehr-'bee-see ohs deh sah-'lood)*
hear (to)	oír	*(oh-'eer)*
hearing aids	audífonos *(los)*	*(lohs ow-'dee-foh-nohs)*
heart	corazón *(el)*	*(ehl koh-rah-'sohn)*
heart attack	ataque cardíaco *(el)*	*(ehl ah-'tah-keh kahr 'dee-ah-koh)*
heart disease	enfermedad cardíaca *(la)*	*(lah ehn-fehr-meh-'dahd kahr-'dee-ah-kah)*
heart murmurs	murmullos en el corazón *(los)*	*(lohs moor-'moo-yohs ehn ehl koh-rah-'sohn)*
heartbeat	ritmo cardíaco *(el)*	*(ehl 'reet-moh kahr-'dee-ah-koh)*
heat	calor *(el)*	*(ehl kah-'lohr)*
heat stroke	postración *(la)*	*(lah pohs-trah-see-'ohn)*
heating	calefacción *(la)*	*(lah kah-leh-fahk-see-'ohn)*
heel	talón *(el)*	*(ehl tah-'lohn)*
height	altura *(la)*	*(lah ahl-'too-rah)*
helicopter	helicóptero *(el)*	*(ehl eh-lee-'kohp-teh-roh)*
help	ayuda *(la)*	*(lah ah-'yoo-dah)*
help (to)	ayudar	*(ah-yoo-'dahr)*
We're going to help the patient.	Vamos a ayudar al paciente.	*('bah-mohs ah ah-yoo-'dahr ahl pah-see-'ehn-teh)*
hemorrhage	hemorragia *(la)*	*(lah eh-mohr-'rah-hee-ah)*

hemorrhoids	hemorroides *(los)*	*(lohs eh-moh-'rroh-ee-dehs)*
hepatitis	hepatitis *(la)*	*(lah ehp-ah-'tee-tees)*
her	su	*(soo)*
here	aquí	*(ah-'kee)*
hereditary	hereditario	*(eh-reh-dee-'tah-ree-oh)*
heroin	heroína *(la)*	*(lah eh-roh-'ee-nah)*
hiccups	hipo *(el)*	*(ehl 'ee-poh)*
highway	carretera *(la)*	*(lah kah-rreh-'teh-rah)*
hip	cadera *(la)*	*(lah kah-'deh-rah)*
his	su	*(soo)*
HIV	VIH *(el)*	*(ehl beh-ee-'ah-cheh)*
hives	urticaria *(la)*	*(lah oor-tee-'kah-ree-ah)*
hold (to)	mantener	*(mahn-teh-'nehr)*
Hold *(request to)*	Mantenga.	*(mahn-'tehn-gah)*
Holter scan	prueba de Holter *(la)*	*(lah proo-'eh-bah deh ohl-'tehr)*
honey	miel *(la)*	*(lah mee-e'ehl)*
hormones	hormonas *(las)*	*(lahs ohr-'moh-nahs)*
hospital	hospital *(el)*	*(ehl ohs-pee-'tahl)*
hot	caliente	*(kah-lee-'ehn-teh)*
hours	horas *(las)*	*(lahs 'oh-rahs)*
visiting hours	horas de visita *(las)*	*(lahs 'oh-rahs deh bee-'see-tah)*
how?	¿cómo?	*('koh-moh)*
how many?	¿cuántos?	*('kwahn-tohs)*
how much?	¿cuánto?	*('kwahn-toh)*
however	sin embargo	*(seen ehm-'bahr-goh)*
hunger	hambre *(el)*	*(ehl 'ahm-breh)*
hungry	hambriento (m.); hambrienta (f.)	*(ahm-bree-'ehn-toh, ahm-bree-'ehn-tah)*
hurricane	huracán *(el)*	*(ehl oo-rah-'kahn)*
husband	esposo *(el)*	*(ehl ehs-'poh-soh)*
hydrogen peroxide	agua oxigenada *(el)*	*(ehl 'ah-gwah ohk-see-heh-'nah-dah)*
hygienist	higienista (m. & f.)	*(ehl (lah) ee-hee-eh-'nees-tah)*
hypertension	hipertensión *(la)*	*(lah ee-per-ten-see-'ohn)*
hypoglycemia	hipoglicemia *(la)*	*(lah ee-poh-glee-'seh-mee-ah)*
hysterectomy	histerectomía *(la)*	*(lah ees-teh-rehk-toh-'mee-ah)*
hysteria	histerismo *(el)*	*(ehl ees-teh-'rees-moh)*
I	yo	*(yoh)*

I.V.	intravenoso	*(een-trah-beh-'noh-soh)*
ice	hielo *(el)*	*(ehl 'yeh-loh)*
ice cream	helado *(el)*	*(ehl eh-'lah-doh)*
ice pack	bolsa de hielo *(la)*	*(lah 'bohl-sah deh ee-'eh-loh)*
identification	identificación *(la)*	*(lah ee-dehn-tee-fee-kah-see-'ohn)*
illness	enfermedad *(la)*	*(lah ehn-fehr-meh-'dahd)*
mental illness	enfermedad mental *(la)*	*(lah ehn-fehr-meh-'dahd mehn-'tahl)*
immediately	inmediatamente	*(eeh-meh-dee-ah-tah-'mehn-teh)*
immunotherapy	inmunoterapia *(la)*	*(lah een-moo-noh-teh-'rah-pee-ah)*
impaction	impacción *(la)*	*(lah eem-pahk-see-'ohn)*
impacted tooth	diente impactado *(el)*	*(ehl dee-'ehn-teh eem-pahk-'tah-doh)*
improve (to)	mejorar	*(meh-hoh-'rahr)*
in, on	en	*(ehn)*
in-patient	paciente interno *(el)*	*(ehl pah-see-'ehn-teh een-'tehr-noh*
inch	pulgada *(la)*	*(lah pool-'gah-dah)*
income	ingreso *(el)*	*(ehl een-'greh-soh)*
indigestion	indigestión *(la)*	*(lah een-dee-hehs-tee-'ohn)*
infant	infante *(el)*	*(ehl een-'fahn-teh)*
infant car seat	asiento para infantes *(el)*	*(ehl ah-see-'ehn-toh 'pah-rah een-'fahn-tehs)*
infected	infectado (m.); infectada (f.)	*(een-fehk-'tah-doh, een-fehk-'tah-dah)*
infection	infección *(la)*	*(lah een-fehk-see-'ohn)*
infertility	infertilidad *(la)*	*(lah een-fehr-tee-lee-'dahd)*
inflamed	inflamado (m.); inflamada (f.)	*(een-flah-'mah-doh, een-flah-'mah dah)*
inflammation	inflamación *(la)*	*(lah een-flah-mah-see-'ohn)*
information	información *(la)*	*(lah een-fohr-mah-see-'ohn)*
ingrown toenail	uña encarnada *(la)*	*(lah 'oo-nyah ehn-kahr-'nah-dah)*
inhale (to)	aspirar	*(ahs-'pee-rahr)*
Inhale *(request to)*	Aspire.	*(ahs-'pee-reh)*
injection	inyección *(la)*	*(lah een-yehk-see-'ohn)*
injury	herida *(la)*	*(lah eh-'ree-dah)*
injured	herido (m.); herida (f.)	*(eh-'ree-doh, eh-'ree-dah)*
Are you injured?	¿Está herido?	*(eh-'stah eh-'ree-doh)*
inlay	incrustación *(la)*	*(lah een-kroos-tah-see-'ohn)*
insanity	locura *(la)*	*(lah loh-'koo-rah)*

insect bite	mordedura de insecto *(la)*	*(lah mohr-deh-'doo-rah deh een-'sehk-toh)*
insecticide	insecticida *(el)*	*(ehl een-sehk-tee-'se-dah)*
inside	adentro de	*(ah-'dehn-troh deh)*
insomnia	insomnio *(el)*	*(ehl een-'sohm-nee-oh)*
instrument	instrumento *(el)*	*(ehl een-stroo-'mehn-toh)*
insurance	seguro *(el)*	*(ehl seh-'goo-roh)*
accident insurance	seguro de accidente *(el)*	*(ehl seh-'goo-roh deh ahk-see-'dehn-teh)*
health insurance	seguro de salud *(el)*	*(ehl seh-'goo-roh deh sah-'lood)*
insurance company	compañía de seguros *(la)*	*(lah kohm-pah-'nyee-ah deh seh-'goo-rohs)*
life insurance	seguro de vida *(el)*	*(ehl seh-'goo-roh deh 'bee-dah)*
Do you have insurance?	¿Tiene seguro?	*(tee-'eh-neh seh-'goo-roh)*
Intensive Care	sala de cuidados intensivos *(la)*	*(lah 'sah-lah deh kwee-'dah-dohs een-tehn-'see-bohs)*
intermediate care	cuidado intermedio *(el)*	*(ehl kwee-'dah-doh een-tehr-'meh-dee-oh)*
intermittent	intermitente	*(een-tehr-mee-'tehn-teh)*
interpreter	intérprete (m. & f.)	*(ehl (lah) een-'tehr-preh-teh)*
intoxication	intoxicación *(la)*	*(lah een-tohk-see-kah-see-'ohn)*
intravenous fluids	líquidos intravenosos *(los)*	*(lohs 'lee-kee-dohs in-trah-veh-'noh-sohs)*
iron	hierro *(el)*	*(ehl ee-'ehr-roh)*
irritated	irritado (m.); irritada (f.)	*(eer-ree-'tah-doh, eer-ree-'tah-dah)*
itch (to)	picar	*(pee-'kahr)*
itching	picazón *(la)*	*(lah pee-kah-'sohn)*
jacket	chaqueta *(la)*	*(lah chah-'keh-tah)*
January	enero	*(eh-'neh-roh)*
jaundice	ictericia *(la)*	*(lah eek-teh-'ree-see-ah)*
jaw	mandíbula *(la)*	*(lah mahn-'dee-boo-lah)*
jelly	jalea *(la)*	*(lah hah-'leh-ah)*
jewelry	joyas *(las)*	*(lahs 'hoh-yahs)*
joint	articulación *(la)*	*(lah ahr-tee-koo-lah-see-'ohn)*
juice	jugo *(el)*	*(ehl 'hoo-goh)*
July	julio	*('hoo-lee-oh)*
June	junio	*('hoo-nee-oh)*
jungle	selva *(la)*	*(lah 'sehl-bah)*
keep (to)	guardar	*('gwahr-dahr)*

Keep *(request to)*	Guarde.	*('gwahr-deh)*
kick (to)	patear	*(pah-teh-'ahr)*
kidney	riñón *(el)*	*(ehl ree-'nyohn)*
kidney stones	cálculos en los riñones *(los)*	*(lohs 'kahl-koo-lohs ehn lohs ree-'nyoh-nehs)*
knee	rodilla *(la)*	*(lah roh-'dee-yah)*
kneecap	rótula *(la)*	*(lah 'roh-too-lah)*
knife	cuchillo *(el)*	*(ehl koo-'chee-yoh)*
label	etiqueta *(la)*	*(lah eh-tee-'keh-tah)*
labor pains	dolores de parto *(los)*	*(doh-'loh-rehs deh 'pahr-toh)*
laboratory	laboratorio *(el)*	*(ehl lah-boh-rah-'toh-ree-oh)*
laborer	obrero *(el)*	*(ehl oh-'breh-roh)*
lack (to)	faltar	*(fahl-'tahr)*
lake	lago *(el)*	*(ehl 'lah-goh)*
lane	pista *(la)*	*(lah 'pees-tah)*
language	lenguaje *(el)*	*(ehl lehn-'gwah-heh)*
laparoscopy	laparoscopia *(la)*	*(lah lah-pah-roh-'skoh-pee-ah)*
lard	manteca *(la)*	*(lah mahn-'teh-kah)*
last	último	*('ool-tee-moh)*
last (to)	durar	*(doo-'rahr)*
late	tarde	*('tahr-deh)*
later	más tarde	*(mahs 'tahr-deh)*
law	ley *(la)*	*(lah 'leh-ee)*
lawyer	abogado (m.); abogada (f.)	*(ehl ah-boh-'gah-doh, lah ah-boh-'gah-dah)*
laxative	laxante *(el)*	*(ehl lahk-'sahn-teh)*
learn (to)	aprender	*(ah-prehn-'dehr)*
leave (to)	salir	*(sah-'leer)*
left	izquierdo (m.); izquierda (f.)	*(ees-kee-'ehr-doh, ees-kee-'ehr-dah)*
to the left	a la izquierda	*(ah lah ees-kee-'ehr-dah)*
leg	pierna *(la)*	*(lah pee-'ehr-nah)*
lemon	limón *(el)*	*(ehl lee-'mohn)*
lesions	lesiones *(las)*	*(lahs leh-see-'oh-nehs)*
less	menos	*('meh-nohs)*
lettuce	lechuga *(la)*	*(lah leh-'choo-gah)*
leukemia	leucemia *(la)*	*(lah leh-oo-'seh-mee-ah)*
lice	piojos *(los)*	*(lohs pee-'oh-hohs)*

lie down (to)	acostarse	*(ah-cost-'ahr-se)*
Lie down *(request to)*	Acuéstese.	*(ah-'kweh-steh-se)*
Lie on your back.	Acuéstese de espalda.	*(ah-'kwehs-teh-seh deh ehs-'pahl-dah)*
Lie on your side.	Acuéstese de lado.	*(ah-'kweh-steh-seh deh 'lah-doh)*
life	vida *(la)*	*(lah 'bee-dah)*
ligament	ligamento *(el)*	*(ehl lee-gah-'mehn-toh)*
light	luz *(la)*	*(lah loos)*
light switch	interruptor de la luz *(el)*	*(ehl een-tehr-roop-'tohr deh lah loos)*
like (to)	gustar	*(goos-'tahr)*
Do you like the bed?	¿Le gusta la cama?	*(leh 'goos-tah lah 'kah-mah)*
liniment	linimento *(el)*	*(ehl lee-nee-'mehn-toh)*
lip	labio *(el)*	*(ehl 'lah-bee-oh)*
liquid	líquido *(el)*	*(ehl 'lee-kee-doh)*
liquor	licor *(el)*	*(ehl lee-'kohr)*
listen (to)	escuchar	*(ehs-koo-'chahr)*
Listen *(request to)*	Escuche.	*(ehs-'koo-cheh)*
liters	litros *(los)*	*(lohs 'leet-rohs)*
live (to)	vivir	*(bee-'beer)*
He/she is not going to live.	No va a vivir.	*(noh bah ah bee-'beer)*
liver	hígado *(el)*	*(ehl 'ee-gah-doh)*
loan	préstamo *(el)*	*(ehl 'prehs-tah-moh)*
lobby	salón *(el)*	*(ehl sah-'lohn)*
lobe	lóbulo *(el)*	*(ehl 'loh-boo-loh)*
look (to)	mirar	*(mee-'rahr)*
Look *(request to)*	Mire.	*('mee-reh)*
look for (to)	buscar	*(boos-'kahr)*
loose	flojo (m.); floja (f.)	*('floh-hoh, 'floh-hah)*
lose (to)	perder	*(pehr-'dehr)*
lotion	loción *(la)*	*(lah loh-see-'ohn)*
lots of times	muchas veces	*('moo-chahs 'beh-sehs)*
lower (to)	bajar	*(bah-'hahr)*
Lower *(request to)*	Baje.	*('bah-heh)*
lozenge	pastilla *(la)*	*(lah pahs-'tee-yah)*
lump	bulto *(el)*	*(ehl 'bool-toh)*
lungs	pulmones *(los)*	*(lohs pool-'moh-nehs)*
lunch	almuerzo *(el)*	*(ehl ahl-moo-'ehr-soh)*

machine	máquina *(la)*	*(lah 'mah-kee-nah)*
magazine	revista *(la)*	*(lah reh-'bees-tah)*
magnesium	magnesia *(la)*	*(lah mahg-'neh-see-ah)*
mailbox	buzón *(el)*	*(ehl boo-'sohn)*
main lobby	salón principal *(el)*	*(ehl sah-'lohn preen-see-'pahl)*
make-up	maquillaje *(el)*	*(ehl mah-kee-'yah-heh)*
malaria	malaria *(la)*	*(lah mah-'lah-ree-ah)*
malignant	maligno	*(mah-'leeg-noh)*
mammogram	mamograma *(el)*	*(ehl mah-moh-'grah-mah)*
man	hombre *(el)*	*(ehl 'ohm-breh)*
manager	gerente (m. & f.)	*(ehl (lah) heh-'rehn-teh)*
maniac	maniático (m.); maniática (f.)	*(mah-nee-'ah-tee-koh, mah-nee-'ah-tee-kah)*
many	muchos (m.); muchas (f.)	*('moo-chohs, 'moo-chahs)*
map	mapa *(el)*	*(ehl 'mah-pah)*
March	marzo	*('mahr-soh)*
margarine	margarina *(la)*	*(lah mahr gah-'ree-nah)*
marijuana	marijuana *(la)*	*(lah mah-ree-'wah-nah)*
marital status	estado civil *(el)*	*(ehl ehs-'tah-doh see-'beel)*
marriage	matrimonio *(el)*	*(ehl mah-tree-'moh-nee-ohv*
married	casado (m.); casada (f.)	*(kah-'sah-doh, kah-'sah-dah)*
mask	máscara *(la)*	*(lah 'mahs-kah-rah)*
mastectomy	mastectomía *(la)*	*(lah mahs-tehk-toh-'mee-ah)*
matches	fósforos *(los)*	*(lohs 'fohs-foh-rohs)*
Maternity Ward	sala de maternidad *(la)*	*(lah 'sah-lah deh mah-tehr-nee-'dahd)*
mattress	colchón *(el)*	*(ehl kohl-'chohn)*
May	mayo	*('mah-yoh)*
measles	sarampión *(el)*	*(ehl sah-rahm-pee-'ohn)*
measure (to)	medir	*(meh-'deer)*
meat	carne *(la)*	*(lah 'kar-neh)*
mechanic	mecánico *(el)*	*(ehl meh-'kah-nee-koh)*
medicine	medicina *(la)*	*(lah meh-dee-'see-nah)*
meditation room	sala de meditación *(la)*	*(lah 'sah-lah deh meh-dee-tah-see-'ohn)*
member	miembro (m. & f.)	*(mee-'ehm-broh)*
memory	memoria *(la)*	*(lah meh-'moh-ree-ah)*
meningitis	meningitis *(la)*	*(lah meh-neen-'hee-tees)*
menstrual cycle	ciclo menstrual *(el)*	*(ehl 'seek-loh mehn-stroo-'ahl)*

menstruate (to)	menstruar	*(mens-troo-'ahr)*
meters	metros *(los)*	*(lohs 'meht-rohs)*
mild	moderado	*(moh-deh-'rah-doh)*
milk	leche *(la)*	*(lah 'leh-cheh)*
minerals	minerales *(los)*	*(lohs mee-neh-'rah-lehs)*
mirror	espejo *(el)*	*(ehl ehs-'peh-hoh)*
miscarriage	pérdida *(la)*	*(lah 'pehr-dee-dah)*
mixture	mezcla *(la)*	*(lah 'mehs-klah)*
molar	muela *(la)*	*(lah 'mweh-lahv)*
mold	molde *(el)*	*(ehl mohl-deh)*
molestation	vejación sexual *(la)*, molestia sexual *(la)*	*(lah beh-hah-see-'ohn sehk-soo-'ahl, lah moh-'lehs-tee-ah sehk-soo-'ahl)*
Monday	lunes	*('loo-nehs)*
money	dinero *(el)*	*(ehl dee-'neh-roh)*
monitor	monitor *(el)*	*(ehl moh-nee-'tohr)*
mononucleosis	mononucleosis *(la)*	*(lah moh-noh-noo-kleh-'oh-sees)*
month	mes *(el)*	*(ehl mehs)*
more	más	*(mahs)*
morphine	morfina *(la)*	*(lah mohr-'fee-nah)*
mosquito	zancudo *(el)*	*(ehl sahn-'koo-doh)*
mother	madre *(la)*	*(lah 'mah-dreh)*
mother-in-law	suegra *(la)*	*(lah 'sweh-grahv*
motorcycle	motocicleta *(la)*	*(lah moh-toh-see-'cleh-tah)*
mountain	montaña *(la)*	*(lah mohn-'tah-nyah)*
mouse	ratón *(el)*	*(ehl rah-'tohn)*
mouth	boca *(la)*	*(lah 'boh-kah)*
Do you have a sore mouth?	¿Le duele la boca?	*(leh 'dweh-leh lah 'boh-kah)*
Do you have a sore tongue?	¿Le duele la lengua?	*(leh 'dweh-leh lah 'lehn-gwah)*
Do your gums bleed often?	¿Le sangran las encías con frecuencia?	*(leh 'sahn-grahn lahs ehn-'see-ahs kohn freh-'kwehn-see-ah)*
Has your mouth felt swollen?	¿Siente hinchada la boca?	*(see-'ehn-teh een-'chah-dah lah 'boh-kah)*
Has your sense of taste changed?	¿Tiene problemas con su sentido del gusto?	*(tee-'eh-neh proh-'bleh-mahs kohn soo sehn-'tee-doh dehl 'goos-toh)*
move (to)	mover	*(moh-'vehr)*
Move *(request to)*	Mueva.	*('mweh-bah)*

movie theater	cine *(el)*	*(ehl 'see-neh)*
MRI	imagen por resonancia magnética *(la)*	*(lah ee-'mah-hen pohr reh-soh-'nahn-see-ah mag-'neh-tee-kah)*
mucous	mucoso (m.); mucosa (f.)	*(moo-'koh-soh, moo-'koh-sah)*
mucus	moco *(el)*	*(ehl 'moh-koh)*
mucus	mucosidad *(la)*	*(lah moo-koh-see-'dahd)*
mud	lodo *(el)*	*(ehl 'loh-doh)*
multiple sclerosis	esclerosis múltiple *(la)*	*(lah ehs-kleh-'roh-sees 'mool-tee-pleh)*
mumps	paperas *(las)*	*(lahs pah-'peh-rahs)*
murder (to)	matar	*(mah-'tahr)*
muscle	músculo *(el)*	*(ehl 'moos-koo-loh)*
pulled muscle	músculo rasgado *(el)*	*('moos-koo-loh rahs-'gah-doh)*
muscular dystrophy	distrofia muscular *(la)*	*(lah dees-'troh-fee-ah moos-koo-'lahr)*
mushroom	hongo *(el)*	*(ehl 'ohn-goh)*
my	mi	*(mee)*
nail	uña *(la)*	*(lah 'oon-yah)*
name	nombre *(el)*	*(ehl 'nohm-breh)*
father's last name	apellido paterno *(el)*	*(ehl ah-peh-'yee-doh pah-'tehr-noh)*
first name	primer nombre *(el)*	*(ehl pree-'mehr 'nohm-breh)*
mother's last name	apellido materno *(el)*	*(ehl ah-peh-'yee-doh mah-'tehr-noh)*
nap	siesta *(la)*	*(lah see-'ehs-'tah)*
napkin	servilleta *(la)*	*(lah sehr-bee-'yeh-lah)*
nationality	nacionalidad *(la)*	*(lah nah-see-oh-nah-lee-'dahd)*
natural childbirth	parto natural *(el)*	*(ehl 'pahr-toh nah-too-'rahl)*
nausea	náusea *(la)*	*(lah 'now-seh-ah)*
navel	ombligo *(el)*	*(ehl ohm-'blee-gh)*
near	cerca de	*('sehr-kah deh)*
near-sighted	miope	*(mee-'oh-peh)*
necessary	necesario	*(neh-seh-'sah-ree-oh)*
neck	cuello *(el)*	*(ehl 'kweh-yoh)*
necklace	collar *(el)*	*(ehl koh-'yahr)*
need (to)	necesitar	*(neh-seh-see-'tahr)*
needle	aguja *(la)*	*(lah ah-'goo-hah)*
nephew	sobrino *(el)*	*(ehl soh-'bree-noh)*
nerve	nervio *(el)*	*(ehl 'nehr-bee-oh)*
nervous	nervioso (m.); nerviosa (f.)	*(nehr-bee-'oh-soh, nehr-bee-'oh-sah)*

nervous breakdown	postración nerviosa *(la)*	*(lah pohs-trah-see-'ohn nehr-bee-'oh-sah)*
nervous system	sistema nervioso *(el)*	*(ehl sees-'teh-mah nehr-bee-'oh-soh)*
neuro-psychiatric unit	unidad neurosiquiátrica *(la)*	*(lah oo-nee-'dahd neh-oo-roh-see-kee-'ah-tree-kah)*
neurologist	neurólogo *(el)*	*(ehl neh-oo-'roh-loh-goh)*
neurosis	neurosis *(la)*	*(lah neh oo-'roh-sees)*
never	nunca	*('noon-kah)*
new	nuevo	*('noo-eh-boh)*
newborn	recién nacido (m.); recién nacida (f.)	*(reh-see-'ehn nah-'see-doh, reh-see-'ehn nah-'see-dah)*
newspaper	periódico *(el)*	*(ehl peh-ree-'oh-dee-koh)*
next	siguiente	*(see-gee-'ehn-teh)*
next to	al lado de	*(ahl 'lah-doh deh)*
niece	sobrina *(la)*	*(lah soh-'bree-nah)*
night	noche *(la)*	*(lah 'noh-cheh)*
last night	anoche	*(ah-'noh-cheh)*
nightstand	mesa de noche *(la)*	*(lah 'meh-sah de 'noh-cheh)*
nipple	pezón *(el)*	*(ehl peh-'sohn)*
none	ninguno (m.); ninguna (f.)	*(neen-'goo-noh, neen-'goo-nah)*
noodle	fideo *(el)*	*(ehl fee-'deh-oh)*
normal	normal	*(nohr-'mahl)*
normally	normalmente	*(nohr-mahl-'mehn-teh)*
nose	nariz *(la)*	*(lah nah-'rees)*
Do you feel pain in your nose?	¿Siente dolor en la nariz?	*(see-'ehn-teh doh-'lohr ehn lah nah-'rees)*
Do you feel stuffiness often, and when?	¿Siente la nariz taponada a menudo y cuándo?	*(see-'ehn-teh lah nah-'rees tah-poh-'nah-dah ah meh-'noo-doh ee 'kwahn-doh)*
Do you get nosebleeds often?	¿Le sangra la nariz a menudo?	*(leh 'sahn-grah lah nah-'rees ah meh-'noo-doh)*
Do you sneeze all the time?	¿Estornuda todo el tiempo?	*(ehs-tohr-'noo-dah 'toh-doh ehl tee-'ehm-poh)*
Have you ever injured your nose?	¿Se ha lesionado la nariz alguna vez?	*(seh ah leh-see-oh-'nah-doh lah nah-'rees ahl-'goo-nah behs)*
Is the nose constantly runny?	¿Le gotea la nariz continuamente?	*(leh goh-'teh-ah lah nah-'rees kohn-tee-noo-ah-'mehn-teh)*
nostril	fosa nasal *(la)*	*(lah 'foh-sah nah-'sahl)*
nothing	nada	*('nah-dah)*

November	noviembre	*(noh-bee-'ehm-breh)*
now	ahora	*(ah-'oh-rah)*
nowadays	ahora	*(ah-'oh-rah)*
numb (to)	adormecer	*(ah-dohr-meh-'sehr)*
numbness	adormecimiento *(el)*	*(ehl ah-dohr-meh-see-mee-'ehn-toh)*
nurse	enfermero (m.); enfermera (f.)	*(ehn-fehr-'meh-roh, ehn-fehr-'meh-rah)*
nurse (to)	lactar	*(lahk-'tahr)*
nursery	guardería *(la)*	*(lah gwahr-deh-'ree-ah)*
nursing bottle	biberón *(el)*	*(ehl bee-beh-'rohn)*
nursing care	cuidado con enfermera *(el)*	*(el kwee-'dah-doh kohn ehn-fehr-'meh-rah)*
nut	nuez *(la)*	*(lah noo-'ehs)*
obesity	obesidad *(la)*	*(lah oh-beh-see-'dahd)*
observe (to)	observar	*(ohb-sehr 'bahr)*
obstetrician	obstetriz (m. & f.)	*(ehl (lah) ohb-steh-'trees)*
October	octubre	*(ohk-'too-breh)*
of	de	*(deh)*
office	oficina *(la)*	*(lah oh-fee-'see-nah)*
oil	aceite *(el)*	*(ehl ah-'seh-ee-teh)*
old	viejo	*(hee-'eh-hoh)*
older	mayor	*(mah-'yohr)*
on	en	*(ehn)*
once	una vez	*('oo-nah behs)*
oncology	oncología *(la)*	*(lah ohn-koh-loh-'hee-ah)*
onion	cebolla *(la)*	*(lah seh-'boh-yah)*
open (to)	abrir	*(ah-'breer)*
Open *(request to)*	Abra.	*('ah-brah)*
Open your hand.	Abra la mano.	*('ah-brah lah 'mah-noh)*
operate (to)	operar	*(oh-peh-'rahr)*
Operating Room	sala de operaciones *(la)*	*(lah 'sah-lah deh oh-peh-'rah-see-'oh-nehs)*
operation	operación *(la)*	*(lah oh-peh-rah-see-'ohn)*
To prepare you for the operation.	Prepararle para la operación.	*(preh-pah-'rahr-leh 'pah-rah lah oh-peh-rah-see-'ohn)*
ophthalmologist	oftalmólogo *(el)*	*(ehl ohf-tahl-'moh-loh-goh)*
opinion	opinión *(la)*	*(lah oh-pee-nee-'ohn)*
optometrist	optometrista *(el)*	*(ehl ohp-toh-meh-'trees-tah)*

or	o	*(oh)*
orange (color)	anaranjado (m.); anaranjada (f.)	*(ah-nah-rahn-'hah-doh, ah-nah-rahn-'hah-dah)*
orderly	practicante *(el)*	*(ehl prahk-tee-'kahn-teh)*
organ	órgano *(el)*	*(ehl 'ohr-gah-noh)*
orthodontist	ortodoncista (m. & f.)	*(ehl (lah) ohr-toh-dohn-'sees-tah)*
orthopedic surgeon	cirujano ortopédico *(el)*, cirujana ortopédica *(la)*	*(ehl see-roo-'hah-noh ohr-toh-'peh-dee-koh, lah see-roo-'hah-nah ohr-toh-'peh-dee-kah)*
orthopedics	ortopedia *(la)*	*(lah ohr-toh-'peh-dee-ah)*
ounces	onzas *(las)*	*(lahs 'ohn-sahs)*
our	nuestro (m.); nuestra (f.)	*('nwehs-troh, nwes-trah)*
outlet	enchufe *(el)*	*(ehl ehn-'choo-feh)*
ovary	ovario *(el)*	*(ehl oh-'bah-ree-oh)*
overdose	dosis excesiva *(la)*	*(lah 'doh-sees ehk-seh-'see-bah)*
ovum	óvulo *(el)*	*(ehl 'oh-boo-loh)*
oxygen	oxígeno *(el)*	*(ehl ohk-'see-heh-noh)*
P.M.	de la tarde	*(deh lah 'tahr-deh)*
pacemaker	marcapasos *(el)*	*(ehl mahr-kah-'pah-sohs)*
pacifier	chupete *(el)*	*(ehl choo-'peh-teh)*
pain	dolor *(el)*	*(ehl doh-'lohr)*
constant pain	dolor constante *(el)*	*(ehl doh-'lohr kohn-'stahn-teh)*
pain in the chest	dolor en el pecho *(el)*	*(ehl doh-'lohr ehn ehl 'peh-choh)*
Have you had this pain before?	¿Ha tenido este dolor antes?	*(ah teh-'nee-doh 'eh-steh doh-'lohr 'ahn-tehs)*
I have a lot of pain.	Tengo mucho dolor.	*('tehn-goh 'moo-choh doh-'lohr)*
This is for the pain.	Esto es para el dolor.	*('eh-stoh ehs 'pah-rah ehl doh-'lohr)*
Was it a sharp or dull pain?	¿Fue un dolor agudo o sordo?	*(fweh oon doh-'lohr ah-'goo-doh oh 'sohr-doh)*
paint	pintura *(la)*	*(lah peen-'too-rah)*
painter	pintor (m.); pintora (f.)	*(ehl peen-'tohr, lah peen-'toh-rah)*
pajamas	pijamas *(las)*	*(lahs pee-'hah-mahs)*
palate	paladar *(el)*	*(ehl pah-lah-'dahr)*
palm	palma de la mano *(la)*	*(lah 'pahl-mah deh lah 'mah-noh)*
palpitations	palpitaciones *(las)*	*(lahs pahl-pee-tah-see-'oh-nehs)*
pan	bacín *(el)*	*(ehl bah-'seen)*
pancreas	páncreas *(el)*	*(ehl pahn-kreh-ahs)*
panties	bragas *(las)*	*(lahs 'brah-gahs)*

pants	pantalones *(los)*	*(lohs pahn-tah-'loh-nehs)*
pap smear	examen de Papanicolao *(el)*	*(ehl ehk-'sah-mehn deh pah-pah-nee-koh-'lah-oh)*
paper	papel *(el)*	*(ehl pah-'pehl)*
paralysis	parálisis *(la)*	*(lah pah-'rah-lee-sees)*
parasites	parásitos *(los)*	*(lohs pah-'rah-see-tohs)*
park	parque *(el)*	*(ehl 'pahr-keh)*
parking lot	estacionamiento *(el)*	*(ehl ehs-tah-see-oh-nah-mee-'ehn-toh)*
part	parte *(la)*	*(lah 'pahr-teh)*
partner	socio *(el)*	*(ehl 'soh-see-oh)*
pathologist	patólogo *(el)*	*(ehl pah-'toh-loh-goh)*
patient	paciente (m. & f.)	*(ehl (lah) pah-see-'ehn-teh)*
pay (to)	pagar	*(pah-'gahr)*
pea	chícharo *(el)*	*(ehl 'chee-chah-roh)*
pediatrician	pediatra (m. & f.)	*(ehl (lah) peh-dee-'ah-trah)*
pelvis	pelvis *(la)*	*(lah 'pehl-bees)*
pen	lapicero *(el)*	*(ehl lah-pee-'seh-roh)*
pencil	lápiz *(el)*	*(ehl 'pah-pees)*
penicillin	penicilina *(la)*	*(lah peh-nee-see-'lee-nah)*
penis	pene *(el)*	*(ehl 'peh-neh)*
people	gente *(la)*	*(lah 'hehn-teh)*
pepper	pimienta *(la)*	*(lah pee-mee-'ehn-tah)*
percent	porcentaje *(el)*	*(ehl pohr-sehn-'tah-heh)*
period (menstrual)	regla *(la)*; período *(el)*	*(lah 'reh-glah; ehl peh-'ree-oh-doh)*
When was your last period?	¿Cuándo fue su última regla?	*('kwahn-doh fweh soo 'ool-tee-mah 'reh-glah)*
permission	permiso *(el)*	*(ehl pehr-'mee-soh)*
person	persona *(la)*	*(lah pehr-'soh-nah)*
perspire (to)	sudar	*(soo-'dahr)*
pharmacist	farmacéutico *(el)*	*(ehl fahr-mah-'seh-oo-tee-koh)*
pharmacy	farmacia *(la)*	*(lah fahr-'mah-see-ah)*
phlegm	flema *(la)*	*(lah 'fleh-mah)*
physical exam	examen físico *(el)*	*(ehl ehk-'sah-mehn 'fee-see-koh)*
physical therapy	fisioterapia *(la)*	*(lah fee-see-oh-teh-'rah-pee-ah)*
pie	pastel *(el)*	*(ehl pahs-'tehl)*
pill	píldora *(la)*	*(lah 'peel-doh-rah)*
pillow	almohada *(la)*	*(lah ahl-moh-'ah-dah)*
pillowcase	funda *(la)*	*(lah 'foon-dah)*

pimple	grano *(el)*	*(ehl 'grah-noh)*
pin	alfiler *(el)*	*(ehl ahl-fee-'lehr)*
pineapple	piña *(la)*	*(lah 'pee-nyah)*
pink	rosado (m.); rosada (f.)	*(roh-'sah-doh, roh-'sah-dah)*
pitcher	jarra *(la)*	*(lah 'har-rah)*
placenta	placenta *(la)*	*(lah plah-'sehn-tah)*
plague	plaga *(la)*	*(lah 'plah-gah)*
plan	plan *(el)*	*(ehl plahn)*
planning	planificación *(la)*	*(lah plah-nee-fee-kah-see-'ohn)*
plaque	placa *(la)*	*(lah 'plah-kah)*
plate	plato *(el)*	*(ehl 'plah-toh)*
plumber	plomero *(el)*	*(ehl plo-'meh-roh)*
pneumonia	pulmonía *(la)*	*(lah pool-moh-'nee-ah)*
podiatrist	podiatra (m. & f.)	*(ehl (lah) poh-dee-'ah-trah)*
point (to)	señalar	*(seh-nyah-'lahr)*
Point *(request to)*	Señale.	*(seh-'nyah-leh)*
poison	veneno *(el)*	*(ehl beh-'neh-noh)*
poison ivy	hiedra venenosa *(la)*	*(lah 'yeh-drah beh-neh-'noh-sah)*
poison oak	encina venenosa *(la)*	*(lah ehn-'see-nah beh-neh-'noh-sah)*
police	policía *(la)*	*(lah poh-lee-'see-ah)*
police officer	policía (m. & f.)	*(ehl (lah) poh-lee-'see-ah)*
policy	póliza *(la)*	*(lah 'poh-lee-sah)*
polio	polio *(el)*	*(ehl 'poh-lee-oh)*
pollen	polen *(el)*	*(ehl 'poh-lehn)*
polyp	pólipo *(el)*	*(ehl 'poh-lee-poh)*
poor	pobre	*('poh-breh)*
porcelain	porcelana *(la)*	*(lah pohr-seh-'lah-nah)*
post-op	después de la operación	*(dehs-'pwehs deh lah oh-peh-rah-see-'ohn)*
postcard	tarjeta postal *(la)*	*(lah tahr-'heh-tah pohs-'tahl)*
potassium	potasio *(el)*	*(ehl poh-'tah-see-oh)*
potato	papa *(la)*	*(lah 'pah-pah)*
pound	libra *(la)*	*(lah 'lee-brah)*
pray (to)	rezar	*(reh-'sahr)*
pregnant	embarazada	*(ehm-bah-rah-'sah-dah)*
You are pregnant.	Está embarazada.	*(eh-'stah ehm-bah-rah-'sah-dah)*
premature	prematuro (m.); prematura (f.)	*(preh-mah-'too-roh, preh-mah-'too-rah)*

prenatal care	atención prenatal *(la)*	*(lah ah-tehn-see-'ohn preh-nah-'tahl)*
prepare (to)	preparar	*(preh-pah-'rahr)*
pretty	bonito (m.); bonita (f.)	*(boh-'nee-toh, boh-'nee-tah)*
prescription	receta médica *(la)*	*(lah reh-'seh-tah 'meh-dee-kah)*
Take this prescription.	Tome esta receta.	*('toh-meh 'eh-stah reh-'seh-tah)*
press (to)	apretar	*(ah-preh-'tahr)*
Press *(request to)*	Apriete.	*(ah-pree-'eh-teh)*
prevent (to)	prevenir	*(preh-beh-'neer)*
priest	sacerdote *(el)*	*(ehl sah-sehr-'doh-teh)*
private	privado (m.); privada (f.)	*(pree-'bah-doh, pree-'bah-dah)*
private care	cuidado privado *(el)*	*('ehl kwee-'dah-doh pree-'bah-doh)*
probe	sonda *(la)*	*(lah 'sohn-dah)*
procedure	procedimiento *(el)*	*(ehl proh-seh-dee-me-'ehn-toh)*
proceed (to)	proceder	*(proh-seh-'dehr)*
proctologist	proctólogo *(el)*	*(ehl prohk-'toh-loh-goh)*
proctology	proctología *(la)*	*(lah prohk-toh-loh-'hee-ah)*
proctoscopy	proctoscopía *(la)*	*(lah prohk-toh-skoh-'pee-ah)*
prohibit (to)	prohibir	*(proh-hee-'beer)*
prohibited	prohibido	*(proh-ee-'bee-doh)*
protect (to)	proteger	*(proh-teh-'hehr)*
protein	proteína *(la)*	*(lah proh-teh-'ee-nah)*
provider	proveedor (m.); proveedora (f.)	*(proh-beh-eh-'dohr, proh-beh-eh-'doh-rah)*
psychiatric hospital	hospital psiquiátrico *(el)*	*(ehl ohs-pee-'tahl see-kee-'aht-ree-koh)*
psychiatrist	psiquiatra (m. & f.)	*(ehl (lah) see-kee-'ah-trah)*
The psychiatrist will help you.	El psiquiatra (m. & f.) le ayudará.	*(ehl (lah) (see-kee-'ah-trah leh ah-yoo-dah-'rah)*
psychiatry	psiquiatría *(la)*	*(lah see-kee-ah-'tree-ah)*
psychologist	psicólogo (m.); psicóloga (f.)	*(see-'koh-loh-goh, see-'koh-loh-gah)*
psychology	psicología *(la)*	*(lah see-koh-loh-'hee-ah)*
psychotherapy	psicoterapia *(la)*	*(lah see-koh-teh-'rah-pee-ah)*
pull (to)	jalar	*(hah-'lahr)*
Pull *(request to)*	Jale.	*('hah-leh)*
pulse	pulso *(el)*	*(ehl 'pool-soh)*
Your pulse is very fast.	Su pulso es muy rápido.	*(soo 'pool-soh ehs 'moo-ee 'rah-pee-doh)*

Your pulse is very slow.	Su pulso es muy lento.	*(soo 'pool-soh ehs 'moo-ee 'lehn-toh)*
pump	bomba *(la)*	*(lah 'bohm-bah)*
pump (to)	bombear	*(bohm-beh-'ahr)*
purify (to)	purificar	*(poo-ree-fee-'kahr)*
purple	morado (m.); morada (f.)	*(moh-'rah-doh, moh-'rah-dah)*
pus	pus *(el)*	*(ehl poos)*
push (to)	empujar	*(ehm-poo-'har)*
Push *(request to)*	Empuje.	*(ehm-'poo-heh)*
put (to)	poner	*(poh-'nehr)*
Put on *(request to)*	Póngase.	*('pohn-gah-seh)*
Put *(request to)*	Ponga.	*('pohn-gah)*
pyorrhea	piorrea *(la)*	*(lah pee-oh-'rreh-ah)*
question	pregunta *(la)*	*(lah preh-'goon-tah)*
Do you have a question?	¿Tiene una pregunta?	*(tee-'eh-neh 'oo-nah preh-'goon-tah)*
quickly	rápidamente	*('rah-pee-dah-mehn-teh)*
rabbit	conejo *(el)*	*(ehl koh-'neh-hoh)*
race	raza *(la)*	*(lah 'rah-sah)*
radiation	irradiación *(la)*	*(lah eer-rah-dee-ah-see-'ohn)*
radiation therapy	radioterapia *(la)*	*(lah rah-dee-oh-teh-'rah-pee-ah)*
radiologist	radiólogo (m.); radióloga (f.)	*(rah-dee-'oh-loh-goh, rah-dee-'oh-loh-gah)*
radiology	radiología *(la)*	*(lah rah-dee-oh-loh-'hee-ah)*
radiotherapy	radioterapia *(la)*	*(lah rah-dee-oh-teh-'rah-pee-ah)*
rain	lluvia *(la)*	*(lah 'yoo-bee-ah)*
raise (to)	levantar	*(leh-bahn-'tahr)*
Raise *(request to)*	Levante.	*(leh-'bahn-teh)*
rape	violación *(la)*	*(lah bee-oh-lah-see-'ohn)*
rape (to)	violar	*(bee-oh-'lahr)*
rashes	sarpullidos *(los)*	*(lohs sahr-poo-'yee-dohs)*
rat	rata *(la)*	*(lah 'rah-tah)*
razor blade	hoja de afeitar *(la)*	*(lah 'oh-hah de ah-feh-ee-'tahr)*
read (to)	leer	*(leh-'ehr)*
readmit (to)	readmitir	*(reh-ahd-mee-'teer)*
receipt	recibo *(el)*	*(ehl reh-'see-boh)*
receive (to)	recibir	*(reh-see-'beer)*
recommend (to)	recomendar	*(reh-koh-mehn-'dahr)*

Recovery Room	sala de recuperación *(la)*	*(lah 'sah-lah deh reh-koo-peh-rah-see·'ohn)*
rectum	recto *(el)*	*(ehl 'rehk-toh)*
recuperate (to)	recuperar	*(reh-koo-peh-'rahr)*
recuperation	recuperación *(la)*	*(lah recuperación)*
red	rojo (m.); roja (f.)	*('roh-hoh, 'roh-hah)*
redhead	pelirrojo (m.); pelirroja (f.)	*(peh-lee-'rroh-hoh, peh-lee-'rroh-hah)*
refrigerator	refrigerador *(el)*	*(ehl reh-free-heh-rah-'dohr)*
register (to)	registrar	*(reh-hees-'trahr)*
relationship (family)	parentezco *(el)*	*(ehl pah-rehn-'tehs-koh)*
relaxed	relajado (m.); relajada (f.)	*(reh-lah-'hah-doh, reh-lah-'hah-dah)*
release (to)	dar de alta	*(dahr deh 'ahl-tah)*
relieve (to)	aliviar	*(ah-lee-bee-'ahr)*
religion	religión *(la)*	*(lah reh-lee-hee·'ohn)*
remedy	remedio *(el)*	*(ehl reh-'meh-dee·oh)*
remember (to)	recordar	*(reh-kohr-'dahr)*
remove (to)	sacar	*(sah-'kahr)*
We're going to remove the stitches.	Vamos a sacarle los puntos.	*('bah-mohs ah sah-'kahr-leh lohs 'poon-tohs)*
repair (to)	reparar	*(reh-pah-'rahr)*
replace (to)	remplazar	*(rehm-plah-'sahr)*
research (to)	investigar	*(een-behs-tee-'gahr)*
resist (to)	resistir	*(reh-sees-'teer)*
resources	recursos *(los)*	*(lohs reh-'koor-sohs)*
respirator	respirador *(el)*	*(ehl rehs-pee-rah-'dohr)*
rest (to)	descansar	*(dehs-kahn-'sahr)*
restaurant	restaurante *(el)*	*(ehl rehs-tow-'rahn-teh)*
restless	inquieto (m.); inquieta (f.)	*(een-kee-'eh-toh, een-kee-'eh-tah)*
return (to)	regresar, volver	*(reh-greh-'sahr, bohl-'behr)*
Are you going to return?	¿Va a regresar?	*(bah ah reh-greh-'sahr)*
rheumatic fever	fiebre reumática *(la)*	*(lah fee-'eh-breh reh-oo-'mah-tee-kah)*
rib	costilla *(la)*	*(lah kos-'tee-yah)*
rice	arroz *(el)*	*(ehl ah-'rrohs)*
rich	rico (m.); rica (f.)	*('rree-koh, 'rree-kah)*

right	derecho (m.); derecha (f.)	*(deh-'reh-choh, deh-'reh-chah)*
to the **right**	a la derecha	*(ah lah deh-'reh-chah)*
ring	anillo *(el)*	*(ehl ah-'nee-yoh)*
rinse (to)	enjuagar	*(ehn-hwah-'gahr)*
Rinse *(request to)*	Enjuáguese.	*(ehn-'hwah-geh-seh)*
risky	arriesgado (m.); arriesgada (f.)	*(ahr-ree-ehs-'gah-doh, ahr-ree-ehs-'gah-dah)*
river	río *(el)*	*(ehl 'ree-oh)*
road	camino *(el)*	*(ehl kah-'mee-noh)*
robe	bata *(la)*	*(lah 'bah-tah)*
rock	piedra *(la)*	*(lah pee-'eh-drah)*
room	cuarto *(el)*	*(ehl 'kwahr-toh)*
root	raíz *(la)*	*(la rah-'ees)*
root canal	tratamiento del nervio dental	*(ehl trah-tah-mee-'ehn-toh dehl 'nehr-bee-oh dehn-'tahl)*
run (to)	correr	*(koh-'rrehr)*
sad	triste (m. & f.)	*('trees-teh)*
safe	seguro	*(seh-'goo-roh)*
salad	ensalada *(la)*	*(lah ehn-sah-lah-dah)*
salesperson	vendedor (m.); vendedora (f.)	*(ehl behn-deh-'dohr, lah behn-deh-'doh-rah)*
saliva	saliva *(la)*	*(lah sah-'lee-bah)*
salt	sal *(la)*	*(lah sahl)*
same	mismo (m.); misma (f.)	*('mees-moh, 'mees-mah)*
sample	muestra *(la)*	*(lah 'mwehs-trah)*
sand	arena *(la)*	*(lah ah-'reh-nah)*
sane	cuerdo (m.); cuerda (f.)	*('kwehr-doh, 'kwehr-dah)*
satisfied	satisfecho (m.); satisfecha (f.)	*(sah-tees-'feh-choh, sah-fees-'feh-chah)*
Saturday	sábado *(el)*	*(ehl 'sah-bah-doh)*
sauce	salsa *(la)*	*(lah 'sahl-sah)*
say (to)	decir	*(deh-'seer)*
Say *(request to)*	Diga.	*('dee-gah)*
scab	costra *(la)*	*(lah 'kos-trah)*
scale (of skin)	costra *(la)*	*(lah 'kohs-trah)*
scale (on teeth)	sarro *(el)*	*(ehl 'sah-rroh)*
scale (weighing)	báscula *(la)*	*(lah 'bahs-koo-lah)*

scar	cicatriz *(la)*	*(lah see-kah-'trees)*
scared	espantado (m.); espantada (f.)	*(ehs-pahn-'tah-doh, ehs-pahn-'tah-dah)*
scarf	bufanda *(la)*	*(lah boo-'fahn-dah)*
scarlet fever	escarlatina *(la)*	*(lah ehs-kahr-lah-'tee-nah)*
schedule	horario *(el)*	*(ehl oh-'rah-ree-oh)*
schizophrenic	esquizofrénico (m.); esquizofrénica (f.)	*(ehl ehs-kee-soh-'freh-nee-koh, lah ehs-kee-soh-'freh-nee-kah)*
school	escuela *(la)*	*(lah ehs-'kweh-lah)*
scissors	tijeras *(las)*	*(lahs tee-'heh-rahs)*
scorpion	escorpión *(el)*	*(ehl ehs-kohr-pee-'ohn)*
scratch (to)	rascar	*(rahs-'kahr)*
scrotum	escroto *(el)*	*(ehl ehs-'kroh-toh)*
sea	mar *(el)*	*(ehl mahr)*
second	segundo *(el)*	*(ehl seh-'goon-doh)*
secretary	secretario (m.); secretaria (f.)	*(seh-kreh-'tah-ree-oh, seh-kreh-'tah-ree-ah)*
security	seguridad *(la)*	*(lah seh-goo ree-'dahd)*
sedative	sedante *(el)*	*(ehl seh-'dahn-teh)*
see (to)	ver	*(behr)*
seizures	ataques *(los)*	*(lohs ah-'tah-kehs)*
semen	semen *(el)*	*(ehl 'seh-mehn)*
send (to)	mandar	*(mahn-'dahr)*
senile	senil	*(seh-'neel)*
senile dementia	demencia senil *(la)*	*(lah deh-'mehn-see-ah seh-'neel)*
senility	senilidad *(la)*	*(lah seh-nee-lee-'dahd)*
sensitivity	sensibilidad *(la)*	*(lah sehn-see-bee-lee-'dahd)*
September	septiembre	*(sehp-tee-'ehm-breh)*
serious	grave	*('grah-beh)*
servant	criado *(el)*, criada *(la)*	*(ehl kree-'ah-doh, lah kree-ah-dah)*
service	servicio *(el)*	*(ehl sehr-'bee-see-oh)*
seventh	séptimo	*(sehp-tee-moh)*
severe	muy fuerte	*('moo-ee 'fwehr-teh)*
severe	severo (m.); severa (f.)	*(seh-'beh-roh, seh-'beh-rah)*
sew (to)	coser	*(koh-'sehr)*
sex	sexo *(el)*	*(ehl 'sehk-soh)*
sexual relations	relaciones sexuales *(las)*	*(lahs reh-lah-see-'oh-nehs sehk-soo-'ah-lehs)*

shallow (person)	superficial	*(soo-pehr-fee-see-'ahl)*
sharp	agudo	*(ah-'goo-doh)*
sharp (edge)	afilado	*(ah-fee-'lah-doh)*
sharp (sound)	agudo	*(ah-'goo-doh)*
shave (to)	afeitar	*(ah-feh-ee-'tahr)*
she	ella	*('eh-yah)*
sheet	sábana *(la)*	*(lah 'sah-bah-nah)*
shellfish	mariscos *(los)*	*(lohs mah-'rees-kohs)*
ship	barco *(el)*	*(ehl 'bahr-koh)*
shirt	camisa *(la)*	*(lah kah-'mee-sah)*
shoe	zapato *(el)*	*(ehl sah-'pah-toh)*
shoot (to)	disparar	*(dees-pah-'rahr)*
shortness of breath	falta de aliento *(la)*	*(lah 'fahl-tah deh ah-lee-'ehn-toh)*
shorts	calzoncillos *(los)*	*(lohs kahl-sohn-'see-yohs)*
shoulder	hombro *(el)*	*(ehl 'ohm-broh)*
dislocated shoulder	hombro dislocado *(el)*	*(ehl 'ohm-broh dees-loh-'kah-doh)*
shower	ducha *(la)*	*(lah 'doo-chah)*
shower (to)	ducharse	*(doo-'chahr-seh)*
sick	enfermo (m.); enferma (f.)	*(ehn 'fehr-moh, ehn-'fehr-mah)*
When did he/she get sick?	¿Cuándo se enfermó?	*('kwahn-doh seh ehn-fehr-'moh)*
sickness	enfermedad *(la)*	*(lah ehn-fehr-meh-'dad)*
sidewalk	acera *(la)*	*(lah ah-'seh-rah)*
sight	vista *(la)*	*(lah 'bees-tah)*
sign (to)	firmar	*(feer-'mahr)*
Sign *(request to)*	Firme.	*('feer-meh)*
Sign your name.	Firme su nombre.	*('feer-meh soo 'nohm-breh)*
signature	firma *(la)*	*(lah 'feer-mah)*
silver	plata *(la)*	*(lah 'plah-tah)*
simple	sencillo	*(sehn-'see-yoh)*
single (person)	soltero (m.); soltera (f.)	*(sohl-'teh-roh, sohl-'teh-rah)*
sink	lavamanos *(el)*	*(ehl lah-bah-'mah-nohs)*
sister	hermana *(la)*	*(lah ehr-'mah-nah)*
sister-in-law	cuñada *(la)*	*(lah koo-'nyah-dah)*
sit down (to)	sentarse	*(sehn-'tahr-seh)*
Have a seat.	Siéntese.	*(see-'ehn-teh-sah)*

sixth	sexto	*('sehks-toh)*
size	tamaño *(el)*	*(ehl tah-'mahn-yoh)*
skeleton	esqueleto *(el)*	*(ehl ehs-keh-'leh-toh)*
skin	piel *(la)*	*(lah pee-'ehl)*
skin cancer	cáncer de la piel *(el)*	*(ehl 'kahn-sehr deh lah pee-'ehl)*
skin disease	enfermedad de la piel *(la)*	*(lah ehn-fehr-meh-'dahd deh lah pee-'ehl)*
skin rash	erupción en la piel *(la)*	*(lah eh-roop-see-'ohn ehn lah pee-'ehl)*
skirt	falda *(la)*	*(lah 'fahl-dah)*
sleep (to)	dormir	*(dohr-'meer)*
sleeping pill	somnífero *(el)*	*(ehl sohm-'nee-feh-roh)*
sleepy	soñoliento (m.); soñolienta (f.)	*(soh-nyoh-lee-'ehn-toh, soh-nyoh-lee-'ehn-tah)*
Are you sleepy?	¿Tiene sueño?	*(tee-'eh-neh 'sweh-nyoh?)*
sleeve	manga *(la)*	*(lah 'mahn-gah)*
sling	cabestrillo *(el)*	*(ehl kah-behs-'tree-yoh)*
slippers	pantuflas *(las)*	*(lahs pahn-'too-flahs)*
slow	lento (m.); lenta (f.)	*('lehn-toh, 'lehn-tah)*
slowly	lentamente, despacio	*(lehn-tah-'mehn-teh, dehs-'pah-see-oh)*
small	chico (m.); chica (f.)	*('chee-koh, 'chee-kah)*
smallpox	viruela *(la)*	*(lah bee-roo-'eh-lah)*
smear	frotis *(el)*	*(ehl 'froh-tees)*
smell (to)	oler	*(oh-'lehr)*
smile	sonrisa *(la)*	*(lah sohn-'ree-sah)*
smoke	humo *(el)*	*(ehl 'oo-moh)*
smoke (to)	fumar	*(foo-'mahr)*
snack	merienda *(la)*	*(lah meh-ree-'ehn-dah)*
snake	culebra *(la)*	*(lah 'koo-'leh-brah)*
poisonous snake	víbora venenosa *(la)*	*(lah 'bee-boh-rah beh-neh-'no-sah)*
snake bite	mordedura de culebra *(la)*	*(lah mohr-deh-'doo-rah deh koo-leh-brah)*
sneeze (to)	estornudar	*(ehs-tohr-noo-'dahr)*
snow	nieve *(la)*	*(lah nee-'eh-beh)*
so	así que	*(ah-'see keh)*
soap	jabón *(el)*	*(ehl hah-'bohn)*
Social Security number	número de seguro social *(el)*	*(ehl 'noo-meh-roh deh seh-'goo-roh soh-see-'ahl)*

social worker	trabajador social *(el)*, trabajadora social *(la)*	*(ehl trah-bah-hah-'dohr soh-see-'ahl, lah trah-bah-hah-'doh-rah soh-see-'ahl)*
socks	calcetines *(los)*	*(lohs kahl-seh-'tee-nehs)*
sodium	sodio *(el)*	*(ehl 'soh-dee-oh)*
soft	blando (m.); blanda (f.)	*('blahn-doh, 'blahn-dah)*
soft drink	refresco *(el)*	*(ehl reh-'frehs-koh)*
sole	planta del pie *(la)*	*(lah 'plahn-tah dehl pee-'eh)*
solution	solución *(la)*	*(lah soh-loo-see-'ohn)*
some	unos (m.); unas (f.)	*('oo-nohs, 'oo-nahs)*
something	algo	*('ahl-goh)*
sometimes	a veces	*(ah 'beh-sehs)*
son	hijo *(el)*	*(ehl 'ee-hoh)*
son-in-law	yerno *(el)*	*(ehl 'yehr-noh)*
sonogram	sonograma *(el)*	*(ehl soh-noh-'grah-mah)*
soon	pronto	*('prohn-toh)*
sore (person)	dolorido (m.); dolorida (f.)	*(doh-loh-'ree-doh, doh-loh-'ree-dah)*
sore (wound)	llaga *(la)*	*(lah 'yah-gah)*
sound	sonido *(el)*	*(ehl soh-'nee-doh)*
soup	sopa *(la)*	*(lah 'soh-pah)*
spasm	espasmo *(el)*	*(ehl ehs-'pahs-moh)*
speak (to)	hablar	*(ah-'blahr)*
Do you speak English?	¿Habla inglés?	*(ah-'blah een-'glehs)*
I speak a little Spanish.	Hablo un poquito de español.	*('ah-bloh oon poh-'kee-toh deh ehs-pah-'nyohl)*
special	especial	*(ehs-peh-see-'ahl)*
specialist	especialista (m. & f.)	*(ehl (lah) ehs-peh-see-ah-'lees-tah)*
speed (amphetamine)	anfetamina *(la)*	*(lah ahn-feh-tah-'mee-nah)*
sperm	esperma *(la)*	*(lah ehs-'pehr-mah)*
spicy	picante	*(pee-'kahn-teh)*
spicy food	comida picante *(la)*	*(lah koh-'me-dah pee-'kahn-teh)*
spinal fluid	líquido cefaloraquídeo *(el)*	*(ehl 'lee-kee-doh seh-fah-loh-rah-'kee-deh-oh)*
spice	especia *(la)*	*(lah ehs-'peh-see-ah)*
spider	araña *(la)*	*(lah ah-'rah-nyah)*
spinal column	columna vertebral *(la)*	*(lah koh-'loom-nah behr-teh-'brahl)*
spinal tap	punción lumbar *(la)*	*(lah poon-see-'ohn loom-'bahr)*

spit (to)	escupir	*(ehs-koo-'peer)*
spleen	bazo *(el)*	*(ehl 'bah-soh)*
splinter	astilla *(la)*	*(lah ahs-'tee-yah)*
sponge	esponja *(la)*	*(lah ehs-'pohn-hah)*
spoon	cuchara *(la)*	*(lah koo-'chah-rah)*
spot	mancha *(la)*	*(lah 'mahn-chah)*
spring	primavera *(la)*	*(lah pree-mah 'bch rah)*
sputum	esputo *(el)*	*(ehl ehs-'poo-toh)*
squeeze (to)	apretar	*(ah-preh-'tahr)*
stab (to)	apuñalar	*(ah-poo-nyah-'lahr)*
stable	estable (m. & f.)	*(ehs-'tahb-leh)*
stairs	escaleras *(las)*	*(lahs ehs-kah-'leh-rahs)*
stamps	estampillas *(las)*	*('lahs ehs-lahm-'pee-yahs)*
stand (to)	pararse	*(pah-'rahr-seh)*
stand up (to)	levantarse	*(leh-bahn-'tahr-seh)*
start (to)	empezar	*(ehm-peh-'sahr)*
station	estación *(la)*	*(lah ehs-tah-see-'ohn)*
stay (to)	quedarse	*(keh-'dahr-seh)*
steak	bistec *(el)*	*(ehl bees-'tehk)*
step	escalón *(el)*	*(ehl ehs-kah-'lohn)*
sterilize (to)	esterilizar	*(ehs-teh-ree-lee-'sahr)*
stethoscope	estetoscopio *(el)*	*(ehl ehs-teh-toh-'skoh-pee-oh)*
stillborn	nacido muerto	*(nah-'see-doh 'mwehr-toh)*
stimulant	estimulante *(el)*	*(ehl ehs-tee-moo-'lahn-teh)*
stitches	puntos *(los)*	*(lohs 'poon-tohs)*
stockings	medias *(las)*	*(lahs 'meh-dee-ahs)*
stomach	estómago *(el)*	*(ehl ehs-'toh-mah-goh)*
stomachache	dolor de estómago *(el)*	*(ehl doh-'lohr deh ehs-'toh-mah-goh)*
stones	cálculos *(los)*	*(lohs 'kahl-koo-lohs)*
store	tienda *(la)*	*(lah tee-'ehn-dah)*
straight ahead	adelante	*(ah-deh-'lahn-teh)*
straight jacket	camisa de fuerza *(la)*	*(lah kah-'mee-sah deh 'fwehr-sah)*
straighten (to)	enderezar	*(ehn-deh-reh-'sahr)*
strangulation	estrangulamiento *(el)*	*(ehl ehs-trahn-goo-lah-mee-'ehn-toh)*
strawberry	fresa *(la)*	*(lah 'freh-sah)*
street	calle *(la)*	*(lah 'kah-yeh)*
stretcher	camilla *(la)*	*(lah kah-'mee-yah)*

stress	estrés *(el)*	*(ehl ehs-'trehs)*
stroke	ataque *(el)*	*(ehl ah-'tah-keh)*
stroller	cochecillo *(el)*	*(ehl koh-cheh-'see-yoh)*
strong	fuerte	*('fwehr-teh)*
student	estudiante (m. & f.)	*(ehl (lah) ehs-too-dee-'ahn-teh)*
study (to)	estudiar	*(ehs-too-dee-'ahr)*
stuffy nose	nariz tapada *(la)*	*(lah nah-'rees tah-'pah-dah)*
subway	metro *(el)*	*(ehl 'meh-troh)*
suck (to)	chupar	*(choo-'pahr)*
suffer (to)	sufrir	*(soo-'freer)*
suffocation	sofocación *(la)*	*(lah soh-foh-kah-see-'ohn)*
sugar	azúcar *(el)*	*(ehl ah-'soo-kahr)*
suicide	suicidio *(el)*	*(ehl soo-ee-'see-dee-oh)*
He committed suicide.	Se suicidó.	*(seh soo-ee-see-'doh)*
suit	traje *(el)*	*(ehl 'trah-heh)*
summer	verano *(el)*	*(ehl beh-'rah-noh)*
sun	sol *(el)*	*(ehl sohl)*
Sunday	domingo	*(doh-'meen-goh)*
sunstroke	insolación *(la)*	*(lah een-soh-lah-see-'ohn)*
suppositories	supositorios *(los)*	*(lohs soo-poh-see-'toh-ree-ohs)*
Sure!	¡Claro!	*('klah-roh)*
surgeon	cirujano *(el)*, cirujana *(la)*	*(ehl see-roo-'hah-noh, lah see-roo-'hah-nah)*
surgery	cirugía *(la)*	*(lah see-roo-'hee-ah)*
surprised	sorprendido (m.); sorprendida (f.)	*(sohr-prehn-'dee-doh, sohr-prehn-'dee-dah)*
suture	sutura *(la)*	*(lah soo-'too-rah)*
swallow (to)	tragar	*(trah-'gahr)*
sweat	sudor *(el)*	*(ehl soo-'dohr)*
sweater	suéter *(el)*	*(ehl 'sweh-tehr)*
sweating	sudor *(el)*	*(ehl soo-'dohr)*
sweaty	sudoroso (m.); sudorosa (f.)	*(soo-doh-'roh-soh, soo-doh-'roh-sah)*
sweet	dulce *(el)*	*('dool-seh)*
swelling	hinchazón *(la)*	*(lah een-chah-'sohn)*
symptom	síntoma *(el)*	*(ehl 'seen-toh-mah)*
syndrome	síndrome *(el)*	*(ehl 'seen-droh-meh)*

syphilis	sífilis *(la)*	*(lah 'see-fee-lees)*
syringe	jeringa *(la)*	*(lah heh-'reen-gah)*
table	mesa *(la)*	*(lah 'meh-sah)*
tablespoon	cucharada *(la)*	*(lah koo-chah-'rah-dah)*
tablet	tableta *(la)*	*(lah tah-'bleh-tah)*
take (to)	tomar	*(toh-'mahr)*
Take *(request to)*	Tome.	*('toh-meh)*
take off (clothes) (to)	quitarse	*(kee-'tahr-seh)*
Take off *(request to)*	Quítese.	*('kee-teh-seh)*
talcum powder	talco *(el)*	*(ehl 'tahl-koh)*
tape	cinta *(la)*	*(lah 'seen-tah)*
tartar	sarro *(el)*	*(ehl 'sah-rroh)*
taste (to)	saborear	*(sah-boh-reh-'ahr)*
tea	té *(el)*	*(ehl teh)*
teacher	maestro *(el)*, maestra *(la)*	*(ehl mah-'ehs-troh, lah mah-'ehs-trah)*
teacup	taza *(la)*	*(lah 'tah-sah)*
teaspoon	cucharadita *(la)*	*(lah koo-chah-rah-'dee-tah)*
technician	técnico (m. & f.)	*(ehl (lah) 'tehk-nee-koh)*
telephone	teléfono *(el)*	*(ehl teh-'leh-foh-noh)*
telephone number	número de teléfono *(el)*	*(ehl 'noo-meh-roh deh teh-'leh-foh-noh)*
television	televisión *(la)*	*(lah teh-leh-bee-see-'ohn)*
tell (to)	decir	*(deh-'sihr)*
Tell *(request to)*	Diga.	*('dee-gah)*
Tell me.	Dígame.	*('dee-gah-meh)*
Tell the nurse.	Diga a la enfermera.	*('dee-gah ah lah ehn-fehr-'meh-rah)*
temperature	temperatura *(la)*	*(lah tehm-peh-rah-'too-rah)*
temple	sien *(la)*	*(lah 'see-ehn)*
tendon	tendón *(el)*	*(ehl tehn-'dohn)*
test	examen *(el)*	*(ehl ehk-'sah-mehn)*
testicles	testículos *(los)*	*(lohs tehs-'tee-koo-lohs)*
tests	pruebas *(las)*	*(lahs proo-'eh-bahs)*
tetanus	tétano *(el)*	*(ehl 'teh-tah-noh)*
that	ese (m.); esa (f.)	*('eh-seh, 'eh-sah)*
then	entonces	*(ehn-'tohn-sehs)*
therapist	terapeuta (m. & f.)	*(ehl (lah) teh-rah-'peh-oo-tah)*
therapy	terapia *(la)*	*(lah teh-'rah-pee-ah)*

there	allí	*(ah-'yee)*
therefore	por eso	*(pohr 'eh-soh)*
there is/there are	hay	*('ah-ee)*
thermometer	termómetro *(el)*	*(ehl tehr-'moh-meh-troh)*
thermostat	termostato *(el)*	*(ehl tehr-moh-'stah-toh)*
these	estos (m.); estas (f.)	*('ehs-tohs, 'ehs-tahs)*
they	ellos (m.); ellas (f.)	*('eh-yohs, 'eh-yahs)*
thick	grueso (m.); gruesa (f.)	*(groo'eh-soh, groo-'eh-sah)*
thigh	muslo *(el)*	*(ehl 'moos-loh)*
thin	delgado (m.); delgada (f.)	*(dehl-'gah-doh, dehl-'gah-dah)*
thing	cosa *(la)*	*(lah 'koh-sah)*
think (to)	pensar	*(pehn-'sahr)*
third	tercero	*(tehr-'seh-roh)*
thirsty	sediento (m.); sedienta (f.)	*(seh-dee-'ehn-toh, seh-dee-'ehn-tah)*
this	este (m.); esta (f.)	*('ehs-teh, 'ehs-tah)*
those	esos (m.); esas (f.)	*('eh-sohs, 'eh-sahs)*
thread	hilo *(el)*	*(ehl 'ee-loh)*
throat	garganta *(la)*	*(lah gahr-'gahn-tah)*
sore throat	dolor de garganta *(el)*	*(ehl doh-'lohr de gahr-'gahn-tah)*
Do you feel a choking sensation when not eating?	¿Tiene sensación de ahogo cuando no está comiendo?	*(tee-'eh-neh sehn-sah-see-'ohn deh ah-'oh-goh 'kwahn-doh noh eh-'stah koh-mee-'ehn-doh)*
Do you have a sore throat often?	¿Le duele la garganta con frecuencia?	*(leh 'dweh-leh lah gahr-'gahn-tah kohn freh-'kwehn-see-ah)*
Is it difficult to swallow food?	¿Le es difícil tragar comida?	*(leh ehs dee-'fee-seel trah-'gahr koh-'mee-dah)*
Is it hard to swallow liquids?	¿Le es difícil tragar líquido?	*(leh ehs dee-'fee-seel trah-'gahr 'lee-kee-doh)*
throbbing	pulsante	*(pool-'sahn-teh)*
Thursday	jueves	*('hweh-behs)*
thyroid	tiroides *(la)*	*(lah tee-'roh-ee-dehs)*
thyroid disease	enfermedad de la glándula tiroides *(la)*	*(lah ehn-fehr-meh-'dahd deh lah 'glahn-doo-lah tee-'roh-ee-dehs)*
ticks	garrapatas *(las)*	*(lahs gahr-rah-'pah-tahs)*
time	tiempo *(el)*	*(ehl tee-'ehm-poh)*
tingling	hormigueo *(el)*	*(ehl ohr-mee-'geh-oh)*

tie	corbata *(la)*	*(lah kohr-'bah-tah)*
tingling	hormigueo *(el)*	*(ehl ohr-mee-'geh-oh)*
tired	cansado (m.); cansada (f.)	*(kahn-'sah-doh, kahn-'sah-dah)*
tissue	tejido *(el)*	*(ehl teh-'hee-doh)*
to	a	*(ah)*
today	hoy	*('oh-ee)*
toe	dedo del pie *(el)*	*(ehl 'deh-doh dehl 'pee-eh)*
toilet	excusado *(el)*	*(ehl ehks-koo-'sah-doh)*
toilet (personal hygiene, grooming)	aseo personal *(el)*	*(ehl ah-'seh-oh pehr-soh-'nahl)*
toilet paper	papel higiénico *(el)*	*(ehl pah-'pehl ee-hee-'eh-nee-koh)*
tomato	tomate *(el)*	*(ehl toh-'mah-teh)*
tomorrow	mañana	*(mah-'nyah-nah)*
tongue	lengua *(la)*	*(lah 'lehn-gwah)*
tongue depressor	pisalengua *(la)*	*(lah pee-sah-'lehn-gwah)*
tonight	esta noche	*('eh-stah 'noh-cheh)*
tonsillitis	amigdalitis *(la)*	*(lah ah-meeg-dah-'lee-tees)*
tonsils	amígdalas *(las)*	*(lahs ah-'meeg-dah-lahs)*
too much	demasiado	*(deh-mah-see-'ah-doh)*
tooth	diente *(el)*	*(ehl dee-'ehn-teh)*
toothache	dolor de muela	*(ehl doh-lohr deh 'mweh-lah)*
toothbrush	cepillo de dientes *(el)*	*(ehl seh-'pee-yoh deh dee-'ehn-tehs)*
toothpaste	pasta de dientes *(la)*	*(lah 'pahs-tah deh dee-'ehn-tehs)*
tornado	tornado *(el)*	*(ehl tohr-'nah-doh)*
tourniquet	torniquete *(el)*	*(ehl tohr-nee-'keh-teh)*
towel	toalla *(la)*	*(lah toh-'ah-yah)*
toy	juguete *(el)*	*(ehl hoo-'geh-teh)*
traction	tracción *(la)*	*(lah trahk-see-'ohn)*
train	tren *(el)*	*(ehl trehn)*
tranquil	tranquilo (m.); tranquila (f.)	*(trahn-'kee-loh, trahn-'kee-lah)*
transplant (to)	trasplantar	*(trahs-plahn-'tahr)*
transportation	transporte *(el)*	*(ehl trahns-'pohr-teh)*
trapeze	trapecio *(el)*	*(ehl trah-'peh-see-oh)*
trash	basura *(la)*	*(lah bah-'soo-rah)*
trashcan	cesto de basura *(el)*	*(ehl 'cehs-toh deh bah-'soo-rah)*
trauma	trauma *(el)*	*(ehl 'trah-oo-mah)*

tray	bandeja *(la)*	*(lah bahn-'deh-hah)*
treatment	tratamiento *(el)*	*(ehl trah-tah-mee-'ehn-toh)*
tree	árbol *(el)*	*(ehl 'ahr-bohl)*
truck	camión *(el)*	*(ehl kah-mee-'ohn)*
truck driver	camionero *(el)*	*(ehl kah-mee-oh-'neh-roh)*
try (to)	tratar	*(trah-'tahr)*
Try to *(request to)*	Trate de.	*('trah-teh deh)*
t-shirt	camiseta *(la)*	*(lah kah-mee-'seh-tah)*
tubal ligation	ligadura de las trompas *(la)*	*(lah lee-gah-'doo-rah deh lahs 'trohm-pahs)*
tube	tubo *(el)*	*(ehl 'too-boh)*
tuberculosis	tuberculosis *(la)*	*(lah too-behr-koo-'loh-sees)*
Tuesday	martes	*(ehl 'mahr-tehs)*
turkey	pavo *(el)*	*(ehl 'pah-boh)*
turn (to)	voltear	*(bohl-teh-'ahr)*
Turn around *(request to)*	Voltéese.	*(bohl-'teh-eh-seh)*
Turn off *(request to)*	Apague.	*(ah-'pah-gue)*
Turn on *(request to)*	Prenda.	*('prehn-dah)*
Turn *(request to)*	Dé vuelta.	*(deh 'bwehl-tah)*
turn oneself over (to)	voltearse	*(bohl-teh-'ahr-seh)*
tweezers	pinzas *(las)*	*(lahs 'peen-sahs)*
twin	gemelo (m.); gemela (f.)	*(heh-'meh-loh, heh-'meh-lah)*
typhoid	fiebre tifoidea *(la)*	*(lah fee-'eh-breh tee-foh-ee-'deh-ah)*
ugly	feo (m.); fea (f.)	*('feh-oh, 'feh-ah)*
ulcer	úlcera *(la)*	*(lah 'ool-seh-rah)*
ultrasound	ultrasonido *(el)*	*(ehl ool-trah-soh-'nee-doh)*
umbilical cord	cordón umbilical *(el)*	*(ehl kohr-'dohn oom-bee-lee-'kahl)*
uncle	tío *(el)*	*(ehl 'tee-oh)*
uncomfortable	incómodo (m.); incómoda (f.)	*(een-'koh-moh-doh, een-'koh-moh-dah)*
unconscious	inconsciente (m. & f.)	*(een-kohn-see-'ehn-teh)*
under	debajo de	*(deh-'bah-hoh deh)*
understand (to)	entender	*(ehn-tehn-'dehr)*
I don't understand!	¡No entiendo!	*(noh ehn-tee-'ehn-doh)*
Do you understand?	¿Entiende?	*(ehn-tee-'ehn-deh)*
underwear	ropa interior *(la)*	*(lah 'roh-pah een-teh-ree-'ohr)*
up	arriba de	*(ah-'rree-bah deh)*

urethra	uretra *(la)*	*(lah oo-'reh-trah)*
urinal	orinal *(el)*	*(ehl oh-ree-'nahl)*
urinate (to)	orinar	*(oh-ree-'nahr)*
urologist	urólogo *(el)*, uróloga *(la)*	*(ehl oo-'roh-loh-goh, lah oo-'roh-loh-gah)*
use (to)	usar	*(oo-'sahr)*
uterus	útero *(el)*	*(ehl 'oo-teh-roh)*
vaccinate (to)	vacunar	*(bah-koo-'nahr)*
vaccination	vacuna *(la)*	*(lah bah-'koo-nah)*
vagina	vagina *(la)*	*(lah bah-'hee-nah)*
valve	válvula *(la)*	*(luh 'buhl-boo-lah)*
varicose veins	venas varicosas *(las)*	*(lahs 'beh-nahs bah-ree-'koh-sahs)*
vasectomy	vasectomía *(la)*	*(lah bah-sehk-toh-'mee-ah)*
vaseline	vaselina *(la)*	*(lah bah-seh-'lee-nah)*
vegetable	legumbre *(la)*	*(lah leh-'goom-breh)*
vein	vena *(la)*	*(lah 'beh-nah)*
venereal disease	enfermedad venérea *(la)*	*(lah ehn-fehr-meh-'dahd beh-'neh-reh-ah)*
ventricle	ventrículo *(el)*	*(ehl behn-'tree-koo-loh)*
verify (to)	verificar	*(beh-ree-fee-'kahr)*
very	muy	*('moo-ee)*
vision	visión *(la)*	*(lah bee-see-'ohn)*
double vision	doble visión *(la)*	*(lah 'doh-bleh bee-see-'ohn)*
visit	visita *(la)*	*(lah bee-'see-tah)*
visit (to)	visitar	*(bee-see-'tahr)*
When was the doctor's last visit?	¿Cuándo fue la última visita del doctor?	*('kwahn-doh fweh lah 'ool-tee-mah bee-'see-tah dehl dohk-'tohr)*
visitor	visitante (m. & f.)	*(ehl (lah) bee-see-'tahn-teh)*
vital signs	signos vitales *(los)*	*(lohs 'seeg-nohs bee-'tah-lehs)*
vitamin	vitamina *(la)*	*(lah bee-tah-'mee-nah)*
voice	voz *(la)*	*(lah bohs)*
vomit (to)	vomitar	*(boh-mee-'tahr)*
vulva	vulva *(la)*	*(lah 'bool-bah)*
waist	cintura *(la)*	*(lah seen-'too-rah)*
wait (to)	esperar	*(ehs-peh-'rahr)*
Wait *(request to)*	Espere.	*(ehs-'peh-reh)*
waiter	mesero *(el)*	*(ehl meh-'seh-roh)*
Waiting Room	sala de espera *(la)*	*(lah 'sah-lah deh ehs-'peh-rah)*
wake up (to)	despertar	*(dehs-pehr-'tahr)*

Wake up *(request to)*	Despiértese.	*(dehs-pee-'ehr-teh-seh)*
walk (to)	caminar	*(kah-mee-'nahr)*
walker	caminadora *(la)*	*(lah kah-mee-nah-'doh-rah)*
wall	pared *(la)*	*(lah pah-'rehd)*
want (to)	querer	*(keh-'rehr)*
Do you want something else?	¿Quiere algo más?	*(kee-'eh-reh 'ahl-goh mahs)*
warehouse	almacén *(el)*	*(ehl ahl-mah-'sehn)*
wart	verruga *(la)*	*(lah beh-'rroo-gah)*
washcloth	toallita *(la)*	*(lah toh-ah-'yee-tah)*
wash oneself (to)	lavarse	*(lah-'bahr-seh)*
Wash *(request to)*	Lávese.	*('lah-beh-seh)*
watch	reloj de pulsera *(el)*	*(ehl reh-'loh deh pool-'seh-rah)*
water	agua *(el)*	*(ehl 'ah-gwah)*
water fountain	fuente de agua *(la)*	*(lah 'fwehn-teh deh 'ah-gwah)*
watery	aguado (m.); aguada (f.)	*(ah-'gwah-doh, ah-'gwah-dah)*
we	nosotros	*(noh-'soh-trohs)*
weak	débil (m. & f.)	*('deh-beel)*
weakness	debilidad *(la)*	*(lah deh-bee-lee-'dahd)*
weather	clima *(el)*, tiempo *(el)*	*(ehl 'klee-mah, ehl tee-'ehm-poh)*
Wednesday	miércoles	*(mee-'ehr-koh-lehs)*
week	semana *(la)*	*(lah seh-'mah-nah)*
weigh (to)	pesar	*(peh-'sahr)*
How much do you weigh?	¿Cuánto pesa?	*('kwahn-toh 'peh-sah)*
weight	peso *(el)*	*(ehl 'peh-soh)*
welfare	bienestar social *(el)*	*(ehl bee-'ehn-ehs-'tahr soh-see-'ahl)*
well	bien	*('bee-ehn)*
wet	mojado (m.); mojada (f.)	*(moh-'hah-doh, moh-'hah-dah)*
What?	¿Qué?	*(keh)*
When?	¿Cuándo?	*('kwahn-doh)*
Where?	¿Dónde?	*('dohn-deh)*
Which?	¿Cuál?	*('kwahl)*
white	blanco (m.); blanca (f.)	*('blahn-koh, 'blahn-kah)*
Who?	¿Quién?	*(kee-'ehn)*
whooping cough	tos ferina, tos convulsiva *(la)*	*(lah tohs feh-'ree-nah, tohs kohn-bool-'see-bah)*

Whose?	¿De quién?	*(deh kee-'ehn)*
Why?	¿Por qué?	*(pohr keh)*
widow	viuda	*(vee-'oo-dah)*
widower	viudo	*(vee-'oo-doh)*
wife	esposa *(la)*	*(lah ehs-'poh-sah)*
wind	viento *(el)*	*(ehl bee-'ehn-toh)*
window	ventana *(la)*	*(lah behn-'tah-nah)*
wine	vino *(el)*	*(ehl 'bee-noh)*
winter	invierno *(el)*	*(ehl een-bee-'ehr-noh)*
with	con	*(kohn)*
without	sin	*(seen)*
woman	mujer *(la)*	*(lah moo-'hehr)*
word	palabra *(la)*	*(lah pah-'lah-brah)*
Another word, please.	Otra palabra, por favor.	*('oh-trah pah-'lah-brah pohr fah-'bohr)*
Word by word.	Palabra por palabra.	*(pah-'lah-brah pohr pah-'lah-brah)*
work (to)	trabajar	*(trah-bah-'hahr)*
workman's compensation	compensación de obrero *(la)*	*(lah kohm-pehn-sah-see-'ohn deh oh-'breh-roh)*
worm	gusano *(el)*	*(ehl goo-'sah-noh)*
worried	preocupado (m.); preocupada (f.)	*(preh-oh-koo-'pah-doh, preh-oh-koo-'pah-dah)*
worse	peor (m. & f.)	*(peh-'ohr)*
worsen (to)	empeorar	*(ehm-peh-oh-'rahr)*
Wow!	¡Caramba!	*(kah-'rahm-bah)*
wrist	muñeca *(la)*	*(lah moo-'nyeh-kah)*
write (to)	escribir	*(ehs-kree-'beer)*
wrong	equivocado (m.); equivocada (f.)	*(eh-kee-boh-'kah-doh, eh-kee-boh-'kah-doh)*
X ray	radiografía *(la)*	*(lah rah-dee-oh-grah-'fee-ah)*
X rays	rayos equis *(los)*	*(lohs 'rah-yohs 'eh-kees)*
yard	patio *(el)*	*(ehl 'pah-tee-oh)*
year	año *(el)*	*(ehl 'ah-nyoh)*
yellow	amarillo (m.); amarilla (f.)	*(ah-mah-'ree-yoh, ah-mah-'ree-yah)*
yes	sí	*(see)*
yesterday	ayer	*(ah-'yehr)*
yet	todavía	*(toh-dah-'bee-ah)*

yogurt	yogur *(el)*	*(ehl yoh-'goor)*
you	usted (respectful), tú (familiar)	*(oo-'stehd, too)*
you (plural)	ustedes	*(oo-'steh-dehs)*
young	joven	*('hoh-behn)*
young person	muchacho *(el)*, muchacha *(la)*	*(ehl moo-'chah-choh, lah moo-'chah-chah)*
younger	menor	*(meh-'nohr)*
your	su (respectful), tu (familiar)	*(soo, too)*
youth	joven (m. & f.)	*('hoh-behn)*
zip code	zona postal *(la)*	*(lah 'soh-nah pohs-'tahl)*

.

English-Spanish Expression Finder

Bless you!	¡Salud!	*(sah-'lood)*
Calm down!	¡Cálmese!	*('kahl-meh-seh)*
May I come in?	¿Se puede?	*(seh 'pweh-deh)*
May I help you?	¿Puedo ayudarle?	*('pweh-doh ah-yoo-'dahr-leh)*
Congratulations!	¡Felicitaciones!	*(feh-lee-see-tah-see-'oh-nehs)*
Danger!	¡Peligro!	*(peh-'lee-groh)*
Don't worry!	¡No se preocupe!	*(noh seh preh-oh-'koo-peh)*
Excuse me!	¡Perdón! or ¡Disculpe! or ¡Con permiso!	*(pehr-'dohn, dees-'kool-peh, kohn pehr-'mee-soh)*
Get well soon!	¡Qué se alivie pronto!	*(keh seh ah-'leee-bee-eh 'prohn-toh)*
Go ahead!	¡Pase!	*('pah-seh)*
Go with God!	¡Vaya con Dios!	*('bah yah kohn 'dee-ohs)*
Good afternoon.	Buenas tardes	*('bweh-nahs 'tahr-dehs)*
Good evening or Good night.	Buenas noches.	*('bweh-nahs 'noh-chehs)*
Good luck!	¡Buena suerte!	*('bweh-nah 'swehr-teh)*
Good morning.	Buenos días.	*('bweh-nohs 'dee-ahs)*
Good-bye.	Adiós.	*(ah-dee-'ohs)*
Happy Birthday!	¡Feliz cumpleaños!	*(feh-'lees kool-pleh-'ah-nyohs)*
Have a nice day!	¡Que le vaya bien!	*(keh leh 'bah-yah 'bee-ehn)*
Hi!	¡Hola!	*('oh-lah)*
How are you?	¿Cómo está?	*('koh-moh eh-'stah)*
How do you feel?	¿Cómo se siente?	*('koh-moh seh see-'ehn-teh)*
How do you say it?	¿Cómo se dice?	*('koh-moh seh 'dee-seh)*
How do you write it?	¿Cómo se escribe?	*('koh-moh seh ehs-'kree-beh)*
How do you spell it?	¿Cómo se deletrea?	*('koh-moh seh deh-leh-'treh-ah)*
How much does it cost?	¿Cuánto cuesta?	*('kwahn-toh 'kwehs-tah)*
How old are you?	¿Cuántos años tiene?	*('kwahn-tohs 'ah-nyohs tee-'eh-neh)*
How's it going?	¿Qué tal?	*(keh tahl)*
Hurry up!	¡Apúrese!	*(ah-'poo-reh-seh)*
I appreciate it!	¡Muy amable!	*('moo-eh ah-'mah-bleh)*
I'm sorry!	¡Lo siento!	*(loh see-'ehn-toh)*
More slowly.	Más despacio.	*(mahs dehs-'pah-see-oh)*
Nice to meet you.	Mucho gusto.	*('moo-choh 'goos-toh)*
Please.	Por favor.	*(pohr fah-'bohr)*

See you tomorrow.	Hasta mañana.	*('ahs-tah mah-'nyah-nah)*
Take it easy!	¡Cúidese bien!	*('kwee-deh-seh 'bee-ehn)*
Thank you.	Gracias.	*('grah-see-ahs)*
That's great!	¡Qué bueno!	*(keh 'bweh-noh)*
Very good!	¡Muy bien!	*('moo-ee 'bee-ehn)*
We'll see you!	¡Nos vemos!	*(nohs 'beh-mohs)*
Welcome!	¡Bienvenido!	*(bee-ehn-beh-'nee-doh)*
What does it mean?	¿Qué significa?	*(keh seeg-nee-'fee-kah)*
What time is it?	¿Qué hora es?	*(keh 'oh-rah ehs)*
What's happening?	¿Qué pasa?	*(keh 'pah-sah)*
What's the date?	¿Cuál es la fecha?	*(kwahl ehs lah 'feh-chah)*
What's wrong?	¿Qué pasó?	*(keh pah-'soh)*
What's your name?	¿Cuál es su nombre?	*(kwahl ehs soo 'nohm-breh)*
Where are you from?	¿De dónde es?	*(deh 'dohn-deh ehs)*
You're welcome!	¡De nada!	*(deh 'nah-dah)*

Spanish-English Word Finder

a	to	agarrar	grab (to)
a veces	sometimes	agencia	agency
abajo de	down	agosto	August
abandono	abandonment	agotado, agotada	exhausted
abeja	bee	agua	water
abogado, abogada	lawyer	agua oxigenada	hydrogen peroxide
aborto	abortion	aguacate	avocado
abril	April	aguado, aguada	watery
abrir	open (to)	agudo	sharp (sound)
absceso	abscess		
abuela	grandmother	aguja	needle
abuelo	grandfather	ahogarse	drown (to)
aburrido, aburrida	bored	ahora	now
abuso	abuse	aire acondicionado	air conditioning
abuso de las drogas	drug abuse	ajo	garlic
abuso de los niños	child abuse	al lado de	next to
accidente	accident	alarma	alarm
acción	action	alcohólico, alcohólica	alcoholic
aceite	oil	alergias	allergies
acera	sidewalk	alfiler	pin
ácido	acid	algo	something
acrílico	acrylic	aliento	breath
acostarse	lie down (to)	falta de aliento	shortness of breath
acumular	accumulate (to)		
adelante	straight ahead	alimentar	feed (to)
adentro de	inside	aliviar	relieve (to)
adicto, adicta	addict	almacén	warehouse
administración	administration	almohada	pillow
adopción	adoption	almuerzo	lunch
adoptar	to adopt	altura	height
adormecer	numb (to)	allí	there
adormecimiento	numbness	amamantamiento	breast feeding
aeropuerto	airport	amamantar	breast feed (to)
afeitar	shave (to)	amarillo	yellow
afilado	sharp (edge)	ambulancia	ambulance

amígdalas	tonsils
amigdalitis	tonsillitis
amoníaco	ammonia
ampolla(s)	blister(s)
amputación	amputation
amputar	amputate (to)
anaranjado	orange
anciano, anciana	elderly person
ancianos	elderly
anemia	anemia
anestesia	anesthesia
anfetamina	speed (amphet-amine)
angiograma	angiogram
anillo	ring
animal	animal
animales de peluche	stuffed animals
ano	anus
anoche	last night
anormal	abnormal
ansiedad	anxiety
antebrazo	forearm
anteojos	glasses
antes	before
antibiótico	antibiotic
anticoncepción	birth control
año	year
aorta	aorta
apellido materno	mother's last name
apellido paterno	father's last name
apendectomía	appendectomy
apéndice	appendix
apetito	appetite
aplicar	apply (to)
apoyo	headrest
aprender	learn (to)

apretar	squeeze (to)
apuñalar	stab (to)
aquí	here
araña	spider
árbol	tree
arbusto	bush
ardor	burning
área	area
arena	sand
aretes	earrings
armadura de yeso	cast
arriba	up
arriesgado, arriesgada	risky
arroz	rice
arteria	artery
articulación	joint
artificial	artificial
artritis	arthritis
ascensor	elevator
aseo personal	toilet (personal hygiene, grooming)
así que	so
asiento para infantes	infant car seat
asma	asthma
astigmatismo	astigmatism
astilla	splinter
ataque	stroke
ataque cardíaco	heart attack
ataques	fits, seizures
atención prenatal	prenatal care
atender	assist (to)
audífonos	hearing aids
aurícula	auricle
autobús	bus
automóvil	automobile
axila	armpit

ayer	yesterday
ayuda	help
ayudante	assistant
ayudar	help (to)
azúcar	sugar
azul	blue
bacín	pan
bacinete	bassinet
bacteriólogo	bacteriologist
bañarse	bathe (to)
bañera	bathtub
baño	bathroom
banco	bank
bandeja	tray
barandas de la cama	bedrails
barbilla	chin
barbitúricos	barbiturates
barco	boat
báscula	scale (weighing)
bastante	enough
bastón	cane
basura	trash
bata	robe
bautismo	baptism
bazo	spleen
bebé	baby
beber	drink (to)
bebida	beverage
beneficios	benefits
benigno	benign
biberón	nursing bottle
bicarbonato	baking soda
bicicleta	bicycle
bien	well
bienestar social	welfare
bifocales	bifocals

billetera	billfold
biopsia	biopsy
bistec	steak
blanco	white
blando	soft
blusa	blouse
boca	mouth
bolsa	handbag
bolsa amniótica	amniotic sac
bolsa de hielo	ice pack
bomba	pump
bombear	pump (to)
bombero	fireman
bonito	pretty
borracho, borracha	drunk
bosque	forest
botas	boots
botella	bottle
bragas	panties
brazalete	bracelet
brazo	arm
broche	clasp
bueno	good
bufanda	scarf
bulto	lump
buscar	look for (to)
buzón	mailbox
cabello	hair
cabestrillo	sling
cabeza	head
cable	wire
cadera	hip
café (bebida)	coffee
café (color)	brown
cafetería	cafeteria
cajero, cajera	cashier
cajón	drawer

calambres	cramps
calcetines	socks
cálculos	stones
cálculos en la vesícula	gallstones
cálculos en los riñones	kidney stones
calefacción	heating
calendario	calendar
caliente	hot
calle	street
callo	corn
callos	calluses
calmado, calmada	calm
calor	heat
calvo	bald
calzoncillos	shorts
cama	bed
cambiar	change (to)
camilla	stretcher
caminadora	walker
caminar	walk (to)
camino	road
camión	truck
camionero	truck driver
camisa	shirt
camisa de fuerza	straight jacket
camiseta	t-shirt
campesino, campesina	farmer
campo	countryside
canal cervical	cervical canal
cáncer	cancer
cansado	tired
cansancio	exhaustion
capilla	chapel
cápsula	capsule
cara	face
¡Caramba!	Wow!
cardiólogo	cardiologist

cargo	charge
carie	cavity
carne	meat
carpintero	carpenter
carretera	highway
carro	car
cartílago	cartilage
casi	almost
casado, casada	married
catarata	cataract
catéter	catheter
causar	cause (to)
cebolla	onion
ceja	eyebrow
célula	cell
cemento	cement
cena	dinner
cenicero	ash tray
cepillo de dientes	toothbrush
cerca	near
más cerca	closer
cereal	cereal
cerebro	brain
cereza	cherry
cerrado	closed
cerrar	close (to)
certificar	certify (to)
cerveza	beer
cesto de basura	trashcan
chaqueta	jacket
chata	bedpan
cheque	check
chícharo	pea
chicle	gum
chico, chica	small
chocar	crash (to)
chocolate	chocolate

chupar	suck (to)
chupete	bottle nipple
cianuro	cyanide
cicatriz	scar
ciclo menstrual	menstrual cycle
ciego	blind
cielo raso	ceiling
cigarrillo	cigarette
cine	movie theater
cinta	tape
cinta adhesiva	adhesive tape
cintura	waist
cinturón	belt
circuncisión	circumcision
cirugía	surgery
cirujano, cirujana	surgeon
cirujano ortopédico	orthopedic surgeon
cistoscopía	cystoscopy
cita	appointment
ciudad	city
¡Claro!	Sure!
clase	class
clavícula	collarbone
clima, tiempo	weather
cobija	blanket
cocaína	cocaine
cocinar	cook (to)
cocinero, cocinera	cook
cochecillo	stroller
codeína	codeine
codo	elbow
colchón	mattress
cólera	anger
cólera	cholera
cólico	colic
colon	colon

color	color
columna vertebral	spinal column
collar	necklace
comenzar	begin (to)
comer	eat (to)
comida	food
entre comidas	between meals
¿Cómo?	how?
cómodo	comfortable
compañero, compañera	buddy
compañía	company
compañía de seguros	insurance company
compensación de obrero	workman's compensation
complejo	complex
común	common
con	with
con frecuencia	frequently
condón	condom
conejo	rabbit
confusión	confusion
confuso, confusa	confused
congelamiento	frostbite
consciente	conscious
consejería	counseling
consejero, consejera	counselor
consejos	counseling
constante	constant
consultar	consult (to)
contestar	answer (to)
contracciones	contractions
controlar	control (to)
convulsión	convulsion
copa	cup
corazón	heart
corbata	tie

cordón umbilical	umbilical cord	cuerdo, cuerda	sane
corona	crown	cuerpo	body
correcto	correct	cuidado	care
corredor	hallway	cuidado ambulatorio	ambulatory care
correr	run (to)		
cortar	cut (to)	cuidado con enfermera	nursing care
corte	cut		
corte de pelo	haircut	cuidado del niño	childcare
cortinas	curtains	cuidado intermedio	intermediate care
cosa	thing		
coser	sew (to)	cuidado privado	private care
cosméticos	cosmetics	culebra	snake
costilla	rib	cuñada	sister-in-law
costo	cost	cuñado	brother-in-law
costra	scab	cuna	crib
crack (drug)	crack	curar	cure (to)
cráneo	cranium, skull	curita	Band-Aid®
		daltónico	color-blind
crecer	grow (to)	dar	give (to)
crema	cream	dar de alta	discharge (to)
criado, criada	servant	de	of
criminal	criminal	¿De quién?	Whose?
Cruz Azul	Blue Cross	debajo de	under
cruzar	cross (to)	débil	weak
cuadra	city block	debilidad	weakness
¿Cuál?	Which?	decir	say (to)
¿Cuándo?	When?	dedo	finger
¿Cuánto?	How much?	dedo del pie	toe
¿Cuántos?	How many?	deducible	deductible
cuarto (cuarta parte)	fourth	defecar	defecate (to)
cuarto (pieza)	room	defecto de nacimiento	birth defect
cuchara	spoon	delgado	thin
cucharada	tablespoon	demasiado	too much
cucharadita	teaspoon	demencia senil	senile dementia
cuchillo	knife	dentaduras postizas	false teeth
cuello	neck	departamento	department
cuello uterino	cervix	depósito	deposit
		depresión	depression

derecho, derecha	right
a la derecha	to the right
dermatólogo	dermatologist
desayuno	breakfast
descafeinado	decaffeinated
descansar	rest (to)
descongestionante	decongestant
descuento	discount
desear	to want
deseo	desire
deshidratación	dehydration
desierto	desert
desinfectante	disinfectant
desinfectar	disinfect (to)
desmayarse	faint (to)
desodorante	deodorant
despejado	clear
despierto	awake
después	after
detectar	detect (to)
detergente	detergent
detrás de	behind
día	day
diabetes	diabetes
diafragma	diaphragm
diagnóstico	diagnosis
diarrea	diarrhea
diciembre	December
diente	tooth
diente impactado	impacted tooth
dieta	diet
dieta blanda	bland diet
dieta limitada	restricted diet
dieta para diabéticos	diabetic diet
dietista	dietician
diferente	different
difícil	difficult

difteria	diphteria
dinero	money
dirección	address
disparar	shoot (to)
disponible	available
distrofia muscular	muscular dystrophy
disturbio	disturbance
divorcio	divorce
doblado, doblada	bent
doblar	bend (to)
doble	double
doctor, doctora	doctor
dolor	pain
dolor agudo	sharp pain
dolor constante	constant pain
dolor de cabeza	headache
dolor de estómago	stomachache
dolor de garganta	sore throat
dolor de muela	toothache
dolor de oído	earache
dolor en el pecho	pain in the chest
dolor sordo	dull pain
dolores de espalda	backaches
dolores de parto	labor pains
dolorido	sore (person)
domingo	Sunday
¿Dónde?	Where?
dormido, dormida	asleep
dormir	sleep (to)
dosis	dosage
dosis alta	high dosage
dosis baja	low dosage
dosis excesiva	overdose
drogas	drugs
drogadicción	drug addiction

drogadicto, drogadicta	drug addict	encías	gums
		encima de	above
droguero, traficante de drogas	drug dealer	encina venenosa	poison oak
		encontrar	find (to)
relacionado con drogas	drug-related	enchufe	outlet
		enderezar	straighten (to)
ducha	shower	endurecimiento	hardening
ducharse	shower (to)	enema	enema
dulce (sabor)	sweet	enero	January
dulce (golosina)	candy	enfermarse	get sick (to)
durar	last (to)	enfermedad	sickness
duro	hard	enfermedad cardíaca	heart disease
edad	age	enfermedad de la glándula tiroides	thyroid disease
edificio	building		
efectivo	cash	enfermedad de la piel	skin disease
ejercicio	exercise	enfermedad mental	mental illness
ejote	green bean	enfermedad venérea	venereal disease
él	he		
electricidad	electricity	enfermero, enfermera	nurse
electrocardiograma	ECG	enfermo, enferma	sick
electroencefalograma	EEG	enfisema	emphysema
ella	she	engordar	gain (weight) (to)
ellos, ellas	they		
embarazada	pregnant	enjuagar	rinse (to)
embrión	embryo	enojado, enojada	angry
emergencia	emergency	ensalada	salad
emocionado, emocionada	excited	entender	understand (to)
		entonces	then
empastar	fill (teeth) (to)	entrada	entrance
empaste	tooth filling	entre	between
empezar	start (to)	epidemia	epidemic
empleado, empleada	employee	epilepsia	epilepsy
empleo	job, employment	epiléptico, epiléptica	epileptic
empeorar	worsen (to)	equilibrio	balance
empresario, patrón, jefe	employer	equipo	equipment
		equivocado	wrong
empujar	push (to)	eructar	burp (to)
en	at, in, on	erupción	rash

erupción en la piel	skin rash	estación	station
escaleras	stairs	estacionamiento	parking lot
escalofríos	chills	estado	condition
escalón	step	estado civil	marital status
escarlatina	scarlet fever	estampillas	stamps
esclerosis múltiple	multiple sclerosis	estar, ser	be (to)
		este, esta	this
escorpión	scorpion	esterilizar	sterilize (to)
escribir	write (to)	estetoscopio	stethoscope
escritorio	desk	estilete	probe
escroto	scrotum	estimulante	stimulant
Escudo Azul	Blue Shield	estómago	stomach
escuela	school	estornudar	sneeze (to)
escupir	spit (to)	estos, estas	these
ese, esa	that	estrangulamiento	strangulation
esmalte	enamel	estreñimiento	constipation
esófago	esophagus	estrés	stress
esos, esas	those	estudiante	student
espalda	back	estudiar	study (to)
espantado, espantada	scared	etiqueta	label
espasmo	spasm	evaluar	evaluate (to)
especia	spice	evitar	avoid (to)
especial	special	examen	exam
especialista	specialist	examen de Papanicolao	pap smear
espejo	mirror		
esperma	sperm	examen físico	physical exam
espinazo	backbone	examinar	examine (to)
esponja	sponge	excusado	toilet
esposa	wife	exhalar	exhale (to)
esposo	husband	explicar	explain (to)
espuma	foam	extracción	extraction
esputo	sputum	extraer	extract (to)
esqueleto	skeleton	fábrica o factoría	factory
esquina	corner	fácil	easy
esquizofrénico, esquizofrénica	schizophrenic	faja	girdle
		falda	skirt
estable	stable	faltar	lack (to)

familia	family	frenillos	braces
farmacéutico	pharmacist	frente	forehead
farmacia	pharmacy	frente de	front of
fatiga	fatigue	fresa	strawberry
febrero	February	frío	cold
fecha	date	frotis	smear
fecha de nacimiento	birthdate	fruta	fruit
feliz	happy	fuego, incendio	fire
feo	ugly	fuente de agua	water fountain
fertilización	fertilization	fuerte	strong
feto	fetus	fumar	smoke (to)
fibra	fiber	funcionar	function (to)
fibrosis cística	cystic fibrosis	funda	pillowcase
fideo	noodle	gabinete	cabinet
fiebre	fever	galleta	cookie
fiebre del heno	hay fever	garganta	throat
fiebre reumática	rheumatic fever	garrapatas	ticks
fiebre tifoidea	typhoid	gas	gas
fijo	fixed	gasa	gauze
firma	signature	gastos	expenses
fisioterapia	physical therapy	gastroenterología	gastroenterology
		gastroenterólogo	gastroenterologist
flatulencia	flatulence		
flema	phlegm	gastrointestinal	gastrointestinal
flojo, floja	loose	gastritis	gastritis
flor	flower	gatear	crawl (to)
florero	flower vase	gato	cat
flujo	discharge	gemelo, gemela	twin
fórmula	formula	genes	genes
formulario	form	genitales	genitals
formulario de consentimiento	consent form	genitourinario	genitourinary
		gente	people
fosa nasal	nostril	gerente	manager
fósforos	matches	ginecólogo	gynecologist
fracaso	failure	glándula	gland
frazada	blanket	glaucoma	glaucoma
frecuencia	frequency	globos	balloons

golpear	beat (to)
goma	glue
gonorrea	gonorrhea
gordo	fat (person)
gota (enfermedad)	gout
gotas	drops
gotas para los ojos	eye drops
gráfico	chart
gramos	grams
grande	big
grano	pimple
grasa	fat (food)
gratis	free
grave	serious
gris	gray
grueso, gruesa	thick
grupo	group
guantes	gloves
guardería	nursery
gusano	worm
gustar	like (to)
hablar	speak (to)
hacer	do (to)
hacer gárgaras	gargle (to)
hambre	hunger
hambriento	hungry
harina	flour
hay	there is/there are
hebilla	barrette
helado	frozen, ice cream
helicóptero	helicopter
hemorragia	hemorrhage
hemorroides	hemorrhoids
hepatitis	hepatitis
hereditario	hereditary
herida	injury
herida de bala	gunshot wound
herido, herida	injured
hermana	sister
hermano	brother
heroína	heroin
hiedra venenosa	poison ivy
hielo	ice
hierba	grass
hierro	iron
hígado	liver
higienista	hygienist
hija	daughter
hijo	son
hilo	thread
hilo dental	dental floss
hinchazón	swelling
hipertensión	hypertension
hipo	hiccups
hipoglicemia	hypoglycemia
histerectomía	hysterectomy
histerismo	hysteria
hoja de afeitar	razor blade
hombre	man
hombro	shoulder
hombro dislocado	dislocated shoulder
hongo	mushroom
horario	schedule
horas	hours
horas de visita	visiting hours
hormigueo	tingling
hormonas	hormones
horquilla	bobby-pin
hospital	hospital
hoy	today

hueso	bone	intoxicación	intoxication
hueso roto	broken bone	intravenoso	I.V.
huevo	egg	líquidos intravenosos	I.V. fluids
humo	smoke	inundación	flood
huracán	hurricane	investigar	research (to)
ictericia	jaundice	invierno	winter
identificación	identification	inyección	shot
iglesia	church	ir	go (to)
imagen por resonancia magnética	MRI	irradiación	radiation
		irritado, irritada	irritated
impacción	impaction	izquierdo, izquierda	left
incapacidad	disability	a la izquierda	to the left
incómodo, incómoda	uncomfortable	jabón	soap
inconsciente	unconscious	jalar	pull (to)
incrustación	inlay	jalea	jelly
indigestión	indigestion	jarabe para la tos	cough syrup
infante	infant	jardinero	gardener
infección	infection	jarra	pitcher
infectado, infectada	infected	jeringa	syringe
infertilidad	infertility	joven	young
inflamación	inflammation	joven	youth
inflamado, inflamada	inflamed	joyas	jewelry
información	information	juanete	bunion
ingle	groin	juego	game
ingreso	income	jueves	Thursday
injerto	graft	jugo	juice
inmediatamente	immediately	juguete	toy
inmunoterapia	immunotherapy	julio	July
inquieto, inquieta	restless	junio	June
insecticida	insecticide	labio	lip
insolación	sunstroke	laboratorio	laboratory
insomnio	insomnia	lactar	breast-feed (to)
instrucciones	directions	lago	lake
instrumento	instrument	laparoscopia	laparoscopy
intermitente	intermittent	lapicero	pen
intérprete	interpreter	lápiz	pencil
interruptor de la luz	light switch	lata	can (container)

lavamanos	sink
lavarse	wash oneself (to)
laxante	laxative
leche	milk
lechuga	lettuce
leer	read (to)
legumbre	vegetable
lengua	tongue
lenguaje	language
lentamente, despacio	slowly
lentes de contacto	contact lenses
lento	slow
lesiones	lesions
leucemia	leukemia
levantarse	stand up (to)
ley	law
libra	pound
libro	book
licencia de manejar	driver's license
licor	liquor
ligadura de las trompas	tubal ligation
ligamento	ligament
lima	file (nailfile)
limar	file (to)
limón	lemon
limpiar	clean (to)
linimento	liniment
líquido	liquid
líquido cefaloraquídeo	spinal fluid
litros	liters
llaga	sore (wound)
llamar	call (to)
llamas	flames
llenar	fill out (to)
lleno	full

llevar	carry (to)
llorar	cry (to)
lluvia	rain
lóbulo	lobe
loción	lotion
loco, loca	crazy
locura	insanity
lodo	mud
lunes	Monday
luz	light
madre	mother
maestro, maestra	teacher
magnesia	magnesium
maíz	corn (food)
mal	bad
malaria	malaria
maligno	malignant
malo	bad
mamograma	mammogram
mañana	tomorrow
por la mañana	a.m.
mancha	spot
mandar	send (to)
mandíbula	jaw
manejar	drive (to)
manga	sleeve
maniática, maniático	maniac
manicomio	psychiatric hospital
mano	hand
manteca	lard
mantequilla	butter
manzana	apple
mapa	map
maquillaje	make-up
máquina	machine

máquina de movimiento continuo	continuous passive motion machine
mar	sea
marcapasos	pacemaker
mareado, mareada	dizzy
mareos	dizziness
margarina	margarine
marijuana	marijuana
mariscos	shellfish
martes	Tuesday
marzo	March
más	more
más tarde	later
máscara	mask
mastectomía	mastectomy
masticar	chew (to)
matar	murder (to)
matrimonio	marriage
mayo	May
mayor	older
mecánico	mechanic
medias	stockings
medicina	medicine
médico, médica	physician
medir	measure (to)
médula	bone marrow
mejilla	cheek
mejor	better
mejorar	improve (to)
memoria	memory
meningitis	meningitis
menor	younger
menos	less
menstruar	menstruate (to)
merienda	snack
mes	month

mesa	table
mesa de noche	nightstand
mesero	waiter
metro	subway
metros	meters
mezcla	mixture
mi	my
miedo	fear
miel	honey
miembro	member
miércoles	Wednesday
minerales	minerals
ministro	minister
miope	near-sighted
mismo	same
mitad	half
moco	mucus
moderado	mild
mojado, mojada	wet
molde	mold
monitor	monitor
mononucleosis	mononucleosis
montaña	mountain
morado	purple
mordedura	bite
mordedura de culebra	snake bite
mordedura de insecto	insect bite
mordedura de perro	dog bite
morder	bite (to)
morena	brunette
morfina	morphine
morir	to die
motocicleta	motorcycle
muchacho, muchacha	young person
muchas veces	lots of times
muchos	many
mucoso	mucous

muebles	furniture	nervio	nerve
muela	molar	nervioso, nerviosa	nervous
muerte	death	neurólogo	neurologist
muerto, muerta	dead	neurosis	neurosis
muestra	sample	nieta	granddaughter
mujer	woman	nieto	grandson
muñeca (cuerpo)	wrist	nieve	snow
muñeca (juguete)	doll	ninguno	none
murmullos en el corazón	heart murmurs	niño, niña	child
		noche	night
músculo	muscle	esta noche	tonight
músculo rasgado	pulled muscle	nombre	name
muslo	thigh	normal	normal
muy	very	normalmente	normally
muy fuerte	severe, very strong	nosotros	we
		novia	girlfriend
nacer	be born (to)	noviembre	November
nacido muerto	stillborn	novio	boyfriend
nacimiento	birth	nublado	cloudy
nacionalidad	nationality	nuera	daughter-in-law
nada	nothing	nuestro	our
nalga	buttock	nuevo	new
narcotráfico	drug traffic	nuez	nut
nariz	nose	número	number
dolor de nariz	nose pain	número de seguro social	Social Security number
goteo de nariz	nose drip	número de teléfono	telephone number
sange de nariz	nosebleed		
nariz tapada	stuffy nose	nunca	never
náusea	nausea	o	or
necesario	necessary	obesidad	obesity
necesitar	need (to)	obrero	laborer
negocio	business	observar	observe (to)
negro, negra	black	obstetriz	obstetrician
hombre negro	black man	octavo	eighth
mujer negra	black woman	octubre	October
niña negra	black girl	ocupado, ocupada	busy
niño negro	black boy		

ocho	eight
oficina	office
oftalmólogo	ophthalmologist
oído	ear
dolor de oído	earache
sangre del oído	earbleed
sordera	deafness
oír	hear (to)
ojo	eye
dolor de ojo	eyepain
ojos llorosos	crying eyes
ver puntos	to see spots
ver borroso	blurred vision
vision doble	double vision
oler	smell (to)
ombligo	navel
once	eleven
oncología	oncology
onzas	ounces
operación	operation
antes de la operación	pre-op
después de la operación	post-op
operación cesárea	cesarean section
operación de emergencia	emergency operation
preparar para la operación	to prepare for the operation
operar	operate (to)
opinión	opinion
optometrista	optometrist
órgano	organ
orilla	curb
orinal	urinal
orinar	urinate (to)
oro	gold
ortodoncista	orthodontist
ortopedia	orthopedics
otoño	fall
ovario	ovary
óvulo	ovum
oxígeno	oxygen
paciente	patient
paciente externo	outpatient
paciente interno	in-patient
padrastro (familia)	stepfather
padrastro (uña)	hangnail
padre	father
pagar	pay (to)
pájaro	bird
palabra	word
paladar	palate
palma de la mano	palm
palpitaciones	palpitations
pan	bread
pañal	diaper
paño higiénico	feminine napkin
páncreas	pancreas
pantalones	pants
pantorrilla	calf
pantuflas	slippers
papa	potato
papel	paper
papel higiénico	toilet paper
paperas	mumps
parálisis	paralysis
parálisis cerebral	cerebral palsy
pararse	stand (to)
parásitos	parasites
pared	wall
pareja	couple
parentezco	relationship

párpado	eyelid	persona	person
parque	park	pesar	weigh (to)
parte	part	pescado	fish
partida de nacimiento	Certificate of	peso	weight
vivo	Live Birth	pestaña	eyelash
parto	childbirth	pezón	nipple
parto natural	natural	picadura de abeja	bee sting
	childbirth	picante	spicy
pasta de dientes	toothpaste	comidas picantes	spicy foods
pastel	pie	picar	itch (to)
pastilla	lozenge	picazón	itching
patear	kick (to)	pie	foot
patio	yard	piedra	stone
patólogo	pathologist	piel	skin
patrón	employer	cáncer de la piel	skin cancer
pavo	turkey	pierna	leg
pecho	chest	pijamas (las)	pajamas
pediatra	pediatrician	píldora	pill
peine	comb	píldoras	birth control
pelear	fight (to)	anticonceptivas	pills
peligroso	dangerous	pimienta	pepper
pelirrojo, pelirroja	redhead	piña	pineapple
pelota	ball	pintor, pintora	painter
pelvis	pelvis	pintura	paint
pene	penis	pinzas	tweezers
penicilina	penicillin	piojos	lice
pensar	think (to)	piorrea	pyorrhea
peor	worse	pisalengua	tongue
perder	lose (to)		depressor
pérdida	miscarriage,	piso	floor
	loss	pista	lane
pérdida de	blackout	placa	plaque
conocimiento		placenta	placenta
perforar	drill (to)	plaga	plague
periódico	newspaper	plan	plan
permiso	permission	planificación	planning
pero	but	planta del pie	sole
perro	dog		

plata	silver	présbito	far-sighted
plátano	banana	presión de la sangre	blood pressure
plato	plate	préstamo	loan
playa	beach	prevenir	prevent (to)
plomero	plumber	prieto	dark-skinned
pobre	poor		(coll.)
pocos	few	primavera	spring
poder	be able (to)	primer nombre	first name
podiatra	podiatrist	primer piso	first floor
polen	pollen	primero	first
policía	police officer	primeros auxilios	first aid
polio	polio	primo, prima	cousin
pólipo	polyp	privado, privada	private
póliza	policy	problemas emocionales	emotional
polvo	dust		problems
pollo	chicken	proceder	proceed (to)
pómulo	cheekbone	procedimiento	procedure
poner	put (to)	proctología	proctology
por, para	for	proctoscopía	proctoscopy
por eso	therefore	producto químico	chemical
¿Por qué?	Why?	productos lácteos	dairy products
porcelana	porcelain	profundo, profunda	deep
porcentaje	percent	prohibido	prohibited
porque	because	prohibir	prohibit (to)
postizo	false	pronto	soon
postración	heat stroke	proteger	protect (to)
postración nerviosa	nervous	proteína	protein
	breakdown	protuberancia(s)	bump(s)
postre	dessert	proveedor, proveedora	provider
potasio	potassium	pruebas	tests
practicante	orderly	prueba de CAP	CAP test
pregunta	question	prueba de Holter	Holter scan
preguntar	ask (to)	psicólogo, psicóloga	psychologist
prematuro, prematura	premature	psicoterapia	psychotherapy
preocupado,	worried	psiquiatra	psychiatrist
preocupada		puente	bridge
preparar	prepare (to)	puerta	door

pulgada	inch	ratón	mouse
pulgas	fleas	rayos equis	X rays
pulmones	lungs	raza	race
pulmonía	pneumonia	readmitir	readmit (to)
pulsante	throbbing	receta médica	prescription
pulso	pulse	recibir	receive (to)
pulso irregular	irregular pulse	recibo	receipt
pulso lento	slow pulse	recién nacido,	newborn
pulso rápido	fast pulse	recién nacida	
punción lumbar	spinal tap	recomendar	recommend (to)
puntos	stitches		
purificar	purify (to)	reconocimiento	checkup
puro	cigar	recordar	remember (to)
pus	pus	recto	rectum
¿Qué?	What?	recuento	count
quedarse	stay (to)	recuento de la sangre	blood count
quemante	burning	recuperación	recuperation
quemar	burn (to)	recuperar	recuperate (to)
querer	want (to)	recursos	resources
queso	cheese	refresco	soft drink
¿Quién?	Who?	refrigerador	refrigerator
quinto	fifth	regalo	gift
quiropráctico	chiropractor	registrar	register (to)
quiste	cyst	regla, período	period (menstrual)
quitarse	take off (clothes) (to)	regresar, volver	return (to)
radiografía	X ray	relaciones sexuales	sexual relations
radiología	radiology	relajado, relajada	relaxed
radiólogo, radióloga	radiologist	religión	religion
radioterapia	radiation therapy	reloj	watch
		remedios	drugs (legal)
raíz	root	remplazar	replace (to)
rápidamente	quickly	reparar	repair (to)
rápido	fast	repollo	cabbage
rascar	scratch (to)	resfrío	cold (illness)
rasurar	shave (to)	resistir	resist (to)
rata	rat	respiración	breathing

respirador	respirator	sala de maternidad	Maternity Ward
respirar	breathe (to)	sala de meditación	meditation room
restaurante	restaurant		
resucitación cardiopulmonar	CPR	sala de operaciones	Operating Room
		sala de partos	delivery room
revista	magazine	sala de recuperación	Recovery Room
rezar	pray (to)	salida	exit
rico, rica	rich	salir	leave (to)
riñón	kidney	saliva	saliva
río	river	salón	lobby
ritmo cardíaco	heartbeat	salón principal	main lobby
rodilla	knee	salsa	sauce
rojo	red	salud	health
romo	dull (edge)	¡Salud!	Bless you!
ropa	clothing	sangre	blood
ropa interior	underwear	sarampión	measles
ropero	closet	sarpullidos	rashes
rosado, rosada	pink	sarro	tartar
rótula	kneecap	satisfecho, satisfecha	satisfied
rubéola	German measles	seco, seca	dry
		secretario, secretaria	secretary
rubio, rubia	blond	sedante	sedative
sábado	Saturday	sediento	thirsty
sábana	sheet	seguir	follow (to)
saborear	taste (to)	segundo	second
sacar	remove (to)	seguridad	security
sacarse	take off (to)	seguro (a salvo)	safe
sacerdote	priest	seguro	insurance
sal	salt	compañía de seguros	insurance company
sal de epsom	epsom salt		
sala	room, unit, ward	seguro de accidente	accident insurance
sala de conferencias	conference room		
		seguro de salud	health insurance
sala de cuidados intensivos	Intensive Care		
		seguro de vida	life insurance
sala de emergencia	Emergency Room	selva	jungle
		semana	week
sala de espera	Waiting Room	semen	semen

sencillo	simple
senos, pechos	breasts
sensibilidad	sensitivity
sentarse	sit down (to)
sentir	feel (to)
septiembre	September
séptimo	seventh
sequía	drought
servicio	service
servicios de salud	health care
servilleta	napkin
severo, severa	severe
sexo	sex
sexto	sixth
sí	yes
SIDA	AIDS
prueba del SIDA	AIDS test
siempre	always
sien	temple
siesta	nap
sífilis	syphilis
signos vitales	vital signs
siguiente	next
silla	chair
simpático	cute
sin	without
sin embargo	however
síndrome	syndrome
síndrome del alcohol fetal	fetal alcohol syndrome
síntoma	symptom
sistema nervioso	nervous system
sobre	about
sobre (de carta)	envelope
sobrina	niece
sobrino	nephew
socio	partner

sodio	sodium
sofocación	suffocation
sol	sun
solo, sola	alone
soltero, soltera	single (person)
solución	solution
somnífero	sleeping pill
soñoliento, soñolienta	sleepy
sonido	sound
sonograma	sonogram
sonrisa	smile
sopa	soup
sordo	dull (sound)
sordo, sorda	deaf
sorprendido, sorprendida	surprised
sótano	basement
sostén	brassiere
su	her/his/your
subir	go up (to)
sucio, sucia	dirty
sudar	perspire (to)
sudor	sweating
sudoroso	sweaty
suegra	mother-in-law
suegro	father-in-law
sueños	dreams
suéter	sweater
sufrir	suffer (to)
suicidarse	to commit suicide
suicidio	suicide
superficial	shallow (person)
supositorios	suppositories
sutura	suture
tableta	tablet
taladro	drill

talco	talcum powder	tijeras	scissors
talón	heel	timbre	bell
tamaño	size	tío	uncle
también	also	tipo de sangre	blood type
tapar	cover (to)	tiroides	thyroid
tarde	late	toalla	towel
por la tarde	p.m.	toallita	washcloth
tarjeta	card	tobillo	ankle
tarjeta de crédito	credit card	tobillo torcido	sprained ankle
tarjeta de saludo	greeting card	todavía	yet, still
tarjeta postal	postcard	todo	all
taza	teacup	tomar	take (to)
té	tea	tomate	tomato
técnico	technician	tomografía	CT scanning
tejido	tissue	computarizada	
teléfono	telephone	tornado	tornado
televisión	television	torniquete	tourniquet
temperatura	temperature	toronja	grapefruit
temprano	early	torta; bizcocho	cake
tenazas	forceps	tos	cough
tendón	tendon	tos dolorosa	painful cough
tenedor	fork	tos ferina, tos	whooping cough
tener	have (to)	convulsiva	
tener que	have to (to)	toser	cough (to)
terapeuta	therapist	trabajador social	social worker
terapia	therapy	trabajar	work (to)
tercero	third	tracción	traction
terminar	end (to)	tragar	swallow (to)
termómetro	thermometer	traer	bring (to)
termostato	thermostat	traje	suit
terremoto	earthquake	tranquilo	calm
testículos	testicles	transfusión de sangre	blood transfusion
tétano	tetanus		
tía	aunt	transporte	transportation
tiempo	time	trapecio	trapeze
tienda	store	trasplantar	transplant (to)
tienda de regalos	gift shop	trastorno	disorder
tierra	dirt	tratamiento	treatment

tratamiento del nervio dental	root canal
tratar	try (to)
trauma	trauma
tren	train
triste	sad
tristeza	grief
trompas de falopio	fallopian tubes
tu	your
tuberculosis	tuberculosis
tubo	tube
úlcera	ulcer
último	last
ultrasonido	ultrasound
un, una	a
uña	nail
uña encarnada	ingrown toenail
una vez	once
unidad neurosiquiátrica	neuro-psychiatric unit
unos, unas	some
uretra	urethra
urólogo	urologist
urticaria	hives
usar	use (to)
usted, tú	you
ustedes	you (plural)
útero	uterus
uva	grape
vacío	empty
vacuna	vaccination
vacunar	vaccinate (to)
vagina	vagina
válvula	valve
varicela	chicken pox
vasectomía	vasectomy
vaselina	vaseline

vaso	glass (drinking)
vejación sexual, molestia sexual	molestation
vejiga	bladder
infección de la vejiga	bladder infection
vena	vein
venas varicosas	varicose veins
vendaje	bandage
vendedor, vendedora	salesperson
veneno	poison
venir	come (to)
ventana	window
ventilador	electric fan
ventrículo	ventricle
ver	see (to)
verano	summer
verde	green
verificar	check (to)
verificar	verify (to)
verruga	wart
vestido	dress
vestirse	get dressed (to)
víbora venenosa	poisonous snake
vida	life
viejo	old
viento	wind
viernes	Friday
VIH	HIV
vino	wine
violación	rape
violar	rape (to)
viruela	smallpox
visión	vision
doble visión	double vision
visita	visit

visitante	visitor	**vulva**	vulva
visitar	visit (to)	**y**	and
vista	sight	**ya**	already
vitamina(s)	vitamin(s)	**yerno**	son-in-law
vivir	live (to)	**yo**	I
vivo, viva	alive	**yogur**	yogurt
voltearse	turn oneself over (to)	**zanahoria**	carrot
		zancudo	mosquito
vomitar	vomit (to)	**zapato**	shoe
voz	voice	**zona postal**	zip code